SLAUGHTER
ON THE
EASTERN FRONT

SLAUGHTER
ON THE
EASTERN FRONT

HITLER AND STALIN'S WAR 1941–1945

ANTHONY TUCKER-JONES

The History Press

Cover illustrations
Front: Soviet tanks destroyed at the gates of Moscow. (Scott Pick)
Back: Stalled before Moscow, the German Army was woefully ill-equipped to cope with the harsh Russian winter. (Scott Pick)

First published 2017
This paperback edition published 2019

The History Press
97 St George's Place, Cheltenham
Gloucestershire, GL50 3QB
www.thehistorypress.co.uk

British Library Cataloguing in Publication Data.
A catalogue record for this book is available from the British Library.

ISBN 978 0 7509 9269 5

Map illustrations by Thomas Bohm, User Design, Illustration & Typesetting

Typesetting and origination by The History Press
Printed and bound in Great Britain by TJ International Ltd

CONTENTS

Appendices

Stalin's Gathering Armies

General Mikhail Ivanovich Kazakov stood on the edge of Tashkent Airfield. It was warm – this time of year temperatures in Uzbekistan reached a stifling 34°C. Out in the sun it did not take long for the standard Red Army issue khaki cotton shirt and single-breasted tunic to become soaked. He dug a handkerchief from his pocket and mopped his brow and then his neck.

Kazakov was not a fan of the Soviet Central Asian Republics. Career wise, the region was a complete backwater – European Russia or Siberia was where most officers wanted to be. Tashkent lacked the opportunities of, say, Moscow, Minsk, Kharkov and Leningrad, or even Vladivostok, for that matter.

Kazakov had found himself ordered to Moscow in early June 1941 to brief the General Staff on the readiness of the Central Asian Military District. He reassured himself it was a routine trip, but in the back of his mind there was a nagging doubt. A few years ago, such an order could mean a brief and often painful interview with Stalin's dreaded internal security forces, followed by the Gulag or firing squad. Kazakov had heard what had happened to tough Red Army veterans like Konstantin Rokossovsky. He spent three vicious years in the Gulag, where he had been subjected to mock executions and had his ribs broken and his teeth knocked out. Only because Stalin had need of such men had Rokossovsky been released. Kazakov later, very briefly, worked for Rokossovsky and was highly impressed by the man.

He knew war with neighbouring China to the east was highly unlikely. The country had been brought to its knees by decades of violent internal political turmoil. Besides, China was a good trade partner and was distracted by recent Japanese aggression in Manchuria and Mongolia. To the south, Kazakov appreciated that no one in their right mind would tangle with the bloodthirsty tribes of Afghanistan. Its greatest value was as a useful buffer to British colonial interests in India. Only Iran, to the south-west, was of interest to Moscow because of its vast oil reserves and access to the Arabian Sea. The Red Army watched with amusement as the British and Americans squabbled over oil rights in the region.

Kazakov lit up a Machorka cigarette just to calm any last-minute nerves before his flight. He was used to the high nicotine content, which was three times that of regular tobacco. Many officers preferred European cigarettes, but in Tashkent they were not so easy to get hold of. He pondered his trip. It was slightly worrying that he had been at the military's central headquarters in Moscow earlier in the year and now six months on he had been called back.

His relationship with the military district commander was good, so he was not aware of any problems in the chain of command. In the Red Army, where bullying was institutionalised, it paid to have a good relationship with your immediate superior, otherwise it could make for a very unpleasant working environment and a short-lived career. If anything, Kazakov was slightly envious of his 42-year-old boss, Major General Sergei Trofimenko. He was a veteran of the Russian Civil War and in recent years had been involved in the campaigns in Poland and Finland. After promotion, Trofimenko had arrived to take command of the Central Asian Military District in early 1941.

Across the runway the loadmaster of a DB long-range bomber motioned to Kazakov. This aircraft had proved to be vulnerable to nationalist fighters during the Spanish Civil War and, in many instances, was now relegated to transport duties. He stubbed out his cigarette and straightened his furashka officer's peaked cap.

Flying north, the pilot picked up the Trans-Siberian Railway as an easy way to navigate to Moscow, and below Kazakov saw trainload after trainload of troops from the Soviet Far East, all heading west. Kazakov was unaware of any large-scale military manoeuvres, so Stalin must be gathering his armies – it seemed war was brewing in Europe. Now he knew why he had been summoned to Moscow.

Meanwhile, in his office in the Central Arbat District of Moscow, General Filipp Golikov, head of Military Intelligence, knew exactly what was going on. He had watched as Adolf Hitler massed three powerful army groups in Prussia, Nazi-occupied western Poland and then Romania. There had also been unending border violations by German spy planes. His credible and well-placed sources all indicated that Hitler was poised to strike between mid-May and mid-June 1941. Golikov had direct access to 'the Boss' in the Kremlin and was regularly at his side. When it came to briefing Joseph Stalin, he did not even have to bother going through the General Staff.

The Soviet Union was well prepared to face any threat posed by Hitler, or so he thought. Golikov was relatively new in the post and he understood that it was best not to disagree with the Boss. He had replaced Ivan Proskurov, who had been sacked for not sugar-coating the intelligence about Hitler's intentions. Proskurov had gone the way of his six predecessors and would face a firing squad in four months' time.

Golikov appreciated that being head of Military Intelligence for someone like Stalin was a poisoned chalice. To survive the rigours of life in the Red Army, you always kept your head down. The Boss, naturally supported by Golikov, had very set views on what was going on. In his mind, Hitler's build-up was all part of an elaborate plan to force England to the negotiating table. Therefore, it was very clear to Stalin and Golikov that war with Germany was not imminent.

At Wünsdorf, south of Berlin, Colonel Eberhard Kinzel, head of German intelligence-gathering in Eastern Europe, was slightly worried about his conclusions which had been backed by the Luftwaffe's intrusive reconnaissance flights over the Soviet Union. These had confirmed two very important things: firstly, the Red Army seemed to have no strategic reserves east of their old frontier, and this posed the question, where *were* Stalin's reserves? Secondly, the Red Air Force was very obligingly lining its aircraft up wingtip to wingtip on its forward airfields. This meant that the Luftwaffe would be able to easily destroy the Red Air Force on the ground and once Hitler's blitzkrieg had stormed through eastern Poland, the road to Moscow would be wide open.

Kinzel had in recent months made a very thorough study of the Red Army deployed in the border areas, and overall it was in a lamentable state. Everything indicated that a swift victory could be achieved. His superior, General Franz Halder, Chief of the German General Staff, was very pleased with his work in building up a meticulous picture of Stalin's defences. However, Kinzel had also studied Stalin's manpower reserves and industrial strength. Should Hitler attack the Soviet Union, the war would clearly be a race against time, not only against the Russian winter but also Stalin's mobilising reserve armies.

Rumour of war was rife across the rest of Eastern Europe; there was no hiding it. In Bucharest's Calea Victoriei Boulevard and Cişmigiu Park people talked of nothing else. Sitting at his desk in a city affectionately known as 'Little Paris', Jewish writer Iosif Hechter was anxious about Romania's relationship with Hitler's Nazi Germany. Better known by his pen name 'Mihail Sebastian', the playwright and novelist had connections with the country's intellectuals who supported the Fascist Iron Guard.

By early June, men were being called up and the Romanian government had ordered everyone to build an air-raid shelter in their yards within the next two weeks. The city had also been subject to a series of blackouts. Writing in his journal almost every day, Hechter fretted about four things: the fate of Europe's Jews, his creativity, unending money problems and the growing likelihood of war with the Soviet Union. He had little idea of the key role the Romanian military would play in Hitler's war against Stalin.

On the other side of the world in Tokyo, man about town Richard Sorge was feeling rather pleased with himself. By anyone's reckoning he was a chancer who got a thrill from taking risks. A Soviet citizen turned Nazi journalist he was actually on Golikov's payroll. He came from Baku but had grown up and worked in Germany for many years. After a stint in China he had been sent to Japan in the early 1930s. During his time in China he had provided intelligence on Sino-Japanese tensions. Reporting from Shanghai had been particularly exhilarating. In Tokyo he had been very discreet whilst building up his contacts and keeping above suspicion of the Japanese secret police.

He had just come from a meeting with the German military attaché Lieutenant Colonel Erwin Scholl. It had been a very valuable chat; Scholl had his confidence and had been criminally indiscreet. Scholl had informed Sorge that Hitler was poised to attack the Soviet Union on about 20 June 1941. Sorge hastened home to radio Moscow – he would be hailed a hero for saving Mother Russia.

Sorge knew that part of the equation was missing. When Hitler attacked the Soviet Union how would Japan react? Would the Japanese attack at the same time? His sources told him that elements of the Japanese military felt the Soviet Union should be punished for interfering in Mongolia. If that were the case it meant a two front war for Stalin. Sorge's energies would now be directed at confirming Tokyo's intentions. What Richard Sorge did not know was that Stalin despised him, as he did all spies. Sorge in Stalin's opinion was little better than a brothel keeper and a peddler of misinformation. When the time came later in the year he would abandon Sorge to the Japanese, torture and the hangman's noose. Such was the Boss's gratitude.

INTRODUCTION

COLLECTIVE MADNESS

To people born and raised in Western Europe, the slaughter that occurred on the Eastern Front during 1941–45 is, without doubt, beyond comprehension. The campaigns fought in the west were bloody and brutal affairs, but they pale into insignificance against the simply enormous battles fought in the east and the resulting death toll. In addition, beyond military circles there is little appreciation that so many different nationalities shared in the appalling bloodletting.

In the summer of 1941 a collective madness overtook Adolf Hitler and his senior generals. Contrary to their intelligence, they convinced themselves that they could take on and defeat a superpower in the making – the Soviet Union. Foolishly, they thought they could smash the disorganised Red Army in a swift campaign and force Joseph Stalin to sue for peace. However, even at the start Hitler had insufficient manpower for such an enterprise and he was forced to rely on the inadequate armies of his Axis allies – Finland, Italy, Hungary, Romania, Slovakia and even Spain. Bulgaria also became involved indirectly, by freeing up German troops in the Balkans.

Hitler indulged in tunnel vision; it was his victorious Wehrmacht that would deliver the decisive knock-out blow against the Red Army while his Axis allies simply held the southern flank. In reality though, the Italians, Hungarians and Romanians were key players in the disaster that unfolded for Hitler's war effort in the east. Hitler bullied and cajoled the Hungarian and Romanian leadership into joining his anti-Bolshevik crusade against Stalin. Their motives for doing so were based more on mutual distrust of each other than on any great antipathy toward the Soviet Union. They would learn to regret their alliance with the devil.

Crucially, Hitler wilfully ignored the Siberian factor and Stalin's enormous manpower reserves. By the summer of 1940 there was rumour of war amongst the Soviet military authorities in the cities of Chita, Tashkent, Sverdlovsk and

Saratov. This rumour pointed not to the Far East of the sprawling Soviet Union, where there had been open hostilities with Japan, but to the west where Hitler's aggressive expansion in Europe was a growing cause for concern.

The popular perception is that Stalin was caught completely by surprise by Hitler's assault on the Soviet Union – but this is complete rubbish. In the spring of 1941 Soviet generals in these far-flung outposts were ordered to ship their troops west to form the Reserve Front. This act would help save Moscow from Nazi occupation and stall Hitler's invasion at a critical moment in the battle. On four occasions, German Intelligence failed to predict the creation of Soviet reserve fronts with catastrophic results: first at Moscow, then Stalingrad, Kursk and finally Minsk.

Three little-known intelligence officers were partially responsible for the appalling slaughter on the Eastern Front, thanks to their impact on Stalin and Hitler. First, General Filipp Golikov, in charge of Soviet Military Intelligence, on the very eve of war helped convince Stalin that Hitler would not attack in the summer of 1941. Despite warnings from his most experienced senior generals, Stalin felt he knew best. As a result, the Red Army was neither fully mobilised nor fully equipped and the Wehrmacht was able to strike it at the optimum moment. Second, Colonel Eberhard Kinzel, responsible for German intelligence on the Eastern Front, failed to impress upon Hitler the danger posed by Stalin's Reserve Front and the reserve armies gathering beyond the Volga. The Reserve Front coalesced around Moscow to hold off Operation Typhoon while the reserve armies were mobilising. This meant Hitler had one chance and one chance only to capture Moscow before losing momentum. Kinzel was subsequently sacked for being the bearer of bad tidings.

Likewise, his successor, Colonel Reinhard Gehlen, tried to warn Hitler of the danger gathering on the Volga and the threat this posed to the German Army and its Axis allies at Stalingrad, in the winter of 1942. Hitler refused to listen and would not authorise a tactical withdrawal. Massed Soviet forces cut across the Don and surrounded Stalingrad with ease. Gehlen then tried call off Hitler's Kursk Offensive in the summer of 1943, warning that it was another trap, but left it too late. The following year he again tried to warn that Army Group Centre was at risk from a third Soviet reserve front, but once again failed to get Hitler to withdraw. As a consequence, Army Group Centre was annihilated before Minsk and the remnants driven all the way back to Warsaw.

What possessed Hitler to believe he could defeat Stalin's vast army, which had more manpower, and was equipped with more tanks, artillery and aircraft? Hitler's blitzkrieg had brought Poland, Scandinavia, Western Europe and the Balkans to its knees, and even the combined might of the British and French armies had been unable to stave off defeat. Through a combination of new tactics and daring, Hitler's generals had run circles around their opponents – quite literally, in many cases. By June 1941 the Wehrmacht stood undefeated and undisputed master of Europe, and Moscow seemed within Hitler's grasp. Even so, challenging the Red Army still seems a tall order.

Stalin's purges of his officer corps in the late 1930s and the Red Army's lamentable performance against Finland during the brief Winter War also convinced Hitler that such a feat was possible. On top of this, the Soviet High Command chose to ignore the mobile warfare possibilities presented by the tank. To them it was a support weapon rather than an armoured fist. They looked to their experiences during the Spanish Civil War and drew the wrong conclusions – despite the recent lessons of Hitler's blitzkrieg across Europe where the panzer had reigned supreme. The political intrigue of Marshals Voroshilov and Budenny ensured the death of leading tank advocate Tukhachevsky, the Soviet answer to Britain's Fuller, Germany's Guderian and France's Estienne; all of whom were champions of the tank.

Stalin's collectivisation programmes had wrought untold suffering on the Soviet population. Ukraine, in particular, endured the most appalling famine with a horrific death toll. Stalin violently dragged the Soviet Union into the twentieth century, whether it liked it or not. Collectivisation was enforced at the barrel of a gun and any signs of nationalism within the Soviet Union's member states was stamped out. As a result, the Soviet Union appeared to be in a state of political and military chaos. To Hitler and his generals there could be only one outcome – if attacked with sufficient force, the mighty Red Army would collapse and Stalin would be ousted by a military coup.

To his cost, Hitler chose to ignore the dire warning provided by an up-and-coming Soviet general, who shaped modern armoured warfare tactics with notable flare just before Hitler's blitzkrieg was unleashed on Poland. This was where the crucial Siberian factor came in. During the summer of 1939, Georgi Zhukov crushed the Japanese Army on the steppes of Mongolia with such ease that Japan never meddled in Soviet affairs again. It ensured that Stalin was free to fight on just one front rather than two when the time came. When Hitler's armies reached Moscow, Zhukov was there waiting for them with his wealth of experience and winter-hardened Siberian divisions.

In addition, after the invasion Hitler chose to ignore the anti-Soviet sentiments that were widespread within the Nazi-occupied territories. At grassroots level, collectivisation had fired a hatred of Stalin's repressive regime. The Baltic States and Ukraine wanted independence and initially welcomed the Nazis as liberators, but Hitler and his despotic cronies chose to ride roughshod over them and treated them as subjugated peoples. The opportunity to raise large armies of nationalist forces from the Baltic States was left too late. Early 'volunteers' were consigned to menial support roles within the German military, or became brutal police units who simply alienated the local population even more.

Attempts at raising anti-Stalinist Ukrainian and even Russian forces were simply too little too late. Those units instigated in the name of political change in the Soviet Union suffered predictable fates. Some ended up in the unenviable position of being trapped in the middle, disowned by all. Only the Don and Kuban Cossacks were embraced with any great enthusiasm by the German armed forces. Even then, the powerful Cossack Corps ended up fighting in Italy, far from the Red Army.

The opening stages of Hitler's assault on the Soviet Union were an unexpected and unsurpassed triumph. In June 1941, in a campaign conducted at breathless speed the German and other Axis armies rolled triumphantly across the Baltic States, Byelorussia and Ukraine. The Red Army and Red Air Force were completely smashed and scattered across the Russian Steppes. Desperate to save their necks, the Soviet generals set about blaming each other for the ineptitude that had permitted Hitler to reach the very gates of Moscow.

Then, dramatically, with the onset of the Russian winter Hitler faltered before the Soviet capital and Leningrad. Stalin's insistence on a premature counter-offensive at Moscow was a dismal failure, but it caused Hitler's armies, who were ill-equipped to cope with the bitter weather, to pause for breath. Although Moscow was the real centre of gravity, Hitler became needlessly distracted by events on his flanks; the allure of Leningrad, Sevastopol, Stalingrad and Baku became too great. In particular, Stalingrad was where the slowly but surely rejuvenating Red Army was able to prove its new-found mettle. It was a battle that neither Hitler nor Stalin would give up on.

From 1941–42 the losses on the Eastern Front were extremely heavy, but nothing like the subsequent slaughter that occurred with appalling regularity from 1942–45. Thanks to their intelligence, Hitler's generals knew that the Soviet Union's massive population would throw a vital lifeline to the battered Red Army on a scale that was impossible for the Wehrmacht. The real question was how quickly the Red Army could recover and if Stalin would survive.

The German intelligence assessment was that with the capture of vital raw materials concentrated in the Caucasus, the Red Army would be starved of resources. Notably, General Georg Thomas, head of the German economic office just before the Eastern Front opened, estimated that Stalin would lose two thirds of his heavy industry, which would make it impossible to re-arm the Red Army. He could not conceive that Stalin's factories would be shifted, wholesale, east of the Urals and that they would not only resume production of military equipment but also step it up to levels with which Germany could not compete.

The regeneration of the shattered Red Army and Red Air Force was little short of a miracle. Reinhard Gehlen, head of German Intelligence on the Eastern Front, noted that despite staggering Soviet losses at Kiev, Vyazma and Bryansk, by January 1942 the Red Army was still maintaining a front-line strength of 4.5 million men and there were as many Red Army divisions confronting the Wehrmacht as when Hitler first attacked the Soviet Union. General Halder, Chief of the German General Staff, estimated total German losses on the Eastern Front on 28 February 1942 to be 1 million casualties. Whatever the true figure, even by Halder's reckoning, as of November 1941 Hitler had lost almost a quarter of his forces on the Eastern Front and by February 1942 this had risen to almost a third. This shattered the illusion of a swift victory.

At the same time, Stalin began to release his vice-like grip on the conduct of the war as this had so clearly led to defeat in early 1942. Instead, he finally began to rely on the expert judgement of his deputy, Zhukov. In turning the tide in late 1942, Stalin chose to strike Hitler's Achilles heel at Stalingrad. First, he routed the ill-equipped Italian, Hungarian and Romanian armies, and then he trapped and crushed an entire German Army between the banks of the Don and Volga, while the Luftwaffe was also dangerously weakened trying to save it. A shudder ran through the ranks of the German armed forces; this was not supposed to happen.

Hitler had deliberately chosen to ignore the warning signs. His efforts to wrest back the initiative received a further deathblow at Kursk, where Stalin sprang another well-concealed trap. Hitler's depleted armies were now bleeding to death and the slaughter continued in earnest.

When Stalin launched his version of D-Day the following year, he tore the beating heart out of the Wehrmacht and overran Hungary and Romania. From then on it was a fighting retreat for the Germans. Hitler marshalled his dwindling manpower for one last attempt to stop the Red tide in the spring of 1945, but it was to no avail and the Red Army was on its way to Berlin.

Extensive analysis of German intelligence reveals the blunders that led to the shocking and needless destruction of Hitler's armed forces as early as the winter of 1941–42. The myth is that the regeneration of the Red Army cost Hitler the war, thanks to his defeats at Stalingrad and Kursk, but it was ultimately his will-o'-the-wisp strategy and fortress mentality that fatally hamstrung his war effort. In refusing to cede ground, Hitler took away the Wehrmacht's ability to conduct mobile warfare and fight on the ground of their choosing. Inevitably, the initiative increasingly passed over to the Red Army. Despite this, Hitler's war machine fought to its very last against a relentless enemy knowing that defeat was inevitable.

ENEMIES OF THE PEOPLE

The Red Army did everything it could to win the Second World War, but before the conflict broke out, Soviet dictator Joseph Stalin did all he could to prevent it from doing so. Representing one of the worst crimes against humanity of the twentieth century, his brutal administration of the Soviet Union during the 1930s caused up to 30 million deaths. His vindictive persecution of the Red Army inadvertently contributed to another 20 million deaths during the Great Patriotic War against Hitler. Stalin's unbridled Terror, or Great Purge, was all encompassing within the Soviet armed forces, making the Red Army's hard-won victory in Europe in May 1945 even more remarkable.

On the eve of war with Germany there were over 100,000 Red Army officers on active duty, but up to half of these were removed. This was the first time that the officers of a loyal and undefeated army had been so systematically decimated by their own government during peacetime.

Stalin's paranoia was to cost him dearly. Adolf Hitler concluded that the Wehrmacht had the ability to bring the Soviet Union to its knees in the summer of 1941. This would give his rapidly expanding Third Reich the *Lebensraum*, or 'living space', and raw materials that it required to prosper and from which it could dominate Europe. It was Soviet leader Joseph Stalin himself who convinced Hitler he had the ability to crush the superficially formidable but nonetheless weakened Red Army.

The previous December, Hitler had set out his military plans for the Soviet Union in 'Directive No. 21: Case Barbarossa':

The Wehrmacht must be prepared, even before the conclusion of the war against England, *to crush Soviet Russia in a rapid campaign* ('Case Barbarossa').
[…]

The bulk of the Russian Army stationed in western Russia will be destroyed by daring operations led by deeply penetrating armoured spearheads. Russian forces still capable of giving battle will be prevented from withdrawing into the depths of Russia.

The enemy will then be energetically pursued and a line will be reached from which the Russian Air Force can no longer attack German territory. The final objective of the operation is to erect a barrier against Asiatic Russia on the general line Volga–Archangel. The last surviving industrial area of Russia in the Urals can then, if necessary, be eliminated by the Luftwaffe.[1]

While strong on general intentions, it was at best fuzzy on military and political practicalities. Fundamentally Hitler presupposed that the Soviet Union could be successfully partitioned once the Red Army had been defeated and Stalin had fallen from power. Even in 1940, to imagine that the Asian portion of the Soviet Union would leave European Russia under Nazi rule seemed a massive leap of faith. What convinced Hitler that such an outcome was possible, that the Red Army would never be able to recover sufficiently to claim it back?

Before Stalin's purges, Nikita Khrushchev, Soviet Military Council member and Politburo representative (and future Soviet premier), felt that the Red Army would have been more than a match for Hitler:

There's no question that we would have repulsed the fascist invasion much more easily if the upper echelons of the Red Army command hadn't been wiped out. They had been men of considerable expertise and experience. Many of them had graduated from military academies and gone through the Civil War. They were ready to discharge their soldierly duties for the sake of the Homeland, but they never had a chance.[2]

Meddling political control of the Red Army first appeared to ease in 1934 when dual oversight was ended. The commissars now found their role was purely to provide political advice and education rather than exercise power. This seemed to imply Stalin's seal of approval of the professionalism and loyalty of the Red Army's officers. Shortly after, military titles were reinstated.

The five most senior military officials were promoted to Marshal of the Soviet Union. These were Mikhail Tukhachevsky, a former Guards officer; Klimet Voroshilov, Commissar of Defence, veteran of the Bolshevik's 1st Cavalry Army and confidant of Stalin; Alexander Yegorov, chief of staff and another veteran of the 1st Cavalry Army; Semyon Budenny, another cavalryman; and Vasily Blyukher, commander of the Army of Siberia.

However, Stalin's new-found seal of approval was to be very short-lived. When Stalin's Terror was unleashed in 1937 almost the entire Red Army High Command were accused of being part of a German military-political conspiracy. Approximately 90 per cent of the general officers and 80 per cent of the colonels disappeared; three of the five Marshals of the Soviet Union and thirteen out of fifteen senior generals were eliminated, as were seventy-five of the eighty members of the Supreme Military Council and eleven Vice Commissars of Defence. Regional commands and more junior officers were not spared either.

Command and control of the ten Soviet military districts, tasked with defending the Soviet Union's borders, was decimated. Out of eighty-five corps commanders, fifty-seven were gone within a year, and of 406 brigade commanders, 220 were dead by the close of 1938. Some 40,000 senior and medium-grade officers were removed from post and executed, imprisoned or sent to the labour camps of the Gulag. As a result, Hitler was completely duped into believing that the Wehrmacht could crush the decapitated Red Army and so he greenlighted Operation Barbarossa.

But, what first drove Stalin to emaciate his armed forces to such an extent that Hitler felt confident enough to attack his well-armed neighbour? By 1929, in the wake of the turmoil of the Russian Revolution and Civil War, Stalin was firmly in control of the Soviet Union and had no intention of relinquishing it, regardless of the cost. Within two years, fearing the influence of his exiled arch-rival Leon Trotsky (the number two figure, after Lenin, during the 1917 Bolshevik Revolution), he turned his attentions to the Red Army, making changes amongst the senior appointments. This was one of Stalin's initial minor bloodless purges of the armed forces. Those involved could count themselves extremely lucky, for they were simply removed from post and in many cases simply dismissed. Relatively painlessly, Stalin promoted his own cronies. As a dress rehearsal of things to come this minor purge, conducted in 1929–30, saw just 4.7 per cent of the military membership expelled from the Communist Party; again, in 1933–34, 6.7 per cent of the military membership was excluded or demoted.

Stalin launched his first 'five-year plan' in 1928. Its goal was to industrialise an agricultural system that largely remained rooted in the Middle Ages. The Red Army was also to be modernised; particularly in terms of equipment and mechanisation. The second 'five-year plan', launched in 1932, saw Stalin turn his attention on the hapless wealthy peasants, for he wished to collectivise their farms which meant appropriating their land. The Soviet Union had some 25 million peasant farmers who worked their own land. The richest numbered some 2 million, to whom Stalin ruthlessly attached the name '*kulak*' ('usurer' or crooked rural trader). There were 18 million middle peasants and some 5 million who were semi-destitute.

Stalin ordered that the *kulaks* be liquidated as a class, accusing them of being enemies of the state. The tragedy was that many of them were former loyal Red Army veterans who had returned to claim their land after fighting in the Civil War. In response to Stalin's mass appropriation of their property, the *kulaks* slaughtered their own livestock rather than let the state take it and, in some cases, resisted. Red Army morale plummeted and in many units there was mass desertion by peasant soldiers, who hastened home to their villages, with or without rifles, to wreak vengeance on the executives of the collectives. By 1936 it has been estimated that 7 million people died in the collectivisation famine and forced deportations.

At the same time, new military vehicles began to roll out of Soviet factories at a rate previously unknown, and by the end of the year the Red Army had approximately as many tanks as France, which was at the time the pre-eminent European military power – by 1935 the Red Army had a fleet of 10,000 tanks.

Stalin, however, soon began to fear that a revived and enhanced Red Army would pose a threat to his power base. In addition, the Red Army had been divided by the wanton persecution of the *kulaks*. Stalin's following actions were to have ramifications that even his warped mind could not have conceived.

First, he moved to stamp out potential political opposition in the key city of Leningrad. When Sergei Kirov, an old Stalin supporter, was assassinated (allegedly on Stalin's orders) this unleashed a gradual purge which was to gather momentum until it became the all-encompassing Great Purge. This was to affect every element of Soviet society, including the Red Army. Stalin's instrument of terror and destruction was to be the Peoples' Commissariat of Internal Affairs – the dreaded NKVD – which came into being in 1934 as the forerunner of the KGB.

That year, on a December afternoon, Kirov (Leningrad Party leader for whom the ballet was named) was shot dead. It appeared the assassin acted on his own, but thirteen accomplices were killed along with him. Then, in the spring of 1935 thousands of Leningrad Party members, tainted by association with Kirov, were deported to the Gulag.

In Moscow, Stalin's supporters moved quickly, the Central Committee of the Communist Party had 70 per cent of its 200 members liquidated. A few faced kangaroo courts, the rest just vanished from their homes. A show trial was conducted in 1937 where seventeen politicians were accused of conspiring with Leon Trotsky, the Germans and the Japanese.

No previous persecutions had ever reached the scale of Stalin's. He made Ivan the Terrible's reign of terror look tame. Under Stalin, state-authorised executions reached up to 1,000 a day. Between 1936 and 1938 approximately 500,000–1 million people were executed, with a further 8 million imprisoned.

Colonel General Andrei Trofimovich Stuchenko, who attended the prestigious MV Frunze Academy (the Soviet Union's second highest military school) in 1936, recalled:

> It was a terrifying time. People began to fear one another. Anything might serve as grounds for arrest: national origin, failure on the job, or even an incorrect interpretation of some word. It was particularly dangerous to be suspected of having connections with 'enemies of the people'. [...]
>
> The arbitrariness and violations of socialist legality which were spawned by Stalin's personality cult caused us to lose many experienced military comrades. The critical shortage of commanders began to be felt by the troops.[3]

Once Stalin's political enemies were exterminated, the *Yezhovshchina* (as the Great Terror became known – named after NKVD head, Nikolai Yezhov) fell firmly upon the Red Army with a vengeance in 1937. Ironically, the year before, the US Military Attaché in Moscow had observed that the loyalty of the Red Army to the government appeared beyond doubt.

Stalin had already murdered Defence Commissar Mikhail Frunze in 1925 (he was forced to undergo a gall stone operation despite a weak heart), in order to replace him with Kliment Voroshilov. The latter was a *political* general rather than a professional soldier. The initial step in tightening Stalin's grip was the reintroduction of Communist Party political deputies (military commissars) into units of divisional size or larger.

Author Alexandr Solzhenitsyn, a Red Army veteran and guest of the Gulag who became the Soviet Union's leading dissident, wrote with gallows humour of the strain these purges put on the Gulag's metaphorical sewage system:

> Although I have no statistics at hand, I am not afraid of erring when I say that the wave of 1937 and 1938 was neither the only one nor the main one, but only one, perhaps, of the three biggest waves which strained the murky, stinking pipes of our prison sewers to bursting.
>
> *Before* it came the wave of 1929 and 1930 ... which drove a mere fifteen million peasants ... into the permafrost.
>
> After it there was a wave of 1944 to 1946 ... when they dumped whole *nations* down the sewer pipes, not to mention millions and millions of others who (because of us!) had been prisoners of war, or carried off to Germany and subsequently repatriated.
>
> But the wave of 1937 swept up and carried off to the Archipelago [Gulag] people of position ...[4]

One of the *Yezhovshchina*'s first senior military victims was General Gamarnik, head of the army's Main Political Administration (MPA). Marshal Blyukher visited him on 31 May 1937, informing him of the spreading arrests throughout the army. That afternoon, when the NKVD came, Gamarnik either committed suicide or was killed resisting arrest.

With the head of the MPA out of the way, the NKVD had free rein. Marshal Mikhail Tukhachevsky and seven other senior generals were arrested without fuss and taken to the dreaded Lubyanka Prison in Moscow. Amongst them were the commanders of the Soviet Union's key western military districts (Leningrad, Byelorussia, Kiev and Volga) and the Moscow garrison. In one fell swoop Stalin compromised the whole of the western Soviet Union's defences. Tukhachevsky's real crime was in being everything that Stalin was not – educated, talented and very able. Also, he hated Generals Voroshilov and Budenny, which won him no friends at Stalin's Red Court.

Tukhachevsky has been described as Stalin's most gifted general. A former tsarist cadet, he was energetic and incisive and at 27 had commanded Soviet forces fighting against Poland. At 28, he destroyed the Kronstadt uprising with Trotsky, and at just 31 he became chief of staff. Already viewed as a rival, he had initially been removed by Stalin in 1928 and posted to the provinces. Tukhachevsky may not have known it but he was on borrowed time.

Stalin wanted Tukhachevsky arrested for treason as early as 1930, but his forward thinking with the Red Army had ensured that he remained Deputy Defence Commissar. It was another six years before he slid from power. In May 1936, following a heated row with Stalin's favourite, Voroshilov, Tukhachevsky found himself sacked and sent to the Volga Military District. He was almost immediately arrested and sent back to Moscow. This was at a time when the first generals were being arrested and they were only too willing to implicate him if it meant saving their own necks.

Incriminatingly, Tukhachevsky was close friends with members of the German General Staff; he had been captured during the First World War and had since visited Germany six times. He made impassioned pleas to Stalin and Voroshilov, but to no avail, and under torture eventually 'confessed' to being a German agent. His blood-splattered confession bore testimony to the methods used to gain it. Stalin claimed, at a meeting of the Soviet High Command, that Tukhachevsky had been recruited in a honey trap involving a German female spy.

The growing numbers pouring into the Gulag from all walks of life meant that bureaucratic niceties were soon dispensed with. According to Solzhenitsyn:

Before 1938 some kind of formal documentation was required as a preliminary to torture, as well as specified permission for each case to be under investigation

... then in the years 1937–1938 ... interrogators were allowed to use violence and torture on an unlimited basis ... in 1939 such indiscriminate authorisation was withdrawn and once again written permission was required.[5]

It may have been that Stalin feared, or indeed knew of, a genuine plot amongst the ranks of the Red Army to oust him. Nonetheless, it is equally possible that the following show trial was because of Hitler's attempts to feed Stalin's paranoia and deliberately weaken the Red Army. The marshals' and generals' arrests came after an allegedly secret German document fell into the hands of President Benes of Czechoslovakia, who passed it to Stalin. The German Gestapo and the NKVD are suspected of faking this incriminating evidence. It was passed to Benes via a White Russian émigré, General Nikolai Skoblin, in Paris, who had links with the Gestapo and NKVD. He was to vanish from Paris in September 1937, conveniently tying up any loose ends.

On 11 June 1937, the entire Red Army command, including the chief of the General Staff, the deputy defence commissars, military district commanders, all four army commanders, naval flag officers and four of the Marshals of the Soviet Union, attended the show trial of their comrades. Only Voroshilov was conspicuously missing, although he had branded the accused 'scoundrels and degenerates'. To try the eight accused were eight judges (including two marshals); perversely, five of them were destined to die as well. Apart from Military Jurist of the Army First Class V. Ulrikh (who had considerable experience of show trials), none of them had any legal training. Understandably the judges themselves were uneasy about the whole proceeding. Marshal Blyukher even claimed he was ill and excused himself.

In contrast, Marshal Semyon Budenny, commander of the Moscow Military District, swaggered in full of bravado – even taking time to pose for the cameras. Budenny, a Civil War cavalry veteran who had served with Stalin on the South-Western Front, proceeded to denounce Tukhachevsky's progressive thinking. He referred to the accused as 'scum' and argued the creation of tank corps was a deliberate attempt to wreck the Red Army. Tukhachevsky was understandably flabbergasted. However, Budenny's self-seeking grandstanding did not stop him later falling under the suspicion of the NKVD.

Chief of the General Staff General Boris Mikhailovitch Shaposhnikov was aghast as General Ion Yakir, former commander of the Kiev Military District, stoutly denied the accusations of being a traitor. Shaposhnikov held the key post of commandant of the Frunze Military Academy (the Soviet equivalent of Sandhurst or Westpoint) from 1932 to 1937. He was then elevated to chief of the General Staff of the Red Army, a position he held until 1940 and again during 1941–42.

Yakir demanded of his colleagues, 'Look me in the eyes! Can you really not understand that this is all lies?' Fellow accused, General Primakov, former deputy commander of the Leningrad Military District, realising this was the work of Stalin and that all was lost, replied, 'Give it up, Ion. Don't you see who we are dealing with here?'

It was claimed that all eight were working for German Intelligence and undermining the Red Army, a charge that would have been better levelled at Stalin himself. Strangely, the folder containing the Benes document was never produced as evidence. None of the unfortunate generals pleaded guilty; in the typed trial report, all the 'no' responses were changed in ink to 'yes', apart from Tukhachevsky, who resolutely refused to co-operate. All eight were shot and their bodies were taken to a building site at Khodynka, thrown in a ditch and covered in quicklime and soil. It was a shocking demonstration of Stalin's absolute power over the Red Army. In the coming months, it was to be repeated again and again.

This show trial opened the floodgates and former tsarist officers and Red Army veterans of the Civil War shared the fate of the eight generals. Lubyanka, Butyrka and Lefortovo in Moscow, and Kresty and Shlaperny prisons in Leningrad began to fill up with the 'enemies of the people'.

For the arrests, the NKVD operated in pairs, while three constituted a tribunal. Arrest, sentencing and transportation took just three months, on average, and sentences were either death or a minimum of ten years in the Gulag prison labour system. Nothing could save the accused. Many, thinking that it was some sort of mistake, phoned Voroshilov, but he was Stalin's protégé and their calls for help fell on deaf ears or he would instruct them to remain where they were until someone could come and 'explain'. Voroshilov, far from trying to safeguard the Red Army High Command, personally ordered the arrest of 300 fellow officers – by his own account, 40,000 were arrested and 100,000 new, inexperienced officers promoted.

All the judges were executed, except for Budenny, Shaposhnikov and Ulrikh. Budenny even called Stalin to inform him that he had just warned off the NKVD with machine guns protecting his house. Stalin claimed he had no better idea than Budenny what the NKVD were up to and he was concerned they might come for him next. Budenny somehow survived to fight the Germans.

As a junior officer, Marshal Sergei Biriuzov had similar experiences to General Stuchenko:

> I recalled with a shudder the years of 1937–38. During that dismal period, I studied at the MV Frunze Academy. […] After graduation I was appointed to the 30th Irkutsk Red Banner Division [as chief of staff]. There, an even more stupefying picture unfolded before me.[6]

The military in the Soviet Far East remained untouched until May 1938 when the deputy head of the NKVD arrived. Even Marshal Blyukher, Commander of the Far East, who had sat on the initial tribunals, disappeared in 1938. The 100,000-strong Soviet Kolkhoz Corps was disbanded and the Japanese, underestimating the effect of the purge, were prompted to probe Soviet border defences during 1938 and 1939.

Even those sent to serve in the Spanish Civil War were not immune. Soviet Consul Antonov-Ovseyenko was liquidated in 1939, and General Jan Berzin, former head of Military Intelligence, also fell prey to the Terror. The other services were not spared either. In fact, the navy lost more senior officers than the Red Army. Admiral Orlov, commander-in-chief of the navy, was shot, as was Admiral Muklevich. Four of the five fleet commanders were also executed.

Very few escaped the rolling tide of denunciation and destruction. Amongst them was General Andrei Vedenin. Although accused of being a tsarist sympathiser and buying unhealthy horses for the military, he survived to become commandant at – of all places – the Kremlin. Similarly, Laventi Beria told General Meretskov, who had been forced to confess that he was a British agent by the NKVD, that his claims were nonsense. He was released, given a general's uniform and sent off to the front.

Other survivors were equally brutalised. Solzhenitsyn recalled:

> They say that Konstantin Rokossovsky, the future marshal, was twice taken into the forest at night for a supposed execution. The firing squad levelled rifles at him, and then they dropped them, and he was taken back to prison. And this was also making use of 'the supreme measure' as an interrogator's trick. But it was all right; nothing happened; and he is alive and healthy and doesn't even cherish a grudge about it.[7]

Such forgiving attitudes in the face of appalling physical and mental brutality are hard to fathom. One would expect that Rokossovsky and colleagues who suffered similar experiences would have wanted the Red Tsar and his court dead as soon as possible. Rokossovsky and his comrades not only endured mock executions but also countless brutal beatings. Yet the Russian officers' love for the 'Motherland' overrode any hatred they may have felt for Stalin or the Soviet system. Rather than turning on Stalin, they would readily spill their blood for him. Such loyalty is testimony to the culture of brutality prevalent in the Red Army at the time.

With the Second World War imminent, the timing of Stalin's purge could not have been worse. Prior to the Terror the Red Army was at its strongest and most efficient – all this work was undone in one fell swoop. The removal of the able Tukhachevsky and his colleagues was a disaster. The General Staff was left completely disorganised, with its members constantly looking over their shoulders to see who was next.

Making up for the level of damage wrought by Stalin's purge before Hitler attacked was impossible. While Voroshilov was incompetent, Stalin bore equal blame for also allowing the Red Army's manpower to treble while officer training only doubled. Efforts to make good the purges were clearly insufficient. In the spring of 1940, over 30 per cent of Red Army platoon and company commanders had not attended the prescribed five-month course for junior lieutenants. By the summer of the following year, over 90 per cent of Soviet officers had not received higher military education and almost 40 per cent had not completed intermediate training. On top of this, 75 per cent of all officers had only held their posts for under a year, casting doubt on their competency. The reality was that no one knew what they were doing.

The Red Army's desperate need for experienced officers inevitably began to result in the release of some of those consigned to the Gulag. Solzhenitsyn observed:

> The reverse wave of 1939 was an unheard of incident in the history of the Organs [state security, or NKVD], a blot on their record! But, in fact, this reverse wave was not large; it included about one to two per cent of those who had been arrested but not yet convicted, who had not yet been sent away to far off places and had not yet perished. It was not large, but was put to effective use.[8]

General Ernst Köstring, the German Military Attaché in Moscow in 1940, was predicting it would take the Red Army four years to recover from Stalin's purges. Prior to Barbarossa, the German General Staff produced *A Brief Review of the Soviet Armed Forces*, which provided an assessment of the Soviet officer corps. It concluded:

> At the present time, many positions must be considered vacant as a result of the many arrests. There are attempts to make up for the lack of officers by reducing the period of officer training and by promoting veteran sergeants to junior lieutenants ... The actual strength of the Air Force is about 30 per cent less than the authorised establishment ... Following the execution of Tukhachevsky and a number of generals in the summer of 1937, just a few military leaders have remained. Everything indicates, at this juncture, the middle and senior command personnel represent the weakest element.[9]

During the second half of the 1930s Soviet cinemas had screened a rousing documentary film called *The Fight for Kiev*. Foreign military delegations were invited to watch impressive large-scale Red Army manoeuvres being filmed in Byelorussia and Ukraine. Undoubtedly, the German General Staff could draw conclusions from the exercises and the documentary about how Soviet military thinking was developing. 'We ourselves failed essentially to utilise our rich experience,' said Marshal Biriuzov, 'although we were the first to work out the principles of conducting large-scale combat operations under modern conditions of mechanised war.'[10]

Not surprisingly, the veterans of the 1st Cavalry Army got themselves into positions of power. This was, after all, Stalin's favourite Civil War formation. Despite his purge, an old boys' network of Civil War veterans survived to ensure that the Red Army still retained a few relatively competent commanders, amongst whom were General Semyon Mikhailovich Budenny, Semyon Konstantinovich Timoshenko and Georgi Zhukov.

Budenny was an old-school cavalryman through and through, with a deep-rooted scepticism of tanks, and was not considered very bright by some. His main contribution to the Red Army seems to have been his ridiculously large moustache and a comical looking Civil War era cloth helmet, named after him. Nonetheless, from 1937–39 he held the key post of Commander of the Moscow Military District, followed by the First Deputy People's Commissar of Defence, and during the German invasion commanded the South-Western Front.

Zhukov had served as a squadron commander under Budenny in the 1st Cavalry Army, and more importantly, Zhukov's brigade commander had been Timoshenko. Just under two decades later Timoshenko, by then a marshal and People's Commissar for Defence, ensured that Zhukov gained the post of his principal assistant, chief of the General Staff in January 1941 at the age of 44. Neither Budenny nor Timoshenko would show the flare or survival instincts exhibited by Zhukov before or during the war.

Prior to his appointment as Timoshenko's deputy, Zhukov, future hero of the battles of Moscow, Stalingrad and Berlin, was deputy commander of the Byelorussian Military District. He prudently kept himself away from Soviet politics and escaped Stalin's purges. Zhukov had been appointed commander of the 3rd Cavalry Corps in 1937, but shortly after was offered the 6th Cossack Corps. Zhukov discovered this formation to be in a much better state, and found it contained an old command of his, the Don Cossack Division, as well the 6th Chongar and 29th Cavalry Divisions.

However, Zhukov was not a conservative cavalryman – far from it – he was, in fact, very progressive. During this time, Zhukov recalled, 'It was clear that the future largely belonged to armour and mechanised units. Hence we gave undivided attention to questions of cavalry–armour co-operation, and the organisation of anti-tank defences in combat and in executing manoeuvres.'[11] While commanding the 3rd and then the 6th Corps, Zhukov co-operated closely with the 21st Detached Tank Brigade under M.I. Potapov and the 3rd Detached Tank Brigade under V.V. Novikov. Both commanders were, in Zhukov's own words,'former mates of mine'.[12]

At the end of 1938 Zhukov was offered the Byelorussian post, commanding the cavalry and tank units which were to comprise up to five cavalry divisions, up to four detached tank brigades and other supporting units. Saying goodbye to the Cossack Corps, Zhukov travelled to Smolensk and during May 1939 conducted exercises near Minsk, little realising that this would soon be the scene of bitter battles with Hitler's marauding panzers.

Other notable commanders who served with the 1st Cavalry Army included Grigory Kulik, Semyon Krivoshein, Kirill Meretskov and Klimet Voroshilov. The prominence of these cavalrymen ensured that at the start of the war with Germany the Red Army had thirteen cavalry divisions (four of which were mountain cavalry). By the end of 1941 there were forty-one (although these were only of brigade strength) being used as mounted infantry. Even with the revitalisation of the Red Army's mechanised corps, by 1943 there were still twenty-seven cavalry divisions. This cavalry-orientated legacy of the Russian Civil War simply refused to fade away.

There was another, simpler reason for the continued dominance of the Red Army by the cavalry. Alexander Werth, a reporter for *The Sunday Times*, enjoyed a grandstand view from Moscow and was remarkably able to travel around the country unhindered. Born in St Petersburg and a fluent Russian speaker, he was given unparalleled access to the Red Army:

> Undoubtedly it is the largest cavalry force in the world, but most Russian generals will tell you that they would prefer an armoured division to a cavalry division, and that their relatively wide use of cavalry resulted primarily from inadequate tank and armoured car production.[13]

Ironically, it has been argued that Stalin's purge of the Red Army, although damaging, also served to prune out much dead wood. While Stalin spared his Civil War cronies such as Budenny, Kulik and Voroshilov, they proved to be far from progressive; it was the surviving younger generation of generals such as Zhukov, Vasilevskiy, Rokossovsky, Meretskov, Voronov, Malinovsky, Tolbukhin and Rotmistrov who would eventually surpass Hitler's commanders.

Although Stalin undoubtedly liquidated several very talented and potentially promising generals, it would be wrong to argue that even with them the Red

Army could have withstood the Nazi blitzkrieg any better than the other intact European armies that had been crushed so easily. Popular mythology has it that Stalin decapitated the Red Amy and this contributed to its catastrophic defeat, however, his purge's greater crime was to encourage Hitler to attack in the first place. The reality is that with or without the purge Hitler would have still attacked the Soviet Union.

2

ZHUKOV PULLS NO PUNCHES

In the second half of 1939 Hitler and his High Command watched with great interest as the Red Army fought three brief and very different border wars. In the summer, it was involved in what seemed an inconsequential border squabble with the Japanese. Then in September, sixteen days after Hitler's invasion of Poland, it rolled into eastern Poland under the terms of the Nazi-Soviet Non-Aggression Pact. Polish opposition to the Red Army was negligible, which was just as well, as its conduct proved to be the complete opposite to the Wehrmacht's highly efficient blitzkrieg. Then in the winter, the outnumbered Finnish Army ran circles around the Red Army after it became trapped in Finland's dense forests.

Ironically, the Soviet–Japanese War could not have come at a better time for Zhukov and the Red Army. Zhukov would gain invaluable experience conducting armoured warfare. He would also become familiar with the forces of the Transbaikal Military District guarding the Chinese Manchuria–Manchukuo border. This district had come into being in the mid-1930s as a precautionary measure in response to the Japanese invasion of China. It also helped create a useful reserve for the Red Army.

The main Japanese force in occupied Manchuria, known as Manchukuo, was the Kwantung Army. Japan coveted the Soviet port of Vladivostok, but to keep the Red Army at bay it needed to sever the Trans-Siberian Railway. As a precautionary measure, the Red Army occupied Changkufeng Hill near the mouth of the Tyumen River on the eastern border, south-west of Vladivostok. Throughout the summer of 1938, the Japanese probed Soviet defences with a series of border incidents near Vladivostok at Lake Khasan. The Soviet response was poor, revealing the true extent of Stalin's purge. On 11 July 1938 fighting broke out when the Japanese tried to remove Soviet troops from Changkufeng. However, they had fortified the area and remained in possession of the hill following an armistice on 10 August 1938.

The Imperial Japanese Army risked losing face after the formal ceasefire at Khasan. However, Japanese Emperor Hirohito agreed to the General Staff's plan to act much further west, against Mongolia. Stalin's purges had left the Red Army in disarray and with war brewing with Finland, which would tie up resources and severely stretch its capabilities, and tensions growing over Poland, Stalin looked around for someone he could trust, who would swiftly put an end to Japanese adventurism. He picked Corps Commander Georgi Konstantinovich Zhukov.

Zhukov was ordered to see the People's Commissar of Defence, Marshal Voroshilov in Moscow on 2 June 1939. Voroshilov told him:

> Japanese troops have made a surprise attack and crossed into friendly Mongolia which the Soviet government is committed to defend from external aggression by the Treaty of 12 March 1936. Here is a map of the invasion area showing the situation as of 30 May.[1]

The Kwantung Army had occupied a region along the Khalkhin-Gol River, as this formed much of the boundary between the Outer Mongolian Peoples' Republic to the west and Manchukuo to the east. Based at Hailar, General Michitaro Komatsubara's 23rd Division was responsible for security in western Manchukuo. The Japanese claimed the border was the Khalkhin-Gol River, in contrast to the Mongolians and their Soviet allies who claimed it ran 10 miles (16km) east of the river and just east of the village of Nomonhan.

Pointing to the map, Voroshilov added:

> The Japanese had for a long time carried out provocative attacks on Mongolian frontier guards, and here the Japanese Hailar garrison invaded MPR [Mongolian People's Republic] territory and attached Mongolian frontier units which were covering the area east of Khalkhin Gol.
>
> I think they've started a big military gamble. At any rate, it's only the beginning … Could you fly there right away and if need be assume command of our troops?[2]

Zhukov jumped at the chance of seeing action. He went to see Ivan Smorodinov, acting deputy chief of the General Staff. 'The moment you arrive,' said Smorodinov, 'see what's going on and report to us. But pull no punches.'[3]

Zhukov understood only too well that his new appointment could make or break his career. Simply ousting the Japanese from Outer Mongolia would not be enough; the Japanese would have to be dealt such a blow that they would never consider tackling the Red Army again. In effect, the security of the whole of the Soviet Far East rested in his hands. Accompanied by a small team, at 1600hrs Zhukov flew east, landing first in Chita, headquarters of the Transbaikal Military District. He found the city was a secretive place. The Japanese had briefly occupied it for two years at the end of the First World War, and prior to that it had been the scene of resistance to tsarist rule. Under the Soviet authorities, Chita was closed to most Russians and all foreigners because of its proximity on the strategically important Trans-Siberian Railway and the Chinese–Mongolian borders. Chita boasted a mosque, thanks to its Muslim Tartar population who were ethnic cousins of the Mongolians to the south.

Military District Commander General V.F. Yakovlev and his officers met Zhukov at their headquarters. He knew that Stalin was taking the Japanese incursion into the MPR very seriously if the People's Commissariat of Defence had sent a special envoy with the authority to take charge without recourse to any of the regional commands.

In the first instance, Zhukov needed credible intelligence to make a thorough assessment of the situation. He was informed that General N.V. Feklenko's 57th Special Corps was forward deployed to the south-east in Mongolia and tasked with protecting the republic. This was good news, as it meant that the Red Army had a corps-level command-and-control structure in place in the MPR.

Worryingly, it transpired that the Japanese Air Force had been attacking Soviet troop movements in Mongolia indicating a lack of support from the Red Air Force. Apart from this, Zhukov was very disappointed by the vagueness and lack of detailed intelligence regarding Japanese military intentions and strength. It was immediately clear that Yakovlev's communications with Feklenko were very poor. It was also very evident that Feklenko did not have a firm grip on the situation. The Soviet High Command was not ignorant of Japan's conquest of huge areas of China and that this constituted a very real threat to the Soviet border. In light of previous border fighting, Feklenko's lack of urgency did seem very puzzling.

Just three days after his Moscow meeting, Zhukov arrived at 57th Special Corps HQ at Tamtsak-Bulak in Mongolia and met Feklenko, Regimental Commissar M.S. Nikishev, who was corps commissar, and Brigade Commander A.M. Kushchev, chief of staff. To Zhukov's irritation, the situation was a complete mess. The headquarters had little appreciation of the situation and communication between the Soviet and Mongolian commands was non-existent and co-ordination lacking. Zhukov was very unhappy that none of the commanders, except for Nikishev, had even visited the front and therefore had little idea of what was happening on the ground. Grasping the situation, he travelled up to the front and found that local intelligence was equally poor.

Zhukov quickly came to the conclusion that 57th Corps in its present state was not up to the job of directing operations nor stopping the Japanese.

He immediately sent his report to Voroshilov, stating he planned that Soviet-Mongolian troops should maintain the bridgehead on the right bank of the Khalkhin-Gol while preparing for a counter-offensive. Voroshilov agreed, and the ineffectual Feklenko found himself immediately replaced by Zhukov. The latter's first move was to request reinforcements for the air force, plus three rifle divisions, a tank brigade and artillery.

On 22 June 1939, well over 100 Japanese planes were engaged by ninety-five Soviet fighters over Mongolian territory. The Soviet pilots were led by Y.V. Smushkevich and twenty other 'Heroes of the Soviet Union'. Two days later, the Japanese returned and were again driven off. They, in turn, brought up air aces who had been operating over China and these were thrown into battle over Lake Buir Nor on the 26th. Between 22–26 June the Soviets claimed sixty-four Japanese planes. The dogfights continued on an almost daily basis until 1 July. Zhukov and Voroshilov were greatly encouraged.

It was clear to the Japanese that Stalin had intervened on behalf of the MPR. In retaliation, the Japanese 2nd Air Brigade bombed the Soviet air base at Tamtsak-Bulak on 27 June. This attack, however, was unauthorised and when the Imperial Japanese Army HQ in Tokyo heard of it the Japanese Air Force was ordered not to do it again. Stalin was beginning to feel uneasy, with Germany militarily resurgent in the west and Japan probing his eastern frontiers, the last thing he wanted was a two-front war.

Zhukov had to do something, and fast. By July the Japanese had massed some 38,000 men, supported by 135 tanks and 225 aircraft, east of the Khalkhin-Gol. Zhukov could muster little more than 12,500 Soviet-Mongolian troops, although his main asset was 186 tanks and 226 armoured cars. Notably, the Soviet armour comprised the T-26 light tank and the BT-5 and BT-7 fast tanks, while the Japanese relied on the Type 97 (although they were a match for the BT tanks, they were too few), and the slower Type 89 medium tanks.

The Japanese struck on 2 July and their tanks and infantry soon reached the river. Zhukov decided to bide his time before showing his hand. The following day, the Japanese threw a pontoon bridge over the river near Mount Bain-Tsagan. They pushed 10,000 troops, 100 pieces of artillery and sixty anti-tank guns onto the mountain; the defenders from the Mongolian 6th Cavalry Division could muster barely 1,000 men and fifty guns, including those on the eastern bank of the river. The Japanese seized Bain-Tsagan and advanced south along the west bank. Colonel I.M. Afonin, senior Soviet advisor to the Mongolian Army, arrived to find that the Japanese had driven the Mongolians onto the north-western part of the mountain. He quickly apprised 57th Corps of the desperate situation.

Zhukov, alert to the danger of his forces being cut off on the east bank, ordered a triple-pronged counter-attack with 450 tanks and armoured cars.

At his command, he had the 11th Tank Brigade, equipped with 150 tanks; the 7th Armoured Brigade with another 154 armoured vehicles; and the Mongolian 8th Armoured Battalion, armed with 45mm guns. The 11th Tank Brigade, under Commander Yakovlev, was instructed to strike from the north supported by the 24th Motorised Regiment, which pressed in from the north-west supported by artillery under Colonel Fedyuinsky. In addition, the 7th Armoured Brigade under Colonel Lesovoi was to attack from the south, supported by an armoured battalion from the Mongolian 8th Cavalry Division. Heavy guns were moved up from the 185th Artillery Regiment to support the attack on Bain-Tsagan and the 9th Armoured Brigade in the Khalkhin-Gol bridgehead.

At 0700 hrs on 3 July 1939, the Red Air Force and artillery commenced softening up Japanese positions. At 0900 hrs the tanks of the 11th Tank Brigade moved up, with the full attack being launched at 1045 hrs. Japanese defences and anti-tank guns were inadequate and the Soviets began to make ground. The Japanese response was to launch a counter-attack on the 4th, but it came to grief in the face of Soviet bombers and artillery. The bombers also successfully severed the pontoon bridge.

That night, General Komatsubara gave the order to withdraw and the Japanese were pushed back over the river by 5 July, although their engineers blew the remaining bridges to prevent the Soviet tanks following, leaving many Japanese with little option but to swim for it. Those troops remaining on the eastern slopes of Bain-Tsagan were annihilated. Although Komatsubara and his headquarters made it back across the river, hundreds of his men drowned. He left much of his 10,000-strong force behind, strewn over the mountain.

In the face of a Japanese counter-attack, the Soviets held their ground and on 25 July the Japanese gave up, having suffered over 5,000 casualties. According to Soviet sources, between 23 July and 4 August the Japanese Air Force also lost 116 aircraft. The Japanese counter-attacked on 12 August, driving the Mongolian 22nd Cavalry Regiment from the Bolshiye Peski Height to the south. At this point, it would have been prudent for the Kwantung Army to call it a day and summon the diplomats. Instead, more anti-tank gun units were brought up ready for a counter-attack. They planned to attack along a 43-mile front on 24 August. However, Zhukov was to beat them to it by four days.

Zhukov's Soviet-Mongolian Command was also prepared for a knock-out counter-offensive. Reinforcements were brought up, including two rifle divisions, a tank brigade and two artillery regiments, as well as supporting bomber and fighter units. Stalin, conscious that Nazi Germany would be closely watching events in Central Asia, despatched further reinforcements. These included three infantry and two cavalry divisions and seven independent brigades, including five armoured, additional artillery and air force units, to create the First Army Group. Zhukov had everything he needed.

Soviet reconnaissance aircraft pieced together a good intelligence picture of the Japanese defences. The reconnaissance group from the 149th Motorised Rifle Regiment, under regimental commander I.M. Remizov, also provided a steady stream of prisoners for interrogation. Zhukov and his staff assessed that the Japanese were most vulnerable on their flanks. He knew that the Japanese' greatest weakness was their lack of mobility, effective tank units and motorised infantry. This meant they would not be able to respond quickly to any Soviet attack or breakthrough.

Zhukov's armoured fist consisted of the 4th, 6th and 11th Tank Brigades and the 7th and 8th Mechanised Brigades. He was ready four days before his opponents, and sought to encircle the Japanese using his north, south and central groups, with his armour on the wings. The Soviets deployed 50,000 troops to defend the east bank and then Zhukov prepared to cross to the west on 20 August with three rifle divisions and his armoured forces. Waiting at their jump-off points were thirty-five infantry battalions supported by a mobile force of twenty cavalry squadrons, 498 tanks, 346 armoured cars and 502 guns.

At 0545 hrs on 20 August, Soviet aircraft blasted the Japanese forward positions, followed by a three-hour artillery and mortar bombardment. At 0845 hrs Zhukov's tanks roared forward to overwhelm the remaining Japanese. By the next day, to the south Soviet forces had swung behind the Japanese, reaching the Khalkhin-Gol's east–west tributary, the Khailastyn-Gol. On 23 August the North Group, supported by Zhukov's reserves, the 212th Airborne Brigade fighting as infantry, seized the Palet Heights and swung south. Although trapped, the Japanese resisted to the last and the Soviets lost 600 men clearing the Heights.

The two wings of Zhukov's attack linked up at Nomonhan on 25 August, trapping the Japanese 23rd Division. The following day, Japanese forces outside the pocket tried to get through to them but were met by the Soviet 6th Tank Brigade. The Red Air Force also ensured that the Japanese could not bring up reinforcements. They dropped 190 tons of bombs during 474 sorties in the first week alone.

Having trapped the Japanese, Zhukov spent a week eradicating the survivors. To get at those ensconced on the Remizov Heights his engineers assisted his tanks over the Khailastyn-Gol by reinforcing the riverbed. By 31 August it was all over.

Zhukov's successful campaign at Khalkhin-Gol severely mauled the Kwantung Army. He had passed his first major test of high-level combat command with flying colours. The Japanese claimed they lost 8,440 dead and suffered

8,766 wounded, while the Soviets claimed 9,284 casualties. However, losses for the Japanese have been put as high as 45,000 killed and Soviet casualties well over 17,000. Certainly, of the 60,000 Japanese troops trapped in Zhukov's cauldron, 50,000 were listed as killed, wounded and missing. The Japanese 23rd Division lost 99 per cent of its strength. The Japanese Air Force claimed 1,200 Soviet planes, which seems improbable, and the Soviets claimed 660 Japanese aircraft, which seems equally implausible in four months of fighting.

Meanwhile, Stalin, with war brewing in Europe, was convinced Hitler would not turn on the Soviet Union, and on 19 August 1939 he told the Politburo:

Now let us consider the second possibility, a German victory [over Poland, Britain and France]. Some think that this would confront us with a serious danger. There is some truth in this, but it would be a mistake to regard the danger as so close at hand or as great as has been proposed.

If Germany should prove to be victorious, she will leave the war too weakened to start a war with the USSR within a decade at least. She will have to supervise the occupation of France and England and to restore herself. [...]

Obviously, this Germany will be too busy elsewhere to turn against us.[4]

On 1 September 1939 Adolf Hitler invaded Poland, and when the shooting stopped Stalin occupied the eastern half of the country. Behind the scenes Stalin, alarmed by the ease with which the Wehrmacht had crushed Poland in just four weeks, feared that Finland and the Baltic States might provide a springboard for a Nazi invasion of the Soviet Union. He imposed a mutual defensive agreement on the Baltic States of Estonia, Latvia and Lithuania in October 1939. This involved allowing the Red Army to be based on their soil (in July 1940 they were officially incorporated into the Soviet Union).

Then Stalin invaded Finland on 30 November 1939. In London, the British Foreign Secretary, Lord Halifax, suspected the duplicitous hand of Hitler. He was convinced Hitler and Stalin had cut a deal:

The Russian attack on Finland seems to me to be a direct consequence of German policy. By the agreement which he thought would give him a free hand to attack Poland, it would seem Herr Hitler bartered what was not his property to barter – the liberties of the Baltic people.[5]

Halifax made it clear he felt that Hitler, not Stalin, was to blame:

Germany assisted Finland to maintain her independence in 1918. Now that independence is threatened by a brutal and totally unprovoked aggression for which Germany, by one of the most cynical acrobatic feats in political history, … must bear her own full and heavy share of the blame.[6]

From the start, it seemed that the Russo-Finnish Winter War would be short-lived. The Red Army had ten times the strength of the Finnish armed forces, and in the far north Soviet troops outnumbered the Finns by forty-two to one. The invasion, triggered by a spurious border incident, was publicly designed to punish Finland. The country had become independent from Russia after the First World War, but Stalin harboured lost imperial territorial ambitions. In the south, an attack would push the border away from the strategically important port of Leningrad, and in the north, secure the Finnish port of Petsamo on the Arctic Ocean which, in turn, would help protect Soviet Murmansk.

Following a massive bombardment, General Kirill A. Meretskov threw 600,000 soldiers from the 7th, 8th, 9th and 14th Armies against about 200,000 Finnish troops. In the south, the 7th Army, with nine divisions, attacked the Karelian Isthmus, which was sandwiched between the Gulf of Finland to the west and the vast Lake Ladoga to the east. Here lay the Finns' strongest defences in the shape of the Mannerheim Line, named after Marshal Carl Gustaf Mannerheim, the 72-year-old commander of the Finnish forces. He had served in the Imperial Russian Army when Finland was part of the Russian Empire. Further north, attacks by the Soviet 8th Army were also conducted along the eastern shore of Ladoga and from Petroskoi toward Kollaa and Talvajarvi. The Soviet 9th Army struck toward Suomussalmi, in central Finland, while other units advanced on Salla and Petsamo.

Finnish defences, however, were well prepared and the Finns proved to be masters in conducting highly effective ambushes. Throughout the first half of December the ill-prepared Red Army was given a bloody nose at Taipale, at the eastern end of the Mannerheim Line, and at Summa to the west. Near Suomussalmi, an entire Soviet division was trapped and decimated, losing 5,000 men.

Stalin's invasion was supposed to overwhelm the Finns, and with a three-to-one superiority it should have done. Nikita Khrushchev recalled in his memoirs, 'Stalin was furious with the military, and with Voroshilov – justifiably in my opinion.'[7] At a meeting to discuss progress, the Soviet leader was beside himself with anger. He leapt to his feet and berated Voroshilov, who was responsible for the campaign. He, in turn, red with fury, jumped up and shouted, 'You have yourself to blame for all this! You're the one who had our best generals killed!'[8]

Stalin needed a quick victory for fear that the Western powers would come to Finland's aid. With Britain and France already at war with Hitler, the last thing he wanted to do was find himself in open conflict against them alongside Nazi Germany. In January 1940, Lord Halifax found it hard to conceive that

Hitler would attack France and Britain, let alone the Soviet Union. He noted, 'In Austria, Bohemia, Moravia, and Poland you see Germany being compelled to drain her reserves of military strength by sending divisions to hold down by force the territories which she has incorporated into the Reich.'[9]

After the Red Army's shambolic performance, Stalin moved to shake up his command in Finland. He reorganised the entire leadership of those forces attacking Finland at the end of 1939 – many were shot or replaced. The senior command, though, got off lightly. Despite his outburst, Voroshilov was only demoted from People's Commissar for Defence to Deputy Chairman of the Defence Council, while General Meretskov, commanding the Soviet forces in Finland, was also demoted. The latter was replaced by Marshal Semyon Timoshenko, who had taken part in the occupation of Poland. Timoshenko agreed to his assignment as long as he was not held responsible for Soviet casualties.

Timoshenko massed twenty-five divisions and launched his offensive on 1 February 1940, having selected an area east of Summa for his breakthrough. Six days later, he achieved this near Lake Muolaa, south-east of Viipuri, Finland's second largest city, and attacked Summa twice. The outnumbered Finns were overwhelmed, having by this stage lost almost 30,000 men in the past month. Mannerheim had little choice but to abandon his defence line and the Karelian Isthmus.

By late February the Finns were desperately trying to hold on around Viipuri and by early March the Soviets were threatening to cut the roads leading west from the city. With Sweden refusing to allow British and French troops to transit its territory to help the Finns, on 12 March Finland surrendered.

Stalin moved swiftly in the wake of the Winter War to remove any threat from the indigenous population. 'Finland ceded its isthmus to us with zero population,' says Solzhenitsyn. 'Nevertheless, the removal and resettlement of all persons with Finnish blood took place throughout Soviet Karelia and in Leningrad in 1940.'[10]

The Finns suffered 68,480 casualties and had ceded one-tenth of their territory to Stalin. In order to get this back they were secretly prepared to side with Hitler when the time came and to conduct what they termed the 'Continuation War'. Although defeated, Marshal Mannerheim estimated that the Winter War cost the Red Army 200,000 casualties, 2,300 armoured vehicles and 1,000 aircraft. Khrushchev was later to admit to 1 million casualties, which was two-thirds of the Red Army forces sent to Finland. Admiral N.G. Kuznetsov concluded, 'We had received a severe lesson. We had to profit from it. The Finnish campaign had shown that organisation of military leadership at the centre left much to be desired.'[11] Afterwards, political commissars were abolished and the rank of general and other military ranks reintroduced with appropriate privileges.

The Winter War starkly highlighted the shortage of experienced officers. Once they had calmed down, Stalin and Voroshilov put their heads together. The small number of Soviet veterans who had served in Spain, China, Manchuria and Poland were simply insufficient to undo the damage done by the Great Purge. They were forced to release over 4,000 selected officers who had been imprisoned during the Terror and return them to active service. This, though, was not enough to stave off the disaster looming on the horizon.

Despite Timoshenko's overwhelming victory, the extremely poor performance of the Red Army in Finland greatly influenced Hitler's decision to invade the Soviet Union. Stalin had mobilised half his regular divisions in Europe and western Siberia to fight his tiny neighbour. He had relied on brute strength, tanks and aircraft, but the Soviet troops, while brave, had crucially lacked initiative. Nikita Khrushchev realised the wider ramifications:

> All of us – and Stalin first and foremost – sensed in our victory a defeat by the Finns. It was a dangerous defeat because it encouraged our enemies' conviction that the Soviet Union was a colossus with feet of clay.[12]

The ineptitude of the Red Army in Finland convinced Hitler that Barbarossa would swiftly bring the Soviet Union to its knees. As a result, he chose to ignore Zhukov's resounding victory at Khalkhin-Gol. In contrast, General N.N. Voronov noted:

> We had still not learned how to make use of the full potential of the new equipment. […] The troops were ill-prepared for operations in forests and for coping with freezing weather and impassable roads. The Party demanded that the combat experience accumulated in Khasan, at Khalkhin Gol, and on the Karelian Isthmus be thoroughly taken into account.[13]

Unfortunately for the Soviet Union and the Red Army, the valuable experience gained by Zhukov in Mongolia and during earlier massed military exercises was all but ignored. 'We relegated to oblivion the fundamentals of combat-in-depth tactics and of combined arms manoeuvres which had been widespread before the Finnish campaign,' recalled Marshal Biriuzov.[14]

However, valuable lessons were learned regarding training (in some divisions only 60 per cent of the soldiers had been given military training before being sent to Finland), support services and the performance of weaponry in extreme temperatures. General Voronov observed:

Artillery matériel was of particular concern. During the freezing weather in Finland, the semiautomatic mechanisms in the guns failed. New types of lubricants had to be developed immediately. When the temperature dropped sharply, the 152mm Howitzer behaved in an erratic manner. Large-scale research work had to be carried out. After some improvements, these guns performed brilliantly in the Great Patriotic War.[15]

Ultimately, though, Marshal Biriuzov noted:

The spirit of battles for 'the Mannerheim Line' continued to hover over our tactics and the combat training of our troops, although by 1940 the Germans had taught everyone a lesson that should not have been ignored. After a few months of the 'Phoney War,' the Germans refused to gnaw through the 'Maginot Line' and sent their armoured divisions instead through the unprotected left flank of the French and English armies in Flanders. Their tactics then were exactly the same as those we had to deal with in 1941: massive aerial attacks, tank breakthroughs, pincer movements, and encirclements. And of course, there was nothing like this on the Karelian Isthmus in the winter of 1939–40.[16]

In June 1940, just as France was capitulating in the face of Hitler's blitzkrieg, the Soviet–Japanese dispute was settled with a border treaty. This was a strategic disaster for Hitler as it allowed Stalin to redeploy the bulk of his battle-hardened forces west. Nonetheless, Stalin and his generals were not complacent over the threat still posed by Japan. The Transbaikal forces were reorganised into the newly formed 16th (which was transferred west) and 17th Armies. On the eve of the Nazi attack on the Soviet Union, this military district consisted of the 17th Army, with two tank divisions and three rifle divisions. Following the invasion, the Transbaikal Military District became the Transbaikal Front, whose task remained safeguarding against possible renewed Japanese aggression. The newly created 36th Army bolstered the 17th Army in June 1941.

After Khalkhin-Gol, Zhukov singled out his tank brigades, especially the 11th under Yakovlev, for praise, as well as the 36th Motorised Division under Petrov and 57th Rifle Division under Galanin. The 82nd Division, now under Fedyuninsky, was to distinguish itself fighting the Germans, and Fedyuninsky would end up commanding the 42nd Army at beleaguered Leningrad. Potapov, who had acted as Zhukov's deputy, ended up commanding the 5th Army.

Crucially, thanks to his experiences in the Far East, Zhukov would see to it that the Transbaikal Military District sowed the seeds for the Reserve Front that would help defend the western Soviet Union.

3

HITLER'S WILL-O'-THE-WISP

Any hopes Hitler may have had that Stalin would be forced to fight a two-front war were firmly quashed by the Soviet–Japanese Neutrality Pact. The German Foreign Minister even suggested that Japan should attack British Singapore, when his Japanese counterpart visited Berlin on 27 March 1941. No mention was made, however, of Hitler's Operation Barbarossa (meaning 'Redbeard' in Italian and named in honour of Frederick I, the German Holy Roman Emperor who led the Third Crusade to the Holy Land in 1189) and his impending attack on the Soviet Union. This was a costly blunder.

Hitler felt success against Stalin would encourage the Japanese to attack America, which would stop Roosevelt from openly siding with Britain. He reasoned that America would not want to fight a two-front war, seemingly missing the dangerous implications of his tripartite pact with Japan and Italy. Hitler calculated that the Soviet Union could be defeated in eight to ten weeks, such was his faith in the Wehrmacht's blitzkrieg. He concluded his army would not need cold weather clothing and that he would only have to leave sixty divisions in the Soviet Union during the coming winter.

Hitler was not the only one who held this opinion. Senior figures in Britain and America thought that if Germany attacked, the Red Army would be destroyed in a matter of weeks. On the very eve of Barbarossa, British Prime Minister Winston Churchill believed 'a German attack on Russia is certain and Russia will assuredly be defeated'.[1]

In July 1940 the Soviet High Command assessed that Hitler would attack with the support of Finland, Italy, Romania and possibly Hungary and Japan. According to their intelligence, the enemy would be able to field 270 divisions, 233 of which could be used against the Soviet Union's new western border in Poland. This estimate was 30 per cent too high.

In October 1940, the German General Staff reckoned they would be facing 170 Soviet divisions (they thought this an over-estimate, but it was actually too low). The Führer could not conceive that the vast battles about to be fought on the Eastern Front were doomed from the very start; but was the defeat of the Red Army really a strategic possibility?

The driving force behind Hitler's Nationalist Socialist (Nazi) Party was extreme nationalism and anti-Semitism. *Lebensraum*, the 'drive for living space', provided German nationalism with an appealing cause and was seductive propaganda. During the mid-1930s, at his Nuremberg rallies Hitler spoke passionately of the raw material wealth of the east.

Beyond Germany's borders, observers were not convinced by Hitler's rationale for *Lebensraum*. British Foreign Secretary Lord Halifax said:

> It is noteworthy that this claim to 'living space' is being put forward at a moment when Germany has become an immigration country, importing workers in large numbers from Czechoslovakia, from Holland, and from Italy to meet the needs of her industry and agriculture. How then can Germany claim to be overpopulated?[2]

Hitler's demand for *Lebensraum politik*, while having a broad appeal at home, was not initially firmly rooted. His economic goals, geographical limits and military objectives for the Third Reich were dealt with in the vaguest of terms. More important was the primacy of the Führer's ideology of biological determinism. Coupled with his lifelong dislike for Communism, he saw Bolshevism as a Jewish plot for world domination. The destruction of the Soviet Union as a political entity would permit Hitler to achieve both his economic and ideological goals in one fell swoop.

After the Wehrmacht's incredibly successful blitzkrieg campaigns of September 1939–June 1940, against Poland, Norway, Denmark, the Low Countries (Belgium and the Netherlands) and France, Hitler reached a strategic dilemma. Before he could turn east, for he saw the war in the west as purely pre-emptive, there remained the thorny issue of Churchill's continued defiance across the Channel. Hitler's strategic options were limited. He could invade Britain and risk defeat, join Mussolini in his drive to the Suez Canal, in what he regarded as an unwanted sideshow, or invade the Soviet Union. An attack into the Balkans was not seen as an option by mid-1940, as the Axis position in south-east Europe was, as yet, unthreatened.

Conscious that *Lebensraum* was considered in some German political circles an irrational reason for attacking the Soviet Union, Hitler claimed that a strike against Stalin was a grand strategic means of defeating Britain, by depriving her of a potential continental ally as Napoleon had tried to do in 1812. If this were true, it would have surely meant that a Nazi victory over Britain would render an invasion of the Soviet Union wholly unnecessary.

Hitler's overriding desire was to ensure continuity with his warped ideology and vague military strategy. While there was continuity with his brutal ideological aims, these were to come into direct conflict with his strategic ambitions. Hitler's desire to defeat the Soviet Union dominated everything, and this is illustrated by the debate over the potential invasion of Britain during August–September 1940.

He had failed to take the initiative and prepare viable plans for an invasion of Britain at the same time as the preparation for the campaign in the east. His half-hearted attempts to rectify this with Operation *Seelöwe* (Sealion), combined with the ill-conceived and badly co-ordinated efforts by the Luftwaffe, made it apparent that Hitler's interest after June 1940 lay firmly in the east.

The German High Command considered attacking the Soviet Union in the autumn of 1940, but even Hitler saw the impracticality of that. It seemed as if Hitler's Sealion preparations and the Luftwaffe's Eagle Day operations against Britain were simply marking time until the end of the year. Clearly the Führer needed to deliver a crippling blow to Britain, because he did not want his attack on the Soviet Union delayed any longer than necessary, as this would give Stalin time to build up his forces in the Soviet western military districts. To Hitler, implementing Sealion seemed far too risky and the diminishing size of the proposed operation shows that it was intended to transport an army of occupation rather than a full-blown seaborne assault on the British Isles. Indeed, Hitler hoped that his air offensive during the Battle of Britain would cause a political collapse. In the event, it transpired that the Blitz was useless without the *Krieg* and Churchill resolutely refused to buckle, thanks to RAF Fighter Command.

By the end of the year, Hitler had to convince his generals of the urgency in attacking the Red Army and in 'Führer Directive No. 18', issued on 12 November 1940, he stated:

> Political discussions for the purpose of clarifying Russia's attitude in the immediate future have already begun. Regardless of the outcome of these conversations, all preparations for the East for which verbal orders have already been given will be continued.
>
> Further directives will follow on this subject as soon as the basic operational plan of the Army has been submitted to me and approved.[3]

Hitler now capitalised on tensions over the Balkans, Stalin's attack on Finland and his occupation of the Baltic States and the fear of Soviet attack to justify his actions. In truth, an operational plan for an attack on the Soviet Union was already in hand, but Hitler and his generals could not decide on where their strategic priorities lay. General Erich von Manstein, who was to command the 56th Panzer Corps during Operation Barbarossa, recalled:

> There has been a great deal of argument as to whether the Soviet troop positions were actually defensive or offensive in character. If one went by the strength of the forces assembled in the western parts of the Soviet Union and the powerful concentration of armour in the Bialystok area and around Lwow [Lvov], it was possible to contend – as Hitler did in support of his decision to attack – that sooner or later the Soviet Union would take the offensive. On the other hand, the layout of the Soviet forces on 22 June 1941 did not indicate any *immediate* intention of aggression on the part of the Soviet Union.
>
> I think it would be nearest the truth to describe the Soviet dispositions – to which the occupation of eastern Poland, Bessarabia and the Baltic territories had already contributed very strong forces – as a 'deployment against every contingency'.[4]

Ironically, Zhukov and Timoshenko were grappling with just the same problem in trying to determine Hitler's intentions. While the Soviets were deployed in depth for defence, they could have rapidly changed their stance so there was a latent threat.

It is very notable that there was no serious planning for an attack on the Soviet Union until after the fall of France in June 1940. Hitler's intentions were first recorded in the diary of General Franz Halder, Chief of Army General Staff, on 22 July 1940. These were very imprecise and included no less than three aims:

> To defeat the Russian Army or at least to occupy as much Russian soil as is necessary to protect Berlin from air attack. It is desired to establish our own positions so far east that our own air force can destroy most important areas of Russia.[5]

This general vagueness was to continue.

Nonetheless, on 18 December 1940 the issuing of 'Directive 21: Case Barbarossa', calling for a rapid campaign, showed how committed Hitler was to an invasion:

> The Army will have to employ all available formations to this end, with the reservation that the occupied territories must be insured against surprise attacks.

The Air Force will have to make available for this Eastern campaign supporting forces of such strength that the Army will be able to bring land operations to a speedy conclusion and that Eastern Germany will be as little damaged as possible by enemy air attack. [...]

In certain circumstances I shall issue orders for the deployment against Soviet Russia eight weeks before the operation is timed to begin.[6]

This belief in a 'rapid campaign' was echoed on 14 June 1941 at a staff meeting in Berlin of all the commanders of the army and panzer groups. Hitler seemed completely blind to the potential limitations of what he was proposing. He said they could not defeat Britain and to end the war they must have victory on the continent; only once the Soviet Union was defeated would Germany's dominant position be secure.

General Heinz Guderian, who was to command the 2nd Panzer Group for Barbarossa, noted, 'His detailed exposition of the reasons that led him to fight a preventive war against the Russians was unconvincing.'[7] Despite this, there was no discussion or dissent and Guderian recalled everyone 'dispersed, still in silence and with heavy hearts'.[8] Most of Hitler's generals were undoubtedly very uneasy about the prospect of a two-front war – Germany had tried this in 1914, and been defeated as a result. Privately, some generals must have thought what Hitler was proposing was complete folly, but no one spoke up.

Initial secret planning for the invasion of the Soviet Union was conducted under the code name Operation Otto. The man selected for the job of reviewing all the options was General Erich Marcks. He was a highly experienced officer, having served as chief of staff with 8th Corps during the invasion of Poland and then chief of staff with the 18th Army during the invasion of France.

Marcks drafted an outline plan, 'Operational Draft East', by 5 August 1940, which highlighted Moscow, Ukraine, the Donets Basin and Leningrad as the key strategic goals. There was one crucial omission, as historian Colonel Albert Seaton noted, 'Weighty aims, the destruction of Soviet military power and the occupation of strategic areas immediately relevant to this power formed no part of Marcks' main mission.'[9] The assumption seemed to be that once the Red Army was down it would stay down. Understandably, there was conflict over this and, to further complicate matters, German Armed Forces High Command (*Oberkommando der Wehrmacht* – OKW) and the Army High Command (*Oberkommando des Heeres* – OKH) produced competing plans.

Marcks' 'Operational Draft East' was just that, nothing more than a planning study rather than a fully fledged operational plan. However, it laid down the fundamental strategy for Barbarossa, although it was to be much amended and Hitler and the army's strategic views were to diverge considerably. Most notably, Hitler would see the capture of Leningrad not as a subsidiary objective as advocated by the army but as essential before the drive on Moscow. His desire to take Baku would cause similar problems.

Marcks, who was working under the auspices of General Halder, chief of the General Staff, assumed that the Soviets would not attack first. While the Wehrmacht would only have a small superiority in men, it would make up for this with a distinct superiority in armoured units and quality of equipment. Marcks calculated that, occupation forces aside, Hitler could muster 110 infantry divisions, twenty-four panzer and twelve motorised divisions against ninety-six Soviet rifle divisions, twenty-three cavalry divisions and twenty-eight armoured brigades. Marcks was unaware that Timoshenko was resurrecting the Soviet tank divisions and mechanised corps.

Marcks envisaged allocating the bulk of German forces to an army group striking east across occupied Poland to Moscow, via Minsk and Smolensk, and another attacking south-eastwards toward the Ukrainian capital, Kiev. He advocated a subsidiary German flanking operation against Leningrad to the north, as well as the southern advance against Kiev by German-Romanian forces striking from annexed Bessarabia. The central objectives of Moscow and Kiev were key, as they would ensure the Red Army was trapped and destroyed between the Dvina and Dnepr in nine to seventeen weeks.

When Marcks presented his plan to the OKH it was with Halder's approval that he made Moscow the primary objective. The Red Army would be drawn to defend the Soviet capital and destroyed on the road to the city. The subsidiary operations in the south were designed to protect Romania's oilfields and pre-empt any distracting Soviet counter-attacks. Once Moscow had been captured, the Wehrmacht could swing south to crush the remains of the Red Army in Ukraine. This meant Byelorussia would be the main battlefield and Marcks called for 70 per cent of German armour to be massed north of the vast Pripet Marshes.

A winter campaign was not considered because it was anticipated that the Red Army would have completely collapsed by the end of the year – such was Hitler's optimism. Field Marshal Walther von Brauchitsch, the army's commander-in-chief, and Halder agreed that the main weight of their attack should fall along the Minsk–Smolensk–Moscow land bridge.

Lieutenant Colonel Bernard von Lossberg produced his 'Build-up East' (*Aufbau Ost*) plan for the OKW, which laid greater emphasis on the flanks. Lossberg made the advance beyond Smolensk dependent on what was happening on the flanks. There was a very real concern that the Red Army would hold onto the Baltic States and therefore be a threat to the advance on Moscow. However, the operational plan presented to General Alfred Jodl, chief of the

OKW Operations Staff, on 19 September, also saw the main blow falling north of the Pripet Marshes for a push toward Moscow.

Hitler though chose to ignore the lessons drawn from a war game which had been directed by General Paulus during 28 November to 3 December 1940, concluding that Moscow was not that important. Although Marcks' OKH team advocated the main thrusts be aimed at the cities of Moscow and Kiev, Halder added a strong thrust toward Leningrad in early December 1940. Hitler's subsequent 'Directive No. 21' shifted all the emphasis further north, making the destruction of the Red Army in the Baltic States and the capture of Leningrad a priority, before Moscow. Rightly or wrongly, Hitler wanted to secure his northern flank before the main event (ironically, Stalin would have the same problem on the road to Berlin in 1945).

Despite the consensus between the OKH and OKW, Hitler's eyes were also drawn away from Moscow to protecting Romania's oilfields and securing Ukraine's vast raw materials, which inevitably meant diverting military resources south. The Deployment Directive (*Aufmarschweisung*) Barbarossa, issued on 31 January 1941, added Romania to von Rundstedt's Army Group South's area of responsibility, although there remained the problem of Hungary.

Distractions in Yugoslavia and Greece during April 1941 also further complicated matters and disrupted Hitler's deployment schedules. He wanted to invade the Soviet Union on 15 May 1941. However, Barbarossa could not possibly have started then because spring came late that year. Even by the beginning of June, the Polish–Russian river valleys were still flooded and partly impassable, as a result of exceptionally heavy rainfall.

While Hitler's desire to attack Stalin took precedent over everything else, his unfocused and generalised aims were clearly reflected in the planning process. Indeed, the campaign in the west had completely inflated Hitler's and the OKW's faith in blitzkrieg and this, coupled with the blind superiority of Nazi ideology, was to induce a complete and utter lack of strategic foresight. Von Manstein called Hitler's Barbarossa Directive nothing more than a strategic, or even tactical, formula. It could never replace an operations plan that should have had unanimity in its preparation, purpose and execution. But this was not to be the case, Hitler was in a hurry to carve out an eastern empire without the need for a long and costly coalition war.

In 'Directive 21', Hitler stated, 'In the *North* a quick advance to Moscow. The capture of the city would represent a decisive political and economic success and would also bring about the capture of the most important railway junctions.'[10] Nonetheless, he seemed unable to decide where the strategic heart of Stalin's Soviet Union lay. Von Manstein pointed out, 'Hitler's strategic aims were based primarily on *political* and *economic* considerations.'[11]

Aside from the advance on Moscow, Hitler now wanted to capture Leningrad, the cradle of Bolshevism, to the north, the raw materials of Ukraine to the south, the armaments centres of the Donets Basin and, later, the Caucasus oilfields even further south. He hoped that this would mortally cripple Stalin's war economy.

This was to cause fundamental confusion in conducting Barbarossa and weakened the effectiveness of his panzers. Perhaps understandably, Brauchitsch and Halder felt that the destruction of the Red Army should take precedence over the economic goals. In this respect, the OKH assessed that the Red Army should be defeated on the road to Moscow. The city was the political and communications heart of the Soviet Union, with very important munitions factories just to the east. The German Army saw a powerful drive on Moscow as paramount, in order to divert Soviet forces, split their defences and paralyse their communications. Fatefully, Hitler was against this concentration of effort; he wanted operations settled on the flanks.

Both plans had their merits and disadvantages, but a firm decision was needed one way or the other. Once Barbarossa was underway any dithering or needless diversion of resources would inevitably cost the Wehrmacht dearly in lost time. Ultimately, everything hung on the fate of Moscow. Von Manstein observes that:

> It was on this divergence of basic strategy that the German conduct of operations ultimately foundered. Although Hitler agreed to the distribution of forces proposed by OKH, according to which the bulk of the army was to be committed in two army groups in the north and only one in the area south of the Pripet Marshes, the tug-of-war over strategic objectives continued throughout this campaign. The inevitable consequence was that Hitler not only failed to attain his aims, which were too far-flung anyway, but also confused the issue for OKH.[12]

Subsequently, Hitler's meddling would complicate matters even more and dissipate German resources, particularly in front of Moscow.

The issue that neither Hitler nor his generals wanted to address was whether Barbarossa was a viable long-term strategic solution for dominating the Soviet Union. Von Manstein says their first mistake was in 'underrating the resources of the Soviet Union and the fighting qualities of the Red Army. In consequence, he [Hitler] based everything on the assumption that the Soviet Union could be overthrown by military means in one campaign.'[13] Likewise, General Heinz Guderian was horrified at the idea of a two-front war, commenting, 'No single clear operational objective seemed to be envisaged. [...] it also became increasingly plain to see how inadequate were our preparations for the undertaking.'[14]

Hitler had 153 divisions at most, including reserves available for operations on the Eastern Front by 22 June 1941; Stalin had almost double that number. In total, Hitler could muster about 3 million men; Stalin had 4.5 million at his disposal. Geographically, there was also the problem of the Eastern Front itself, which funnelled out from 1,300 miles to 2,500 miles. This accentuated the problem of maintaining 3 million men and half a million horses in the field.

These logistical problems were compounded by a critical lack of reserves; the German Replacement Army had less than half a million men, just sufficient for replacements during the intended brief summer campaign. Hitler only had three months' reserves of petrol and one month of diesel. This should have set alarm bells ringing amongst Hitler's planners, but he persisted in gambling on a quick victory. Hitler did not seem inclined to consider the long-term value or reliability of his Eastern Front allies, who disliked each other as much as the Bolsheviks.

Equally worrying was the fact that the superiority of German armour was not that marked. Guderian, father of the German panzer forces, believed at the beginning of the campaign that the technical superiority of their tanks would cancel out the Soviets' enormous numerical superiority. The same went for the Luftwaffe and its ability to neutralise the massive Red Air Force. This was true only for a limited period, and new types of Soviet tanks and aircraft were already in the pipeline.

In the spring of 1941, a visiting Soviet commission's comments on seeing Hitler's panzers led German ordnance officials to conclude, 'It seems that the Russians must already possess better and heavier tanks than we do'.[15] Again, this should have set alarm bells ringing – but it did not. The German military should have already come to this conclusion after the Spanish Civil War ended in 1939; it was evident then that Soviet tank design was advancing in leaps and bounds. The Soviet T-34 medium tank just coming into service was equal, and in many cases superior, to existing German tank designs. Notably, it was armed with a larger calibre gun than Hitler's panzers.

There can be little doubting that, politically, Hitler's goals clashed with the strategic feasibility of Barbarossa. He was aware of the ethnic complexity of the Soviet Empire and he believed that its member nations were creaking at the seams. This gave rise to Hitler's mistaken belief that 'one good kick would bring the tottering and rotten structure down'.[16] He believed that the Soviet populace would embrace Nazi ideology, but as soon as Barbarossa began almost everything was done to prevent any such thing taking place. Von Manstein observed that Hitler's policies in the occupied territories ran counter to his military strategy. Not enlisting the support of the multi-racial Soviet peoples was a grave political and military blunder.

Hitler's determination to achieve his ideological goals left him with no other option than the flawed strategic aims of Barbarossa. However, Hitler's desire to crush Bolshevism could never be achieved with the continued existence of a Soviet Empire east of the Volga, or indeed east of the Urals, nor were these geographical stop-lines any ultimate safeguard to Nazi Germany's security. The Russian bear would be able to withdraw and lick its wounds, ready to fight another day. As Colonel Seaton observed, 'Hitler was about to send the German Army into the Soviet Union, on a four year will-o'-the-wisp chase after seaports, cities, oil, corn, coal, nickel, manganese and iron ore'.[17]

Hitler's ideological mania would cause him to do even worse than launch a massive military operation. He ordered the subjugation and economic despoliation of the conquered territories, the extermination of the Jews, Communist intelligentsia and the enslavement of the entire population.

While Hitler indulged himself in the fantasy of an eight to nine-week campaign, he wilfully ignored the potentially swift recovery of the Red Army, both in terms of manpower and equipment. Staff at OKW and OKH knew that Hitler did not like pessimistic intelligence, as it was not what he wanted to hear. Colonel Eberhard Kinzel, head of the General Staff's Branch 12 'Foreign Armies East' intelligence unit, appears to have fallen foul of this aversion. Colonel Reinhard Gehlen, his successor, says:

> Colonel Kinzel had already succeeded in building up a relatively accurate picture of Russian defences, Order of Battle and mobilisation measures, and of Moscow's strategic planning. It was the basis of this information that our 'Barbarossa' campaign had been developed and adjusted to meet each changing circumstance. Kinzel had also instituted detailed surveys of Soviet manpower and industrial reserves.[18]

On the assumption that Barbarossa went according to schedule, the General Staff had to get their assessments of Soviet manpower and, indeed, industrial capacity right because it was vital they predict the Red Army's response. Accurate intelligence regarding Soviet front-line units and reserves was crucial to the success of the entire enterprise. It was these judgements that convinced Hitler firstly to invade and secondly fight the Battle of Moscow in the winter of 1941–42, because he believed it would exhaust the depleted Red Army's reserves.

By the end of June 1941 Zhukov was anticipating being able to deploy just under 150 divisions, running north to south in the Baltic, Western, Kiev and Odessa Military Districts. The manpower of these units was 50 per cent less than an average German division. The Wehrmacht would have to overcome these, plus at least another twenty regular army divisions which were being assembled. There is every reason to believe that Kinzel and his staff at Branch 12 deduced that, despite Stalin's forward defence policy, the Red Army would create a significant reserve on the old Soviet frontier to act as a stop-line. In the spring of 1941 they were in the process of marshalling at least six armies in Byelorussia and Ukraine for this very purpose. The Reserve Front would underpin the key Western Military District and provide troops for the defence of Moscow. Therefore, the German General Staff must have known that they faced a race against time – not only against the weather, but also the gathering Soviet reserve armies.

In addition, Hitler knew perfectly well that thanks to the Soviet–Japanese peace treaty, Stalin could call on General Josif Rodionovič Apanasenko's Far Eastern Front, which fully mobilised on the day of the German invasion and consisted of twenty-five divisions and nine armoured brigades. They had been maintained since tsarist times to defend the frontiers with China, Manchuria, Mongolia and Korea. Initially these were held in place by the fear of renewed Japanese hostilities, but as the Siberian campaigning season shortened the Soviets were able to consider redeploying them west. Throughout the Red Army's defeats during the early summer and autumn, the Far Eastern Army remained untouched. These troops were climate hardened, being used to operating in the coldest of winters, and were equipped accordingly. Apanasenko was another veteran of the Bolshevik's 1st Cavalry Army.

The Far East and other regions plus Muscovite civilian volunteers would provide fifty-one extra divisions for the defence of Moscow. This was without even touching the Supreme High Command's Reserve. To buy time while the Far East units were redeployed, Zhukov was reinforced with fourteen divisions in early October 1941 from the Reserve Army and adjacent fronts. Therefore, just for the defence of Moscow alone the Red Army came up with sixty-five additional divisions. The Supreme Command Reserve was also busy gathering almost double this figure between the Don and Volga rivers.

It beggars belief that Colonel Kinzel and his colleagues had no inkling that such a feat was possible. Kinzel had produced a top-secret handbook on the Red Army in early 1941, but it only dealt with Soviet units in the immediate border area. Two months into the invasion, Halder recorded that they had considerably underestimated Soviet strength – they had anticipated 200 divisions, but by this stage they had already identified 360. Many were drastically under strength, or simply 'ghost' units designed to deceive the Wehrmacht – nonetheless, it showed a quick victory was impossible.

Following Zhukov's winter counter-offensive around Moscow, by March 1942 according to Gehlen, Kinzel was optimistically reporting:

Only a meagre reserve is available over and above the armed forces already existing, and in my view of the prevailing conditions in Russia one must be sceptical as to whether this reserve can be built up to the theoretical estimate.

The Russians will never again be able to throw reserves into the scales as they did in the winter of 1941/1942.[19]

Hitler echoed this wishful thinking when he issued 'Führer Directive No. 41' on 5 April 1942, stating:

The enemy has suffered severe losses in men and material. In an effort to exploit what appeared to him to be an early success, he has expended during the winter the bulk of reserves intended for later operations.[20]

Kinzel, who was sacked shortly before Hitler's directive, claimed that he never held this view and had accurately assessed that there were many new Soviet armies forming. In fact, he warned that Stalin might have some sixty divisions as an operational reserve. Gehlen says his predecessor was sent to join General Friedrich Paulus' 6th Army because he did not get on with Halder. It is more likely that Kinzel was replaced because he did not agree with Hitler and Halder that the Red Army had exhausted all its reserves. Kinzel was to end the war as chief of staff of Army Group Vistula, tasked with defending Berlin. His dismissal had absolutely nothing to do with his abilities – he was a highly competent staff officer and was to gain praise from none other than Field Marshal Montgomery.

Interestingly, Gehlen was Halder's former adjutant from the Operations Department. By his own admission, he had no experience in intelligence. Some might question the wisdom of placing him in charge of Branch 12 at such a critical point in the war.

By June 1942 Gehlen found that despite staggering Soviet losses at Kiev, Vyazma and Bryansk the Red Army was still maintaining the front-line strength of 4.5 million men that had been attained at the beginning of the year. Therefore, there were as many Red Army divisions confronting the Wehrmacht as when it first attacked the Soviet Union. This was bad enough, but what further reserves could Stalin and his generals draw on?

In 1941, after Stalin's territorial expansion, the Soviet Union had a population of 199 million. Statistically the Germans calculated that a country could mobilise about 10 per cent of its population. This meant, theoretically, that the Soviet armed forces could have up to 19 million men under arms. The following year, Gehlen calculated the Soviet Union might have mobilised around 17 million men. From this, he deducted 430,000 killed or wounded after the fighting with Finland in 1939–40 and the Wehrmacht had accounted for a staggering 7.5 million. This left approximately 9.5 million, of whom 7.8 million were active troops, comprising 6 million in the army, 1.5 million in the air force and 300,000 in the navy. By Gehlen's reckoning, this left 1.7 million in reserve which, he guessed, could only be released gradually and even then, large numbers would be tied up with training and logistics. He concluded, 'We were entitled to assume it would not prove possible for Moscow to tap more than a fraction of these ultimate manpower resources.'[21] In essence, Gehlen agreed with Hitler and Halder. When he reported his findings, he covered himself by saying, 'The enemy's numerical superiority in manpower and equipment must not be underestimated'.[22] Even if Gehlen had assumed 50 per cent of Kinzel's figure was correct this would have meant the Red Army could readily call on 400,000 troops.

It is evident that not only did Barbarossa lack clear strategic goals, but also that Hitler deliberately ignored his own intelligence from the very beginning. Kinzel was, in fact, conservative with his intelligence estimates. By 1942 Stalin had mobilised ten reserve armies, each with six or seven divisions with 5,000–8,000 men per division. Allowing for all the supporting units, this equated to about 800,000 men. They were supplemented by two new tank armies plus numerous other independent corps and brigades. They were roughly the equivalent to thirty-eight divisions and amounted to around another 240,000 men.

These calculations are based on the best available figures, but it should be borne in mind that tens of thousands of new recruits were also subsumed into reconstituted existing units. What this means is that within less than a year of Hitler's invasion, despite all his losses, Stalin mobilised around 100 divisions with 1 million men under arms. These forces were to play a key role in the fighting at Voronezh, Stalingrad and Kursk. If you add the Moscow reinforcements, this means that the Red Army could almost replace its entire western defence force. When Halder warned Hitler of this danger in the summer of 1942, he too was sacked. The additional bad news was that the Soviets could still mobilise almost another 1 million men, equivalent to another 100 divisions.

Hitler's intelligence also failed to take into account the Soviet Union's paramilitary organisations such as the NKVD's (People's Commissariat for Internal Affairs) security troops, plus prison and frontier guards. At the beginning of the war, the NKVD was able to form fifteen rifle divisions, and by 1945 this number had expanded to over fifty divisions. Some fought with the Red Army, but most were mainly used for rear-area security and preventing Red Army units from retreating. A number of NKVD border and prison guard units were used to create General Galanin's 70th Army, which had six divisions at the Battle of Kursk.

At the outbreak of war there was a mixed reaction from the NKVD Gulag guards – some were alarmed at losing their cushy jobs and being shipped to the

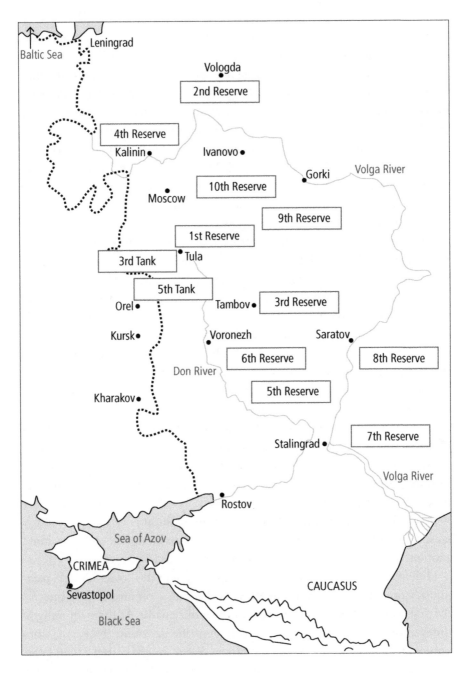

Soviet Reserve Armies, 1942.

front, others fretted that they would not get to defend the Motherland. Within two weeks of war, political prisoner Gustav Herling was amazed:

> There was something incredible in the arrivals at Yercevo of fresh contingents of young and healthy NKVD soldiers to strengthen the garrisons of camps on the shore of the White Sea, while at the same time the names of the towns mentioned in the wireless communiqués made it clear that the front was rapidly moving eastward.[23]

Stalin could also call on the untapped manpower of his Gulag prisoners. In 1941 there were about 2 million people in the camps, representing an enormous reserve. While the number of prisoners was largely constant, there was a high turnover of people passing in and out of the system for various reasons. During the first three years of the war almost 1 million men were released to join the ranks of the Red Army. In addition, as slave labour, inmates produced ammunition and uniforms as well as building airfields, roads and railways. Many Soviet scientists, particularly the aviation engineers, were held in the more benign camps known as *sharashkas*.

Where Gehlen also got it wrong was in underestimating Soviet raw materials. He assumed that Soviet arms production would suffer (in particular, supplies of manganese for steel production). The plan was to capture the Caucasus and knock out most of their raw resources – that, of course, came unstuck at Grozny and Stalingrad. Crucially, General Georg Thomas, head of the OKW's Economic and Armaments Branch just before the Eastern Front opened, calculated that Stalin would lose 75 per cent of his heavy industry; this should make it almost impossible to rearm the Red Army. He failed to predict that the Soviet military industries would be transported by train to east of the Urals and that they would continue building weapons. Nor did he foresee they would step up production to levels with which Hitler could not equal. This was to have severe ramifications.

The failure to predict the massive regeneration of the Red Army, as well as the Red Air Force, was an intelligence blunder of the greatest magnitude. The key players in this grand delusion along with Halder, were General Field Marshal Wilhelm Keitel, chief of the OKW, and his deputy, General Alfred Jodl, chief of operations at OKW. Is it really possible that on the eve of Operation Barbarossa Hitler and his senior generals were unaware that if they struck the Soviet Union they would awaken an industrial monster? It seems inconceivable.

Lieutenant Bernd Freytag von Loringhoven, on the staff of Guderian's 2nd Panzer Group, spent the winter of 1940 planning for Barbarossa. He had read about Napoleon's disastrous 1812 campaign against Russia and was 'distinctly uneasy'. He shared Guderian's concerns, and struggled to understand Hitler's rationale:

> The opening of a second front seemed absurd at a time when Britain was refusing peace negotiations and the United States was on the verge of entering the war. We soon realised that the Wehrmacht High Command had been completely deceived in its estimation of Soviet military capacity. After the Army purges carried out by Stalin and the wretched failings of the Finnish campaign, expert German opinion that the Red Army had been irredeemably weakened proved to be wholly mistaken.[24]

These were a lot of 'ifs' to base Barbarossa's planning assumptions on: if Stalin had fatally decimated the Red Army's officers to the point of making it leaderless; if the Wehrmacht could smash the Red Army in a matter of weeks; if there were insufficient reserves and Stalin's weapon factories could be captured; if the Soviet Union collapsed into internal turmoil and Stalin was unseated – then victory was possible.

In the summer of 1941, Hitler's intelligence largely ran contrary to all this. Nevertheless, he chose to ignore it and so started the slaughter on the Eastern Front. Field Marshal von Rundstedt, Brauchitsch and Halder all subsequently claimed that they were opposed to the invasion. Certainly, they appreciated the enormous challenges, thanks to their experiences of 1914–18 fighting on the Eastern Front. Marcks had his own reservations about Operation Otto and was aware of Halder and Brauchitsch's opposition to Case Barbarossa. The successful defeat and partitioning of France did not mean such a victory was repeatable against a country the size of the Soviet Union. Marcks had a pretty good idea of what could happen if they attacked Stalin, but nonetheless requested a combat command rather than another staff job.

4

SHAMEFUL INTRIGUE

In Bucharest by early 1941, there was a general impression that conflict was inevitable. Iosif Hechter wrote:

> There is an atmosphere of war, of general mobilisation. The grey vehicles used by the German Army are mostly full of mud; they come from afar and are heading afar. The German soldiers, who up to now have sauntered around as in a resort, look hurried and lost in thought.[1]

Hitler was now confident that he could win a war in the east and, having obtained the bulk of Poland to provide a springboard for an attack on the Soviet Union, sought to secure his flanks. Six months before Operation Barbarossa, Hitler secretly allocated Romania a key role. He directed:

> It will be the task of Romania to support the attack of the German southern flank, at least at the outset, with its best troops; to hold down the enemy where German forces are not engaged; and to provide auxiliary services in the rear areas.

Through guile and trading on festering post-First World War border disputes, Hitler enlisted not only Romanian dictator, General Ion Antonescu, but also Hungarian regent, Admiral Miklós Horthy, Slovakian premier, Dr Joseph Tiso, and King Boris III of Bulgaria to his war effort against Stalin.

Antonescu provided, by far, the largest number of satellite troops and his best units, including his fledgling armoured forces. He was to remain loyal to Hitler to the bitter end. Field Marshal von Manstein recorded in his memoirs:

Whatever verdict posterity may pass on him as a politician, Antonescu was a
real patriot, a good soldier and certainly our most loyal ally. He was a soldier
who, having once bound up his country's destiny with that of the Reich, did
everything possible until his overthrow to put Romania's military power and
war potential to effective use on our side.[2]

In 1941 Antonescu provided his 3rd and 4th Armies, numbering about 150,000
men, and his 1st Armoured Regiment was the first Romanian unit to cross into
the Soviet Union when the time came.

After the Munich Agreement, President Hacha's Czechoslovakian government granted autonomy to Slovakia, but received intelligence on 9 March 1939
that Slovak separatists were plotting to overthrow the republic. The Slovak
prime minister, Dr Tiso, was dismissed and promptly flew to Berlin to see Hitler.
He returned to Slovakia and declared independence, rupturing Czechoslovakia.

Hitler's troops occupied Moravská–Ostrava, one of the Czechs' key industrial
towns, and were poised along the border of Bohemia and Moravia. The beleaguered Hacha turned to Hitler, who cunningly announced he would take the
Czech people under his protection. Hacha told his cabinet to surrender.

The annexed Czech lands became the German 'Protectorate of Bohemia
and Moravia' and Hitler also placed Slovakia under his protection. Tiso found
German troops entering his country, and under the Treaty of Protection Hitler
gained exclusive rights to exploit the Slovak economy. Lieutenant General
Ferdinand Catlos, the Slovak defence minister, was allowed to raise just three
infantry divisions from the ruins of the Czechoslovakian Army.

Hostility between Horthy and Antonescu also drove them into their pact
with Hitler. Horthy acceded to the Tripartite Pact on 20 November 1940,
having been promised territory in Yugoslavia and the Soviet Union in return for
taking part in the war against Stalin. Antonescu followed suit on 23 November,
as he wanted Soviet Moldavia and the southern part of Ukraine. Under the
1938 Munich Agreement, Horthy regained southern Slovakia and the following
year he occupied the Czech region of Ruthenia. Then, in August 1940 Hitler
pressured Antonescu to hand back northern Transylvania to Horthy.

Romania lost two very large western border regions to Stalin in 1940, followed by half of Transylvania to Horthy and southern Dobruja to King Boris.
Although the Romanian king abdicated in favour of his son, King Mihai
(Michael), Antonescu held the reins of power and invited in two German divisions to deter Horthy from further aggression.

With Antonescu's permission, by the end of February 1941 Hitler was massing
his troops in Romania ready for his attack on Stalin. However, the Führer was
distracted by the prospect of British forces landing at Salonika to support the

Greek Army in fending off Italian leader Benito Mussolini's forces operating out of Albania. Hitler decided he must first secure southern Thrace, which he would then hand over to King Boris of Bulgaria to police. Boris acceded to the Tripartite Pact on 1 March 1941, and Hitler's troops in Romania crossed the Danube and took up position in Bulgaria ready to invade Greece. The opportunist King Boris provided the Bulgarian 5th Army, equipped with less than sixty wholly inadequate light tanks, to support the invasions of Greece and Yugoslavia.

Hitler and Horthy's blitzkrieg seized the devastated Yugoslav capital, Belgrade, on 13 April. Boris' army followed the panzers across the frontier, occupying most of Yugoslav Macedonia and the Greek regions of Eastern Macedonia and Western Thrace, much to the irritation of Mussolini.

King Boris' greatest concern was his traditional foe, Turkey, and he had no intention of tying up his army in Greece and Yugoslavia. Bulgaria's regular army field divisions remained deployed on the Turkish border, leaving reservist formations to act as occupation forces up until 1944. While King Boris had taken part in the brutal dismemberment of Yugoslavia and Greece (and eventually declared war on Britain and America in December 1941), he was not keen to entangle himself with Stalin. Arguing that his army lacked mechanisation (and they were the least mechanised of all the satellite armies that fought for Hitler), Boris prudently avoided taking part in Operation Barbarossa.

'Everyone talks of war soon against the Russians,' noted Hechter, in his journal at the end of April 1941, 'But I don't believe it. Hitler won't do the British such a favour.'[3] By early June, he had changed his tune:

> Could there be a war between Russia and Germany? For three days everyone has thought one imminent. Since yesterday we have had a climate of mobilisation in Bucharest. On Friday there was a blackout; yesterday an order was issued that air-raid shelters must be built in every yard in a maximum of two weeks. Today a number of trains have been cancelled, probably because of troop movements. There is a wave of call-ups and requisitioning.[4]

Hechter was increasingly fatalistic about the prospect of war. On 12 June he observed, 'Since yesterday, General Antonescu has been in Germany having meetings with [Foreign Minister] Ribbentrop and Hitler. It looks as if the final decisions are being made.'[5] On the eve of Barbarossa, the Romanian government sought to cut its people off from the outside world. Hechter noted, 'Private phones are not working. There is a strange sense of danger, isolation, siege. You feel you can no longer communicate with anyone. The buses no longer run; they are said to have been converted into ambulances.'[6]

Just before Barbarossa commenced, Timoshenko and Zhukov, who held the top posts of commissar for defence and chief of staff respectively, did all they could to warn Stalin of the growing threat of invasion. Zhukov was instructed to prepare State Defence Plan 1941. While this was based on the premise that Red Army operations would be in response to Nazi aggression, the idea was to take the fight to the enemy in an offensive rather than defensive manner.

Zhukov's defence plan and Soviet mobilisation plans envisaged nearly all of the Red Army being deployed in the west, namely in the Special Baltic, Leningrad, Western, Kiev and Odessa Military Districts. This meant that of the Red Army's impressive order of battle, which comprised a total of 303 divisions, the bulk of them (some 237 divisions) would be deployed in the west facing the Nazi threat. However, of this impressive overall total, eighty-eight divisions were still in the process of being formed across the breadth and width of the Soviet Union. Stalin's reluctance to mobilise, and the logistics involved, meant that by the summer of 1941 only 171 divisions were in the field in the western Soviet Union, deployed in three belts comprising fifty-seven, fifty-two and sixty-two divisions respectively. They were to be strengthened by Stalin's twenty new mechanised corps, fielding about 1,800 heavy and medium tanks plus thousands of inadequate light tanks.

As a result, only a third of the Soviet divisions were actually in the crucial first defensive echelon. Under such circumstances it was clearly impossible for the Red Army to conduct a forward-offensive defence. The reality was that the first echelon was little more than a tripwire. To add to the Red Army's difficulties, after moving into eastern Poland it had abandoned and stripped most of the pre-1939 Soviet–Polish frontier defences. This meant the construction of new defences in the western areas of the frontier military districts. These were a logistical headache and not something that could be completed in a hurry.

Ironically, the Communist Soviet Union and Nazi Germany were cut from the same cloth: they were the offspring of the traumatic First World War, and both were considered pariahs by the rest of Europe. Thus, they become strange bed fellows forced together by circumstances largely beyond their control. After the Bolsheviks had seized power in 1917, Lenin had assumed the old order would be swept away. Instead, the Western powers had closed ranks and sought to reinstate the tsarist regime by force. The Bolsheviks found themselves fending off foreign intervention and struggling to gain control of the crumbling Russian Empire. Stalin and the other Russian Civil War veterans never forgave the Western powers for their betrayal of the Russian Revolution.

While Ukraine failed to break free, Finland, Estonia, Latvia, Lithuania and Georgia all escaped Moscow's authority. Likewise Poland, previously divided between Imperial Russia, Germany and Austria–Hungary, gained independence along with chunks of Byelorussia and Ukraine. By the time the Soviet Union was formally established in 1923 it had only managed to assert control of the Russian Far East and Georgia. The world's first socialist state was ostracised by the rest of Europe, forcing it into a relationship with recovering Germany, although Stalin terminated this when Hitler came to power in 1933.

Harbouring a grudge against the Western powers, Stalin was intent on regaining all the lost territories even if this meant making a pact with the devil. Six years later, he and Hitler signed the Nazi-Soviet Non-Aggression Pact. Nonetheless, it seemed as if some duplicity was at hand, as just four months earlier Stalin hasd been offering to enter into a mutual assistance pact with Britain and France. Now Soviet foreign minister, Vyacheslav Molotov was extending the hand of friendship to a dictatorship that was opposed to everything the Soviet Union stood for. However, the pact included a secret agreement for the 'Fourth Partition', in which Hitler and Stalin would divide Poland between them. Poland had been subsumed by Russia following the 'Third Partition' and had only reappeared in 1918 as an independent nation after more than 120 years.

Stalin, under the secret provisions of the pact, was permitted to grab territory that Poland had seized in 1920 (east of the Curzon Line), despite it being recognised by the Treaty of Versailles. In addition, Estonia, Finland, Latvia and Lithuania were also recognised as being in the Soviet sphere. Stalin was intent on regaining the tiny Baltic States as well as the Karelian Isthmus from Finland (to protect Leningrad); this would safeguard the Soviet Union's western borders. In return for giving Hitler a free hand in western Poland, Stalin gained everything he wanted.

Barely a week after the Nazi-Soviet Non-Aggression Pact was signed, at dawn on 1 September 1939 Hitler began the destruction of Poland – a nation that both Britain and France pledged to support in the event of a threat to her independence or territorial integrity. For two weeks Stalin watched as the Wehrmacht crushed the outclassed Polish Army. Then, on 17 September 1939 the Red Army rolled into eastern Poland along an 800-mile front to link up with the victorious Germans. Just ten days later Warsaw surrendered, and by 6 October 1939 the fighting was over. Poland had again ceased to exist as an independent nation. Hitler, in the meantime, now found himself at war with Britain and France.

The Red Army was followed into Poland by the NKVD, which rounded up anyone considered a threat to the Soviet occupation. Amongst them was Gustav Herling, who the NKVD accused of being a 'Polish officer in the pay of the enemy'.[7] Their evidence was based on him being caught in the leather boots of a Polish Army major (he maintained they were a gift from his sister), his name translated into Russian became 'Gerling', supposedly making him a relative of Reichsmarschall Göring, but more seriously he had been caught trying to cross the Soviet border into Lithuania. Such arrests implied the NKVD was fearful that eastern Poland was full of pro-Nazis intent on spying on their new military bases.

In Western capitals, Stalin's land grabs during 1939–40 were seen as nothing more than militaristic opportunism riding on the coat-tails of Nazi expansionism. In fact, there was sound military logic for this as it supported Stalin's forward defence doctrine. These occupied territories added strategic depth to the defence of Byelorussia, western Russia and Ukraine. In the centre, they helped shield the cities of Minsk, Smolensk and Moscow. To the north, they added a security buffer to the approaches to the port of Leningrad, while to the south they added protection to the Ukrainian capital, Kiev, and the industrial heartland of Kharkov.

Stalin told his generals that if the Soviet Union was attacked then the Red Army should move forward to engage the enemy. To his way of thinking, it would be better to fight the Wehrmacht in Poland and the Baltic States rather than on the soil of Mother Russia. Before Zhukov replaced him as chief of the General Staff, Marshal Shaposhnikov advocated an in-depth defence, in order to capitalise on the Soviet Union's old border fortifications. He reasoned that the bulk of their forces in the five western military districts should be positioned behind the old state frontier and that only a covering force be deployed in the newly 'liberated' territories. However, this was not in line with Stalin's concept of forward defence and was ignored.

Following the fall of France in 1940 it soon became apparent that major military preparations in German-occupied Poland, as well as in East Prussia, Romania and Finland, indicated that Hitler was planning to strike the Soviet Union. Stalin had well-placed intelligence sources in the shape of the Red Orchestra or *Rote Kapelle*, a group of anti-Nazis in Berlin, and Richard Sorge, a Soviet agent in Tokyo with access to the German embassy. Hitler reassured Stalin by claiming the troop movements eastwards were simply designed to mislead Churchill into lowering his guard prior to Operation Sealion and the invasion of England. Stalin took Hitler at his word.

According to Zhukov, it was General Filipp Ivanovich Golikov, chief of the Intelligence Directorate, who persuaded Stalin in late March 1941 that Hitler would not attack in the summer. Ironically, he produced an accurate report which warned that three German Army groups were indeed massing on the Soviet Union's western frontier and could strike for Leningrad, Moscow and Kiev between 15 May and 15 June 1941.

Golikov, who had commanded troops during the Soviet invasion of Poland and in the war against Finland, seemed destined for great things. Nikita

Khrushchev, Stalin's Communist Party enforcer in Ukraine recalled, 'I'd often seen him in Stalin's presence when he was head of army intelligence.'[8] Later, at Stalingrad, Khrushchev was to form the opinion that Golikov was a coward.

Like Voroshilov, Golikov was considered a 'political general'. Although he had attended the Frunze Military Academy in the early 1930s, he had started his career as a political commissar. Regular officers tended to look down on the political generals, as they felt they had achieved their positions not through any real military aptitude, but because of their slavish adherence to Communist Party line. Golikov concluded his report by saying that Hitler would not attack until after a victory over England and rumours of war were a result of misinformation coming from the English or German intelligence services.

Admiral Kuznetsov also had credible intelligence from Berlin about an imminent attack, but he considered it false. Stalin, a cunning cynic, clung to the Nazi-Soviet Non-Aggression Pact and believed that Germany's enemies were trying to manipulate him.

Stalin had little time for Golikov's abilities, branding him 'inexperienced and naïve'.[9] He also observed that human intelligence should not be relied upon, 'A spy should be like the devil; no one should trust him not even himself'.[10] Stalin chose to believe none of it. 'This information,' he wrote on it, 'is an English provocation. Find out who the author is and punish him.'[11]

Golikov knew better than to antagonise Stalin. By April he was flagging up the significant German troop movements toward the border and had stopped reassuring his boss about Hitler's intentions. However, he avoided making any assessments that might deviate from Stalin's already set views. Stalin's mantra was, 'Don't tell me what you think. Give me the facts and the source!'[12]

Crucially, these reports and similar ones from the Soviet ambassador in Berlin were sent direct to Stalin, neither Timoshenko nor Zhukov were ever privy to them. Zhukov recalled:

All the information General Golikov had was immediately forwarded to Stalin. What I do not know is what intelligence General Golikov laid before Stalin on his own, by-passing the Defence Commissar and the Chief of the General Staff, as he often did. Naturally, this could not but affect the final situation analysis.[13]

This was all part of Stalin's policy of keeping the Red Army compartmentalised and ensuring the generals never had the bigger picture. It meant that he was relying purely on intuition to determine the veracity of the intelligence landing on his desk. The net result was that he did not canvass the opinions of his experienced senior military leaders. Only in late April did Stalin acquiesce to

Timoshenko and Zhukov's request to mobilise reservists and redeploy troops from the Urals, Siberia and Far East to the west. This deployment, though, could not be completed until 10 July – this was to prove three weeks too late.

British Prime Minister Winston Churchill was appalled at the ineptitude of Soviet intelligence, remarking, 'So far as strategy, policy, foresight, competence are arbiters, Stalin and his commissars showed themselves at this moment the most completely outwitted bunglers of the Second World War'.[14] Ironically, despite his best intentions Churchill had contributed to this state of affairs by trying to forewarn Stalin. He thought, as late as March 1941 and supported by the Joint Intelligence Committee, that a German attack on the Soviet Union was unlikely. Right until the end of 1940 Churchill assumed that Spain was likely to be the next victim of Nazi aggression. This was because General Franco would not give Hitler free passage for his troops to capture the British naval base at Gibraltar.

From mid-March 1941, Bletchley Park's top-secret Ultra intelligence intercepts began picking up indications that Hitler was poised to attack Stalin. Churchill waited a few weeks before he felt moved to warn the Soviet leader. He drafted his warning in early April, but did not want to reveal that Bletchley had broken Hitler's Enigma codes. His message, as a result, was vague and not delivered until 27 April. It mattered little, as Stalin saw this as British subterfuge in order to get him to enter the war against Hitler. In Stalin's mind, this was confirmed by Deputy Führer Rudolf Hess's flight to Scotland the following month. Although this mission was unauthorised, to Stalin it indicated that British–German peace talks were underway.

Soviet commanders on the western frontier knew that trouble was brewing. Amongst them was General Fedyuninsky, veteran of Khalkhin-Gol, who in April 1941 was appointed commander of the 15th Rifle Corps serving with the Kiev Military District. His headquarters were at Kovel, a west Ukrainian town just 30 miles from German-occupied Poland. Fedyuninsky observed:

> At the time of my arrival in Kovel, the situation on our western frontier was becoming more and more tense. From a great variety of sources, and from our army and frontier-guard reconnaissance, we knew that since February German troops had begun to concentrate along our borders.[15]

By early May, after Hitler's successful military operations in the Balkans against Yugoslavia and Greece, Stalin seemed to concede that war with Germany might be a possibility. He grudgingly allowed Timoshenko and Zhukov to strengthen the borders on 12 May by calling up 500,000 reserves – but he wanted to do nothing further to antagonise Hitler. When Timoshenko briefed him about

Luftwaffe reconnaissance flights all along the frontier, Stalin was dismissive, saying, 'I'm not sure Hitler knows about those flights'. He steadfastly refused to take any further defensive measures.

General Voronov, First Deputy Chief of the Artillery Directorate, recalled:

> In April, May, and June documents of great importance were being compiled in the General Staff. They told of the large-scale operational movements of German troops to our western frontiers and cited the number of corps and the infantry and tank divisions. The authors of these documents did not draw any clear-cut conclusion but merely confined themselves to stating the bare facts.[16]

Nonetheless, Timoshenko and Zhukov quietly did all they could to prepare the Red Army without incurring Stalin's wrath. They instigated a massive reorganisation and redeployment so they could counter-attack along the entire frontier.

Their biggest enemy was time. While frontier guards held the new border, the first echelon rifle divisions were up to 40 miles away. The mechanised units in the second echelon were even further back. The General Staff felt these forces could hold the Germans until reserves were summoned. To this end, Timoshenko and Zhukov felt it prudent to create a Reserve Front anchored on the pre-1939 border. In effect, they had accepted that Shaposhnikov was right.

Rumours of a Soviet military build-up and war were rife. The official state media did all it could to deny the redeployments being conducted by Timoshenko and Zhukov. In early June, Tass, the Soviet press agency, issued a categoric denial of rumours in the West that several Siberian divisions had redeployed from the Far East to the banks of the River Bug, which formed the boundary between German- and Soviet-occupied Poland. Political prisoner, Gustav Herling, who heard the broadcast wrote:

> The agency report calmly reassured its listeners that the army movements in question were made within the framework of normal summer manoeuvres, and that the good-neighbourly relations of Germany and the Soviet Union ... could not be destroyed by the shameful intrigues of Western warmongers.[17]

Few were convinced by such platitudes, but while there was substance to such rumours in this instance, the Siberians had not moved.

To the south, in the sunny Crimea, rumours of war did nothing to dampen the holiday atmosphere. Just before the Nazi invasion, a Black Sea Fleet naval officer named Evseev, stationed in Sevastopol, wrote in his diary:

A wonderful Crimean evening … all the streets and boulevards in the city were lit. The white houses were bathed in light, the clubs and theatres beckoned the sailors on shore leave to come inside. There were crowds of sailors and local people, dressed in white, packing the city's streets and parks. As always, the famous Primorsky boulevard was full of people out for a stroll. Music was playing.[18]

5

EVERYTHING IS NORMAL

While the codebreakers of Bletchley Park and Churchill were firmly of the view that Hitler intended to invade the Soviet Union, the British Joint Intelligence Committee (JIC) remained unconvinced by Ultra. 'They appeared only on 12th June to have come to the conclusion that Hitler would attack Russia,' recalled Churchill's scientific advisor, R. V. Jones, 'earning the comment from Churchill, "I had not been content with this form of collective wisdom and preferred to see the originals [messages] myself ... thus forming my own opinion sometimes at much earlier dates".'[1]

This change of heart was due to an intercepted telegram from the Japanese ambassador in Berlin. The JIC reported to Churchill:

> Fresh evidence is now at hand that Hitler has made up his mind to have done with Soviet obstruction to Germany and intends to attack her. Hostilities therefore appear highly probable though it is premature to fix a date for their outbreak. It remains our opinion that matters are likely to come to a head during the second half of June.[2]

JIC Chairman Bill Bentick was instructed to immediately brief the Soviet ambassador. 'I remember saying that the attack would take place on 22 or 29 June,' recalled Bentick, 'and that I would put money on the 22nd.'[3] The ambassador dutifully relayed the warning to the Kremlin.

On 11 June 1941, General M. I. Kazakov, chief of staff of the Central Asian Military District, who was conducting officer training in Tashkent, found himself summoned to Moscow to brief Timoshenko. His district controlled three corps totalling around ten divisions and was responsible for defending the Soviet Union's frontiers with Iran, Afghanistan and western China. Kazakov was not unduly alarmed. Following military district exercises, it was routine for senior officers to attend an annual conference at the People's Commissariat of Defence (Soviet Defence Ministry), but these were normally held in November or December.

Kazakov had been in Moscow during December 1940 and January 1941 when he had attended the conference and participated in a series of important large-scale war games. It was following these that Meretskov's very brief tenure as chief of the General Staff was terminated, with Zhukov taking his place. The gathering of generals has resulted in heated debate over the lessons from the Finnish War and Hitler's victories in Europe. The senior commanders had remained divided over the merits of tank versus cavalry.

Kazakov flew to the capital on 12 June, as requested, and once the transport aircraft was in the air he checked over his report. Afterwards, as conversation was almost impossible above the noise of the engines, he settled down for the long flight and, peering out the windows, noticed:

> A railroad stretched beneath us almost the whole time. A great many trains were moving along it, and it soon became clear to me that these were military trains. They were headed in one direction – north-west. I knew very well that no troops had been despatched from our military district, and that there were no plans to do so. So these were troops from Eastern Siberia or the Transbaikal.[4]

At the General Staff's headquarters in Moscow, Kazakov bumped into commanders from the Transbaikal, Urals and Volga Military Districts, all of whom were in their field uniforms. Kazakov felt, 'It was clear that they were not travelling to manoeuvres.' It transpired that it was indeed forces from the Transbaikal that he had seen moving by rail. General Pavlov, commander of the key Western Military District, was also in Moscow.

Major General M.F. Lukin, from the Transbaikal, met Kazakov in passing but was not at liberty to discuss the destination of his troops. However, his men had been summoned to help create the new Reserve Front. Lukin's 16th Army, some 4,000 miles away, was ordered on 25 May to move to Starokonstantinov in Ukraine, south-west of Kiev. It was to join General I.S. Konev's 19th Army from the North Caucasus and General A.K. Smirnov's 18th Army in the Kharkov Military District as part of the Reserve Front in the Southern Sector.

Lukin's boss, Lieutenant General P.A. Kurochkin, commander of the Transbaikal Military District, was ordered back to Moscow to take command of a new 20th Army, also destined to form part of the Reserve Front armies in the Western Sector. General F.A. Ershakov, commander of the Urals Military District, was instructed to send his men to the Vitebsk area, while the Orel Military District, under General F.N. Remizov, sent troops to the area of the middle Dnieper River. It was clear to Stalin's generals that war was brewing.

All this, however, was simply too late. The strategic east–west redeployment was only partially completed when Hitler attacked. In the case of Lukin's 16th Army, just the 5th Mechanised Corps had reached Ukraine by this stage. The late arrival of the 16th Army meant it would be committed to the battle piece-meal, trying to defend the city of Smolensk.

When Kazakov asked the deputy chief of operations General Aleksandr Vasilevskiy when war would break out, the response was, 'We'll be lucky if it doesn't begin in the next fifteen to twenty days'.[5] Instead of delivering his report, much to Kazakov's dismay he was invited to watch a two-hour Nazi propaganda film about Hitler's invasion of the Balkans. After which Timoshenko and Zhukov calmly went off for dinner together. Despite his best efforts, Kazakov never got to brief Timoshenko and, instead, briefly saw Zhukov before returning to Tashkent on 21 June.

While Kazakov was partially reassured that some sort of mobilisation was taking place, he was perturbed by just how relaxed the General Staff seemed to be. Kazakov may have been irritated about how he was treated, having travelled all that way, but his military district was so far from the centre of operations it is hardly surprising that the General Staff had little time for him. Their minds were on other things. Nevertheless, he must have felt disappointed that forces from the Far East had already been summoned to defend Mother Russia against the Nazi menace while he had been sent back to Tashkent to kick his heels.

When Pavlov, commander of the Western Military District, was asked by a colleague why he was in the capital, he responded, 'Everything is normal with us. And so I decided to take advantage of the calm situation and come to Moscow for one thing and another.'[6] It all sounded so casual. However, this may have been a polite way of saying 'it's on a need to know basis' and that he had been summoned by the General Staff like all the other district commanders. Undoubtedly, when Timoshenko and Zhukov went to dinner their topic of conversation would have been the preparedness of all the military districts and progress in creating the vital Reserve Front.

Regardless of Stalin's apparent tunnel vision on the issue, both generals, despite their denials, must have seen or at least been aware of the contents of the reports produced by Golikov's Intelligence Directorate. For arguments sake, if the predictions were accurate they were within days of the deadline for Hitler's strike. May had come and gone but now it was almost mid-June. Timoshenko and Zhukov knew that they were in danger of missing the proverbial boat if Hitler should attack before they were ready.

The pressure on Timoshenko and Zhukov as they leafed through updates on the trains full of troops chugging west must have been immense. Zhukov acknowledged, 'My thoughts were depressing.' They were amongst a small clique who knew what was happening and it was in everyone's interest that they exuded an air of supreme confidence in their preparations. Secretly they appreciated they had too few forces, which were ill-prepared. The reality was that there were insufficient men in place, and those that were lacked sufficient weapons, ammunition and other equipment. For some, it must have felt like the First World War all over again when mobilisation had been reliant on train timetables.

What Kazakov did not know was that while troops were being shipped toward the frontier there were very severe logistical and training problems. Putting men on trains was one thing, but they needed to be equipped and fed. General Andrei Khrulev, the quartermaster general, was simply not issuing weapons and ammunition quickly enough. This, in turn, was having a negative impact on the efforts of General Meretskov, who was in charge of combat training. In light of Meretskov's lacklustre performance in Finland, it is not entirely clear why he had been given this important job.

Both problems, if not rectified, would inevitably have a highly detrimental impact on the performance of the Red Army. According to Pavlov, his men were 'stamping around in various tactical battalion and regimental exercises'.[7] Such small-unit-level training was wholly inadequate at this stage; it should have been on divisional, corps or even army level.

To make matters worse, the production of the newer types of aircraft and tanks was simply too slow. In particular, the tank plants in Leningrad, producing the KV-1 heavy tank, and in Kharkov, building the T-34 medium tank, had not been put on a war footing. While the rifle divisions were suffering, so too were the tank divisions. During 1940, just 243 KVs and 115 T-34s had been built. This greatly hampered the belated formation of the new mechanised corps. Pavlov cannot have been happy that his 14th Mechanised Corps, with an established strength of 1,024 tanks (including 420 T-34s and 126 KVs), in June 1941 comprised just 508 inadequate T-26 light tanks. He must have relayed these concerns to the General Staff. General Boldin castigated the T-26 as 'only good enough for firing at sparrows'.[8]

Alexander Werth, with *The Sunday Times* in Moscow, observed, 'Russian soldiers and officers, I soon found, were amongst the most candid and uninhibited talkers in the world'. He noted that the Red Army was not only lacking in modern aircraft, tanks and motor vehicles, 'Similarly, the production of guns, mortars and automatic weapons proceeded at "an intolerably slow pace". [...] The production of ammunition in 1941 was lagging behind even that of the guns.'[9]

General Voronov felt that the General Staff did not believe there would be war as a result of Stalin's overbearing influence. Clearly, though, Golikov and Kuznetsov shared the blame. Voronov astutely noted the dilemma faced by Timoshenko and Zhukov:

The troops stationed on our western borders were not moved up to their defence line along the border for fear of provoking war. But at the same time, there were large-scale shifts of troops from the interior of our country to the western borders. Units which were not combat ready, which needed more personnel and armaments, were sent there. They were followed by numerous transports with equipment and munitions. This great activity on the railroads could easily have been discovered by the enemy's intelligence service and by his aerial reconnaissance. There was an obvious contradiction here. What was there to fear from moving our troops directly to the borders and deploying them along these defence lines if at this time we were already making major operational shifts and massing troops in certain regions?[10]

Rather unfairly, as a divisional commander, General Biriuzov blamed Zhukov for this state of affairs:

The new Chief of the General Staff G.K. Zhukov, who had replaced B.M. Shaposhnikov shortly before the war, failed to appreciate the significance of his predecessor's proposals, and, knowing Stalin's negative attitude to them, he evidently did not press for their fulfilment.[11]

This was simply not true. Both Timoshenko and Zhukov lobbied Stalin to take decisive steps until the very last moment, but he would not listen. Their creation of the Reserve Front drew on Shaposhnikov's thinking. The net result, though, was that the Red Army was ill-prepared for the coming conflict.

The overall strength of Stalin's armed forces in early 1941 was almost 5 million men – 2.6 million in the west, 1.8 million in the Far East. The Soviet armed forces were divided into five elements: the ground forces, navy, air force, national air defence and armed forces support. The ground forces accounted for the largest proportion of personnel with just over 79 per cent, the Red Air Force had just over 11 per cent and the navy just under 6 per cent. The Red Air Force consisted of four key elements: the *Voenno-Vozdushnye Sily* (VVS – Air Force), *Protivovozdushnaya Oborona* (PVO – Air Defence), the Fleet Air Force and the *Gosudarstvenny Komitet Oborony* (GKO – State Committee for Defence) Air Reserve.

Zhukov's campaign on the Mongolian border provided evidence, contrary to the fighting in Finland, of the Red Army's capabilities when it was efficiently led. While the West did not take much notice of the campaign in Mongolia, Finland was, after all, on everyone's doorstep. Timoshenko and others took note. It was clear that Zhukov's victory was largely due to the concentration of his mechanised forces. Waking up to the menace posed by German panzer divisions, in late 1940 the Red Army was finally allowed to set about creating twenty mechanised corps, each of which comprised one or two tank divisions and one or two motorised divisions. These formations were also the result of the hard-won lessons of the Winter War and observing the German blitzkrieg in the West and the Balkans.

While Timoshenko resurrected Tukhachevsky's discredited armoured corps, the commissars were also demoted once more to political advisors to prevent them hampering military decision making. Once in charge, one of Timoshenko's first moves was to re-establish the large mobile formations. This process, however, only began in March 1941, and of the proposed mechanised corps, less than half had been equipped by June. In theory, each of these powerful mechanised corps consisted of 36,000 men with about 1,000 tanks, but on the eve of Barbarossa they were still being formed. In addition, they were widely scattered rather than held as a concentrated potent reserve that could launch a major armoured counter-offensive.

Following the disastrous performance of the Red Army in Finland, Soviet rifle divisions were reorganised to number 14,483 men, consisting of three infantry and two artillery regiments plus anti-tank and anti-aircraft support. As all the armour went to the new mechanised corps, each rifle division was left with just sixteen light tanks. Few, if any, Soviet rifle divisions ever attained this strength. It is notable that the men in these formations at this stage were largely ethnic Slavs, having been recruited from European Russia, Byelorussia and Ukraine.

In Stalin's mind, should Hitler invade he would undoubtedly go after the raw materials of Ukraine, and thus most of his new mechanised forces were with Colonel General M.P. Kirponos' Kiev Military District (South-Western Front from the outbreak of hostilities). This fielded six mechanised corps: the 9th and 22nd (5th Army); the 4th and 15th (6th Army); the 16th (26th Army); and the 8th (12th Army). He also had two reserve corps: the 19th (16th Army) and the 24th (19th Army).

Notably, in the Lvov (Lemberg) area, in what had until recently been eastern Poland but now formed part of Ukraine, was the 4th Mechanised Corps with General Andrei Vlasov. He did not know it, but he was to play a very infamous role in Hitler's war effort on the Eastern Front. His command included the

Soviet 32nd Tank Division equipped with 300 brand new KV-1 tanks. When the time came, elements of this division would offer effective if short-lived opposition to the German panzers. In contrast, Rokossovsky's 9th Mechanised Corps only had a third of its tanks and they were obsolete, with worn-out engines; his so-called motorised infantry lacked even horses and carts. Rokossovsky would work miracles and, like Zhukov, proved to be exactly the type of general his country needed in its hour of need.

Barring the road to Minsk and Moscow was General Pavlov's Western Military District (or West Front). His command also had six mechanised corps, with a total of twelve tank divisions and six supporting motorised divisions. The 6th and 13th Mechanised Corps were supporting the Soviet 10th Army, but the latter had practically no tanks. The 14th Mechanised Corps was on the left with the 4th Army, while the 11th Mechanised Corps with the 3rd Army was on the right. The 17th and 20th Mechanised Corps were held in reserve.

Pavlov was in the unenviable position of holding the Bialystok Salient, trapped between German East Prussia and German-occupied Poland. There was a suspicion that Stalin and Zhukov considered Pavlov's command a sacrificial lamb and that it was the Reserve Front's job to hold Hitler at the old frontier. Certainly, by June 1941, Pavlov's forces were far from up to strength.

By the autumn of 1941, north to south in front of Moscow were Konev's Western Front (22nd, 29th, 30th, 19th, 16th and 20th Armies plus the 24th and 43rd from the Reserve Front), and the Bryansk Front (50th, 3rd, 13th and Operational Group Yermakov). Behind them, the defensive Vyazma Line was held by the 31st, 49th, 32nd and 33rd Armies of the Reserve Front. These comprised eighty-four rifle divisions, nine cavalry divisions, two motorised rifle divisions and a tank division, plus supporting services.

Soviet air strength was never officially confirmed, but 1,540 of the newer aircraft representing 20 per cent of Soviet air power in the western Soviet Union were available when Hitler invaded. Including the older airframes, it was estimated that there were at least 7,300 Soviet aircraft in the west of the country. An additional 3,500–4,000 aircraft were in service in the central Soviet Union and the Soviet Far East, representing a vast reserve, although most were obsolescent types.

The commander of the Moscow Air Defence Zone, General Gromadin, had at his disposal Colonel Klimov's newly formed 6th PVO Fighter Corps with almost 600 fighters, plus the 1st PVO Anti-Aircraft Artillery Corps with nearly 800 anti-aircraft guns. The Western Sector of the Moscow PVO, under Colonel Stefanovski, consisted of eleven fighter regiments; of these, only two were equipped with the outdated I-153 and I-16 fighters. Of the remaining nine fighter regiments, four had new Yak-1s, two had MiG-3s, two had Hurricanes and one had LaGG-3s, while a twelfth regiment was in reserve with P-40s. Colonel Trifonov's Southern Sector was roughly the same, but smaller resources were committed to Colonel Mitenkov and Colonel Yakushin's Northern and Eastern Sectors.

The Leningrad Military District covered not only Leningrad, but also Murmansk and the Karelo-Finnish Soviet Republic. It included the Soviet 7th, 14th and 23rd Armies (19th, 42nd and 50th Rifle Corps and 1st and 5th Mechanised Corps); 1st Fighter Aviation Corps; and 2nd Air Defence Corps and 7th Aviation Corps of the Air Defence Command. These forces totalled fifteen rifle divisions, one rifle brigade, four tank and two motorised divisions and eight fortified regions. Ground forces numbered 404,470 men, with 1,857 tanks, 7,901 guns and 1,336 combat aircraft.

At sea, the Baltic Fleet comprised a surface ship squadron, a light ship detachment, three submarine brigades and two torpedo boat brigades, which could muster a total of 225 combat ships (including two battleships, two cruisers, twenty-one destroyers, sixty-eight submarines, two cannon ships, seven destroyer escorts, four armoured cutters, fifty-five torpedo boats, thirty-four minesweepers and thirty-four submarine hunters). The fleet's coastal artillery also fielded 2,189 guns and mortars. In addition, the Baltic Fleet had considerable air forces numbering 682 aircraft, including 331 fighters, 184 bombers and 167 reconnaissance aircraft. These combined forces totalled 119,645 men. Way to the south, Stalin was confident in the defences of Odessa and Sevastopol as these were supported by the Black Sea Fleet, which included the firepower of an elderly battleship, cruisers, destroyers, motor torpedo boats and submarines.

Luftwaffe intelligence estimated that the Red Air Force and supporting bombers of the long-range aviation units had some 7,300 aircraft deployed in the western Soviet Union. This did not take into account, however, the 1,500 aircraft of the Soviet Navy (supporting the Artic, Baltic and Black Sea Fleets) and the 1,445 aircraft or the PVO air defence regiments. In total, the Red Air Force actually had up to 14,000 aircraft available in the western Soviet Union. In the key five border military districts these numbered some 5,440 aircraft, including 2,736 fighters and 1,688 bombers, but the Luftwaffe only assessed 2,800 of them to be operational.

The Luftwaffe's intelligence suggested that the Red Air Force had 15,000 pilots and 150,000 ground support and aircrew. While the Luftwaffe had good intelligence on the I-16 fighter, it was not so familiar with the newer Yaks and MiGs or the rate at which the Red Air Force was being re-equipped.

According to German sources, the Luftwaffe had just under 2,000 aircraft available for Operation Barbarossa – supporting Army Group North in Luftflotte 1 under Keller, Army Group Centre in Luftflotte 2 under Kesselring and Army Group South with Luftflotte 4 under Löhr. However, only 1,300 of these were serviceable on the day of the invasion. In contrast, Soviet intelligence, including the Romanian Air Force and Luftflotte 5 in Finland and Norway, put the Luftwaffe strength at 3,500.

As noted it was only at the last minute that Stalin and Stavka, the Soviet High Command, acquiesced to the creation of fully fledged mechanised corps, but by then it was too late. These formations were, on the whole, inadequately led, equipped and trained. The Wehrmacht, in the meantime, had perfected its strategy and tactics in Western Europe, Scandinavia and the Balkans. In the face of the Nazis' tried and tested blitzkrieg, the outcome was inevitable.

Voroshilov's and Stalin's stance on beating an enemy on his own territory meant that defensive training was largely ignored. Also, the fixed defences in the western Soviet Union were neglected in favour of a forward defence in Poland, with no real time to prepare. In the late 1930s they had both misread the lessons from the Spanish Civil War and agreed on disbanding the tank and motorised formations so vital for modern mobile warfare. They both carried equal responsibility for leaving the Soviet armed forces equipped only with largely obsolete tanks and aircraft. Over 60 per cent of the tanks were unserviceable and aircraft serviceability was also alarmingly low. Besides this, numbers would count for nothing if they were not leavened with sufficient quality to give them some backbone and this was to be a serious omission in the opening stages of the war in the east. Similarly, naval doctrine was such that the Soviet fleets would ultimately be unable to safeguard Leningrad, Odessa and Sevastopol, despite the extreme weakness of the German surface fleet. Air power was to prove the deciding factor.

Timoshenko, unhappy at the readiness of the forces on the western frontier, instructed them on 14 June 1941 that all problems were to be remedied by the end of the month. Four days later, both he and Zhukov again attempted to prevail upon Stalin to place the Red Army on full alert. Stalin would hear none of it; he did not wish to provoke Hitler into war. This was despite the very evident massing of the Wehrmacht and constant Luftwaffe reconnaissance flights over eastern Poland, Byelorussia and Ukraine.

6

PROVOKING WAR

At the start of the summer Timoshenko and Zhukov had consistently warned Stalin that their intelligence showed war was imminent and urged for full mobilisation. Stalin steadfastly refused to believe Hitler would attack and even dismissed intelligence from a spy within Luftwaffe headquarters, who had confirmed the impending assault.

The Soviet leader continued to dither. Following the military commanders' briefings at the Defence Ministry on 13 June, Timoshenko sought Stalin's permission to bring the border districts to war readiness. Frustratingly, Stalin did not agree to the deployment of the second echelon divisions in the border areas until four days later.

Nikita Khrushchev, who should have been in Kiev monitoring the Ukrainian border, found himself summoned to the Kremlin. He was very concerned by Stalin's complete air of defeatism:

> He'd obviously lost all confidence in the ability of our army to put up a fight. It was as though he'd thrown up his hands in despair and given up after Hitler crushed the French army and occupied Paris. [...] I was with Stalin when he heard about the capitulation of France. He'd let fly with some choice Russian curses and said now Hitler was sure to beat our brains in.[1]

During a Politburo meeting on 18 June, Stalin was extremely dismissive and belittling of his two most senior generals, accusing them of warmongering. 'So you see,' said Stalin:

> Timoshenko's a fine man with a big head but apparently a small brain. I said it for the people, we have to raise their alertness, while you have to realise that Germany will never fight Russia on her own. You must understand this.[2]

He stomped out of the meeting room only to poke his head back in to warn, 'If you're going to provoke the Germans on the frontier by moving troops there without permission, then heads will roll, mark my words', and with that he slammed the door.

Timoshenko and Zhukov privately despaired of their leader's seeming indifference to the threat gathering on their borders. They gained absolutely no support from the Politburo members, who did not wish to displease their leader. Khrushchev tired of kicking his heels and two days later insisted he be allowed to leave for Ukraine:

> Finally I asked him outright, 'Comrade Stalin, war could break out any hour now, and it would be very bad if I were caught here in Moscow or in transit when it starts. I'd better leave right away ...'
>
> 'Yes, I guess that's true. You'd better leave.'
>
> His answer confirmed what I'd suspected: that he hadn't the slightest idea why he'd been detaining me in Moscow. He knew my proper place was in Kiev. He had kept me around simply because he needed to have company, especially when he was afraid. He couldn't stand being alone.[3]

To the very last, the Politburo said exactly what Stalin wanted to hear. On the very eve of Hitler's attack Interior Minister Beria took the opportunity to ingratiate himself with his boss. On 21 June, he denounced Golikov as a liar after his latest warnings and sent Stalin a note declaring, 'My people and I, Iosif Vissarionovich, firmly remember your wise prediction: Hitler will not attack us in 1941'.[4]

Even so, Pavlov's Western Military District received a message from Timoshenko and Zhukov at 0045 hrs on 22 June. It read:

> A surprise attack by the Germans on the fronts of Leningrad, Baltic, Western Special, Kiev Special and Odessa Military Districts is possible during the course of 22–23 June 1941.
>
> The mission of our forces is to avoid proactive actions of any kind ... At the same time, the ... Districts' forces are to be at full combat readiness to meet a surprise blow by the Germans or their allies.[5]

This seemingly contradictory warning was simply too late. The Red Air Force had not been permitted to intercept Luftwaffe incursions over eastern Poland, where its aircraft were lined up on the runways with parade precision ready to be bombed. Many of the Soviet Army's divisions were simply too poorly equipped to fend off Hitler's onslaught. Critically, there was a shortage of weapons and ammunition. The rifle divisions also lacked transport, spares and fuel. The bulk of their communications relied on landlines rather than radio, and this greatly hampered the armoured units.

The ongoing mobilisation was a mess. Anastas Mikoyan, minister for food supplies, acknowledged there were not enough rifles to go around:

> We thought we surely had enough for the whole army. But it turned out that a proportion of our divisions had been assembled according to peacetime norms. Divisions that been equipped with adequate numbers of rifles for wartime conditions held on to them, but they were all close to the front. When the Germans crossed the frontier and began to advance, these weapons ended up in the territory they controlled or else the Germans simply captured them. As a result, reservists going to the front ended up with no rifles at all.[6]

General Voronov admitted:

> Many of our units in border districts did not even have rifle cartridges before the beginning of the war, to say nothing of live artillery shells. With the knowledge of the General Staff, prime movers [gun tractors] were withdrawn from artillery units and used in the construction of fortified regions along the new western border. As a result, the guns were immobilised and could not have been used in the fighting.[7]

Timoshenko had cleverly advised the district military commanders to hold exercises in the direction of the frontier as a surreptitious way of moving their troops forward. This was done, but the artillery was left behind. This was either because they could not be moved or had been sent to the firing ranges for training.

Hitler's titanic assault on Stalin was heralded at 0315 hrs on Sunday, 22 June 1941, when the Luftwaffe hit the Red Air Force's frontier airfields. In the Kremlin, Stalin and his cronies, upon hearing this news, were panic-stricken. Despite clear and compelling evidence to the contrary, Stalin had continually insisted Hitler would not attack; he had now been proved badly wrong.

The Soviet leader's initial response to Hitler's invasion was one of self-denial. He knew he had stayed the hand of the Red Army at the critical moment and was now paying the price. For a brief moment, it appeared as if Stalin might buckle under the enormous strain. There have been claims that he had some sort of nervous breakdown, but there is little evidence to support this. Zhukov called Stalin at Kuntsevo, his dacha retreat outside Moscow, for permission to counter-attack. Just thirty minutes after Hitler's offensive commenced, Stalin summoned the senior leadership of the Politburo, including Timoshenko and Zhukov, to the Kremlin to discuss the situation.

A bemused General Kazakov had flown in to Tashkent on the night of 21/22 June. He spent several hours briefing his superior then went off to get some much-needed sleep. He was awoken on the instructions of the duty officer – an urgent call had just come through from the General Staff in Moscow. The message simply stated, 'It has started'. He strode off to find his boss, Trofimenko. Kazakov must have cursed his luck that he was now thousands of miles away from the action. He was determined to secure a combat command.

In the meantime, the poor leadership of the Red Army showed through immediately. Georgy Semenyak, serving with the Soviet 204th Rifle Division, was numbed by the ferocity of Hitler's blitzkrieg and aghast at the performance of his officers, 'The lieutenants, captains, second lieutenants took rides on passing vehicles … mostly trucks travelling eastwards. [...] The fact they used their rank to save their own lives, we felt this to be wrong.'[8]

Hitler's forces stormed across eastern Poland evicting the Red Army, and on into Byelorussia. Army Group North thrust toward Leningrad, Army Group Centre struck toward Moscow and Army Group South cut into Ukraine. To the far south, combined German, Hungarian and Romanian forces drove toward the Caucasus, while to the far north, in Finland, thrusts were made toward Murmansk and down the Karelian Isthmus as part of the 'Continuation War'. Soviet pre-1939 gains in both Poland and Finland were soon lost.

General Heinz Guderian's powerful 2nd Panzer Group's key armoured formations comprised the 24th, 46th and 47th Panzer Corps (which included the 3rd, 4th, 10th, 17th and 18th Panzer Divisions). General H. Hoth's slightly weaker 3rd Panzer Group included the 39th and 57th Panzer Corps (encompassing the 7th, 12th, 19th and 20th Panzer Divisions). In their path were the Red Army forces of the Western Front's 3rd, 10th and 4th Armies. They launched a series of desperate, ill-organised and poorly co-ordinated counter-attacks. Their attempts to hold the Germans at bay proved futile as the 3rd and 10th Armies, 6th and 11th Mechanised and 6th Cavalry Corps' counter-attacks were crushed and Army Group Centre encircled Minsk.

On 22 June, General Kirponos tried to get his 15th and 22nd Mechanised Corps to counter the Germans' southern and northern flanks. Only a weak element of the 15th Corps' 10th Tank Division was committed, with little effect, and the Germans penetrated 24 miles to Berestechko. Likewise, the 22nd's 215th Motorised and 19th Tank Division were unable to prevent the Germans reaching Lutsk. When mustered, the 15th Corps' weak 10th and 37th Tank Divisions were unable to stop the panzers pushing another 18 miles. Rokossovsky's 9th and Feklenko's 15th Mechanised Corps were ordered to counter-attack north of Dubno, while to the south, Karpezo's 15th and Riabyshev's 8th Mechanised Corps were also to attack. Unfortunately, Zhukov and Kirponos' orders led to Vlasov's 4th Mechanised Corps being dispersed which prevented them from supporting the 8th Corps.

Upon being informed of Hitler's invasion Churchill unexpectedly changed his opinion of the Red Army. 'I will bet you a Monkey to a Mousetrap [racing terms for 500:1] that the Russians are still fighting, and fighting victoriously, two years from now.'[9] Churchill's private secretary was so taken aback by this premonition that he wrote, 'I recorded your words in writing at the time because I thought they were such a daring prophecy, and because it was such an entirely different point of view from that which everybody else had expressed.'[10] Only the previous day, his opinion had been that Stalin would be swiftly defeated. It was as if Churchill had foreseen Stalingrad and Kursk.

Churchill went onto the radio to inform the British public that the country had a new ally. Reading between the lines, there is an almost holier-than-thou attitude to his broadcast. He announced:

> At 4 o'clock this morning Hitler attacked and invaded Russia. […] All this was no surprise to me. In fact, I gave clear and precise warnings to Stalin of what was coming. I gave him warning as I have given warning to others before. I can only hope this warning did not fall unheeded.[11]

This was not true. Churchill's warnings had been so imprecise that they had the reverse effect on Stalin.

Shortly after, Stalin's main counter-attack was launched on 26 June resulting in a massive battle involving over 2,000 tanks. Confusion reigned. During the fighting the 8th Mechanised Corps was surrounded and the 15th Corps achieved little. In the north, the 19th Corps ran into two panzer divisions and were driven back to Rovno. Rokossovsky conducted his attack on the 27th, only to suffer heavy losses, and was ordered back.

While it was a failure, Stalin's counter-offensive delayed the Wehrmacht for a week and convinced Hitler he needed to first secure Ukraine, which would have ramifications for Army Group Centre's drive on Moscow.

Just four days into the invasion, one of the architects of Barbarossa serving with Army Group South was severely wounded in Ukraine. General Erich Marcks, leading the 101st Light Infantry Division in the fighting for Medyka, was hit and lost a leg. He was shipped home and spent a year recovering before being put in the reserves. This gave Marcks ample time to consider the wisdom of Operation Otto. Two of his three sons were to be killed serving on the Eastern Front.

Soviet command and control of the newly instigated armoured formations proved a complete fiasco, thanks to inexperience and the hand of the commissars. 'I've decided to shoot myself,' Major General Nikolai Vashugin, Commissar of the South-Western Front, told Nikita Khrushchev. 'I am guilty of giving incorrect orders to the commanders of the mechanised corps. I don't want to live any longer.'[12]

He received no sympathy from Khrushchev, who responded, 'Why are you talking such foolishness? If you've decided to shoot yourself, what are you waiting for?' Vashugin promptly drew his gun and did the deed.

Vashugin's orders had mattered little, as most of the tank crews were poorly trained and had insufficient ammunition. In many instances, Soviet tanks ran into each other, became stranded in local marshes and swamps, or were abandoned at the roadside by their panic-stricken crews. Most of the older tanks were too thinly armoured and the new T-34s regularly broke down. There was to be no repeat of Khalkhin-Gol, no matter how hard the Red Army tried. They were simply outmatched at every turn.

The Soviet Supreme Command (Stavka), originally employed by Nicholas II during the First World War, was officially set up on 23 June. Timoshenko, Zhukov and Kuznetsov found themselves outnumbered by senior Communist Party officials and old soldiers who had no business running a modern war. Stalin declined the designation of supreme commander, no doubt keen to avoid any blame for the ongoing wholesale destruction of the Red Army. Nonetheless, he continued to act as if he had accepted the role and finally agreed to the formality on 10 July.

Hitler and his staff oversaw the invasion from Forward Headquarters Wolfsschanze (Wolf's Lair) in the woods at Görlitz, 8km from the town of Rastenburg in East Prussia. He arrived on 24 June expecting it to be state of the art and well located. Instead, the secret complex of bunkers had been built in the middle of an insect-infested forest, which soon made life miserable. 'I have midge bites all up my legs which are now covered in thick swellings,' wrote Christa Schroeder, one of Hitler's secretaries.[13]

The results of the Red Army's appallingly bad co-ordination were evident for all to see. Attending Hitler's situation conferences at Wolfsschanze, Schroeder noted, 'It is made clear how furiously the Russian fights; he could match us man for man if the Soviets had proper military planning which, thank God, is not the case'.[14] Six days into Barbarossa, and Hitler was highly delighted by the rapid progress his armies were making. 'The boss said this morning that if the German soldier deserves a laurel wreath it is for this campaign,' observed Schroeder, 'everything is going better than anticipated.'[15]

Byelorussia's capital, Minsk, fell on 28 June to Army Group Centre. With the liquidation of the Minsk pocket, the Germans claimed to have destroyed

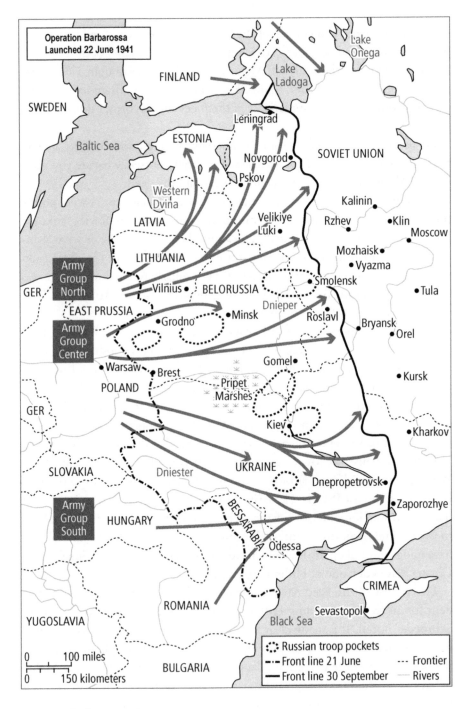

Operation Barbarossa, 22 June 1941.

or captured 4,799 tanks and 9,427 guns and taken 341,000 prisoners of war (POWs). It was a resounding disaster for the Red Army. The subsequent seizure of Smolensk by Army Group Centre yielded similar results and the Germans conducted successful massive encirclements at Vyazma and Bryansk, west of Moscow. On 30 June, Army Group Centre entered Lvov, the Soviet 32nd Tank Division having fled the city and already on the way back to Kiev. Likewise, the rest of Vlasov's 4th Mechanised Corps were long gone.

Just as Minsk was falling, Stalin and his cronies met again. The rapid collapse of the Red Army showed the world what damage his wanton persecution of his generals had done. There was an almighty and ugly row, especially after Zhukov suggested the Politburo should leave the generals alone to get on with it. Stalin was furious with Timoshenko for lack of information over the fate of Minsk and reduced Zhukov to tears, accusing him of gross incompetence. Afterwards, getting into their cars, Stalin allegedly sobbed, 'Everything's lost. I give up. All that Lenin created we have lost forever.'

Stalin retreated to Kuntsevo, almost certain that the Politburo would depose him. Despite summoning them there on 30 June, Stalin wanted to know why they had come; they reassured him that it was to discuss setting up a government committee on defence with him as head. With the Red Army in disarray and Minsk lost, it is quite possible that Stalin feared for his position, his freedom and, indeed, his life. The cynical might argue that the meeting presented him with an opportunity to flush out any would-be plotters, should his leadership be questioned.

Stalin liked staying at the purpose-built Kuntsevo complex because he felt safe there. Surrounded by thick woods, it was fenced in and had a heavily armed special security detachment. Despite being a dacha and single storey, it was quite palatial compared to most summerhouses retained as holiday residences. It was so close to the Kremlin that Stalin's inner circle dubbed it 'Nearby', while his dacha at Semyonovskoe was known as 'Distant', or 'Faraway'. At the end of the day he regularly returned to Kuntsevo rather than remain in his flat in the Kremlin. The emotionally detached Stalin normally slept completely alone in the main house with the guards and servants housed elsewhere. If anyone stayed, it was usually in the guest villas. Such was the life of 'the Boss'.

Partially reassured, Stalin returned to the Kremlin on 1 July. He finally made a long, rambling public radio announcement two days later; his heavy breathing and constant gulping of water betrayed his anxiousness. It was a historic moment, as Stalin had not made a live radio broadcast since 1938 – he had only addressed Communist Party gatherings or his speeches had been pre-recorded.

Stalin indignantly laid the blame for the destruction of the Red Army at the feet of Britain and America because they had not opened a second front against

Germany. The other reason, he said, was the lack of tanks and aircraft. The first claim was ridiculous because Britain and America were simply not in a position to open a second front. Once Japan entered the war later in the year things would go badly for them in the Far East and the Pacific. In addition, Britain was only just holding on in North Africa. The second claim was an outright lie.

However, Stalin did publicly own up to the terrible calamity that was facing the nation:

> In spite of the heroic resistance of the Red Army, and although the enemy's finest divisions and finest air force units have already been smashed and have met their doom on the field of battle, the enemy continues to push forward, hurling fresh forces into the attack.
>
> Hitler's troops have succeeded in capturing Lithuania, a considerable part of Latvia, the western part of Byelorussia, part of western Ukraine. The fascist air force is extending the range of operations of its bombers, and is bombing Murmansk, Orsha, Mogilev, Smolensk, Kiev, Odessa and Sebastopol.
>
> A grave danger hangs over our country.[16]

Even Gulag prisoners got to hear Stalin's frank admission. Gustav Herling, in a labour camp near Archangel, noted, 'It was the speech of a broken old man; he hesitated, his choking voice was full of melodramatic overemphasis and glowed with humble warmth at all patriotic catchphrases'. It gave Herling and the other prisoners warped hope, 'Millions of Soviet slaves prayed for liberation by the armies of Hitler'.[17]

Following Stalin's radio address, it is doubtful that Hitler, Brauchitsch, Halder, Jodl, Keitel or Marcks quite realised the enormity of what they had done with Barbarossa. The Soviets did – even at street level. 'A Russian girl told me today, and it is typical of the sidewalk conversation,' said Erskine Caldwell, a US citizen living in Moscow, 'that winning this war was now the sole objective of her life. If there is any such thing as so-called total war, this is to be it.'[18]

Stalin's vice-like grip on power was such that there would be no dramatic fall from grace. The army was preoccupied and he had Beria's NKVD guarding his back. Voroshilov and Zhukov were sent to the front to try and make sense of the developing chaos and stabilise the situation using whatever methods necessary. This also conveniently served to get his two most senior officers out of Moscow.

In the wake of the Red Army's disintegration, Stalin was determined to stop the rot and reverted to his favourite tactic. The Soviet leader warned, 'There must be no room in our ranks for whimperers and cowards, for panic-mongers and deserters. […] We must wage a ruthless fight against all.'[19] In military terms, the meaning was clear.

The Red Army's failures in the summer of 1941 unleashed a second round of purges. Front, corps, army, divisional and unit commanders were arrested and sent to the firing squad. The NKVD was instructed to shoot every coward, deserter, self-inflicted wounded and shell shock victim they could lay their hands on. It was also made clear that deserters' families would be punished as well. Stalin issued an order that stated, brutally but simply:

> Anyone who removes his insignia during battle and surrenders should be regarded as a malicious deserter, whose family is to be arrested as a family of a breaker of the oath and betrayer of the Motherland. Such deserters are to be shot on the spot. Those falling into encirclement ... and who prefer to surrender are to be destroyed by any means.

The most prominent victim of Stalin's second round of self-inflicted bloodletting was General Pavlov, commander of the Western Military District, followed by Generals Klimovskikh and Klich on his staff. The irony was that Pavlov had indeed contributed to the Red Army's disastrous performance against the Wehrmacht. Pavlov was a veteran of the Spanish Civil War, where he had drawn the wrong conclusions about the use of tanks. He had advocated the French doctrine, whereby armour was used in direct support of the infantry. Voroshilov, eagerly looking to discredit Tukhachevsky's ideas on massing armour, had seized upon this.

Rather than trying to consolidate its precarious position, the Red Army continued to prematurely squander its reserves with ill-fated counter-attacks. Stavka's first counter-strikes saw Lieutenant General P.A. Kurochkin's 30th Army launch the newly arrived mechanised corps at Hoth's 3rd Panzer Group in Byelorussia. In five days of fighting near Senno and Lepel they lost 832 of their 2,000 tanks. This left the Germans free to press on toward Smolensk.

In a desperate move to restore the situation along the Dnepr, Zhukov had instructed Timoshenko's Western Front to conduct counter-attacks along its full length. Timoshenko did this on 6 July, when he threw the 6th and 7th Mechanised Corps, with a total of 700 tanks, at the flanks of the German 39th Panzer Corps north of Orsha. Lacking air cover, they headed for Senno and came across the 17th and 18th Panzer Divisions. A week later, a German breakthrough heralded the encirclement of Smolensk and another 300,000 Soviet troops were cut off between the city and Orsha.

During the first eighteen days of the war, the Soviet Western Front, defending eastern Poland and western Byelorussia, lost more than 417,000 men, killed, wounded or missing, as well as 9,427 guns and mortars, more than 4,700 tanks and 1,797 aircraft. Such terrible losses, though, could be replaced, as over half a million people rallied to the Red Army ranks and about 2 million citizens worked on the construction of defensive zones.

Then, on 14 July 1941 the Red Army took the first very tentative steps toward victory with the official creation of the Reserve Front. This finally formalised Timoshenko and Zhukov's efforts to create a sizeable reserve force and it totalled around forty divisions organised into six armies. These most likely drew on some of the eighty-eight divisions which were still forming earlier in the year.

The reserve armies were initially under General I.A. Bogdanov, until Zhukov personally assumed control. It should be borne in mind that victory was far from assured at this stage and much could, and did, go wrong in the coming months and years for Stalin and his generals.

1

REDBEARD AND BEYOND

The German Army High Command had argued that the Wehrmacht should defeat the Red Army on the road to Moscow. Taking Moscow's rail links would split Stalin's defences and paralyse his communications. Instead, Hitler looked to the flanks. This fundamental divergence over basic strategy saved Stalin and the Red Army from complete destruction in 1941–42. Coupled to this, the Germans grossly underestimated the enormous resources of the Soviet Union and the tough fighting qualities of the Red Army.

Hitler's muddled strategic thinking did not spare Moscow from the violence, however. Luftwaffe bombers totalling 127 aircraft first hit Stalin's capital on the night of 21/22 July 1941, when four waves dropped 104 tons of high explosives and 46,000 incendiary bombs over five and a half hours. The results were poor, though, and Soviet anti-aircraft guns claimed ten bombers, while another twelve fell victim to Soviet night-fighters operating with the searchlight batteries. The German bomber crews had been dazzled by over 300 searchlights and their incendiary bombs failed to penetrate the roof of the Kremlin. The following night, Moscow was attacked by 115 bombers and then by a further 100, but the Luftwaffe had greater priorities and the numbers after that declined to 50, 30 and then just 15. Of the seventy-six raids on the city that year, forces ranging from just three to ten bombers conducted fifty-nine raids.

Valuable time was wasted while Army Groups North and South continued their operations. Crucially, at the end of July 1941, Hitler decided:

Army Group Centre will go over to the defensive, taking advantage of suitable terrain.

Attacks with limited objectives may still be mounted in so far as they are necessary to secure favourable springboards for our offensive against Soviet 21st Army.

2nd and 3rd Panzer Groups will be withdrawn from the front line for quick rehabilitation as soon as the situation allows.[1]

Budenny, that champion of the horse and one of the architects of Tukhachevsky's demise, was woefully ill-equipped to command the armies of the South-Western Front.

Guderian was convinced that the key threat to Army Group Centre was not Budenny's 5th Army, which lay behind him, but the Red Army units gathering on his right flank north of Roslavl. This, in fact, comprised the Soviet 28th Army, with little more than three divisions under Lieutenant General Kachalov, who had been tasked with relieving the Smolensk pocket. Guderian proposed to Field Marshal Fedor von Bock, commander of Army Group Centre, diverting resources south with which to take Roslavl. His attack opened on 2 August and two days later the town had been captured along with 38,000 Soviet prisoners and 200 guns. The ease with which Guderian attained his victory should have warned him that this was not the main threat after all.

Eleven days had been wasted since the decision was taken to destroy Budenny's 5th Army. Not even the destruction of the Soviet 16th Army and the 23rd Mechanised Corps on 5 August, along with elements of the 19th and 20th Armies, resulting in 300,000 prisoners, 3,200 tanks and 3,100 guns taken, could compensate for this failure. Budenny's request to withdraw his forces beyond the Dnepr was approved by Stavka on 19 August. The Soviet 37th Army was ordered to remain in Kiev, but the withdrawn 5th Army and the new 40th Army (made up of remnants of other armies) were directed to form a line running south-east, protecting Chernigov, Konotop and Kharkov. While this was a positive move, Budenny's forces were already expended and he had no reserves left. Everything hung on Yeremenko's Western Front to defend Moscow.

The diversion of part of Army Group Centre's forces to support Army Group South's capture of Kiev from Budenny fatally delayed Hitler's drive on Moscow. However, at Kiev, two-thirds of a million Soviet troops were caught in a pocket the size of Belgium, and for the first and last time the Wehrmacht outnumbered the Red Army.

The German-Hungarian-Romanian Group took Uman on 12 August, capturing another 150,000 enemy troops. By 27 September, Army Group South had put the Red Army to flight, taking 665,000 men, nearly 1,000 tanks and 4,000 guns. Budenny was held responsible for this unmitigated disaster and was sent to take charge of the Reserve Front (a brief command in the Caucasus was then followed by becoming inspector of the cavalry).

Vyazma, to the west of Moscow, fell to Army Group Centre on 2 October taking another 600,000 prisoners. Only by December did Hitler's forces begin to lose steam. All eyes then turned back to Army Group Centre.

The summer of 1941 was catastrophic for the Red Army. Its armoured and air forces were practically wiped out. Only its massive pool of reserves and the iron will of Stalin averted total disaster in the face of Hitler's blitzkrieg. Within the space of five months, Hitler reached the very gates of Moscow. The shattered Red Army lost about 1.5 million killed and 2.5 million captured. The Germans also destroyed or captured 17,000 Soviet tanks and 7,500 aircraft. Red Army tank losses were such that they could only gather 780 tanks for the Battle of Moscow, of which just 140 were heavy and medium tanks.

In the first six weeks of Barbarossa, Leeb's Army Group North cleared nearly all the Baltic States, broke through the Stalin Line and reached a position ready to assault Leningrad itself. In that period, Red Army losses were listed as 35,000 captured, along with 355 tanks, 655 guns and 771 aircraft captured or destroyed. All attempts by the Red Amy to halt Army Group North invariably had the same result. By 25 August, the Soviet 34th and 11th Armies had been forced back to the Lovat River Line, losing 18,000 men captured. During 21 August–9 September the German 18th Army claimed it had captured 9,774 prisoners and destroyed or captured sixty tanks and seventy-seven guns.

During late August, the Germans also encircled a large Soviet force at Molotitsy. The upshot was that the three Soviet armies (11th, 27th and 34th) were destroyed, losing eighteen divisions and a further 35,000 men, 117 tanks and 334 guns. The Germans captured Luga, along with 16,000 men, fifty-one tanks, 171 guns and 1,000 vehicles.

By late September, Army Group North had suffered 60,000 casualties, but the slaughter of the Red Army had been far greater; from 10 July–23 August the Northern Front had lost 55,535 of its 153,000 troops. Similarly, the Leningrad Front, during 23 August–30 September, lost 116,316 from 300,000 and the North-Western Front, during 10 July–30 September, saw its 272,000 troops diminished by 144,788 men.

Although Leningrad's defences were poorly finished and ill-sited, they were still very extensive. There were 5,000 earth, timber and concrete pillboxes; over 370 miles of barbed wire; some 620 miles of earth walls; over 400 miles of anti-tank ditches and 185 miles of wood abates or stakes. Hitler, realising that Army Group North was too weak to overwhelm Leningrad, decided it would besiege the city and starve the defenders into submission under Operation Georg.

It was proposed to keep Leningrad under artillery bombardment from 1 September 1941 while Leeb's forces moved to cut it off. This had been achieved by the 25th, when the Germans reached the Gulf of Finland, west of the city of Schlüsselburg on the southern shore of Lake Lagoda. The Finnish 4th Corps had also secured the Karelian Isthmus north of Leningrad.

Stalin once again called for his key trouble-shooter. On 13 September, Zhukov accompanied by General I.I. Fedyuninsky flew to take charge. The latter assessed the desperate situation:

> The 700,000-man enemy Army Group North which was active along the Leningrad strategic axis, consisted of thirty-two divisions (including four tank and five motorised divisions), with about 1,500 tanks, 1,200 aircraft, and 12,000 guns and mortars. [...] In beginning the campaign, its commander, Field Marshal von Leeb, counted on capturing the Baltic States by means of a strike from East Prussia and, in conjunction with the Finnish Army, on seizing Leningrad. It appeared at the outset that his plans were being realised. Troops of Army Group North succeeded in penetrating far into our territory.[2]

They found conditions in Leningrad grim and near to panic. The city was facing starvation by October, with 11,000 people dying the following month. Zhukov remembered:

> Those days were difficult for all of us who had been through the September fighting for Leningrad. But our forces were succeeding in thwarting the enemy's plans. Because of the unparalleled steadfastness and mass heroism of Soviet soldiers, sailors and non-commissioned officers and the endurance of commanders and political officers, the enemy was encountering insurmountable defence on the approaches to the city.[3]

By 9 November, Leeb had taken Tikhvin, east of Leningrad, cutting road and rail links to Lednevo. Thin ice also hampered getting Soviet supplies over Lake Ladoga. Throughout July to November, German and Italian light naval forces, conducting Operation *Klabautermann* (Bogey Man), attempted to cut the Soviets' supply route across the lake. These efforts were bravely resisted by the crews of the Soviet Ladoga Naval Flotilla.

The Soviets managed to oust the Germans from Tikhvin on 9 December and push them back to the Volkov River. However, by the 20th and since the start of Barbarossa, Army Group North had captured 438,950 prisoners and taken or destroyed 3,847 tanks and 4,950 guns. Regardless of these enormous losses, the Red Army did not sit idly by.

To counter the Red Army's offensive north of Novgorod on the northern shore of Lake Ilmen, the German 18th Army launched Operation *Raubtier* (Beast of Prey). The Soviets had first struck on 7 January 1942 with General K.A.

Meretskov's Volkov Front, formed the previous month, utilising the 4th, 52nd, 59th and 2nd Shock Armies. The latter, under Lieutenant General G.G. Sokolov and supported by the 52nd and 59th Armies, conducted probing attacks over the frozen Volkov with the aim of breaking through German defences and then swinging north to Leningrad. The 54th Army launched a subsidiary offensive south-west from Kirishi. It got to within 15 miles of the 2nd Shock Army, almost trapping General Johannes Blaskowitz's German 1st Corps.

Ten days after the start of Sokolov's 2nd Shock Army's assault, General Georg Lindemann assumed command of the 18th Army after Küchler replaced von Leeb as head of Army Group North. He began to conduct more coherent counter-attacks against the Soviet salient, north of Novgorod. On 19 March, about 130,000 Soviet troops were caught in the Volkov pocket, and when this finally capitulated in June the Red Army lost 33,000 prisoners, 170 tanks and 600 guns.

Beyond Leningrad, the Finns were determined to avenge themselves for the Winter War and regain lost territory, although their troop concentrations were not ready in time for Barbarossa, necessitating a delay in their attack. In return for German arms, Marshal Mannerheim had agreed to allow German bases, as Hitler had his eye on Finnish nickel and a point from which to conduct Operation Silver Fox, an attack on the Soviet naval base at Murmansk.

The plan was for a German offensive with Finnish support to seize the port of Kandalaksha, on the White Sea, in order to trap Red Army forces in the Kola Peninsula. This would enable them to take Murmansk and secure the nickel mining area of Petsamo. There was also to be a push south toward the Lakes of Onega and Ladoga in support of an assault on Leningrad from the north. Lieutenant General V.A. Frolov's Soviet 14th Army (which had five divisions including an armoured one) covered the approaches to the White Sea and Murmansk.

German troops had started moving into Finland in early June. General Nikolaus von Falkenhorst's German Norway Army sent two divisions, and in central Finland, along with one Finnish division, they formed General H. Feige's German 36th Corps. This was to retake Salla (lost by the Finns during the Winter War) and move on Kandalaksha, while in the far north General Eduard Dietl's Mountain Corps, with another two divisions, was to retake Petsamo and attack toward Murmansk. To the south of Dietl, the Finnish 3rd Corps with just one division was to take Kestenga and Ukhta then move to Loukhi, south of Kandalaksha, on the railway from Murmansk to Leningrad.

To the south-east, Mannerheim had thirteen divisions and three brigades supported by a single German division for the drive on Leningrad. Protecting the northern approaches to the city was General Gerasimov's 23rd Army, while

Meretskov's 7th Army was defending the frontier from Lake Ladoga to Yhta. On the Gulf of Finland, the Soviets also had a base at Hanko.

Stalin was under no illusion over Finnish intentions and bombed the country on 25 June. There was to be no blitzkrieg this time. Four days later, Dietl attacked the two divisions of the Soviet 42nd Corps belonging to the 14th Army. The Soviet North Front, under General M.M. Popov, was able to use the lateral rail communications to reinforce the 14th Army and Dietl was only to get as far as the Litsa River. The 36th Corps cleared Salla, but could not get much further than the 1939 frontier. Similarly, the Finnish 3rd Corps struggled to reach Yhta.

In the south, Mannerheim had only enough troops to attack in one sector at a time and decided first to push his Karelian Army down the northern side of Lake Ladoga. This attack started on 10 July and within six days had reached the lake and then swung south-east. Nonetheless, by the end of the month the Soviets had stabilised the situation with the Finns less than halfway to their objectives. It was then that Mannerheim conducted phase two of his plan, attacking down the Karelia Isthmus, striking north of the Vuoksi River and toward occupied Viipuri.

Mannerheim struck on 31 July, trapping two Red Army divisions against the western shore of Ladoga, and beating off attempts to rescue them. On 23 August, he launched his attack toward Viipuri, and four days later his forces cut the main road and railway to Leningrad. Mannerheim sent three divisions to the 1939 frontier, but left assaulting the city itself to the Germans. By 9 September his troops had reached all their objectives, and by that point the Germans had cut Leningrad off by taking Schlüsselburg on the south-western shore of Ladoga.

From that point on, Mannerheim made it clear he would not be party to an attack on Leningrad, although he agreed to press on in Soviet Karelia to the Svir River. Mannerheim's stance greatly hampered Hitler's ability to capture Leningrad and ultimately thwarted his designs on the city. By the end of the year, the small Finnish Army had lost 25,000 dead and over 50,000 wounded and was thoroughly sick of supporting Hitler's war aims. Soviet losses are unknown, although the Finns took 47,000 prisoners. Mannerheim's priority was to hold on to the liberated territories and he knew he would have to prepare his defences for the inevitable Soviet counter-attacks.

Meanwhile, Hitler's allies were playing their part in subduing Ukraine. Way to the south, along with the Wehrmacht, Antonescu's Romanian forces rumbled over the border and into the southern Soviet Union on 22 June 1941. The Romanian 3rd Army's Mountain Corps fought with the German 11th Army, while the Romanian Cavalry Corps worked with the 1st Panzer Army.

In Bucharest, Romanian writer Iosif Hechter recorded in his diary:

In two proclamations to the country and the army, General Antonescu has announced that Romania, alongside Germany, has begun the holy war to liberate Bessarabia and Bukovina and to eradicate Bolshevisim. This morning Hitler issued a long declaration, explaining the reasons for the war that began last night against the Soviets. Before the sun rose, German troops crossed the Russian border at several points and bombarded a number of towns. No precise geographical details are given.[4]

General von Manstein, who controlled the Romanian 3rd Army, recalled that there was:

a noticeable contrast in their fighting qualities. [...] As for the Romanian Army, there is no doubt that it had considerable weaknesses. Although the Romanian soldier ... was usually a capable and brave fighter ... One disadvantage was the absence of a non-commissioned officer corps as we know it.[5]

The Romanian 4th Army, with overwhelming numerical superiority, attempted to seize the Ukrainian port of Odessa on 10 August, but made little headway against dogged Red Army resistance. The attack petered out five days later but was resumed on the 20th, and for a month the Romanians struggled to get within 9 miles of the city. Headway was finally made when the Germans swung down into the Crimea.

After suffering an appalling 98,000 casualties, Antonescu ordered the exhausted 4th Army to be withdrawn home in October for refit. Von Manstein was fulsome in his praise of the average Romanian soldier and their subservience to the German cause:

Despite all the defects and reservations ... the Romanian troops performed their duty as best they could. Above all, they always readily submitted to German military leadership and did not, like other allies of ours, put matters of prestige before material necessity.

In June 1941, the Horthy committed large numbers of Hungarian troops to Barbarossa, including the Hungarian Carpathian Group and the Mobile Corps. Fighting alongside the German 17th Army, the Mobile Corps performed well in Ukraine, but after reaching the Donets was withdrawn home in November. Premier Tiso's Slovak State also provided Army Group South with a Slovak Army Corps of two infantry divisions.

German troops had an affinity with the Hungarians, as many of the officers were German-speaking veterans of the Austro-Hungarian Army or were ethnic *Volksdeutsche*. Hitler once described the Hungarians as 'a nation of daring cavalrymen', however, he had no great affection for Horthy and despaired of the bad blood between the Hungarians and Romanians. 'Our Romanian and Hungarian allies were known to view each other with such mistrust,' recalled von Manstein, 'that they were holding crack troops ready in their respective countries to use against one another if the need arose.'[6]

Mussolini initially sent 62,000 Italian soldiers to join Hitler's other Axis forces in July 1941. They made up the Italian Expeditionary Corps in Russia (CSIR), comprising three divisions, which were placed under the command of the German 11th Army. Lacking tanks, the Italians mainly comprised lightly armed infantry, cavalry and *bersaglieri* (sharpshooters or riflemen). At this stage, the Italian 3rd Mobile Division was equipped with just sixty-one tiny tankettes.

The following month the CSIR was bloodied, fighting the retreating Red Army between the Bug and Dniestr Rivers. Afterwards the Italians were subordinated to General Paul von Kleist and were involved in the attack on Stalino and occupying the neighbouring towns of Gorlovka and Rikovo.

As the battle for Ukraine took place, the conquest of the Crimea was well under way. Despite the Soviets protecting the vital Perekop Isthmus with a 10-mile-deep defence system and contesting every inch of ground, von Manstein says:

> Nevertheless, after warding off strong enemy counter-attacks the corps [54th] took Perekop and crossed Tartars' Ditch on 26 September [1941]. Three more days' intensive fighting saw it through the rest of the enemy's defence zone and, after the capture of the strongly defended locality of Armyansk, out into more open country. The enemy fell back between the Ishun lakes, having suffered heavy losses in killed and left 10,000 prisoners, 112 tanks and 135 guns in our hands.[7]

On 28 October 1941, the Germans barged their way along the Isthmus of Perekop with the intention of seizing Sevastopol and crushing Colonel General F.I. Kuznetsov's 51st Independent Army (under Vice Admiral G.I. Levchenko's Crimea command). General von Manstein's 11th Army, part of Field Marshal Gerd von Rundstedt's Army Group South, found itself fighting in two directions. The first of these was southward toward Sevastopol and the other eastward in pursuit of Kuznetsov's forces which were withdrawing into the Kerch Peninsula.

While Sevastopol was the primary target, the continuing presence of the Soviet 51st Independent Army in the Crimea could not be tolerated. The newly arrived German 42nd Corps, under General H. Graf von Sponeck, was assigned the role of clearing the Kerch under Operation *Trappenfang* (Bustard Trap). By

16 November this had been achieved, with the Soviets forced to evacuate their troops to the Kuban in the northern Caucasus with the loss of all their heavy equipment and weapons.

The Soviets, however, swiftly bounced back. Kuznetsov was replaced by Lieutenant General V.N. Lvov and, along with Lieutenant General S.I. Chernyak's 44th Army, became part of Lieutenant General D.T. Kozlov's Transcaucasus Front. This counter-attacked on 26 December 1941, when 13,000 men of the 51st Army landed at Kerch and 3,000 troops from the 44th landed near the port of Feodosiya at the rear of the Germans. Kozlov, capitalising on his beachheads from 29 December, landed another 23,000 men at Feodosiya.

Recalling this unwelcome development, von Manstein noted with understandable concern:

> The landing of Soviet troops on the Kerch Peninsula, catching 11th Army just when the battle on the northern front of Sevastopol had entered its crucial phase, soon proved to be more than a mere diversionary measure on the enemy's part. Soviet radio stations proclaimed that this was an all-out offensive to re-conquer the Crimea, planned and commanded by Stalin personally, and that it would not end until 11th Army had been wiped off the map.[8]

By the end of 1941, von Manstein's men had conquered the entire Crimea except for the fortress of Sevastopol to the south and the Kerch Straits to the east. Both posed problems, especially after the Red Army pushed its 44th and 51st Armies across the Straits during their 1941–42 winter offensive. They had driven von Sponeck's 42nd Corps from the Kerch Peninsula as far east as the city of Feodosiya. Hitler relieved the general of his command, court-martialled and sentenced him to death, although this became life imprisonment.

This forced von Manstein to divert his 30th Corps from its efforts to reduce Sevastopol, to restore the situation. Von Manstein assumed control near Feodosiya, and on 15 January 1942 counter-attacked eight Soviet divisions with just three reinforced German divisions. Taking up the story, von Manstein states:

> Thanks to the bravery of the troops, the attack succeeded, and by 18 January Feodosiya was ours. In addition to 6,700 dead, the enemy had lost 10,000 prisoners, 177 guns and eighty-five tanks. It now emerged that the Luftwaffe had still done a good job in Feodosiya harbour, in spite of the bad flying conditions, and had sunk a number of transport vessels.[9]

Despite the loss of this port, the Soviets were still able to get reinforcements from the Kuban to the Crimea across the ice. Kozlov was instructed by

Stalin and Zhukov, in no uncertain terms, that he must march to the relief of Sevastopol and whatever the cost prevent the city from falling into Hitler's hands. His Caucasus Front (now renamed the Crimean Front) was sacrificed, attacking again on 27 February 1942, 13 March, 26 March and 9 April, until completely exhausted. However, as well as the 51st, the Soviet 44th Army, under Lieutenant General S.I. Chernyak, and the 47th Army, under Lieutenant General K.S. Kolganov, totalling almost twenty divisions, remained stubbornly in the Soviet bridgehead.

8

THE TYPHOON FALTERS

Finally, almost three months after Barbarossa commenced on 16 September 1941, Field Marshal von Bock issued orders for the capture of Moscow under the code name Operation Typhoon. Three panzer groups would spearhead this, with one of them being withdrawn from the troubled attack on Leningrad. Although Hitler instructed the 3rd and 4th Panzer Groups to conduct two attacks opposite Moscow, following the Kiev victory von Bock had added a third, with Guderian's 2nd Panzer Group advancing from the south-west.

Firstly though, Red Army forces east of Smolensk had to be destroyed by pincer attacks on Vyazma during October 1941, then Bock's Army Group Centre was free to drive on the Soviet capital. While Hitler's armies were unnecessarily distracted on his far flanks, in the centre the culmination of Barbarossa would not be launched until 2 November 1941 with Typhoon. For Hitler's push on the Soviet capital, Army Group Centre gathered 1,929,000 men supported by 1,000 panzers, 14,000 guns and mortars and nearly 1,400 aircraft.

To resist almost 2 million German troops, consisting of three armies, three panzer groups and seventy-eight divisions, were 1,250,000 Soviet troops of Yeremenko's Bryansk Front, Konev's (having replaced Timoshenko in mid-September) Western Front and Budenny's new Reserve Front.

That November, the Red Army launched pre-emptive attacks on Army Group Centre, which got as far as Kashira to the south, the following month. The Soviets liberated Kashira and blunted Hitler's advance on Moscow.

In the meantime, Hitler had opened his initial attack against the Bryansk and South-Western Fronts on 30 September. Guderian's panzers quickly broke through the former and charged toward Orel, to the south of Moscow. His 2nd Panzer Group pushed through the Yermakov Group toward Sevsk and Orel on the Bryansk Front's left flank. In response, Major General D.D. Lelyushenko was sent from Moscow to command the defences at Mtsensk.

Orel fell on 3 October while General Joachim Lemelsen's 47th Panzer Crops swung to the north to cut off the Bryansk Front. Bryansk itself, south-west of Moscow, fell on 6 October just as the first winter snows began to fall. However, Guderian's tanks suffered a reverse near Mtsensk on 6 October, at the hands of the new Soviet T-34, with the 4th Panzer Division suffering heavy losses.

To the north, von Bock's main pincer movement, intended to trap the Soviet West Front before it could fall back on the Vyazma Defence Line, opened on 2 October. The 9th Army and the 4th Panzer Group pierced the junction of the Soviet 30th and 19th Armies north of Dukhovshchina. This enabled the 56th Panzer Corps to attack toward Kholm and Vyazma and the 46th Panzer Corps toward Rzhev on the upper Volga. On 10 October, the northern arm of the pincer cut through the Vyazma Defence Line between Vyazma and Sychevka and worryingly got to Gzhatsk on the railway from Smolensk to Moscow.

The southern arm, made up of the German 4th Army and the 4th Panzer Group, captured Spas Demensk and Kirov on 4 October and reached the approaches of the Mozhaisk (Moscow) Defence Line six days later. In order to escape Army Group Centre, Stalin uncharacteristically permitted both the West and Reserve Fronts to move east of the Vyazma Defence Line. The Soviet 31st and 32nd Armies from Budenny's Reserve Front were given the task of covering the withdrawal. Things did not go well. North of the city the Germans trapped the Soviet 50th Army, while to the south they encircled the Soviet 3rd and 13th Armies. Yeremenko, cut off from Moscow, ordered his troops to break out two days later. Those men still trapped in the pockets (numbering some 50,000) surrendered on 17 and 25 October. It was yet another disaster.

By 7 October, Hitler's 3rd and 4th Panzer Groups also trapped the Soviet 19th, 20th, 24th and 32nd Armies, along with the Boldin Group, in a vast pocket west of Vyazma. Just a week later, on the 13th, resistance collapsed and a staggering 650,000 Soviet troops laid down their arms, including over 1,000 tanks and 4,000 pieces of artillery. This constituted forty-five divisions; almost half of the forces resisting Typhoon.

In the first two weeks of Typhoon, Army Group Centre had inflicted at least 700,000 casualties on the defenders at relatively little cost to itself. It seemed that the Red Army could not recover from such a massive blow and Muscovites began to flee the capital. The weather, combined with Hitler's demands that Tula to the north-east and Kursk to the south be captured, now slowed progress.

Stalin chose this critical moment to reorganise his High Command and the situation slipped further from his grasp. The tried and tested Zhukov was summoned from the defence of Leningrad to organise the Mozhaisk Line. This ran in an arc for over 120 miles from the Moscow Reservoir to the north near Volokolamsk, cutting through the 1812 battlefield of Borodino to west of

Mozhaisk and down to the Ugra and Oka Rivers. Zhukov found it far from complete, but bolstered it with reinforcements comprising six divisions, six armoured brigades, ten artillery regiments and machine-gun battalions.

Every available man was rushed to the front line, including Major General K.K. Rokossovsky's 16th Army, Major General K.D. Golubev's 43rd Army, Lieutenant General I.G. Zakharkin's 49th Army and Major General D.D. Lelyushenko's 5th Army – in total, less than 100,000 men. The question on everyone's mind was, would this be enough? In desperation, Soviet forces from the Far East, North-West and South-West Fronts were also committed to the coming battle for Moscow.

On 10 October, Zhukov assumed command with the West and Reserve Fronts becoming his West Front, while his deputy Konev was sent to create the new Kalinin Front. Units of General Lelyushenko's 5th Army, including the 32nd Division, took up positions at Borodino at the very heart of the Mozhaisk Line on 11 October. Three days later, the Germans broke through at the Shevardino Redoubt and Lelyushenko was wounded in fierce hand-to-hand fighting. Much to Zhukov's annoyance, the 5th Army was forced to abandon Mozhaisk.

While Zhukov strove to consolidate Moscow's defences on the ground, in the air the shaken Red Air Force began to gather its muscle. Each of the four sectors of the Moscow PVO zone were protected by the equivalent of a fighter corps while the 6th PVO Fighter Corps was more the size of an air army. Stalin ensured the fighters deployed to the capital were state of the art. Over half of Klimov's force consisted of modern types. By early July, his command contained 585 fighters – 170 MiG-3, 75 LaGG-3s and 95 Yak-1 fighters, backed by 200 I-16s and 45 I-153s. These were to be later bolstered by British-supplied Hurricanes and American P-40s. Up to 2,000 Soviet fighters took part in the defence of Moscow between July 1941 and January 1942. The result of this was that the Luftwaffe largely avoided the skies over the Soviet capital.

The Moscow Defence Zone was established on 12 October under General Pavel Artemiev (commander of the Moscow Military District) and stretched in a 60-mile radius out from the city. Additional defensive belts were ordered, consisting of an outer belt and three inner ones within the city itself, to be ready within eight days. Some 600,000 Muscovites found themselves digging trenches and tank traps. It was an impossible task for Artemiev to complete by 20 October. Also, more volunteer divisions were called for but only 10,000 men were raised, the best of the volunteers having already gone to war. Nonetheless, five new Moscow Rifle Divisions were created.

Everything now hung in the balance, with both sides having made their preparations. The 3rd Panzer Group was threatening to envelop Moscow from the north after it captured Kalinin on 14 October. It just needed to get around the Volga Reservoir and push along the eastern bank of the Volga Canal to Moscow. Zhukov had no time to do anything with the Mozhaisk Line and it was predictably pierced by General G. Stumme's 40th Panzer Corps at Mozhaisk, General Adolf Kuntzen's 57th Panzer Corps between Borovsk and Maloyaroslavets, and by General Hans Felber's 13th Corps at Kaluga by 18 October. Stalin ordered Moscow into a state of siege the following day. By 30 October the Germans were through the defence along its entire length and just 40 miles from Moscow.

Now that Moscow's outer defences had been pierced the situation looked extremely dangerous. It was vital that Stalin and Zhukov held their nerve. Zhukov was anxious not to squander their reserves with rapid knee-jerk counter-attacks. This was to bring him into conflict with Stalin. The Soviet leader was desperate to drive Hitler away from the Kremlin at any price. In the meantime, the Muscovites bore the brunt of the slaughter.

In reality Army Group Centre was now far too stretched to constitute a real threat to Moscow. With the 2nd Panzer Army tasked to take the armaments city of Tula and envelop Moscow from the south, the 2nd Army striking from Kursk to Voronezh, the 4th Army west of Moscow, the 3rd and 4th Panzer Groups enveloping from the north-west and the 9th Army instructed to help Army Group North, Bock's front had expanded by a third. There were simply not enough troops to go round. He wanted to attack Moscow by the shortest possible route, but found his original front expanded from 400 to 600 miles.

In addition, just three days after Hitler's invasion the Richard Sorge spy network in Tokyo (he had contacts in the German embassy) was able to report that the Japanese preferred the pickings of French Indochina and the Dutch East Indies to any renewed aggression in Mongolia. Once the Sorge spy network had let Japanese intentions toward American interests in the Pacific be known, a trickle of Red Army reinforcements began to head west.

During mid-October, the only new and trained formation to reach the front was the Siberian 310th Motorised Division, although frustratingly it arrived at Zvietkovo Railway Station without its vehicles. At the same time, the reconstituted Soviet 5th, 16th, 43rd and 49th Armies mustered only 90,000 men. These could not provide a continuous defence, so Soviet forces, along with most of the artillery and anti-tank weapons, had to be concentrated on the main axes: Volokolamsk, Istra, Mozhaisk, Maloyaroslavets and Podolsk-Kaluga.

Troops from the Far East only began to arrive in early November in greater numbers; indeed, Zhukov had doubled his strength by the time Hitler's offensive commenced. On 14 October 1941, General Afansy Beloborodov's Siberian 78th Rifle Division, which was 6,000 miles from the front, was ordered to deploy to Moscow. He recalled:

I was very anxious about our debut in combat. We were about to fight a strong and experienced enemy, yet we were being committed to action for the first time. We realised that the first setbacks – and they were inevitable – might put the men off their stroke. I meditated upon the impending engagement while still on the way to the front.[1]

During the long, jolting train journey Beloborodov had plenty of time to ponder. He need not have worried – for its tough performance defending the approaches to the capital, his unit was paid the highest honour and re-titled the 9th Guards Rifle Division. Beloborodov says the enemy was 'mortally afraid of hand-to-hand fighting', such was the savage ferocity of the Siberians.

Before long Stalin's reinforcements were pouring in. The Far Eastern Front provided a very welcome seventeen divisions plus eight tank and one cavalry brigade, equipped with a total of 1,700 tanks and 1,500 aircraft. In addition, Outer Mongolia, Zhukov's old stomping ground, sent one rifle division and two tank brigades; Transbaikalia sent seven rifle, two cavalry divisions and two tank brigades; Ussuri provided five rifle divisions plus one cavalry and three tank brigades; and, finally, Amur provided two rifle divisions and one tank brigade. From these, Zhukov was able to form three new armies, the Soviet 1st Shock, the 10th and the 20th.

Konev's new Kalinin Front, formed by the 22nd, 29th and 31st Armies, had the key task of shielding Moscow to the north around the Sea of Moscow (Ivankovo Reservoir) and the Volga Canal. This gave Zhukov reason for quiet optimism. Nevertheless, despite these powerful reinforcements, Red Army strength was weaker than the Wehrmacht, not only in numbers but also equipment and training.

General Golikov, who had helped contribute to Stalin's delusion that Hitler was not going to invade, was summoned to see the Soviet leader on 21 October. Now that the enemy were approaching the capital, Golikov must have feared that he was in serious trouble; instead, he was given command of the 10th Reserve Army gathering south-east of Moscow. This was drawing divisions from as far afield as the Turkestan and Siberian Military Districts and would be assembled by the first week of November.

The 10th Army was a somewhat ill-fated command. Having first been formed in 1939, it was destroyed at Grodno in mid-1941. Attempts had been made to rebuild it during October, but this had been put on hold. It was the third establishment of which Golikov took charge, and of its nine divisions, seven were new units.

Golikov's experiences were typical of those of other army commanders. He was to discover that most of the officers were reservists and that less than a third were regulars. His command was poorly trained and largely comprised of men with no previous military experience. To make matters worse, they were mustered in summer uniforms and there were shortages of food, ammunition and weapons. Inevitably, training was hampered by cases of frostbite. Golikov and his staff had to constantly badger the chain of command for much-needed supplies. Despite all this, the 10th Army was given just fifteen days' preparation before being sent to the front.

Earlier in the year, Soviet troops had turned up at the front wearing a ragtag mixture of uniforms and headgear. In particular, the Model 1936 helmet had the unfortunate tendency of making the wearer look like a German soldier. Production of the newer Model 1940 helmet had to be increased, but initially could not keep up with demand. Some captured soldiers did not even have helmets, just the *pilotka* side cap or the old Budenovka cloth helmet. Local military depots struggled to equip new recruits and issued them with whatever ancient stock they had to hand. In the run-up to war, Khrulev, the quartermaster general, struggled to arm and equip the Red Army in a timely manner. By the end of the year the logistics system was still creaking at the seams. The creation of the Reserve Front and all the new reserve armies greatly exacerbated the situation. Things would eventually improve, but it was to be a long haul, as Golikov and his comrades discovered.

The Germans knew of these gathering reinforcements but seemed unaware of the full implications. At a meeting of all the army group chiefs of staff held at Orsha in early November, Chief of the General Staff General Halder stated:

> There was good reason to believe that Russian resistance was on the verge of collapse. ... the Führer's plan was to by-pass Moscow and capture the railway junctions beyond it – as OKH [Army High Command] had reports that large reserves, amounting in strength to a fresh army, were on their way from Siberia.[2]

The Führer's plan was wishful thinking. It is noticeable that Halder spoke of an 'army' and not 'armies', indicating they were unaware of the true scale of Zhukov's reinforcements.

The people of Moscow were also rallied to the city's defence, as Zhukov noted with some pride:

> During October and November the working people of Moscow provided five divisions of volunteers to the front. Their total contribution from the start of the war had been seventeen divisions. In addition to these divisions the people's militia, Muscovites formed and armed hundreds of fighting teams and tank-destroyer detachments.[3]

Twelve volunteer divisions had been formed in Moscow by early July; each was given a number and named after the district from where it had been recruited. These totalled 68,000 men and almost 10,500 officers and NCOs. In fact, a target of 200,000 had been set.

Five of these volunteer divisions were trapped at Bryansk and Vyazma, and the 2nd (Stalin), 7th (Bauman), 8th (Krasnaya Presnya), 9th (Kirov) and 13th (Rostokino) had to be disbanded after being completely destroyed in the fighting.

Abram Evseevich Gordon, from Moscow University, volunteered that summer for the capital's citizens' defence units known as *opolchenie*. Initially he found himself simply digging trenches. Then he and his fellow *opolchentsy* were issued with old Polish Army uniforms and Polish rifles and trained as cavalry. In August, his group were transferred to the Red Army to reform the 113th Rifle Division, which had been destroyed earlier in the year. Kitted out in Red Army uniforms and armed with rifles and Molotov cocktails, they were sent to block the Warsaw Highway leading into the capital in October. It was a massacre. The young recruits knew nothing of tactics and fired off all their ammunition before the panzers ever reached them. Just 300 men, including Gordan, survived the encounter but they were surrounded and hunted down. He was captured but managed to slip away and re-join the regular army.

Despite their bravery, the volunteer units were sacrificial lambs. While Zhukov pulled the Red Army's reserves toward Moscow ready for his counter-offensive, he had no intention of committing them to battle before early December. Throughout November, the people of Moscow were to pay the price of this tough decision with their blood. In mid-October, the call had gone out for yet more Muscovite fighters. After just six days, four volunteer divisions were thrown into the fight. 'The Germans took village after village,' reported Walter Kerr, who was in Moscow with the *New York Herald*. 'The Moscow volunteers tried to hold them, failed, but died in the ruins.'[4]

Kerr saw the non-defence factory workers responding to the call to arms, turning up at the recruitment depots carrying 'packs on their backs containing extra clothing, food and tin cups'. He says, 'They were the best Moscow had. They should have been properly trained. They should have been properly equipped. But the Germans were coming on, and the High Command needed time.'[5]

Near Borovsk, south of the highway to Smolensk and Minsk, the 4th Volunteer Division, lacking uniforms and armed with just rifles and light machine guns, was cut to pieces by the advancing Germans. Rather than saving them, Stalin used the Muscovites as pawns in a strategy that was not just about saving Moscow but defeating Hitler. Kerr noted:

The men of Moscow died by the thousand, yet still the Germans advanced. The volunteers fought and died, not knowing, for they could not have known, the plans of the High Command. In the meantime the regular reserve divisions moved up from the east, not to the firing line, but to the woods near the city, to be used when Zhukov was ready to use them.

[...] Hitler ... did not know, any more than the volunteers knew, that the Kremlin was tightening its spring and that one day soon the reserve divisions would be thrown into the battle.[6]

An additional 100,000 workers were given some military training in their spare time. The local Communist Party formed workers' battalions 12,000 strong, and 17,000 women undertook medical training. For these Muscovite workers' battalions, the garrison released just 5,000 rifles and 210 machine guns, but after that the regular forces were instructed not to give up any more arms. The battalions, while numbering 675 men each, were sent to the front with just 295 rifles, 145 revolvers, 120 captured hand grenades, nine machine guns and 2,000 Molotov cocktails. Vasily Grossman, a Soviet war reporter, saw at first hand Moscow's siege mentality, 'Barricades at the outer approaches, and also closer in, particularly around the suburbs, as well as the city itself'.[7]

The German chiefs of staff of Army Groups North and South were against any further advance toward Moscow, while the chief of staff from Army Group Centre opted for a more neutral stance. They knew with the onset of winter they should consolidate their positions and husband their remaining resources. Their advice mattered little, because reaching the railway junctions so far behind the Soviet capital at that time of year was quite impossible.

By November the dreadful slaughter was rising to incredible proportions. The Wehrmacht had lost almost a quarter of its manpower. General Heinz Guderian noted, 'Total casualties on the Eastern Front since 22 June 1941 had now reached the total of 743,000 men; this was twenty-three per cent of our average strength of three and a half million men.'[8]

During a speech made in early November 1941 on the twenty-fourth anniversary of the October Revolution, Stalin grandly claimed:

In four months of war we have lost 350,000 killed, and 378,000 missing, and our wounded number 1,020,000. In the same period the enemy has in killed, wounded and prisoners lost more than four and a half million men.

There can be no doubt that as a result of four months of war Germany, whose reserves of manpower are already being exhausted, has been considerably more weakened than the Soviet Union, whose reserves are only now being mobilised to the full.[9]

In the name of morale-boosting propaganda, he clearly played down the Red Army's staggering losses and deliberately inflated German casualties. It was true, however, that Hitler had exhausted his manpower whereas the Russian bear was only just waking up. Stalin added:

> Hunger and impoverishment reign in Germany today; in four months of war Germany has lost four and a half million men; Germany is bleeding, her reserves of manpower are giving out, the spirit of indignation is spreading not only among the peoples of Europe who have fallen under the yoke of the German invaders, but also the German people themselves, who see no end to the war. The German invaders are straining their last efforts. There is no doubt that Germany cannot sustain such a strain for long.[10]

Exhausted and lacking adequate winter clothing, the German armed forces were in a dire situation. The German High Command assessed that the 101 infantry divisions on the Eastern Front (excluding Finland) had the combat power of just sixty-five and that the seventeen panzer divisions equated to just six. The total German force committed had just over 60 per cent of its established capability; in other words, the real strength of Hitler's forces on the Eastern Front was just seventy-one divisions.

Regardless of his weakening combat power, on 7 November 1941 Hitler optimistically issued orders for Typhoon to be resumed. This was based on the premise that the Red Army before Moscow was getting weaker, not stronger. The West Front, by this stage, had received some 100,000 reinforcements with 300 tanks and 2,000 guns. Typhoon recommenced on 15 November and although the panzers got to within a few miles of Moscow they were unable to make decisive breakthroughs, either to the north or south.

Stalin was weighing his options and asked Zhukov if he could hold Moscow. The latter's response was yes, if he was given two additional armies and 200 tanks. He would get the 1st Shock Army and Golikov's 10th Army but no more tanks. Stalin, impatient to forestall Hitler's final assault on Moscow, instructed Zhukov on 14 November to conduct spoiling attacks south of Moscow and around Volokolamsk.

At this time, considerable Stavka reserves began to arrive in the Moscow area and were used to reinforce the most threatened axes. Notably, the 17th, 18th, 20th, 24th and 44th Cavalry Divisions were used to bolster the 16th Army on the Volokolamsk–Klin axis. Also, General P.A. Belov's Cavalry Corps, the 415th Rifle and 112th Tank Divisions and the 33rd Tank Brigade arrived on the left flank.

Zhukov did not want to waste his precious reserves on an enterprise that was unlikely to produce positive results. Nonetheless, Rokossovsky's 16th Army, which had been employed preparing in-depth defences, was instructed to leave its sanctuary. Pushing forward 1 mile, his men suffered heavy casualties. The 44th Cavalry Division was all but massacred as it arrived fresh from the city of Tashkent. Rokossovsky held Zhukov responsible for his needless losses. In truth, Stalin's micromanagement of the battle was to blame.

Despite all these new forces and the fact that the Western Front had six armies by the middle of November, being stretched along a 375-mile front meant that they had very little depth. However, Stalin and Shaposhnikov called for a pre-emptive attack to disrupt the Germans' preparations. Stalin proposed striking from the Volokolamsk–Novo–Petrovskoye area using the right flank units of Rokossovsky's army, the 58th Tank Division, the Independent Cavalry Divisions and Davtor's Cavalry Corps. While in the Serpukhov area he wanted to use Belov's Cavalry Corps, Getman's Tank Division and part of the 49th Army. Again, Zhukov did not want to exhaust his reserves at the very moment the Germans were about to attack

The Siberians made their presence felt on 18 November, when a newly arrived division supported by an armoured brigade attacked the German 112th Infantry Division, which was guarding 4th Panzer's push on Venev. The unfortunate 112th, having already suffered 50 per cent frostbite casualties, was overrun by Soviet T-34 tanks. A week later, German Intelligence identified more fresh reserves thrown into the fighting which had come from the Far East – the 108th Tank Brigade, and the 31st Cavalry and 299th Rifle Divisions.

Reporter Walter Kerr, with the Red Army, experienced the bitter cold at first hand:

> I saw a column of sledges moving in single file along a forest road. The flanks of the horses were covered with a white frost, and the drivers, muffled against the cold, were walking alongside in an effort to restore the circulation of blood to their feet. [...]
>
> They were taking bandages, splints, containers of blood for transfusions, frozen beef, bread, shells for 122mm gun-howitzers, fodder for the cavalry and rifle ammunition for the infantry. The horses plodded and slipped along and the drivers walked in silence. When it is as cold as this, you do not feel like talking. You just keep going.[11]

Hitler's insistence that the Wehrmacht would not have to fight a winter campaign was now reaping terrible results. Guderian, touring his troops, observed that they were 'insufficiently clothed, half-starved men: and who also saw by contrast the well-fed, warmly clad and fresh Siberians, fully equipped for winter fighting'.[12]

Cold became the Wehrmacht's enemy, as much as the Red Army. During the winter the temperature could drop as low as -40°F. German soldiers who were still in their summer uniforms were left to endure the miseries brought on by the extreme weather. 'The cold soon exceed all bounds. […] Frost gripped my pus infected fingers,' said German infantryman Harald Henry, who was in his early twenties. 'My gloves were so wet I couldn't bear them any longer. I wrapped a towel round my ravaged hands. It was enough to make you want to bawl.'[13]

The men were reduced to relying on clothing parcels from loved ones back home and captured Red Army greatcoats. Using their entrenching spades, German soldiers resorted to breaking up wooden ammunition crates and cutting down trees to create firewood. They also billeted themselves with local farmers by moving into their stout wooden dachas.

The Siberians could endure the conditions better than most Russians, and certainly vastly better than the Germans. Amongst the troops from the Far East was Lieutenant Vladimir Edelman, who was a native Ukrainian. Before redeployment, he and his Siberian troops had been issued with ample winter clothing, which gave them a great advantage over their enemies who were literally freezing on the approaches to Moscow. Edelman saw German prisoners clothed in summer uniforms and light coats without hats. Every now and then one would cry out in agony, '*O Mein Gott! O Mein Gott!*', as they slowly froze to death along the roadside.[14]

However, the Siberian units did not have it all their own way, and were on occasion thwarted by incompetence and their vulnerability to the marauding Luftwaffe. Dispersing from the train depots often did not go unimpeded. Ukrainian Boris Godov arrived in late October with the Siberian 413th Division to defend the city of Tula, an important weapons manufacturing centre south of Moscow. His artillery unit arrived with the wrong ammunition for their guns and paid the price at the hands of the panzers. Although the 413th Division helped save Tula from capture, just 500 of its 15,400 men survived unscathed.

When General Guderian visited the 112th and 167th Infantry Divisions holding the line south of Bielev to the west of Tula, on 14 November 1941, he was dismayed to find that the men were suffering because of a complete lack of winter clothing. Many of them had frostbite and their vehicles were immobilised due to a lack of anti-freeze. In particular, the 112th was at breaking point. 'Snow shirts, boot grease, under clothes and above all woollen trousers were not available,' noted Guderian. 'A high proportion of the men were still wearing denim trousers, and the temperature was eight below zero!'[15] He found the men had been forced to wear Soviet overcoats and fur hats. The 112th Infantry Division had 500 cases of frostbite and their machine guns had packed up because of the cold. In addition, their 37mm anti-tank guns could not overcome the armour of the Soviets' T-34 tank. This left them incapable of fending off Zhukov's Siberians, and for the first time during the campaign a German unit panicked and fled. There was little choice but to relieve the division, as it was no longer capable of effective combat operations.

Guderian was furious, as he had requested warm clothing in September and October, and immediately took steps to find out what was going on. 'All stocks of clothing that the Panzer Army held were immediately sent to the Front, but the shortages were so great that these provided a drop in the ocean.'[16] The army's quartermaster general insisted that winter clothing had been issued. After making a series of telephone calls, Guderian discovered that it had been stranded for several weeks at Warsaw Railway Station due to a lack of trains and disruption to the lines by Polish partisans.

Guderian personally briefed Army Group Centre's commander, Field Marshal von Bock, on 23 November. In light of the desperate situation regarding winter clothing and the threat posed by the arrival of the Siberian units to their inadequately guarded right flank, Guderian requested that his attack be cancelled and that his troops be permitted to go on the defensive during the winter. In response, Bock claimed that OKH was well aware of conditions on the Eastern Front. Nonetheless, he called the army's commander-in-chief with his subordinate listening in. Guderian went away unhappy:

> In view of the manner in which the Commander-in-Chief of the Army and the Chief of the Army General Staff refused my requests it must be assumed that not only Hitler but also they were in favour of a continuation of the offensive.[17]

Rashly, Guderian hoped he could personally make Hitler see sense. When he saw the Führer in late December a heated argument took place over the issue. Guderian pointed out that the cold was causing twice as many casualties as the Red Army and that it was his duty to lessen the 'suffering' of his men. Hitler accused him of not seeing the bigger picture and insisted that winter clothing had been issued. When the quartermaster general was summoned, he had to admit the kit remained in Warsaw. But it was all too late – the damage had been done, Hitler's troops froze, and a week later Guderian was relieved of his command.

By the end of November, Army Group Centre's armour was deployed as follows: 3rd Panzer Division was at Klin on the Kalinin–Moscow road; 7th Panzer had a bridgehead east of the Volga–Moscow Canal at Yakhroma; to the south, 2nd Panzer was battling for Tula and 4th Panzer was east of the city, but could get no closer. The situation was at stalemate.

By this stage, Zhukov was more than satisfied with the Red Army's efforts before Moscow:

In twenty days of the second phase of their offensive, the Germans lost 155,000 dead and wounded, 800 tanks, at least 300 guns and 1,500 planes. The heavy losses, the complete collapse of the plan for a blitzkrieg ending to the war, and the failure to achieve their strategic objectives depressed the spirit of the German forces and gave rise to the first doubts about a successful outcome of the war. The Nazi military-political leadership also lost its reputation of 'invincibility' before world public opinion.[18]

The Red Army was now acting aggressively everywhere except before Moscow on the West and Kalinin Fronts. Here, as Zhukov observed:

The exhausted German enemy, although he had lost his momentum, continued to gnaw his way forward. Army Group Centre was only nineteen miles from the capital and in spite of its severely weakened condition could not be brought to a halt.[19]

According to General Günther Blumentritt, Field Marshal von Kluge's chief of staff, the Russian weather and determined Soviet counter-attacks thwarted Hitler's winter push on Moscow:

The offensive was opened by Hoeppner's panzer group on the left. Its progress was slow, in the face of mud and strong Russian counter-attacks. Our losses were heavy. The weather then turned adverse, with snow falling on the swampy ground. The Russians made repeated counter-attacks from the flank across the frozen Moskwa, and Hoeppner had to divert more and more of his strength to check these thrusts. The 2nd Panzer Division succeeded in penetrating far enough to get sight of the Kremlin, but that was the nearest it came.[20]

There was no hiding Hitler's intelligence failure – Colonel Kinzel and his men, who had built up an 'accurate picture' of Soviet defences, were not to blame. 'We had been badly misled,' said Blumentritt, 'about the quantity of reinforcements that the Russians could produce. They had hidden their resources all too well.'[21]

The bitter weather continued to take a heavy toll on the German soldiers who were ill-equipped to fight in the winter conditions. In contrast, a German doctor with the 276th Infantry Division marvelled at the toughness of their adversaries:

The Russian [was] … completely at home in the wilds. Give him an axe and
a knife and in a few hours he will do anything, run up a sledge, a stretcher, a
little igloo … make a stove out of a couple of old oil cans. Our men just stand
about miserably burning the precious petrol to keep warm. At night they
gather in the few wooden houses which are still standing.[22]

On 2 December von Kluge's 4th Army was launched into the attack and forward elements of the 258th Infantry Division penetrated Moscow's suburbs.
Strong Soviet counter-attacks persuaded von Kluge and Blumentritt that they
were not going to break through and that these advanced units should be withdrawn. This proved to be very prudent action as Zhukov threw 100 divisions at
them in his general counter-offensive three days later.

Despite receiving the divisions from the Far East and the new reserve divisions (which constituted the 1st Shock, 10th and 20th, plus nine rifle and two
cavalry divisions, eight rifle and six tank brigades) from Stavka, Zhukov still
possessed no general superiority. On 1 December, the Western Front mustered
577,726 men, while the Kalinin Front had 118,394 and the right flank of the
South-Western Front supplied 63,398: 1,060,380 men in total. The Germans
held more than three times this number of men just as POWs.

Zhukov was acutely aware that for his counter-offensive he was deficient in
tanks and aircraft:

Late in the evening of 4 December the Chief [Stalin] telephoned me and
asked, 'Is there anything else you need beyond what we gave you?'

I said I still needed air support from Supreme Headquarters reserve and
the air defence forces and at least 200 tanks and crews. The front had too few
tanks and needed more for the rapid development of the counter-offensive.

'We can't give you any tanks; we don't have any,' Stalin said, 'But you'll get
your air support. Arrange it with the General Staff. I am going to call them
now. Just remember that the Kalinin Front Offensive begins on 5 December
and the operational group on the right wing of the South-West Front around
Yelets on the 6th.'[23]

By the time of Zhukov's Moscow counter-offensive, the German Army had
suffered over 100,000 cases of frostbite, of whom 14,357 were so serious that
they required amputations; 62,000 were incapacitated but did not require ampu-
tation; and 36,270 were considered able to return to duty within ten days. On
5 December, Operation Typhoon was formally called off (although two days
earlier some local withdrawals had already been sanctioned).

Stalin's Red Air Force did its utmost to ignore the weather and from 15 November to 5 December 1941 clocked up 15,840 sorties. This equated to nearly five times the flying rates of the Luftwaffe. The 6th PVO Fighter Corps gave the Luftwaffe a tough time in the skies around Moscow. During the last two months of 1941 it claimed to have shot down 250 German planes.

It was then the German Army's turn to be on the receiving end of things when the corps switched from its air defence role to ground-attack and set about the German armies west of Moscow. During June–December 1941 the Soviets lost 21,200 aircraft, of which only about half were destroyed in combat.

Stavka's plan called for an offensive by all three fronts in the Moscow area: Konev's Kalinin, to the north of the Sea of Moscow; Zhukov's Western, either side of the capital; and Timoshenko's South-Western, on Zhukov's left flank. Zhukov would provide the main effort: on his right, the fresh 1st Shock and 20th Armies were to open the attack supported by the 30th and 16th Armies on the flanks. They were to link up with Konev's 29th and 31st Armies. Opposite Moscow, Zhukov's front was to tie down German forces while the 10th and 50th Armies on the southern wing, along with Timoshenko's forces, attacked Guderian's Panzer Group.

Lelyushenko's 30th Army at Dmitrov, to the north of Moscow, made the deepest penetration into German lines on the first day. It advanced to the Moscow–Leningrad Highway, threatening the junction between the German 4th Army and the 4th Panzer Group. After three days, it had got to Klin, and with the 1st Shock Army on the left flank seemed poised to achieve a successful encirclement. Rokossovsky's 16th Army and Vlasov's 20th Army made equally pleasing progress liberating Istra, west of Moscow, by 13 December.

The Soviet 13th and 40th Armies belonging to Timoshenko's South-Western Front pierced the southern face of 3rd Panzer Group's salient, which it had created in November. Timoshenko was threatening the Germans' main supply route, the Orel–Tula Railway by 9 December. In the meantime, the 50th and 10th Armies struck the northern edge of the salient, driving a wedge between Guderian and von Kluge. Once the Soviet 33rd and 43rd Armies had joined the offensive on 18 December, the German 4th Army was increasingly pushed back westward. To the north, Konev's Kalinin Front drove the German 9th Army from Kalinin and thrust south-westward along the upper Volga toward Rzhev. In the far south, von Rundstedt's Army Group South was ejected from Rostov-on-Don on 28 November, having only occupied it five days previously.

'There are lots of broken vehicles,' said Vasily Grossman after witnessing the results of Zhukov's offensive, 'on the roads and in the steppe, lots of abandoned guns, hundreds of German corpses, helmets and weapons lying everywhere.'[24] General Rudolf Hofmann, chief of staff of the German 9th Army, assessed:

The result of the battle for Moscow was to bring both sides temporarily to the end of their strength. Neither side succeeded in attaining its objectives. The Germans did not capture Moscow, though for a while it looked almost within their grasp, and the Russians did not succeed in disintegrating and destroying Army Group Centre.[25]

This belittles the Soviet victory. While the Wehrmacht did not achieve its immediate objective with the capture of Moscow, or indeed its long-term objective with the defeat of the Soviet Union, the Red Army achieved its immediate goal of halting Hitler and pushing the front line away from the Soviet capital. The destruction of Army Group Centre was not achieved because of Stalin's insistence on a general counter-offensive that dissipated their effort.

Zhukov enjoyed his first, if flawed, victory and recalled triumphantly, 'The Hitlerites lost on the battlefields of Moscow a grand total of over half a million men, 1,300 tanks, 2,500 guns, over 15,000 vehicles, and much other materiel.'[26] German sources refute these figures. General Halder, chief of the German General Staff, estimated total German losses on the Eastern Front as of 28 February 1942 to be 1,005,000 casualties (i.e. killed, wounded and missing). Losses for the period, as of 26 November 1941, were 742,000; therefore, German losses for the period of Zhukov's counter-offensive near Moscow in all sectors of the front are estimated at 262,000, which is half of Zhukov's estimate for the Western Strategic Sector alone.

Whatever the true figure, even by Halder's reckoning, as of November 1941 the Germans had lost almost a quarter of their forces on the Eastern Front, and by February 1942 this had risen to almost a third. 'The Battle for Moscow laid the firm foundations for the ensuing defeat of Nazi Germany,' concluded Zhukov.[27]

Despite the mounting losses, Stalin was clearly heartened that the Red Army had managed to hold Hitler at the very gates of Moscow. Every time he addressed the public Stalin now exuded new-found confidence. Gustav Herling, held at the Yercevo labour camp, noted this change:

In December 1941 we heard Stalin give another and very different speech. I shall never forget that strong voice, cold and penetrating, those words hammered out as if with a fist of stone. He said that the German offensive had been arrested at the outskirts of Moscow and Leningrad, that the day of victory over German barbarism was approaching.[28]

Stalin was now determined to launch another counter-offensive. On 5 January 1942, he told his gathered generals:

The Germans are in disarray as a result of their defeat before Moscow. They've prepared badly for the winter. This is the most favourable moment to go over to a general offensive. The Germans hope to hold our offensive until the spring, so that they can resume active operations when they have built up their strength.

Our task is therefore to give the Germans no time to draw breath, drive them to the West, and force them to use up all their reserves before spring comes because by then we will have new reserves and the German reserves will have run out.[29]

Stalin envisaged that the main effort would be against Army Group Centre, with the aim of trapping it west of Vyazma. The Leningrad and Volkhov Fronts were to crush Army Group North and save Leningrad. It would be Timoshenko's job to deal with Army Group South, liberating Kharkov, the Donbass and Sevastopol.

Zhukov did not like the idea of a vast general offensive along the entire Eastern Front stretching from Leningrad to the Black Sea; they simply did not have the strength for such an effort. Manpower and supplies needed to be replenished. He argued that their strength should be directed against Army Group Centre for a single knock-out blow – Stalin did not agree.

Konev opened the attack on 10 January 1942, supported by Rokossovsky's 16th Army and Vlasov's 20th Army. He pierced enemy lines on the Volokolamsk Highway, while Zhukov attacked along the Mozhaisk Highway. However, German reinforcements from Western Europe ensured that things did not go to plan. This culminated in a crisis on the junction of Zhukov's Western Front and the Bryansk Front. The offensive lasted until 20 April and Zhukov pushed up to 155 miles, but in the process the Red Army suffered twice the losses of the Wehrmacht. In the north, the offensive produced no results and in the south managed just 60 miles.

In total, the bitter battle for Moscow lasted six months and cost 926,000 Soviet dead, not to mention the wounded and missing. These colossal losses were greater than Britain and America lost in the whole of the Second World War. The net result was that Zhukov held Moscow and Field Marshal von Bock lost his job to von Kluge.

Hitler was incensed that his generals had not taken Moscow. He promptly sacked Field Marshal von Brauchitsch, commander-in-chief of the army, von Bock, von Leeb and Guderian, while von Rundstedt was transferred west. Thirty-five corps or divisional commanders were also removed from their posts. It was a poor thank you for all the effort and blood that had been expended pushing toward Moscow. It was clear there would be no quick victory on the Eastern Front.

9

OPERATION BLUE

While Zhukov despaired at Stalin's insistence on a wasteful broad-front strategy in the winter of 1941–42, it partially misled Hitler into believing their reserves were spent. When Colonel Gehlen took over as head of Eastern Front intelligence for the German Army's General Staff, he quickly realised it would be foolish to underestimate European Russia and its vast territories east of the Ural Mountains. The Soviet Union was thirty-two times the size of Germany, covering around one-sixth of the earth's surface. Bringing the war to a satisfactory conclusion would not be easy.

Hitler, realising he needed more manpower for his 1942 summer offensive, sent Field Marshal Wilhelm Keitel to Budapest and Bucharest to pressure Horthy and Antonescu for much-needed reinforcements. His deputy, Reichsmarschall Hermann Göring, was sent to Rome to appeal to Mussolini for more Italian troops.

The bolstering of the Eastern Front by other Axis forces was appropriately dubbed 'Operation Mars', after the god of war. These reinforcements began to arrive during the summer of 1942, but Keitel had to agree to them serving as independent national armies rather than under German command. This would inevitably create a muddled chain of command.

Göring reassured Mussolini that Stalin would be defeated in 1942 and that Britain would soon lay down her arms. Count Galeazzo Ciano, the Italian Foreign Minister, was less than impressed by the posturing reichsmarschall, recalling:

We had dinner at the Excelsior Hotel, and during the dinner Göring talked of little else but the jewels he owned. In fact, he had some beautiful rings on his fingers [...] On the way to the station he wore a great sable coat, something between what automobile drivers wore in 1906 and what a high-grade prostitute wears to the opera.[1]

The posturing Mussolini may have felt Göring was a kindred spirit. However, even the German Army saw him as a figure of ridicule and, like Ciano, were aghast at his comic dress sense. Bernd Freytag von Loringhoven later observed:

[He] had the appearance of a clown, dressed like a general in operetta, with a white uniform in mid-winter and jackboots of violet leather fitting over his knees. The eccentricity of the commander-in-chief of the Luftwaffe, rouged and perfumed, fingers covered in rings, made us giggle.[2]

Mussolini promised to send just two divisions in return for artillery but, sensing he was wavering, Hitler summoned him to a personal meeting at Salzburg on 29–30 April. Ciano was shocked at the appearance of Hitler, noting, 'The winter months in Russia have borne heavily upon him, I see for the first time that he has many grey hairs'.[3] According to those closest to him, Hitler had developed a physical revulsion for frost and snow.

Antonescu and Horthy were far more accommodating than Mussolini. Through promises, flattery and outright bullying Hitler and Keitel managed to get the commitment of the equivalent of fifty-two 'allied' divisions for the coming summer campaign, consisting of twenty-seven Romanian, thirteen Hungarian, nine Italian, two Slovak and one Spanish division. Worryingly, this was a quarter of the combined Axis forces and the bulk of the units were to be sent to the southern part of the front where Hitler's main blow was to fall. Of the forty-one fresh divisions sent there, half were 'foreign' and many German generals were uneasy about this – but what could they do in the face of their growing manpower shortage? American war correspondent and historian William Shirer noted, 'But these "allied" armies were all Hitler had.'[4]

Although King Boris of Bulgaria successfully resisted calls to join the war against Stalin, he agreed to provide reinforcements to alleviate pressure on Hitler's security forces in the Balkans. In January 1942, the Bulgarian 1st Army moved into Serbia and from mid-1943 fought Yugoslav partisans in western Serbia. These reinforcements came at a price; in the summer of 1942 Hitler had to intervene in Italian-occupied West Macedonia after clashes between Boris' and Mussolini's troops.

By the summer of 1942 Mussolini, as promised, had greatly expanded his commitment to Hitler, sending four infantry divisions and three mountain divisions. These were incorporated into the Italian 8th Army, which also included two German infantry divisions. By November Mussolini's contribution amounted to over a quarter of a million men in twelve divisions, equipped with 988 guns, 420 mortars, 17,000 vehicles, 25,000 horses and sixty-four aircraft, but crucially very few tanks. These troops were used to operations in East and North Africa and therefore they and their officers were ill-equipped for operations on the unforgiving Russian Steppes. In light of the Axis' fluctuating fortunes in North Africa, this was a massive commitment of resources by Mussolini.

On 5 April 1942 Hitler issued 'Directive 41', striking a positive note, 'The winter battle in Russia is nearing its end. Thanks to the unequalled courage and self-sacrificing devotion on the Eastern Front, German arms have achieved a great defensive success.'[5] He then laid out his plans for the coming summer, which gave the Wehrmacht the task of ejecting the Red Army from the Don region, the Donbas industrial region, the Caucasian oilfields and the Caucasus passes. He hoped that the latter operations would encourage neutral Turkey to finally side with the Axis. Outlining his 'General Plan', Hitler stated:

> In pursuit of the original plan for the Eastern campaign, the armies of the Central sector [Army Group Centre] will stand fast, those in the *North* [Army Group North] will capture Leningrad and link up with the Finns, while those on the *southern flank* [Army Group South] will break through into the Caucasus.
>
> In view of the conditions prevailing at the end of winter, the availability of troops and resources, and transport problems, these aims can be achieved only one at a time.
>
> First, therefore, all available forces will be concentrated on the *main operations in the southern sector*, with the aim of destroying the enemy before the Don, in order to secure the Caucasian oil fields, and the passes through the Caucasus Mountains themselves.[6]

In early 1942 the Germans began to conduct their deception plan dubbed *Kreml* (Kremlin), designed to convince Stalin that Hitler's summer offensive would be directed toward finally capturing Moscow. Leaks were made to the foreign press and Army Group Centre conducted poorly concealed preparations which indicated that Hitler would again attack the Soviet capital in force. Once again Moscow was gripped by war fever.

In the meantime, during the spring the Germans began preparing for their real massive southern summer offensive known as Operation *Blau* (Blue). Their first moves were to secure their flanks. Way to the south, this meant driving the Red Army completely from the troublesome Crimea and capturing the naval base of Sevastopol. This would shield Marshal Fedor von Bock's Army Group South's right flank and enable General Erich von Manstein's 11th Army to cross the Straits of Kerch into the Kuban in support of 1st Panzer Army and 17th Army's offensive along the eastern coast of the Black Sea, once they were across the lower Don and Donets.

Von Manstein moved to eliminate the Red Army's presence in the Kerch Peninsula on 8 May 1942 with Operation *Trappenjagd* (Bustard Hunt). He diverted all his forces except for his 54th Corps and the Romanian Army, which remained before Sevastopol. In total, six German and three Romanian divisions were thrown at the Soviet 44th, 47th and 51st Armies. The Germans, with Luftwaffe support, sliced through the thin Soviet defences. By the evening von Manstein's 30th Corps had pierced the Soviet 44th Army's front and eleven Soviet divisions were driven into the Sea of Azov on 11 May. The rest of von Manstein's forces reached Kerch five days later. At least half of the Red Army divisions were trapped against the Sea of Azov and by 20 May they had been ejected from the Kerch.

The Soviets could not hold on in the Crimea and evacuated. In the chaos that followed they lost 170,000 prisoners, 260 tanks, 1,140 guns and 300 aircraft; the Germans suffered 7,500 casualties. Von Manstein could now devote all his attention to reducing the last remaining Soviet stronghold in the Crimea – Sevastopol. This was defended by about the 100,000 men of Lieutenant General I.E. Petrov's Independent Coastal Command.

Emboldened by their success before Moscow, Stalin and his generals looked to use their freshly raised armies elsewhere. Having stopped Hitler in Russia, Stalin felt he should next be halted in Ukraine and Crimea. Stalin's eyes were drawn south to the city of Kharkov. It was decided that the Red Army's next major blow would fall here, in an effort to defeat Hitler's rampaging war machine. Some in Stavka feared it was too soon – the generals and troops were not experienced enough and Stalin was still micromanaging the war. The latter was not good for the commanders on the ground; they understood the realities of the fight better than Stalin in Moscow. Kharkov was to be a shock to the Red Army's growing confidence.

In Ukraine, while Timoshenko and his South-Western Front was preparing to liberate the city of Kharkov, Bock's Army Group South was planning to destroy the Lozovaya pocket that stretched south-west from Izyum, beyond the Donets. General Friedrich Paulus, to the north, deployed his forces between Belgorod and Balakleya, while Kleist to the south was at Pavlograd. Their intention was to cut off and destroy the Soviet salient, straighten the German line along the Donets and then launch their main offensive. Ironically, Timoshenko obliged von Bock by putting more troops into the noose.

This salient had been created by a Soviet offensive launched in January against Army Group South. They had planned that the Soviet 6th, 57th and 9th Armies of Lieutenant General F.Ya. Kostenko's South-West Front as well as the South Front would drive west over the Donets between Balakleya in the north and Artemovsk in the south, before swinging south to the Sea of Azov at Melitopol trapping German forces in the area. The South Front never got beyond its start point and the South-West Front ground to a halt on 31 January, having created a considerable salient.

Disastrously, two-thirds of the Soviet armour, along with General Kharitonov's 9th Army and General Gorodnyanski's 6th Army, moved into the salient ready to liberate Krasnograd, south-west of Kharkov. This was to be followed by a push on Kharkov and Poltava, way to the west. Their attack was to be supported by the Soviet 28th and 57th Armies, north of Kharkov in the Volchansk bridgehead.

If Bock had struck first he would have had to contend with nearly 600 Soviet tanks, instead Timoshenko beat him to the post by attacking a week earlier on 12 May. Those forces launched from Volchansk to the north of Kharkov made little impression against Paulus' fourteen divisions. In the south, Romanian forces could not prevent the fall of Krasnograd and Kharkov seemed within Timoshenko's grasp. The Soviet 9th Army rolled onto Karlovka, west of Kharkov. Worryingly though, the Red Army was unable to widen the breach south of Izyum and Barvenkov, which meant the pocket was getting bigger but not the breach.

If both the Soviet 6th and 9th Armies had struck toward Merefa, south of Kharkov, things might have gone differently, but with General Kharitonov's forces heading west on 17 May warning signs began to appear. This was the Soviets' first attempt at an armoured offensive on this scale and it had clearly not brought the Germans' main combat strength to battle, which was now identified as lying on their southern flank. Timoshenko prudently contacted Moscow to ask permission to slow down the offensive while he secured his flanks. In response, Stalin was adamant he wanted Kharkov liberated at all costs.

On 18 May the Germans counter-attacked. Eleven German divisions under Kleist drove from Slavyansk-Kramatorsk, striking the Southern Front's 9th and 57th Armies, and within two days he had broken out on the left wing of the South-Western Front in the Pretrovsky region. Kleist was assaulting the left flank of the salient northwards toward Izyum in an attempt to cut off the 57th and 9th Armies as well as the 6th Army and Group Bobrin (the last two had been halted in the preceding days trying to push westward toward Krasnograd on the key railway line south-west of Kharkov). Izyum fell on 18 May and the Soviets fell back in a state of chaos, while the Germans sped on to reach the Oskol River.

Realising the danger, Timoshenko and Khrushchev, serving as the front's commissar, called a halt with a view to helping the 9th Army, only to be over-ridden by Stalin. 'Catastrophe struck a few days later,' says Khrushchev, 'exactly as we expected. There was nothing we could do to avert it. Many generals, colonels, junior officers, and troops perished. The staff of the 57th Army was wiped out completely.'[7] With the noose tightening around the Soviet forces, Timoshenko despatched his deputy General Kostenko to try to save the 6th and 9th Armies. When General Friedrich Paulus' panzers arrived at Balakleya on 23 May, linking up with those of Kleist, the trap was snapped shut. Less than 25 per cent of the two Soviet armies got away, and all their heavy equipment was left littering the west bank of the Donets.

Officially the Soviets acknowledged 5,000 killed (including General Podlas, commander of the 57th Army), 70,000 missing and 300 tanks lost. The Germans claimed to have captured 240,000 men – something which Khrushchev confirmed to Stalin when he reported to Moscow shortly after. This implied that the bulk of the Soviet troops had surrendered. The Germans also claimed to have taken or destroyed 1,200 tanks. Timoshenko only had 845 tanks in total, but the German figure may include all armoured fighting vehicles. It is doubtful that any Soviet armour escaped the southern pocket, although the 28th Army may have saved a few in the north.

The terrible cost of the failed Kharkov Spring Offensive for the Red Army was considerable. While the tank ratio during 1942 had stood at five to one in their favour, it was now ten to one against them, which did not bode well for the coming German summer offensive (Fridericus II) which aimed to clear the Kupyansk area and secure a bridgehead over the Oskol, on 22–26 June. Moving from south-east of Kharkov, the Soviets were again driven back, losing 40,000 more prisoners and sealing the destruction of Kostenko's South-West Front.

Khrushchev, who supported the aim of liberating Kharkov, later blamed Stalin and the planner, General Bagramyan, while Stalin held Timoshenko responsible. Khrushchev was summoned to Moscow to see Stalin and he feared the worse. Khrushchev recalled:

> Later we started to talk things over. What would we do now? What chance was there of building up our defences along the Donets River in order to prevent the enemy from crossing? How could we contain the German advance with our limited resources?[8]

Stalin toyed with him for a few days and even suggested he should hang, but then sent him back to the front. While Khrushchev got off lightly, as a result of the Kharkov disaster Timoshenko was demoted. Zhukov now took over as deputy supreme commander under Stalin.

While the Germans were busy in the south, to the north they also fought the bitter battles of the aptly named Operation *Flaschenhals* (Bottleneck). The German corridor to Schlüsselburg, on the southern shore of Lake Ladoga east of Leningrad, cut the latter off from the rest of the Soviet Union and the

Red Army was determined to eliminate it. On 20 April 1942, General K.A. Meretskov sent his deputy, General Andrei Vlasov (who had distinguished himself with 20th Army west of Moscow), to take command of the trapped Soviet 2nd Shock Army. He was unable to escape and fell into German hands on 12 July. From 13 May until 10 July the Soviets lost 94,751 casualties (including 54,774 killed, captured or missing), most of whom had come from Vlasov's army.

On 19 August 1942, employing the Neva Task Force and the 55th Army of General L.A. Govorov's Leningrad Front and the 8th and 54th Armies of Meretskov's Volkhov Front, the Soviets attempted to cut through the neck of the corridor near the lake. However, by the end of September the Germans had successfully beaten off this offensive, as well as the 42nd Army's attempt to link up with the Soviet Coastal Command in the Oranienbaum beachhead to the west of Leningrad and south of the Gulf of Finland.

In the Crimea, von Manstein assaulted Sevastopol on 7 June. It was defended by about 3,600 fortifications strung out over a depth of 15 miles. There were some 600 guns (including four massive 305mm guns in two twin turrets) and forty tanks. He was understandably concerned about the delay in attacking Sevastopol:

> There could be no shadow of doubt that the assault on the fortress would be even tougher than that of the previous December, the enemy having had half a year in which to tighten up his fortifications, bring his manpower up to strength and stock up with store from across the sea.
>
> The strength of the Sevastopol fortress consisted less in up-to-date fortifications – though a certain number of these did exist – than the extraordinary difficultly of the ground, which was dotted with innumerable smaller defence installations. These formed a thick network covering the entire area from the Belbek valley to the Black Sea Coast.[9]

Von Manstein struck from the north with 54th Corps and from the south with 30th Corps. Although lacking panzers, he had assault guns, 700 artillery pieces and 600 aircraft. However, time was not on von Manstein's side as the Luftwaffe was needed in support of Operation *Blau*. The 54th Corps forced its way down the valley of Belbek and captured Fort Stalin. On 28 June the Germans got across North Bay, thereby turning the Soviets' rear.

Naval officer Evseev was one of those lucky enough to be evacuated. As he drove away to get on a boat he noted, 'The city was unrecognisable. It was dead. The snow-white city of a little while ago, Sevastopol the beautiful, had turned to ruin.'[10] The Soviet garrison withdrew to the Kersones Peninsula where, on 4 July, 30,000 men surrendered. Resistance continued for another five days and the Germans took about 95,000 prisoners for the loss of 24,111 of their own killed and wounded. Von Manstein was promoted to field marshal, and the 11th Army was sent to help capture Leningrad instead of being moved into the Kuban.

Meanwhile, Hitler moved to FHQ Wehrwolf, at Vinnitsa in Ukraine, in the summer of 1942. His staff was confronted by damp, mice and the risk of malaria. Secretary Christa Schroeder was far from happy with the move, 'The living accommodation is similar to Wolfsschanze except we have fortified houses instead of concrete bunkers. They look really attractive but are awfully damp inside. [...] The mosquito plague is worse here than last year.'[11]

Field Marshal von Bock's Army Group South launched Hitler's summer offensive with Operation *Blau* I. This was to push east of Kursk against the Soviet South-West Front to a line on the River Don between Livny and Rossosh and capture Voronezh. Conducted by General von Weichs' German 2nd Army and Hoth's 4th Panzer Army, they were to create left-flank protection for the 'Donet's Corridor', along which Paulus' 6th Army could advance to the city of Stalingrad.

On 28 June, the Germans struck from the Kursk area in the direction of Voronezh, attacking the Bryansk Front's 13th and 40th Armies. Ironically, in the spring of 1942 the Bryansk Front was under the command of General Golikov, the very man who had helped the Soviet Union get into this predicament in the first place. The chief of staff of the Bryansk Front was none other than General Kazakov from the Central Asian Military District. He was later to take command of the 10th Guards Army.

From the start, the Red Army was outgunned and outnumbered. In the face of Hoth's panzers the Soviet 40th Army disintegrated within forty-eight hours and the 13th Army was obliged to withdraw northward. On 30 June, the German 6th Army attacked Ostrogozhsk, penetrating the defences of the 21st and 28th Armies (the latter having been mauled at Volchansk in May) and both were caught in the open by German firepower. Two days later, the Germans struck below Kharkov, with Kleist leading the 1st Panzer Army over the Donets.

Marshal Vasilevskiy, assessing the situation, noted:

The situation on the Voronezh sector deteriorated rapidly at the end of 2 July. The defences at the junction of the Bryansk and South-Western Fronts had been torn open to a depth of 80km. The Front's reserves on this sector were thrown into the fighting. There was a clear danger of the enemy's strike force breaking through the Don and capturing Voronezh.[12]

In response, Stalin released the 6th and 60th Armies, which were instructed to take up positions on the right bank of the Don between Zadonsk and Pavlovsk;

the 5th Tank Army also concentrated south of the Yelets River. Once committed to the fighting in the Voronezh area, these three armies quickly helped to stabilise the situation, but were unable to remove the threat of a German breakthrough across and along the Don toward Stalingrad.

Operation *Blau* II saw Paulus' 6th Army push forward to the west of the Don to then take Stalingrad at the apex of the westward bend of the Volga River. The ineffectual resistance of the South-West Front saw it reorganised into the Voronezh and Stalingrad Fronts. Launching itself from Kharkov, the 6th Army reached Kachalinskaya by 22 July on the eastward bend of the Don. On 9 July 1942 Army Group South was divided into Army Groups A and B, with von Weichs assuming command of B.

Meanwhile, in the spring of 1942 under the designation of *Nordpol* (North Pole), it was planned for Army Group Centre to capitalise on the exhaustion of the Red Army's Winter Offensive at Moscow and to secure the exposed German flanks. The Soviets were completely exhausted by April 1942. In the Nelidovo and Belyy areas, Lieutenant General I.S. Konev's Kalinin Front had cut through the German lines creating a salient that threatened Vitebsk and Smolensk before being halted by General Hermann Hoth's 3rd Panzer Army at Velizh and Demidov. This left the Soviet 4th Shock Army just north of the Moscow Highway and far behind the 9th Army's left flank. Although both the 3rd Panzer Army and the 9th Army were granted permission by Hitler to fall back to the Winter Line, they were still in a far from ideal position.

On 2 July, *Nordpol* 1942 was launched as Operation *Feuerzauber* (Magic Fire), driving back the Soviet 39th Army and 22nd Cavalry Corps between Belyy to the west and Sychevka to the east. Conducted by the 9th Army, this offensive took 50,000 Soviet prisoners and shortened the German defensive line by about 130 miles before Moscow. However, this success was not followed up due to the requirements of Operation *Blau*.

Zhukov was very aware that after the loss of the Crimea and the Red Army's defeats in the Barvenkovo area, in the Donbas and at Voronezh, Hitler had once again successfully seized the initiative from the Red Army. He observed:

> By mid-July the enemy had driven back our troops across the Don between Voronezh and Kletskava and from Surovikino to Rostov and were fighting in the Great Bend of the Don in an attempt to break through to Stalingrad.[13]

The newly created Stalingrad Front absorbed the battered South-Western Front, which was reinforced with the newly formed 1st and 4th Tank Armies and remaining units from the 28th, 38th and 57th Armies. The Volga Naval Flotilla was also placed under the Stalingrad Front. By 22 July, the Stalingrad Front numbered thirty-eight divisions. Some sixteen divisions (the 62nd and 63rd Armies, as well as two divisions from the 64th Army and one from each of the 1st and 4th Tank Armies) were deployed in the main defensive zone. It was their job to fend off the eighteen divisions of Paulus' 6th Army. According to Zhukov, the balance of forces was in the Germans' favour as they had the advantage of 20 per cent more manpower, 100 per cent more tanks and 260 per cent more aircraft. Only in artillery and mortars were the two sides roughly equal.

Four days later, the Germans pierced the defences of the 62nd Army, reaching the Kamensky region. The 1st and 4th Tank Armies were instructed to halt them, but with only two infantry divisions and 240 tanks were unable to achieve much. The fighting also spread to the 64th Army's positions. The fighting spilled over into August and with such a broad front line the Stalingrad Front was split in two, with the creation of the South-Eastern Front. The former remained under Lieutenant General V.N. Gordov and consisted of the 63rd, 21st and 62nd Armies as well as the 4th Tank Army and the 16th Air Army. The latter was placed under Colonel General A.I. Yeremnko, with the 51st, 57th and 64th Armies as well as the 1st Guards Army and the 8th Air Army.

Operation *Fischreiher* (Heron) was an extension of *Blau* II, with the push across the Don toward Stalingrad. This was when Hitler's ambitious plans began to become unstuck, because whereas Army Group B's mission of creating a defensive front along the Don had been a subsidiary to Army Group A's southward thrust, it had now become a strategic offensive in its own right. Paulus' forces were not up to the job and Stalin was understandably determined not to lose a city named in his honour.

The third component of Hitler's offensive saw Field Marshal Wilhelm List's Army Group A launching the 1st Panzer Army and the 17th Army in a push between Izyum on the Donets and Taganrog on the Sea of Azov, to protect the 6th Army's right flank. List's forces were so successful that the offensive was extended into the northern Caucasus with the aim of taking the vital oilfields at Maikop, Grozny and Baku, as well as the port of Batumi. 'If I do not get the oil of Maikop and Grozny,' Hitler told General Paulus, commander of the ill-fated 6th Army, just before Operation *Blau* began, 'then I must end this war.'[14]

Stalin was in the same position; he needed this oil to fuel the Red Army and his industries. If Hitler took control of Stalingrad, then he could block the last major route via the Caspian Sea and the Volga into the central Soviet Union. This would effectively strangle his war effort. This, and only this, stood a chance of finally forcing Stalin to the negotiating table.

As part of Operation *Blau* III, the Germans conducted Operation Edelweiss in an attempt to capture Baku and its oilfields on the Caspian Sea. This task was given to General Kleist's 1st Panzer Army. It meant that while Army Group B was striking east toward Stalingrad, Army Group A was now moving ever further southwards. Group Ruoff was directed south-west toward the Strait of Kerch and the Black Sea coast between Novorossiysk and Batumi. The 1st Panzer Army headed south-east toward Baku and the Caspian. Edelweiss was halted in the Caucasus Mountains just north of Grozny.

General Ewald von Kleist was initially ignorant of the significance of Stalingrad, stating:

> The capture of Stalingrad was subsidiary to the main aim. It was only of importance as a convenient place, in the bottleneck between the Don and the Volga, where we could block an attack on our flank by Russian forces coming from the east. At the start, Stalingrad was no more than a name on a map to us.
>
> Hitler said that we must capture the oilfields by the autumn, because Germany could not continue the war without them. When I pointed out the risks of leaving such a long flank exposed he said he was going to draw on Romania, Hungary and Italy for troops to cover it. I warned him, and so did others, that it was rash to rely on such troops, but he would not listen.[15]

Fortunately for Stalin, Army Group A was soon very overextended and came to a halt along the Terek River by mid-November in the face of resistance from the Soviet Caucasus and Transcaucasus Fronts. In the meantime, the Germans had fought their way over the Kerch Straits from the Crimea and the 4th Panzer Army had been diverted from Army Group B.

On Stalin's orders, which included not evacuating the civilian population, preparations were made to hold Stalingrad. The city was defended by the 66th, 4th Tank, 62nd, 1st Tank, 64th, 51st and 57th Armies, running north to south in three defensive lines. The Germans attacked the first line on 17 August, with General Gustav von Wietersheim's 14th Panzer Corps breaking through five days later to reach the Volga, north of Stalingrad, on 23 August. In the same month, Zhukov was appointed deputy commissar of defence and first deputy commander-in-chief of the Soviet armed forces. His star had now completely eclipsed Timoshenko's.

The 14th Panzer Corps split the Stalingrad defence near Vertyachi. The 62nd Army was cut off from the Stalingrad Front and was transferred to Yeremenko's South-Eastern Front, which had responsibility for the city. The Luftwaffe's bombers pounded Stalingrad into rubble and the following day the panzers attacked toward the Tractor Works, but were cut off for several days by a Soviet counter-attack. To the south of the city, the South-Eastern Front was forced to withdraw on the outer and then the inner defences. General W. Freiherr von Langermann und Erlencamp's 24th Panzer Corps and the 48th Panzer Corps from the 4th Panzer Army reached Stalingrad's second line of defence by the end of the month, and the third line of defence by mid-September.

'Early in the battle the enemy subjected Stalingrad to the cruellest air raids,' recalled Khrushchev. 'Wave after wave of German planes bombed the city. Stalingrad was in flames. We found ourselves cut off from the left bank of the Volga.'[16] Khrushchev and Yeremenko gained Stalin's permission to move their headquarters to the 'left' bank of the river, to better direct the battle, leaving newly selected Chuikov in command of the city's defences. Their Stalingrad headquarters was in a ravine on the Tsaritsa River, a western tributary of the Volga, in a rather luxurious command post allegedly prepared for Stalin. It seems that Khrushchev got his left and right muddled, as he and Yeremenko withdrew to the other side of the Volga, setting up shop at Yamy.

Khrushchev recalled in his memoirs, his suspicions about the origins of the Tsaritsa HQ, 'It was decorated very much according to Stalin's taste. The walls had oak plywood trimming, just like Stalin's dachas. The place was very well equipped. It was even fitted out with a toilet.'[17] The implication was that had Hitler taken Moscow, Stalin was secretly planning to make a stand in his namesake city. This would have made sense if he intended to hold the line of the Volga and draw on the reserve armies assembling just to the east. Stalin understood that the loss of the city would cut the south off from the centre, and mean the loss of their main waterway as well as access to the south's oil. 'I never heard, before or since,' wrote Khrushchev, 'for whom this command post had originally been prepared.'[18]

Golikov, who had turned up in the city on Stalin's instructions as first deputy commander of the front, was ordered to stay and liaise with the defenders. It is probable that Khrushchev viewed Golikov as Stalin's stooge. He had known Golikov since the invasion of Poland and his days as head of Military Intelligence, but had no real impression of the man. It may have been that Khrushchev partly blamed Golikov's faulty intelligence for the mess they were now in. In a panic, Golikov pleaded with Khrushchev not to be left behind. 'Stalingrad is doomed!' he begged. 'Don't leave me behind. Don't destroy me. Let me go with you.'[19]

Khrushchev was unmoved, 'I never saw anyone, soldier or civilian, in such a state during the whole war.'

Golikov remained in the city, but was later relieved of his post having 'gone completely off his head'.[20]

Just before they moved, Khrushchev's faith in their ability to hold Stalingrad seemed to be flagging. Writer Konstantin Simonov, arriving at the Tsaritsa bunker, found he 'was gloomy and replied monosyllabically ... took out a packet of cigarettes and tried lighting one match after another, but the flame died at once because the ventilation in the tunnel was so bad'.[21]

Apart from the deteriorating situation in the city, Khrushchev had good reason to be despondent. Several days earlier, burning oil from a nearby storage dump had flooded the gorge and almost burned everyone alive. No one had thought to inform Simonov that they were evacuating, and in the morning he discovered everyone had gone.

Chuikov, the former deputy commander of the 64th Army and a veteran of the Russian Civil War and the Winter War, fully appreciated that his 62nd Army was being used as bait. 'Chuikov told us that he knew in September that the High Command was planning a counter-offensive,' recalled war correspondent Walter Kerr, during a visit to the city, 'and that his army's assignment was to hold Stalingrad and in doing so hold the German 6th Army where it could be struck in the counter-offensive.'[22] He also appreciated that he had insufficient forces for the job while significant reserves were massed to the north and south of the city.

Chuikov may have been a tough soldier, but the enormous stress he was under manifested itself as severe eczema. This resulted in his hands having to be bandaged. He and his men stayed put in the rubble that had once been Stalingrad. 'They made their gains not because we retreated,' recalled Chuikov, 'but because our men were killed faster than they could be replaced. The Germans advanced only over our dead. But we prevented him from breaking through to the Volga.'[23]

Kerr adds:

The Germans reached the river at only two places, to the north of the Barricades factory for a total distance of about four miles. The remaining sixteen miles of the Volga shore were never surrendered by the 62nd Army.[24]

The battle turned into bitter urban warfare that dragged on until 18 November, by which time the Germans had reached the limit of their offensive. From that point on they were on the defensive.

Stalingrad was Khrushchev's finest moment. He served in the thick of it as political advisor to Yeremenko, who remained responsible for the city until Zhukov launched his counter-offensive. Khrushchev even prevented Stalin from sacking Yeremenko, who unfairly felt he was not doing a good enough job and for his treatment of Golikov.

During the defence of Stalingrad, Khrushchev noticed a change in the Red Army:

When the Battle of Stalingrad started, our armed forces were still very weak. We were suffering from a shortage of heavy artillery, machine guns, anti-aircraft and anti-tank weapons. The Germans were still pressing us hard. But now our troops had begun to put up a stubborn resistance. There was none of the disorderly flight which had characterised the situation earlier in the war. Our troops were now fighting heroically and retreated only when there was no other way out. They retreated in a disciplined fashion from one position to another and never allowed themselves to be routed.[25]

The Red Army was to stand and die on the streets of Stalingrad. The Soviet leader had determined that, along with Leningrad and Moscow, the city was to be denied to Hitler.

10

DISASTER ON THE DON

While Hitler ignored the Wehrmacht's persistent manpower shortages, he had what General Halder called a 'pathological over-estimation of his own strength and a criminal under-estimation of the enemy's'. Halder recalled:

> Once when a quite objective report was read to him showing that still in 1942 Stalin would be able to muster from one to one and a quarter million fresh troops in the region north of Stalingrad and west of the Volga, not to mention half a million men in the Caucasus, and which provided proof that Russian output of front-line tanks amounted to at least 1,200 a month, Hitler flew at the man who was reading with clenched fists and foaming in the corners of his mouth and forbade him to read any more of such idiotic twaddle.
>
> You didn't have to have the gift of a prophet to foresee what would happen when Stalin unleashed those million and a half troops against Stalingrad and the Don flank.[1]

Hitler was simply not receptive to Halder's urgent warning that Stalin had created ten reserve armies with the equivalent of 100 divisions, and sacked him on 24 September 1942.

Halder appreciated that Stalin would never relinquish his namesake city and would do all he could to save it from Hitler's clutches. Formerly called Tsaritsyn, it had been renamed in honour of Stalin's victory over General Denikin's troops between the Don bend and the city during the Russian Civil War. Halder was alarmed by the striking similarities in 1942 – Stalin had exploited Denikin's weak defences along the Don, and Halder was very concerned by the prospect of the same thing happening again. The unfortunate Halder, after losing his job, was eventually arrested and sent to a concentration camp until he was liberated by the Americans at the end of the war.

Before mid-July 1942 a total of nineteen rifle divisions were assigned to the Stalingrad commanders from the Soviet Strategic Reserve, plus another sixteen regular divisions from the shattered front-line armies. Another fifty divisions were assigned up to 24 September 1942. After General Halder's dismissal a further twenty-nine rifle divisions were assigned to the Stalingrad command. This meant that 114 divisions were assigned to the Stalingrad Front alone, regardless of what was going on elsewhere on the Eastern Front. It could only spell disaster for Hitler.

By the autumn of 1942, the fate of Hitler's stalled ambitions for conquering the Soviet Union rested firmly on the shoulders of two ill-equipped Romanian armies. What followed was a disaster of epic proportions, heralding the slow death of the German Army on the Eastern Front. Hitler was about to rue the day he ever decided to rely on Antonescu, Horthy and Mussolini's Axis satellite armies.

Hitler's Eastern Front allies' acute shortcomings were no secret. His generals appreciated only too well that the Romanian 3rd and 4th Armies, the Hungarian 2nd Army and the Italian 8th Army were not even equivalent to one German corps. On top of their military shortcomings, the Germans also culturally looked down on their allies. Only the Romanian mountain troops and Slovak mobile forces were viewed with any degree of respect.

The Red Army soon targeted these satellite armies with propaganda leaflets urging them not to die for Hitler and his stooges. Hungarian minorities were particularly prone to desertion on the Eastern Front. Morale within the Hungarian forces became so bad that the authorities stopped the troops writing home. While the Romanian Army experienced problems with training and equipment, the Hungarians were under strength and poorly led, a factor that was common amongst all the satellite armies. Mussolini's army in the Soviet Union suffered from numerous inadequacies, especially in leadership and equipment. Overall, they all had a crucial deficiency in modern anti-tank weapons.

Stalin's operations during the summer of 1942 misled Hitler into believing that the full weight of any Soviet counter-stroke would fall on Army Group Centre. Instead, the Soviets gathered their forces for a strike toward Stalingrad and Army Group B. The Soviet South-Western Front and Stalingrad Front forces were to link up between Kalach and Sovietsky behind the Axis armies, thereby encircling the Germans at Stalingrad. Stavka knew that a successful offensive in the Stalingrad area would have one of two results – force the Germans to retreat, or fight from a pocket. Either way it was a winning scenario.

Stalin and Zhukov were concerned not only with local German efforts against Stalingrad, but the wholesale destruction of all German forces supporting the offensive. It was an ambitious undertaking intent on reversing the course of the war, which up to this time had been characterised by Hitler holding the strategic initiative. Operation Uranus was planned to reverse this trend. For Hitler, like Denikin before him, defeat was looming along the banks of the mighty River Don.

In the spring of 1942, Hitler ordered:

> In the first instance, units of our allies will be used to hold the Don Front … Allied troops will be mainly disposed so that the Hungarians are farthest north, then the Italians, and the Romanians furthest to the south-east.[2]

In June, the Hungarian 2nd Army under General Jany reached the front at Kursk and moved to hold the line along the Don, south of Voronezh. In the face of the Russian winter and T-34 tanks, Hungarian morale soon fell.

By the end of August, General Italo Gariboldi's Italian 8th Army had become a serious cause for concern to the Germans, convincing them that the Italians were not fit for warfare on the Eastern Front. The German deputy chief of staff, General Blumentritt, was appalled by what he found:

> General Halder had sent me on a flying visit to the Italian sector, as an alarming report had come in that the Russians had penetrated it. However, I found the attack had been made by only one Russian battalion, but an entire Italian division had bolted.[3]

It was evident that the rot had set in.

Blumentritt warned that the supply railheads were too far away, that there was little timber for building adequate defences and that it was not safe to hold such a long defensive flank over the winter. His boss, General Halder, agreed and urged Hitler to halt all offensive operations during the bad weather – he was promptly removed.

By October 1942 it was clear that Hitler's plans on the Eastern Front were starting to become unravelled. Enormous losses were forcing the Germans to go over to the defensive, abandoning large-scale offensive operations. This inevitably meant that they were losing the initiative. The Romanian 3rd Army, under Colonel General Dumitrescu, came back into the line in October 1942 to the north-west of Stalingrad. William Shirer observed, 'Even the rankest amateur strategist could see the growing danger to the German armies in southern Russia as Soviet resistance stiffened in the Caucasus and at Stalingrad and the season of the autumn rains approached.'[4]

To Dumitrescu's left was Mussolini's Italian 8th Army. Shirer adds:

Because of the bitter hostility of Romanians and Hungarians to each other their armies had to be separated by the Italians. Aside from their doubtful fighting qualities, all these armies were inadequately equipped, lacking armoured power, heavy artillery and mobility. Furthermore, they were spread out thinly.[5]

Another Romanian Corps, part of their 4th Army, moved into place on the southern flank, followed by a second in November, providing six divisions to the German 4th Panzer Army. Perhaps as window dressing, Hitler suggested that General Constantinescu's 4th Army should take charge of the 4th Panzer Army. He also proposed that the Romanian 3rd and 4th Armies along with the German 6th Army should form Army Group Don under Marshal Antonescu. The forthcoming Soviet offensive prevented such plans being implemented.

Von Manstein recalled:

> Every Commander-in-Chief must run risks if he wants to succeed. The risk undertaken by the Supreme Command in the late autumn of 1942, however, should never have consisted of tying down the most hard-hitting forces of Army Group B at Stalingrad over a long period in which it was content to leave the Don Front covered by such an easily destructible screen.[6]

Major General von Mellenthin noted somewhat despondently:

> It became known that Hungarian, Italian and Romanian armies had occupied positions on the Don from Voronezh southwards; this certainly did not serve to encourage the German troops. The fighting value of our allies was never overestimated, nor was there poor equipment calculated to enhance their reputation … In November a new panzer corps, consisting of a German and a Romanian armoured division, moved into the Don bend. This was the 48th Panzer Corps, and at the end of November I was appointed its chief of staff.[7]

All the chess pieces were now in place for the drama that was about to unfold. Soviet intelligence on enemy dispositions was good. Zhukov knew:

> The main forces of Army Group B were in the Middle Don area, at Stalingrad, and also southwards in the vicinity of Sarpinskiye Lakes. They comprised the 8th Italian Army, the 3rd and 4th Romanian armies and the German 6th and 4th Panzer armies. Each division held from 15 to 20 kilometres. The effective strength of this group totalled over one million officers and men, 675 tanks and assault weapons, over 10,000 guns and mortars. Numerically the confronting

forces were nearly equal, with the exception of a slight superiority in tanks on the Soviet side.[8]

Although Zhukov does not mention the presence of the Hungarian 2nd Army just to the north of the Italians, they were not to escape unscathed either.

According to Soviet figures, by early November 1942 German strength on the Eastern Front totalled about 6.2 million men organised into 266 divisions and equipped with 5,080 tanks and assault guns, 51,700 pieces of artillery and mortars and 3,500 combat aircraft. Soviet industrial muscle had ensured that, by this stage, the Red Army's massive losses of 1941 had been made good. Stalin's manpower stood at about 6.6 million men under arms equipped with 7,350 tanks, 77,800 guns and mortars and 4,500 combat aircraft. On top of this, Stalin still had considerable reserves.

The main attack of Stalin's' Operation Uranus was to be launched over 100 miles west of Stalingrad and would cut south-east. Unfortunately, the Romanian 3rd Army did not have the strength to occupy a 40-mile-long bend south of the Don, so this left the Red Army with the Serafimovich bridgehead, which was to provide the main springboard that would seal the fate of the Germans battling to capture Stalingrad.

General Dumitrescu, commander of the Romanian 3rd Army, was not blind to the threat. He had argued that the whole of the riverbank should be secured to provide an anti-tank obstacle at the end of September. The Germans' ability to furnish their Romanian allies with assistance was limited, as General Paulus' 6th Army and part of the 4th Panzer Army were entangled in fighting in the immediate Stalingrad area. Army Group A had been planning Operation Winter Tales, which would have launched the Italian 8th Army in an offensive against the Soviet bridgehead over the River Don in September, but it came to nothing, largely because the Italians were not up to the job.

Major General von Mellenthin, chief of staff of the newly arrived 48th Panzer Corps, had a different view of the situation:

Nobody could understand why Romanian formations had given up part of the huge Don bend, allegedly to save troops for other purposes, but actually yielding an area which it would have been easy to defend, and thus handing over a most valuable bridgehead to the Russians.[9]

Stalin's build-up did not go unnoticed and the Romanians reported it to Army Group B on 29 October. Marshal Antonescu even approached Hitler about the dangers facing his forces, but to no avail. The Luftwaffe and Romanian Air Force witnessed what was going on and diverted some of their support from the

6th Army to attack the gathering Red Army opposite the Romanian 3rd Army. The Soviets, however, continued their massive preparations largely unhindered.

Halder's replacement was General Kurt Zeitzler, who had been serving as von Rundstedt's chief of staff in the west. When Zeitzler plucked up courage to advise that General Paulus that his 6th Army be withdrawn from Stalingrad to the elbow in the Don considering the threat to the northern flank, Hitler remained unreceptive. 'Where the German soldier sets foot, there he remains,' was the Führer's terse reply.[10]

Zeitzler fretted about the ongoing Soviet build-up in the Stalingrad area. Army intelligence had informed him that Stalin had gathered thirteen armies and thousands of tanks. An unconcerned Führer, accompanied by Keitel and Jodl, left Rastenburg on 7 November 1942 and travelled by train to Munich to deliver his annual speech celebrating the anniversary of his failed Beer Hall Putsch.

During his speech, the following evening in the Löwenbräukeller, he showed just how outwardly relaxed he was about Stalingrad:

> I wanted to reach the Volga, and I wanted to get there at a particular spot, at a particular city. It just so happened that the city bore the name of Stalin himself. … it is a very important strategic point. I could cut off 30 million tons of river traffic at that point, including nine million tons of oil traffic. All the grain from the vast open spaces of the Ukraine and the Kuban flows though there. That is where all the manganese ore is taken … All there is left to take is a couple of little scraps of land. […] Time is of no importance.[11]

Hitler was soon preoccupied with the Allied landings in North Africa, which commenced on 8 November and threatened to trap Rommel in Libya.

At the very end of his speech made the day before for the 25th anniversary of the Bolshevik Revolution, Stalin hinted that something was about to happen, 'The day is not far distant when the enemy will feel the force of new blows of the Red Army. There will be celebrations in our streets.'[12]

Colonel Reinhard Gehlen and his Foreign Armies East Intelligence Branch tried vainly to warn of the developing threat in the Stalingrad area:

> By 9 November 1942, ten days before the beginning of the Soviet counter-attack, which was to lead eventually to the Stalingrad disaster, my branch had clearly predicted precisely where the blow would fall and which of our armies would be affected. The Stalingrad tragedy marked the turn of the tide in the eastern campaign; it heralded the final defeat of the Third Reich. Since the complete file of our branch's 'Brief Enemy Situation Reports' is

available, it can be seen that our claim to have given good warning is more than substantiated.[13]

Zhukov knew from the interrogation of prisoners that Romanian combat effectiveness was poor and that unless the Germans rushed in reinforcements the Red Army would have considerable local numerical superiority. Lieutenant General N.F. Vatutin's South-Western Front, spearheaded by the 1st Guards Army and 5th Tank Army, was to fall on the 3rd Romanian Army, pierce its defences and race south-east to reach the Don's southern loop at Kalach. This would cut off the Germans' lines of retreat from Stalingrad. The Soviets also held a bridgehead at Beketonskaya, 6 miles south of Stalingrad on the western banks of the Volga River. South of the city, the 4th Romanian Army was to receive similar treatment at the hands of the Soviets' 51st, 57th and 64th Armies.

Stalin's artillery and rocket launchers opened fire on the Romanian 3rd Army's positions at 0630 hrs on 19 November 1942. Their log bunkers and dugouts were blown apart as the barrage ranged in. Romanian soldiers staggered out into the maelstrom in a deafened daze as their inadequate defences collapsed in the face of Stalin's concerted onslaught. Then came the Red Army's T-34 tanks, rumbling across the snow-draped landscape followed by supporting infantry. Many of the Romanian defenders took fright and surrendered on the spot or fled in panic.

The Soviets broke through in two places. This was achieved by Lieutenant General P.L. Romanenko's 5th Tank Army launching itself from the bridgehead south-west of Serafimovich and Major General I.M. Chistyakov's 21st Army attacking from the Kletskaya bridgehead to the south-east.

Some Romanian units fought bravely and attempted to hold their ground. The Romanian 13th Infantry Division beat off a Soviet infantry attack, followed by a tank attack. The diary of a Romanian artillery officer recalls the sense of terror and helplessness experienced by most of the 3rd Army on 19 November, 'Gun-fire so heavy the ground shudders and the windows shatter ... Enemy tanks appear ... raced through our positions ... our guns having no effect'. The following day, he noted with despair, 'Currently we are encircled by enemy troops. In pocket are the 5th, 6th and 15th Divisions and remnants of the 13th Division'.[14]

The Romanian 1st Tank Division and 7th Cavalry Division were thrown into the fight to halt Romanenko. The tank division was brushed aside and the Romanian 5th Corps headquarters overrun. Some of the Romanians fled, but most simply threw away their weapons and surrendered.

While German troops had suffered the previous winter before Moscow for the want of adequate winter clothing, a year on, certainly little had changed for

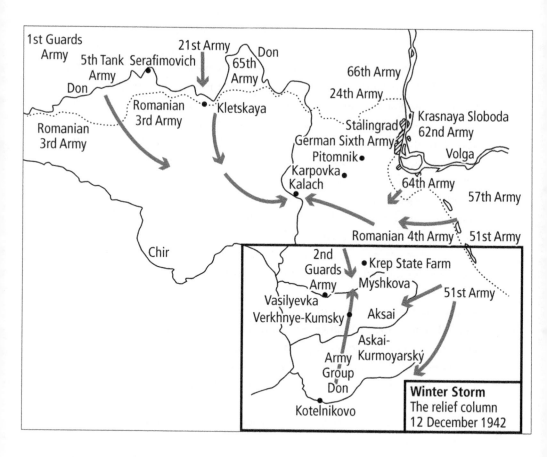

Operation Uranus, December 1942.

the Romanians. Petr Zhulyev, a gunner with the 21st Army moving forward with his battery, almost felt sorry for them:

> More and more often we came across Romanian soldiers with white flags. They were a laughable sight. [...] I have to say that the Romanians did not look much like proper soldiers. They were like one big gypsy caravan, and their uniforms were a strange mish-mash: battered sheepskin hats, all sorts of rags around their necks and feet. They weren't enjoying the Russian frosts.[15]

On their way back from Munich, Hitler and his entourage had stopped off at his mountain residence at the Berghof near Berchtesgaden to take the Alpine air. A phone call from Zeitzler informed them of the alarming news. Despite what was happening, there was no sense of urgency at the Berghof. Hitler was adamant he would not withdraw from the Volga and should the 6th Army become surrounded, despite the weather, it could be resupplied from the air. Hitler did not return to Rastenburg until four days after Stalin's Stalingrad Offensive had commenced. By this time the situation was catastrophic.

General von Weichs, commander of Army Group B on which the 6th Army, 4th Panzer and the Hungarian, Italian and Romanian forces relied, was immediately alert to the situation. On the night of the Soviet offensive he issued the following orders, 'The situation developing on the front of the 3rd Romanian Army dictates radical measures in order to disengage forces quickly to screen the flank of 6th Army and to assure the protection of supplies'.[16] He went on to order units to bolster the Romanians, not realising that the Red Army was planning to attack his right flank the very next day.

Just two days after the assault started, the writing was on the wall for the beleaguered Romanian 3rd Army. The Romanian artillery officer wrote:

> Friends staring at snapshots of their loved ones, wives and children. It hurts to think of my mother, brother, sisters and relatives. We're putting on our best clothing, even two sets of underclothes. We figure very tragic end in store ... Everyone's talking and arguing about our situation ... but we haven't lost hope ... We think German troops will come to our aid.[17]

However, the Germans were far too busy fending off Soviet attacks to worry about the fate of the trapped Romanians. General Mazarini, 5th Division commander, assumed overall command of the 3rd Army pocket and after conferring with his fellow officers accepted the Soviet offer of surrender on 23 November. The Romanians' fighting spirit was crushed as Henry Shapiro, Moscow correspondent for *United Press*, witnessed at first hand, 'Well behind the fighting-line there were now thousands of Romanians wandering about the steppes, cursing the Germans and desperately looking for Russian feeding points, and anxious to formally surrender'.[18]

The Soviet 21st and 5th Armies captured 30,000 officers and men, including several generals, as well as much of their equipment. General Mihail Lascăr, with the remains of four divisions, found himself trapped between Chir and Kletskaya. The Soviets called on him to surrender, but he directed 4,000 men to try to reach von Mellenthin's 48th Panzer Corps before handing himself over. By the end of November, the remnants of the Romanian 3rd Army had been driven back between Chernyshevskaya to the north and Oblivskaya to the south.

Marshal Zhukov confidently reported:

The enemy buckled and, panic-stricken, fled or surrendered. German units holding positions behind the Romanian forces, mounted a powerful counter-attack in an attempt to check our advance, but were crushed by the 1st and 26th Tank Corps. The tactical breakthrough on the South-Western Front was now an accomplished fact.[19]

On the night of 22/23 November, the 26th Tank Corps' advance guard seized a bridge over the southern leg of the Don. The German guards mistook the attack for an exercise using captured Soviet tanks and the armour rumbled over the bridge. Kalach lay just 2km away, but the German defenders were not so easily overwhelmed until Soviet reinforcements arrived.

It seems that, despite the lessons of Moscow, Hitler was once more happy to let his soldiers freeze to death. 'The German prisoners I saw were mostly young fellows, and very miserable,' observed Henry Shapiro. 'In thirty degrees of frost they wore ordinary coats, and had blankets tied round their necks. They had hardly any winter clothing at all.'[20]

Far to the south-east, the Romanian 4th Army suffered a similar fate. Just twenty-four hours after the South-Western and Don Fronts had opened the offensive, the 51st, 57th and 64th Armies of Yeremenko's Stalingrad Front joined the attack. Initially he was held up for two hours by thick fog and he soon had the Kremlin breathing down his neck demanding he 'get on with it'. Yeremenko recalled:

> It got to nine o'clock. Everybody was nervously awaiting the signal. The infantry were hugging the ground, ready to go in. The gunners loaded their cannon and stood to, holding the cord. From somewhere behind us came the growl of tanks as their engines warmed up.
>
> Then the fog started to lift and scatter. At 09.30 the order was given to start the barrage at ten. [...] The katyushas played their music first. Then the artillery and the mortars began their busy work. [...] Out of their foxholes rose the endless lines of our soldiers. I could hear the long, continuous cries of 'hurrah!' and the workmanlike clatter of the tanks.[21]

Soldiers of the Romanian 20th Infantry Division fought bravely against the advancing 64th Army, but with completely inadequate anti-tank guns did little to hinder the Soviets' progress. Major General Tolbukhin's 57th Army swung north-west toward Kalach, while on his left flank the 64th, under Lieutenant General Shumilov, drove on Gavrilovka and Varvarovka.

In the path of Major General Trufanov's 51st Army lay the Romanian 4th Army. His objective was Abganerovo, well behind Romanian lines. On the whole, the Romanians surrendered and many were shot out of hand. Within a few hours 10,000 Romanian troops had been taken prisoner. The Romanian 1st, 2nd, 18th and 20th Divisions were steamrollered out of the way, as was the German 29th Motorised Division. In an attempt to stem the 57th Army's advance on Kalach, the 16th and 24th Panzer Divisions, redirected from Stalingrad, foolishly got in the way.

Günther Toepke, 6th Army's quartermaster, was near Pitomnik Airfield to the west of Stalingrad on 21 November and had then driven to the south-west to their main supply dump. Passing through Kalach, he heard rumours of Soviet advances. Heading south and then east he was alarmed by reports of Soviet tanks in the area:

> Suddenly it dawned on me. Damn it all, it looked like the Russians were attempting a large-scale pincher movement to box the 6th Army into Stalingrad. Kalach was the meeting point.
> […] I knew that there were no troops there in the south apart from Romanians. So the Russians had gone for the Romanians both in the north and the south, and had apparently broken through. […] The divisions inside Stalingrad had no idea of what was going on … in their rear.[22]

By 1600 hrs on 23 November the Soviets were near Sovietsky, to the east of Kalach. It was not long before a link-up was effected with the South-Western Front, trapping the Germans deployed between the Don and the Volga. The next stage was to destroy the German forces trapped in the *Kessel* (Cauldron), as the Stalingrad pocket became known.

The Romanian Army on the Eastern Front had gone from twenty-two divisions to just four – nine had been decimated in the fighting and another nine had simply run away. Also, within five days the Red Army had succeeded in encircling twenty German divisions between the Don and the Volga.

Colonel Gehlen, who had done all he could to warn of the impending disaster, observed:

> The two arms of the Soviet pincher movement met at Kalach, encircling our 6th Army at Stalingrad and a number of lesser formations – a quarter of a million of our finest troops, with 100 tanks, 1,800 guns and over 10,000 motorised vehicles. The rest of the tragedy belongs to history.
> I was understandably bitter about the outcome.[23]

General Weichs sent the following to the German High Command: 'With the total dissolution of the Romanian 3rd Army, 6th Army is now the only fighting formation capable of inflicting damage on the enemy.'[24] Weichs accepted General Paulus' proposal for the fighting withdrawal of the 6th Army, knowing full well that it was impossible to supply his twenty divisions by air. It was clear that the 6th Army would run out of ammunition before help could fight their way through to them, so Weichs suggested Paulus and his men be allowed to break out in a south-westerly direction.

Paulus signalled Hitler on 23 November:

The Army is facing annihilation at short notice unless the enemy, who is attacking from the south and the west, can be destroyed by a concentration of all our forces. To that end all divisions from Stalingrad should be withdrawn forthwith as well as the necessary larger forces on the northern front.[25]

Hitler was having none of it, the 6th Army would stand and fight.

General von Mellenthin states, 'According to information provided by the quartermaster general's branch, 270,000 men found themselves encircled on 24 November 1942. The destruction of these divisions was bound to alter the whole balance of power on the Eastern Front.'[26] Surrounded at Stalingrad were 6th Army's HQ staff, the HQ staff of five corps, thirteen infantry divisions, three panzer divisions, three motorised divisions and an aircraft division. These included elements of the 4th Panzer Army that had been cut off as well. There were also two weak Romanian divisions and a Croat regiment. The suffering of the German troops before Moscow was nothing compared to the depravations endured by those trapped in Stalingrad.

Reichsmarschall Göring boastfully promised Hitler that the Luftwaffe would save the 6th Army. After all, he had successfully rescued 100,000 troops trapped at Kholm and Demyansk, south of Leningrad. But this time it was a promise he could not keep; the task was simply too enormous. During a conference with Hitler on 27 November, Zeitzler called Göring a liar when the reichsmarschall reassured the Führer he could keep Paulus resupplied. Looking at the rotund Göring, who was one of the best-fed men in the whole of the Third Reich, the cruel irony of the situation was not lost on Zeitzler.

Paulus estimated he needed around 600 tons of supplies a day to stay in the fight. The Luftwaffe claimed they could manage just 300 tons, but only about 70 tons was flown in daily. There were simply not enough transport aircraft available and those that flew the air bridge were rapidly shot from the sky.

At this crucial moment, the Anglo-American landings in North Africa impacted on the battle for Stalingrad. Some 500 of Göring's transport aircraft were used to rush German troops to Tunisia to halt the Allied advance from Algiers; 400 of these were diverted from the Stalingrad air bridge.

The reorganised and vengeful Red Air Force prowled the 200-mile long air corridor setting about transports and escorts with equal ferocity. In futilely trying to maintain the air bridge, Göring lost 490 transport planes and many of his crews. The Luftwaffe's greatest achievement was to evacuate 29,000 wounded, but this would be little consolation.

Elsewhere, Stalin's other winter offensives were also major undertakings. While they cleared the approaches to Moscow of the Wehrmacht, they did not achieve their principal aim of defeating Army Group Centre. This was partly because of the failure of the flank offensives, which simply served to dissipate Red Army efforts and produced few operational results.

On 25 November 1942, Stalin launched Operation Mars, designed to destroy the German forces in the Rzhev salient. This involved the Kalinin Fronts' 22nd (supported by the 3rd Mechanised Corps), the 39th and 41st Armies (supported by the 1st Mechanised Corps), as well as the Western Front's 20th, 31st and 30th Armies (supported by the 5th, 6th and 8th Tank Corps and the 2nd Guards Cavalry Corps). The Soviet 3rd Shock Army also attacked German forces at Velikiye Luki.

The Western Front's 5th and 33rd Armies, with the 9th and 10th Tank Corps supported by 3rd Tank Army, were assigned to a follow-up operation designated Jupiter, along the Vyazma axis, which was to complete the destruction of Army Group Centre forces in the Rzhev–Vyazma salient. Unlike Uranus, this offensive was not destined to be a resounding success. The intended victims were not ill-prepared and ill-equipped Romanians, but battle-hardened German divisions who were well dug in. Furthermore, help was at hand. At Rzhev, the German 9th Army had the 1st and 9th Panzer and Grossdeutschland and 14th Panzergrenadiers in operational reserve, while the 19th and 20th Panzer were also within reach; the Western Front was faced by the 5th Panzer Division.

On 25 November, the 22nd and 41st Armies, spearheaded by the two mechanised corps, broke German defences north and south of Beylic; only bad weather and determined German resistance finally brought them to a halt. To the north, the 39th Army hit the Germans north-east of Rzhev, while to the west the 39th Army struggled to cut the Rzhev–Olenio Railway.

During December, German reserves succeeded in destroying the 1st Mechanised Corps and the 6th Rifle Corps. The 3rd Mechanised was driven back and the 30th and 39th Armies contained. The Western Front alone lost 42,000 dead and 1,655 tanks by 14 December. Stalin was not altogether happy, but elsewhere things were definitely going his way.

Meanwhile, approximately a quarter of a million men were now very firmly trapped in the Stalingrad *Kessel*, including up to 13,000 Romanians. Those Romanian soldiers in the pocket proved just as unreliable as those originally deployed either side of the 6th Army. The German 297th Infantry Division, under attack from the Soviet 64th Army, soon found it had a half a mile gap in its flank after the Romanian 82nd Regiment fled. Soviet tanks poured through the hole and only a determined counter-attack by the Germans drove the Red Army back. Paulus and those under his command had little choice but tough it out while their superiors decided what to do next. If the Luftwaffe could not keep the *Kessel* resupplied, then it was imperative a relief force reached it as soon as possible.

II

NO CHAMPAGNE OR COGNAC

Once back at Rastenburg, Hitler wasted a whole week after Paulus had been cut off. His relief of Stalingrad, Operation *Wintergewitter* (Winter Storm), was first planned in early December, but it was almost two weeks before an assault force could be put together. In attempting to rescue Paulus' men, von Manstein cleverly tried to force Hitler's hand into permitting a withdrawal from the city. Von Manstein's intention was that while he cut his way to the north-east and protected his flanks, Paulus should fight his way to the south-west to link up with him.

Von Manstein knew perfectly well that it would take all the 6th Army's offensive strength and the last of its panzers to facilitate the link-up. This meant Paulus would be unable to hold the eastern and northern perimeters around the Stalingrad pocket for more than a few days, once the Red Army was alerted to what was happening. Forced to conduct a fighting retreat, Hitler would have no choice but to give up Stalingrad and let the 6th Army escape. This, of course, could not be spelt out explicitly in von Manstein's operational orders or Hitler would have immediately countermanded such a move. It was up to Paulus to co-operate with von Manstein's subterfuge and save his men.

Von Manstein's highly capable and experienced 11th Army HQ was hurriedly formed into new Army Group Don to co-ordinate Winter Storm. This mission was assigned to the rump of the 4th Panzer Army remaining outside Stalingrad, now grandly named Army Group Hoth under General Herman Hoth. It was intended that Hoth would make a single concerted thrust using General Friedrich Kirchner's 57th Panzer Corps, comprising the 6th and 23rd Panzer Divisions and later bolstered by the 17th Panzer.

Looking at the map, both von Manstein and Hoth realised that the shortest route to Stalingrad was from Nizhne-Chirskaya. However, this was not the best path for success. In the region lay the 5th Tank and 5th Shock Armies of

Lieutenant N.F. Vatutin's South-Western Front, the key players in the success of Operation Uranus. It was quickly decided that Winter Storm was to be conducted not from Nizhne-Chirskaya but further south from Kotelnikovo. The logic was that it would give the relief force a greater element of surprise, the going was better, and Major General N.I. Trufanov's 51st Army, part of Yeremenko's Stalingrad Front, was the weakest of the Soviet armies in the region.

The situation for the trapped Germans was desperate and everyone on the ground appreciated that this was a one-shot deal. In the north-west, the flanks of Army Group Hoth were to be protected by General Karl Hollidt's Army Group, while in the south-east the remains of General C.A. Constantinescu's Romanian 4th Army would hold the Red Army at bay. Von Manstein was uncertain just how long they could successfully defend their flanks.

After assessing his forces, it was depressingly clear to von Manstein that he simply did not have the strength to cut his way through to the 6th Army:

> When Hitler rejected all Don Army Group's requests for the speedy reinforcement of 4th Panzer Army at the end of December, the fate of 6th Army was finally sealed. In vain had we staked the last available man and the last available shell on the liberation of 6th Army! In vain had we striven till the last possible moment to get the relief operation carried out and thrown the fate of the whole Army Group into the balance to do so![1]

With just 230 tanks of the 6th and 23rd Panzer plus air support from the Luftwaffe's 4th Fliegerkorps, the operation commenced on 12 December. Von Manstein recalled this perilous and desperate mission, which cast a shadow over all German forces in the region:

> We and the enemy now set off on a race for life or death. Our own goal was to save the life of 6th Army. But to do so we stake the very existence not only of Don Army Group but also Army Group A.
>
> It was a race to decide whether the relief group of 4th Panzer Army would manage to join hands with 6th Army east of the Don before the enemy forced us to break off the operation. This he might achieve by overrunning our weak front on the Chir or the left wing of the Army Group (and possibly the right wing of Army Group B as well) and putting himself in a position to cut all the rear communications of Don Army Group and Army Group A.[2]

Initially, Winter Storm made some headway through the Soviet 126th and 302nd Rifle Divisions, but Trufanov had the 4th and 13th Mechanised in reserve. Once

Kirchner was over the River Aksai these units began to make their presence felt. The Soviets quickly realised what was going on and ensured that Yeremenko not only committed his 4th Cavalry Corps, but the front was bolstered with the 7th Tank Corps and the 2nd Guards Army belonging to the South-Western Front.

Colonel Helmut Ritgen with the 6th Panzer recalled:

> From the late morning of 19 December 11th Panzer-Regt. was engaged in attacks. The Soviets finally withdrew after prolonged, hard fighting, despite the deployment in this sector of Guards units. The tanks struggled forward through an area of ravines, treacherous obstacles with a thinly iced snow cover.[3]

They were then directed to Wassiljewka to create a bridgehead, which required clearing the Soviets from Hill 147.

Against such forces, the likelihood of von Manstein making any significant progress seemed very small. Indeed, the relief force was stopped between Kapinsky and Nizhne-Kumsky along the line of the River Myshkova. In an act of pure fantasy, Hitler clung to the notion that the 6th Army would be relieved and the Red Army thrown out of Stalingrad.

In the meantime, having smashed the Romanians so effectively, the Red Army set about crushing the other satellite armies. Operation Saturn, which followed the encirclement of Stalingrad, was to smash Mussolini's 8th Army to create a larger pocket of trapped German forces. On 16 December, the Soviet troops crashed into the Italian front line. The following day it fell to pieces, and on 18 December the ring closed south of Boguchar, and the 8th Army under General Italo Gariboldi rapidly collapsed into a state of chaos. The Italian 2nd and 35th Corps disintegrated almost immediately, leaving the Alpine Corps on its own and a massive hole in the front line. The Italian-Croat Legion, fighting alongside the Italian 3rd Mobile Division, was also destroyed during the flight from the Don.

By 19 December the Red Army had penetrated 40 miles and the 3rd Guards Army had captured 15,000 frightened Italian prisoners at Verchnyakovski. The dazed survivors from the 8th Army were regrouped in Ukraine, but Hitler had such little faith in their fighting ability that they were packed back off to Italy. German reinforcements had to be rushed in, including the 6th Panzer Division, to prevent the remains of the Romanian Army being cut off on the upper reaches of the Chir River.

Hoth spent a week cutting his way to within some 40 miles of the southern perimeter of Stalingrad. By 19 December he was within 30 miles and his force's artillery flashes and flares were tantalisingly visible at night to the men of the 6th Army. It was at this stage that von Manstein claims he directed the 6th Army to 'commence breaking through to the south-west forthwith'. This is not strictly true, as his signal to Paulus was very ambiguous. It stated that the 6th Army was to begin the 'attack earliest possible' and if necessary there should be a 'sector-by-sector evacuation of the fortress area'.

Paulus read this to mean that he should let von Manstein know as soon as he had authorisation from Hitler to move. He chose to ignore the implied order to act now, which was made apparent by the instructions from von Manstein to deploy all his artillery and heavy equipment into the south-western corner of the *Kessel*. Paulus must have understood what this meant, but again he chose to ignore it as it would compromise his ability to hold onto Stalingrad. The tragedy was that neither was prepared to openly defy Hitler.

Hoth's 4th Panzer Army did not have the strength to go any further. A two-day window of opportunity existed, but Hitler refused to take it. If Paulus had acted some of his men would almost certainly have been able to fight their way through to Hoth and this could have saved thousands of German lives. Together, Hoth and Paulus could then have conducted a fighting withdrawal.

A highly despondent Paulus claimed that he was not in a position to break out. He argued that he had insufficient fuel for his remaining panzers to bridge the gap. They had enough for just 20 miles. Von Manstein reasoned that if Paulus threw his remaining 100 panzers to the south-west this would alleviate the pressure on Hoth who would be able to cover the remaining distance. It was a highly dangerous gamble but it was better than the alternative. Paulus made it clear he would not move until the 4th Panzer Army was 20 miles away or the Luftwaffe had brought his fuel stocks up to the required level. Both were simply impossible demands, and von Manstein must have felt that Paulus was being spineless.

Despairing, Zeitzler finally gained Hitler's permission on 21 December for Paulus to break out, as long as his forces kept control of the city as part of Operation Thunderclap. The chief of staff was nearly driven 'insane' by such a ridiculous demand. At this stage, Hoth still had up to 25 miles to go; if he could cover some of this then Paulus might still have a chance of linking up. However, the Soviet 2nd Guards Army had been redeployed from the destruction of the 6th Army to stop Hoth. The three corps of the 2nd Guards were reinforced by the 7th Tank Corps and the 6th Mechanised Corps, meaning Hoth could not move forward nor could he stay put.

It was vital that Paulus abandon Stalingrad and implement an evacuation under Thunderclap. 'On the following evening,' Zeitzler says, 'I begged Hitler to authorise the break-out. I pointed out that this was absolutely our last chance to save the two hundred thousand men of Paulus' army.' He adds:

Hitler would not give way. In vain I described to him conditions inside the so-called fortress: the despair of the starving soldiers, their loss of confidence in the Supreme Command, the wounded expiring for the lack of proper attention while thousands froze to death. He remained as impervious to arguments of this sort as to those of others which I had advanced.[4]

As time ran out, Hitler remained in denial. His actions could have but one outcome. General von Mellenthin remembered:

With a heavy heart Manstein was compelled to detach the 6th Panzer Division from Hoth's Army and send it north-west by forced marches to try and stem the Russian flood. This was the best division at Hoth's disposal, it was still intact, and if it had remained under his command it is possible that he would have broken through to Paulus.[5]

Ritgen, concluding the account of the attempted relief of Stalingrad, says:

6th Panzer Division had approached within 48km [29 miles] of Stalingrad, but its impetus had been used up. The advance could not be maintained, and the Soviets built up a strong defence. For three days the division held its bridgehead in the hope that the Stalingrad garrison would break out and link up with them. The break-out never happened. On 23 December, deeply grieved the division withdrew.[6]

By this point, Winter Storm had completely ground to a halt and in desperation von Manstein hoped Paulus might try to reach the Myshkova. This was the only prospect of saving some of the 6th Army, but Paulus adhered to orders and refused to move. His opportunity rapidly evaporated as the Red Army commenced major flanking offensives around Army Groups Hollidt and Hoth, which pushed the Germans back south of Kotelnikovo by 31 December.

In the Stalingrad pocket Hans-Erdmann Schönbeck, a 20-year-old officer with 24th Panzer Division, remembered:

The noise of battle from the relief army had been getting closer day by day. We geared up for the last leap westwards, to meet our liberators. But only in our minds, for we knew that were almost out of fuel and ammo. With the first day of Christmas came the full, awful certainty. The relief troops were unable to make it, the battle sounds were getting fainter and moving to the west. Our thoughts of escape had been in vain.[7]

After its liberation Walter Kerr, a reporter with the *New York Herald Tribune*, was invited to visit Kotelnikovo. He recalled the journey witnessing the detritus of war:

> As we drove across the Kalmuk steppes we passed some of the great battle-fields south of Stalingrad. There was almost no snow on the ground. As far as you could see there was brown steppe grass showing through the white. Then we would pass an area where a tank battle had taken place, and you could almost reconstruct the scene by the position of the damaged machines. Forty or fifty Russian tanks would be scattered about, all pointing toward the west – the direction they were headed when stopped by anti-tank shells or bombs. The thirty or forty yards beyond them, would be fifty or sixty German machines, pointing to the east, rusty, burned out and useless. Here and there were smashed anti-tank guns, hundreds of empty shell-cases, with the bodies of their crews spread around for seventy-five feet. It was over this area the Russian forces south of Stalingrad had moved in the early days of the 19 November counter-offensive.[8]

Zeitzler, having singularly failed to influence the Führer, in the name of solidarity with the 6th Army went on hunger strike at the end of December. He insisted on only eating the same rations as those being issued in Stalingrad. It is unlikely that he was only consuming 100g of bread and defrosted horsemeat daily, but he began to visibly lose weight. 'He did not succeed in persuading Hitler to change his mind,' noted Guderian.[9] By 5 January, Hitler was tired of Zeitzler's behaviour and ordered him to eat properly. Bizarrely, Hitler then instructed that no champagne or cognac be drunk over the next few weeks. At least the Führer had the good grace to acknowledge that there was no cause for celebration. He did not, however, change his mind about the fate of the 6th Army.

Rokossovsky massed some 5,000 guns ready to finish Paulus. However, he could see little point in expending further lives and ammunition in liquidating the *Kessel*. Von Manstein's relief effort had been abandoned so there was clearly nowhere for Paulus and his men to go. On 8 January 1943, Rokossovsky drafted surrender terms and sent them with three officers under a white flag to Paulus' northern perimeter. Rokossovsky stated:

> The situation of your troops is desperate. They are suffering from hunger, sickness and cold. The cruel Russian winter has scarcely yet begun. [...] Your soldiers are unprovided with winter clothing and are living in appalling sanitary conditions ... Your situation is hopeless, and any further resistance senseless.[10]

He went on to say that he would 'guarantee the lives' of those who surrendered. If they did not comply, Rokossovsky spelt out in no uncertain terms what would happen:

> If you choose to reject our proposal for your capitulation, be warned that the forces of the Red Army and the Red Air Force will be compelled to take steps to destroy the surrounded German troops, and that you will bear the responsibility for their annihilation.[11]

Paulus was given twenty-four hours, but the decision was not his. After the text was signalled to Rastenburg the response was negative. Rokossovsky waited another day, then on 10 January his guns opened up a massive artillery bombardment. The Red Air Force also joined in.

Stalin ensured there was no let-up from the unrelenting pressure being exerted by the Red Army across the Eastern Front. Stavka unleashed a third major offensive on 15 January 1943, south of Voronezh against Horthy's Hungarian 2nd Army. Major General von Mellenthin recalls in his memoirs:

> The Hungarian troops were of a better quality than the Romanians or Italians, but they could not withstand the flood. The Russian columns poured through a gap 175 miles wide, and by the end of January had captured Kursk, and were over the Donetz to the south-east of Kharkov.[12]

Horthy's forces lost 30,000 casualties, 50,000 POWs and all their heavy equipment. It was the worst military disaster ever suffered by the Hungarian Army, which was quick to blame Hitler for abandoning them to their fate. Horthy ordered the remains of the 2nd Army home in March, leaving behind two weak corps for half-hearted security duties. The Führer had no sympathy for the suffering and losses endured by Antonescu, Horthy and Mussolini's troops. 'I never want to see another soldier of our Eastern allies on the Eastern Front,' he lamented, after these calamities.[13] He only had himself to blame.

One of the very last to fly out of Stalingrad on 20 January before the airfield was overrun was Captain Bernd Freytag von Loringhoven. He had been commanding a much-depleted panzer battalion and his conduct had impressed his superiors. He was entrusted with a special life-saving mission to take final despatches and messages to von Manstein. Loringhoven was relieved but felt dreadfully guilty about leaving his men. He recalled, 'They wished me good luck, without a trace of envy.'[14]

The filthy, unshaven, half-starved Loringhoven, weighing just 52kg, arrived in Melitopol still in his lice-ridden panzer overalls. He immediately briefed von Manstein on the conditions in the pocket, then:

I explained with some emotion how the majority of soldiers of the 6th Army still believed, with an iron will, the Führer's promise to rescue them from this hell. [...] Manstein heard me out attentively but without reacting or displaying the slightest emotion.[15]

In the Stalingrad pocket things went from bad to worse. Perhaps surprisingly those remaining Axis forces bravely fought and died alongside the Germans. Don Headquarters reported on 24 January 1943, 'Romanian 1st Division and Romanian 20th Division fought to the last with distinction, shoulder to shoulder with their German comrades'.[16] Two days later, it added:

Croatian 369th Infantry Regiment participated in the fighting around Stalingrad with 1st Croatian Artillery Division, and distinguished itself outstandingly. Heavy enemy artillery fire over the entire town area. Defence of same massively hampered because of 30,000–40,000 unattended wounded and scattered personnel. [...] Apart from a few scraps, all rations have been used up.[17]

In a triumphal Order of the Day issued by Stalin on 25 January 1943, he informed the country:

As a result of two months of offensive engagements, the Red Army has broken through the defences of the German-fascist troops on a wide front, routed 102 divisions, captured over 200,000 prisoners, 13,000 guns and a large quantity of their war material, and advanced 252 miles. Our troops have won an important victory. The offensive of our troops continues.[18]

The Red Army broke through to the Volga in the area of the Mamayev Kurgan on 26 January, splitting German resistance and creating two smaller *kessels*, in the north and south of the city. Paulus' forces were then further isolated in three small pockets by the 28th. Just two days later, it was the tenth anniversary of the Nazis coming to power.

Paulus' divisional commanders did everything they could. General von Hartmann, commanding the 71st Infantry Division, was shot in the head during the bitter close-quarter fighting. Other generals took their own lives or were overrun and captured. The commander of the 297th Infantry Division, General von Drebber was taken in his command post. In desperation, Paulus signalled Hitler:

Troops are without ammunition and food. We have contact with some elements of six divisions only. There are signs of disintegration on the southern, western and northern fronts. Unified command is no longer possible. Little change on the eastern side. We have 18,000 wounded who are without any kind of bandages or medicines at all. […] Collapse is inevitable. The Army requests permission to surrender so as to save the lives of those that remain.[19]

A few desperate bands of German soldiers attempted to escape their fate. Breaking west, they were swiftly killed or captured. Deputy Chief Quartermaster Karl Binder from the 305th Infantry Division managed to get 30 miles to the west of Stalingrad before his group was caught by the Red Army at Karpovka. Binder, who was photographed on Christmas Eve, at that stage looked far from malnourished. During the second week of January, he had managed to secure two and half weeks' worth of rations for his division from the last airfield before it was overrun, it had done them no good.

Von Manstein's efforts to break through to the beleaguered 6th Army were nullified by Hitler's stubborn refusal to allow them to break out. It was a cruel death sentence. Newly promoted Field Marshal Friedrich Paulus surrendered on 31 January 1943, and the 6th Army ceased to exist after the loss 60,000–100,000 dead and 120,000 starving, frostbitten POWs. Stalin signalled General Rokossovsky to say, 'I congratulate you and the troops of the Don Front on the successful completion of the annihilation of the enemy forces surrounded at Stalingrad'.[20]

News of Hitler's humiliation spread quickly. In Bucharest, Iosif Hechter recorded in his journal:

The Battle of Stalingrad is over. General Paulus, appointed marshal yesterday, has ended all resistance today. A stunning chapter of the war is drawing to a close. No one in September would have ventured to consider today's epilogue as a faint possibility, let alone to predict it.[21]

Interestingly, nowhere in his preceding diary entries did he mention the two Romanian armies that had been almost entirely destroyed. Hechter was reliant on German communiqués for information. He did mourn the loss of his long-term friend Lieutenant Emil Gulian, who had been captured in November, but of the fate of tens of thousands of other Romanian troops, he knew nothing.

Walter Kerr was there at the very end:

I saw Paulus on Thursday, 4 February. He came out of a peasant's hut followed by [Chief of Staff General Arthur] Schmidt and [Colonel Wilhelm] Adam, the adjutant of the Army. Paulus was six feet four, Schmidt short and stocky, Adam of medium height with a boyish face. They stood there in silence in the snow before the doorway, Paulus wearing a hat of grey rabbit fur and a long grey overcoat without medal, decorations, or service ribbons. His insignia were those of a colonel general, the rank to which he was promoted at the end of November.[22]

Alexander Werth was also there, enduring the -20°C temperature to interview the captured German generals. He wrote:

> One thing was astonishing about these generals. They had been captured only a couple of days before – and yet they looked healthy and not at all undernourished. Clearly, throughout the agony of Stalingrad, when their soldiers were dying of hunger, they continued to have more or less regular meals. There could be no other explanation for their normal, or almost normal, weight and appearance.
>
> The only man who looked in a poor shape was Paulus himself. We weren't allowed to speak to him … Paulus looked pale and sick, and had a nervous twitch in his left cheek. He had a more natural dignity than the others, and wore only one or two decorations.[23]

Afterwards, Major General Moritz von Drebber was asked, 'What do you think of the Red Army?'

'It has fought well,' he replied.

'What happened to the 6th Army?'

He gestured with his right hand and said, 'The Russians came in from the north. The Russians came in from the south. We were in the middle. We were cut off. We had no ammunition, no food. We lost our last airfield.'

His interrogators asked, 'Did Hitler order you to keep on fighting?'

General Drebber shook his head, 'No. But we had orders from von Paulus to stop fighting when we were forced to abandon certain lines of resistance.'

'Could the encircled army have fought its way out if it had received the order in time?'

'We could have fought our way out, but we never received the order.'[24]

Drebber blamed Paulus, but it was Hitler who had played into Stalin and Zhukov's hands. They anticipated he would do exactly the same when reacting to Operation Bagration two years later.

The privations suffered by the 6th Army at Stalingrad were truly appalling, although in many cases were no worse than those endured across the Eastern Front. Photographic evidence of soldiers going into captivity showed that some remained tolerably well fed and in reasonable health. These men, if they had been given the chance, probably had the strength to fight their way out. Photographs of the officers corroborate Werth's observations. The famous photo of a defeated Paulus shows a gaunt ghost of a man; in contrast, General Arthur Schmidt and Colonel Wilhelm Adam who accompanied him, while dirty and unkempt, do look like they had not missed too many meals.

Hitler was furious about the surrender, but seemed more perturbed by Paulus' failure to take his own life rather than the needless loss of a quarter of a million men. Zeitzler, who had resumed eating, remarked to the Führer, 'It's quite impossible to explain how this happened'. He knew only too well how it had happened.

The effect of this defeat on Hitler's Eastern Front allies was catastrophic. Zhukov noted astutely:

> Because of the rout of the German, Italian, and Romanian armies in the Volga and the Don area and later of the Hungarian armies in the Ostrogozh-Rossosh operation, Germany's influence on its allies declined drastically. Discord and friction set in when the allies lost faith in Hitler's leadership and wanted to break out of the web of war in which he had enmeshed these countries.[25]

Despite it being all his own fault, the Führer took the loss of Stalingrad and the 6th Army extremely badly. 'Before the disaster at Stalingrad … Hitler would organise an evening of record music from time to time,' recalled his secretary, Christa Schroeder, 'His favourites were Beethoven symphonies, extracts from Wagner operas … After Stalingrad, Hitler could no longer relax to music.'[26] Instead, he bored his staff with interminable rambling monologues.

Hitler had refused to heed the warnings about Stalin massing his reserves on the Volga and paid the price. His generals might have hoped he had learned from this and perhaps step back from micromanaging the war as Stalin had done.

In the wake of the disaster on the Don, Hitler was shortly to taste defeat again – this time at Kursk.

Despite intelligence indicating a massive military build-up by Adolf Hitler in the summer of 1941, Joseph Stalin could not conceive that Nazi Germany would attack the Soviet Union. (All images via author and Scott Pick)

Hitler and Italian dictator, Benito Mussolini. Hitler recruited all the hard men of Europe to his anti-Bolshevik crusade.

The Nazi leader with Hungarian
ruler Admiral Miklos Horthy, who
supported Operation Barbarossa.

Marshal Ion Antonescu. The
Romanian dictator would play a key
role in Hitler's war on the Eastern
Front.

Marshal Mannerheim of Finland also supported Barbarossa in the name of reclaiming territory lost to Stalin.

King Boris III of Bulgaria. While avoiding involvement with Barbarossa, his troops occupied parts of the Balkans in support of the Nazis.

General Franz Halder was one of the chief architects of Operation Barbarossa.

General Heinz Guderian. The founder of Hitler's Panzer forces was alarmed by Barbarossa's lack of strategic focus.

German and other Axis troops struck the Soviet Union on 22 June 1941.

The Red Army was only partially mobilised and was caught at the worst possible moment.

The Luftwaffe swiftly eliminated the Red Air Force, destroying most of its aircraft on the ground.

Stalin lost tens of thousands of tanks and aircraft in the face of the Nazi onslaught.

Red Army counter-attacks simply resulted in ever-growing pockets of trapped Soviet troops.

The T-34 tank had just entered service; the tank crews were ill-trained and the tank was initially unreliable.

The Soviet Union's massive rivers did not prove an obstacle to Hitler's advancing armies.

Finland's Army also struck the Soviet Union north of Leningrad.

During the summer of 1941 the *Wehrmacht* swiftly occupied the Ukrainian city of Kharkov, which was one of the Soviet Union's key industrial regions.

In the south, Romanian forces eventually captured the port of Odessa after a protracted siege.

Millions of Soviet troops were captured.

By the winter of 1941, Hitler's panzers were at the very gates of Moscow.

Hitler dithered over taking Moscow, choosing to secure his flanks first – this meant that Operation Barbarossa became a needlessly protracted campaign.

Stalin refused to abandon Moscow and mobilised the city's population.

Crucially, many of Stalin's weapons factories escaped Hitler's clutches and were relocated east of the Ural Mountains – this enabled the Red Army to re-equip.

Stalled before Moscow, the German Army was woefully ill-equipped to cope with the harsh Russian winter.

Zhukov's 1941–42 Winter Offensive, despite suffering heavy losses, successfully thwarted Hitler's attempt to take Moscow.

This Romanian cavalryman faced an uncertain fate. By the summer of 1942, Hitler was increasingly reliant on Axis manpower. Two Romanian armies were deployed to the north and south of a city on the Volga called Stalingrad.

North of Stalingrad, separating the Romanian and Hungarian armies, were the men of Mussolini's ill-fated Italian 8th Army.

Hungarian troops with their German liaison officer.

In November 1942 Soviet armoured forces sliced through Romanian lines.

The German 6th Army was trapped at Stalingrad and Hitler steadfastly refused to allow it to surrender.

Attempts to reach Stalingrad were stopped by powerful Red Army attacks.

In the summer of 1943, despite intelligence showing Hitler was outnumbered, he persisted in launching his Kursk Offensive.

At Kursk, Hitler's Panzers soon found themselves under counter-attack and suffered heavy losses, signalling Hitler's second major defeat of the war.

In the summer of 1944
Army Group Centre,
under Field Marshal
Busch (centre), was
smashed by Stalin's
Operation Bagration.

T-34/85 tank crew – by
the summer of 1944
the Red Army was
advancing on all fronts
and reached the gates
of Warsaw.

During June 1944
Stalin sought to punish
the Finns and launched
a major offensive.

Mannerheim was forced to agree to a peace agreement with Stalin on 19 September 1944.

Soviet artillery bombarding Budapest. Hungary changed sides but Hitler clung to the city.

Hitler's last major offensive was at Lake Balaton in Hungary, in March 1945 – it ended in defeat.

After the loss of his Axis allies, by early 1945 Hitler's manpower shortages were such that he had to call up schoolboys and old men to defend Germany's cities.

At the end of April 1945, the Soviets and Americans linked up on the Elbe cutting Nazi Germany in two.

Victorious Soviet tanks west of Berlin.

The Red Army fighting on the streets of Berlin.

The Berlin garrison resisted to the very last and continued even after Hitler's suicide.

Field Marshal Keitel surrendered to Marshal Zhukov on 8 May 1945, finally bringing the slaughter on the Eastern Front to an end.

ZEITZLER'S COMEBACK PLAN

Following the intelligence blunders of Barbarossa and Stalingrad, Hitler was to suffer a third major setback in the summer of 1943. After Stalin's victory on the Volga, Army Group A's 17th Army was isolated in the Kuban bridgehead to the east of the Crimea. Battered Army Group B was placed into reserve and its formations given to Army Group Centre and Don. Hitler's tank forces had been terribly depleted and by early 1943 he had less than 500 panzers deployed on the Eastern Front; whereas Stalin soon had almost 10,000 tanks and self-propelled guns. Stalin's tank factories were churning out 2,000 a month. In terms of replacing lost armour, Hitler simply could not compete in numbers and was increasingly pinning his hopes on technical superiority.

After Stalingrad, Golikov sought to make amends and Stalin entrusted him with a combat command. Stalin wanted to capitalise on his victory and turned his attention once again to Kharkov. However, while the Wehrmacht had received a grievous blow at Stalingrad, it was down, but certainly not out of the war. Indeed, the German Army and the Waffen-SS still had a few tricks up their proverbial sleeves.

In his haste to build on his winter triumph, Stalin was about to needlessly squander his newly raised armies in spectacular fashion. As Golikov was to discover, Kharkov was not to be another Stalingrad. Von Manstein, still smarting over the failure of Winter Storm, would make sure of that by turning defeat into a stunning victory.

One of Stalin's priorities was to liberate Kharkov, the second city of Ukraine, as soon as possible. As well as thrusting south-west to Kharkov he also opted to punch west toward Kursk, to exploit the 200-mile gap torn between Field Marshal von Kluge's Army Group Centre and Army Group Don (shortly renamed South). On 1 February 1943, Stalin launched Operation Star with the 13th and 38th Armies of Golikov's Voronezh Front attacking toward Kursk and his 60th, 40th and 3rd Tank Armies striking for Kharkov. In the meantime, the 6th Army and 1st Guards Army from General N.F. Vatutin's South-Western Front swung south-west to take Mariupol on the Sea of Azov, cutting Army Group Don's communications with Army Group A in the Caucasus.

Spearheading Operation Star was Lieutenant General P.S. Rybalko's 3rd Tank Army on Golikov's southern flank. By 5 February (just three days after the last pocket in Stalingrad had surrendered) he had reached the Donets, east of Kharkov. Golikov liberated Volchansk, Belgorod, Oboyan and Kursk, and by 11 February had successfully reached the very outskirts of Kharkov. The South-Western Front was also soon deep in the rear of Army Group Don.

Stalin had every prospect of trapping the 1st Panzer Army, 4th Panzer Army and Army Group Hollidt against the Sea of Azov. Only after the personal intervention of von Kluge and von Manstein did Hitler reluctantly agree to a withdrawal to the River Mius.

At Kharkov, the newly arrived SS Panzer Corps under General Paul Hausser stood in the Red Army's way, but was pushed back. Hausser, fearing Kharkov could become another Stalingrad, disobeyed Hitler's explicit orders to stand firm and evacuated the city on 15 February. In the meantime, the main Soviet threat was a salient thrusting toward Dnepropetrovsk containing the 1st Guards and 6th Armies, as well as Group Popov. While the Germans held the Red Army west of Kharkov, von Manstein orchestrated a counter-attack on 19 February using the SS Panzer Corps striking south from Krasnograd, south-west of Kharkov toward Pavlograd. Three days later, Hermann Hoth's 4th Panzer Army linked up with the SS at Pavlograd.

To the east, on the southern side of the salient the 1st Panzer Army's 40th Panzer Corps joined the attack, defeating Group Popov near Krasnoarmeysk. The Soviets interpreted all this as a means of covering the 1st Panzer Army and Army Group Hollidt's withdrawal from the Mius to the Dnepr. In response, the South-Western Front was instructed to hold the Germans on the Mius. However, von Manstein's success at Pavlograd enabled his forces to push forward 150 miles, thereby threatening recently liberated Kharkov. Indeed, von Manstein had unhinged the junction of the South-Western and Voronezh Fronts. In the fighting the Soviet advances were stopped, having lost 23,000 dead, 9,000 captured, 615 tanks and 354 artillery pieces.

Rybalko's 3rd Tank Army swung south to take on the SS Panzer Corps on 24 February. The SS withdrew to lure them into a trap, which resulted in the Red Army losing another 9,000 dead, sixty-one tanks, sixty motor vehicles and 225 guns. Rybalko's defeat left newly liberated Kharkov open to the Germans once more. His 3rd Tank Army had to fight its way from the Kharkov area and Stalin agreed to a withdrawal to the Donets, 40 miles away. In the Donbas, von Manstein threw back the South-Western Front and the Western Front failed in the Zhizdra area.

Rokossovsky's offensive was delayed until 25 February. His Don Front (renamed the Central Front) was to be spearheaded by the 2nd Tank Army and the 70th Army from Stavka reserves, with the 65th and 21st Armies redeployed from Stalingrad. Within two weeks, the 2nd Tank Army had gained Sevsk, while a Cavalry Rifle Group from the 2nd Guards Cavalry Corps reached Trubchevsk and Novgorod-Severskii. However, south of Orel the progress of the 65th and 70th Armies was slow and on the left flank the 38th and 60th Armies were tied up trying to turn the German 2nd Army's left flank.

Rokossovsky was denied victory by the delayed arrival of the 21st Army from Stalingrad (which was subsequently diverted to Oboyan to counter von Manstein's move on Belgorod), as well as bad weather and von Manstein's counter-stroke that smashed the Voronezh Front, south of Kharkov. The fighting continued until 23 March, but Rokossovsky's troops gave up Sevsk to take up positions that would significantly become the northern and central face of the Kursk salient.

Von Manstein was then able to launch the second phase of his powerful counter-offensive on 6 March, and by 14 March was back in control of Kharkov. The Germans claimed to have killed another 50,000 Soviets and captured 19,594, as well as destroying 1,140 tanks and 3,000 guns. In just over two months the SS Panzer Corps sustained over 11,000 casualties; the 1st SS Panzer Division lost 4,500 of these during the recapture of Kharkov.

Von Manstein recorded with some satisfaction his remarkable victory at Kharkov, but also noted a lost opportunity against the Soviets' Kursk salient:

> On 14 March Kharkov fell to the SS Panzer Corps. At the same time, on the northern wing Army Detachment Kempf, the 'Gross-Deutschland' Division moved swiftly to Belgorod. The enemy once again threw in strong armoured forces to oppose it, but these were wiped out at Gaivoron.
>
> The capture of Kharkov and Belgorod marked the conclusion of Army Group's second counter-blow, as the increasing muddiness of the ground did not permit any further operations. As a matter of fact the Army Group would have liked to wind up by clearing out, with the help of Central Army Group, the enemy salient extending some distance westwards of Kursk in order to shorten the German front. The scheme had to be abandoned, however, as Central Army Group declared itself unable to co-operate. As a result the salient continued to constitute a troublesome dent in our front.[1]

Alarmed by the situation in the south, Stalin summoned his deputy supreme commander to Moscow on 14 March. Zhukov found himself sent to the

Voronezh Front, where his prognosis was dire: 'All available forces from Stavka's reserves must be deployed here; otherwise, the Germans will capture Belgorod and continue their offensive on the Kursk sector.'[2]

Stalin had already decided to despatch the 1st Tank Army, 21st Army and 64th Army to the Belgorod area, but they could not be in place quick enough to save the city, which fell to von Manstein on 18 March. Nonetheless, the Soviet 21st and 64th Armies moved into blocking positions north-east of Belgorod and this frustrated von Manstein's attempt on Kursk. Once the Soviet 52nd Guards, 67th Guards Rifle and 375th Rifle divisions from the 21st Army had taken up defensive positions, the Germans were unable to dislodge them. The 1st Tank Army deployed south of Oboyan and the 64th Army along the Seversky Donets River.

Zhukov had managed to stabilise things by 26 March and the spring thaw brought mobile warfare to a halt. The Germans, in turn, dug in. General von Mellenthin was fulsome in his praise for von Manstein's remarkable achievements:

> Having regard to the problems which faced Manstein between December 1942, and February 1943, it may be question whether any achievement of generalship in World War II can approach the successful extrication of the Caucasus armies, and the subsequent riposte to Kharkov.[3]

In a stroke of military genius, von Manstein had defeated Operation Star. He had saved Army Group South and put the Germans back on the Mius–Donets line. However, while impressive, such a victory could not offset the disaster at Stalingrad. Although checked by the SS Panzer Corps, the Red Army threatened the whole region from Kharkov via Belgorod to Kursk. Despite von Manstein's success, superior German leadership could not keep the Red Army at bay for much longer.

Both sides now bided their time during the spring thaw and heavy rains that served to stabilise the huge Eastern Front by hampering all road movement. This gave Stalin time to continue mobilising his reserves. In early April 1943, a second Soviet reserve front was created that included seven armies and subsequently became Ivan Konev's Steppe Front.

A few months earlier the Red Army had taken charge of the rather unusual and newly created 70th Army, formed the previous year in Siberia using border and Gulag prison guards drawn from Central Asia, the Far East and Transbaikal. Hitler could simply not compete with the Red Army's continued regeneration capabilities. It also signified that yet another Soviet offensive was being prepared.

Nevertheless, in the run-up to the spring of 1943 General Kurt Zeitzler, the German Army chief of staff, was preoccupied with Hitler's Operation *Zitadelle* (Citadel). The previous Red Army operations had left them in possession of a vast salient around the town of Kursk, flanked by German bulges in the front line and anchored in the south on Belgorod and Kharkov and in the north on Orel. Hitler's intention was to snip off the Soviet Kursk salient at its neck and smash those Soviet forces trapped in an enormous pocket. To that end, he began to mass his armoured forces.

This plan had first been discussed in April, with the view to decisively weakening the Red Army's offensive strength. In light of Stalingrad and the unravelling of the German southern front, such large-scale offensive operations seemed completely out of the question.

Hitler and his generals had reconvened in early May to discuss the matter. Few of them were enthusiastic. General Model was firmly against the operation. He pointed out that his aerial intelligence showed that the Soviets were strengthening their defences exactly where Hitler's two army groups were to attack. In addition, the Red Army had withdrawn most of its mobile forces from the forward area of the salient. Guderian was not happy either, 'If we attacked according to the plan of the chief of the General Staff we were certain to suffer heavy tank casualties, which we would not be in a position to replace in 1943.'[4] He felt they should be looking ahead to the inevitable opening of the Western Front by the Allies in 1944 and that a mobile armoured reserve should be built up there. Von Manstein felt the chances of success were doubtful. Only Field Marshal von Kluge was unequivocally in favour of Zeitzler's plan. Hitler remained undecided.

General Walter Warlimont, who was the OKW's deputy chief of operations staff, observed that Hitler 'did not seem to believe in success'. He felt Hitler only went ahead with Operation Citadel because he did not want to cede the strategic initiative to the Red Army, and 'his eventual consent to the execution of this attack was mainly because, otherwise, he could not have evaded the necessity for a deliberate strategic retreat in the East on a larger scale'.[5] It seems crazy that Hitler would commit exactly the same mistake he had made at Stalingrad.

What the Führer failed to acknowledge was that the Red Army's build-up at Kursk was not defensive but intended to destroy the German Orel and Belgorod salients. If Hitler attacked toward Kursk, he was essentially walking into a massive trap.

At the same time, Stavka debated whether to attack first or wait for Hitler and then counter-attack. The Red Army was very well informed of Hitler's intentions and Zhukov reported to Stalin on 8 April 1943:

> At the present time, the enemy has as many as twelve tank divisions lined up along the Central and Voronezh Fronts and by taking in three or four tank

divisions from other sectors he could pitch as many as fifteen or sixteen tank divisions with some 2,500 tanks against our Kursk grouping. [...]

I do not believe it is necessary for our forces to mount a preventive offensive in the next few days. It will be better to wear the enemy out in defensive action, destroy his tanks and then, taking in fresh reserves, by going over to an all-out offensive we will finish off the emery's main grouping.[6]

Stalin heeded Zhukov's counsel and decided to bide his time.

Citadel was initially scheduled to commence a month later, on 6 May, but sufficient numbers of the brand-new Panther tank were not ready in time. There were frustrating delays with crew training when those Panthers already issued had to be sent back to the factory for modifications. This derailed Reinhard Gehlen's propaganda operation, known as 'Silver Lining'.

In anticipation of the start date on 3 May, some 18 million leaflets were released over Soviet lines. This welcomed deserters, urging them to join Vlasov's non-existent Russian Liberation Army. Gehlen had a panic when it was realised that Silver Lining was also a Luftwaffe code word for chemical warfare using poison gas. As Citadel subsequently slipped back several months, there was no offensive to back up the leaflets and encourage an increase in the Soviet desertion rate. As Gehlen noted, somewhat sourly, the whole operation 'went off at half cock'.

Hitler's intelligence was very poor and underestimated Stalin's strength at Kursk. In June, the OKH calculated that the Red Army had 1,500 tanks in the salient, which was way too conservative. This was, in part, testament to improving Soviet deception measures, which fooled Luftwaffe photoreconnaissance flights. In contrast, Soviet intelligence accurately identified almost every single German division gathered for Citadel, and this meant the Red Army knew that Hitler's southern pincher was the more powerful of the two so could plan accordingly.

Holding the northern half of the enormous Kursk salient was Rokossovsky's Central Front, with six armies (48th, 13th, 70th, 65th and 60th, with the 2nd Tank Army in reserve). The Voronezh Front was now under Vatutin and had six armies with which it defended the southern half (38th, 40th, 6th Guards and 7th Guards, with the 1st Tank and 69th Armies held in reserve). Behind them was the new Theatre Reserve, consisting of General Konev's Steppe Front (5th Guards, 27th, 47th, 53rd and 5th Guards Tank Armies). Total Soviet armour strength was about 5,000 vehicles, almost five times the German intelligence estimate.

Von Manstein's victory at Kharkov seems to have made the German High Command over-optimistic about their chances of success at Kursk. Operation Citadel was madness – even if Hitler's offensive broke through, he did not have the reserves to exploit a breach.

The lack of credible intelligence regarding Stalin's strategic reserves, most notably Konev's forces and Pavel Rotmistrov's very powerful 5th Guards Tank Army, was extremely worrying. Rotmistrov's command gave the front commanders the ability to quickly seal any German breach. In the air, Rokossovsky was supported by Lieutenant General S.I. Rudenko's 16th Air Army; while Vatutin was supported by Lieutenant General S.A. Krasovsky's 2nd Air Army and Konev by Lieutenant General S.K. Goryunov's 5th Air Army. These air forces totalled some 3,600 aircraft. On the ground the Soviets' massed firepower was devastating, with 13,000 guns, 1,000 rocket launchers and 6,000 anti-tank guns covering highly elaborate in-depth defences.

Konev's forces were very much a combat command designed to act as a manoeuvre force and specifically tasked to counter enemy breakthroughs. Zhukov highlighted the evolution of the role played by the Red Army's reserve armies:

> The Steppe Front fundamentally differed in its composition and purpose from the Reserve Front, which had been in operation on the approaches to Moscow in the Autumn of 1941. At that time, the Reserve Front was essentially a second operational echelon deployed by the main forces on the rear lines of the Western Front.[7]

Whatever way you looked at it, Hitler was outnumbered and outgunned from the very start. The Red Army was not only extremely well prepared to rebuff his offensive but also to switch over to its own counter-offensive once the Germans had been stopped in their tracks. While perhaps quietly confident in the enormous defensive belts created in the Kursk salient, Rokossovsky and Vatutin must have been slightly uncomfortable at having their fronts wedged into the exposed bulge. Both had lost armies that were surrounded in the early stages of the war. In addition, there was no guarantee of victory, a lot depended on just how well the Red Army had learned from its previous battles. If any units collapsed, then the ever-flexible Germans would exploit the gap.

Initially, Reinhard Gehlen's Foreign Armies East intelligence unit and the German War Department continued to support Hitler and Halder's optimistic view that a victory was achievable at Kursk. However, Operation Citadel was delayed for over two months and, Gehlen says, 'by late June we were certain of defeat'.[8] This change of heart was because:

> By the time 'Citadel' was finally launched on 5 July, it was clear that we had lost the advantages of both strategic and tactical surprise. I had taken every opportunity, as the files of Foreign Armies East show, to warn the German

command against this major offensive. Since Hitler refused to be dissuaded, on 3 July I wrote an emphatic warning of the likely outcome, under the title 'Appreciation of the Enemy's Moves if Operation "Citadel" is Carried Out'.[9]

Two days later, Gehlen said, 'I repeated my opposition in even more emphatic terms: From the point of view of the general war situation, there is not one ground that could justify launching operation "Citadel" at the present juncture.'[10] Hitler and his senior generals were not receptive to such concerns. Besides it was simply too late to call a halt as everything was in place and poised to go.

On the German right, von Manstein's Army Group South, spearheaded by Hoth's 4th Panzer Army and General Werner Kempf's Army Group, was to attack northward from Belgorod with seven Corps. Hoth's forces comprised three corps (General Eugen Ott's 52nd Corps, General Otto von Knobeldorff's 48th Panzer Corps and General Paul Hausser's 2nd SS Panzer Corps) and Kempf also deployed three corps (General Hermann Breith's 3rd Panzer Corps, General Erhard Raus' 11th Corps and General Franz Mattenklott's 42nd Corps). Von Manstein had General Walter Nehring's 24th Panzer Corps held in reserve. This combined force totalled 350,000 men, about 1,269 panzers and 245 assault guns.

On the far left, Model's 9th Army from von Kluge's Army Group Centre was to push southward. They were to link up with von Manstein at Kursk, cutting off Soviet forces that were to be subsequently annihilated. This northern arm of Hitler's offensive was slightly less formidable, with the 9th Army comprising six corps (General Johannes Friessner's 23rd Corps, General Josef Harpe's 41st Panzer Corps, General Joachim Lemelsen's 47th Panzer Corps, General H. Zorn's 46th Panzer Corps and General Rudolf Freiherr von Roman's 20th Corps). The reserve consisted of Korps Group von Esebeck. In all, Model had about 335,000 troops and 900 panzers at his disposal.

The Luftwaffe mustered 1,800 aircraft to support Citadel, representing 75 per cent of their strength on the Eastern Front. In the north, air support was provided by Luftflotte 6's 1st Fliegerdivision with 730 aircraft, and in the south, 8th Fliegerkorps with 1,100 aircraft.

Von Manstein, Hoth, Hausser and Kempf, all very experienced panzer commanders, cannot have been happy with the basic concept of Citadel. This was not mobile armoured warfare designed to turn an enemy's flank, it was going to be a head-on battle of attrition. Hoth was going to have to bludgeon his way between Belgorod and Gertsovka, cutting a route to Oboyan and on to Kursk. In light of the Soviets' dense defences around Oboyan, the town of Prokhorovka to the north-east looked an 'easier' route.

Rokossovsky and Vatutin, looking at their situation maps, would have come to the same conclusion – the panzers might attempt a left hook against their defences. In the north, Soviet defences were anchored on Olkhovatka and Ponyri.

The bulk of Hitler's armour comprised the older Panzer Mk III and IV. His 'zoo' of newer T-34 killers were simply not available in sufficient numbers – panzer units could muster just 195 Panthers, 144 Tigers and eighty-nine Ferdinands. The northern element of the assault had no Panthers and just forty-five Tigers, while to the south no Ferdinands were available.

His powerful, newly designed Tiger and Panther tanks were introduced in 1942–43. The former, armed with an 88mm gun, was able to stand off and kill enemy tanks at ranges of over 1,500m, thus well out of range of Soviet tank guns. However, the Tiger was slow, difficult to recover from the battlefield and costly to build. The Panther combined armament, armour and mobility, but the early models were mechanically troublesome, in part due to them being rushed into production too soon at Hitler's insistence. Armed with the 75mm L/70 gun, which was an improved version of that in the Panzer Mk IV, it could knock out Soviet tanks almost as easily as the Tiger.

As a result of the Tiger's inauspicious debut in the Leningrad area in the summer of 1942, the Red Army had got hold of a number of examples. This meant that Soviets knew where the Tiger's weak spots were. Soviet infantry were issued leaflets showing how to deal with the panzers, in particular, the Tiger. If the anti-tank guns, artillery and Red Air Force did not stop the enemy's tanks, the infantry were trained to stay put in their trenches and let them pass before attacking them from behind.

13

PROKHOROVKA BLOODBATH

Thanks to Stalin's spy ring in Berlin, the Soviets were not only expecting Citadel but also knew all the details. With the knowledge that Hitler was planning to attack sometime between 3–6 July, Rokossovsky and Vatutin put their fronts on full alert. Across the Kursk salient, Soviet troops made their final defensive preparations, checking and cleaning their weapons and breaking out extra ammunition. The summer heat was oppressive and their uniforms were stained with sweat and grubby from the earth dug from the miles of trenches. The gunners rehearsed their fire plans and checked the funnel points for the panzers that would drive them onto the anti-tank '*pakfronts*'.

German preparations confirmed what Rokossovsky needed to know. Sappers were out late on 4 July, undertaking the thankless task of trying to map and clear the endless Soviet minefields. One group was careless and were jumped on by a Soviet patrol, and rather than fight it out they threw up their hands. The forlorn party was escorted back to Soviet lines where one man, fearful for his life, confirmed the German attack would commence the next day at 0330 hrs. It seems highly unlikely that a lowly sapper would be privy to such information, but the fact that the Germans were clearing the minefields indicated that an attack was imminent.

Zhukov recalled that Rokossovsky was uncertain whether to contact Stavka or take matters in hand. He bluntly told Rokossovsky to get on with it while he telephoned Stalin. Both Zhukov and Rokossovsky expected Model's main thrust to be toward Ponyri, held by General Pukhov's 13th Army. The latter was backed by the 2nd Tank Army, the 19th Tank Corps and the bulk of the front's artillery units. There were almost 100 guns and mortars per kilometre. Notably, the 4th Artillery Corps was deployed near Ponyri with 700 field guns and mortars.

When Rokossovsky's headquarters phoned the 4th Artillery they discovered the Central Front's artillery commander, V.I. Kazakov, was with them. Orders were issued to the gunners to open up with everything they had. Although it was still dark, the gunners hastily broke open the wooden crates containing artillery shells, mortar bombs and Katyusha rockets. These were stacked ready next to their weapons, until 0220 hrs when the gunners began a sudden and furious spoiling bombardment of Model's 9th Army. The darkness was immediately lit up by muzzle flashes and rockets streaking skyward. To the south, Vatutin had also been forewarned by German prisoners, and at 0230 hrs both the 6th and 7th Guards Armies let loose with their artillery. An hour later, the 4th Panzer Army responded.

For the massed German formations, this bombardment was unwelcome. The German infantry, panzergrenadiers and panzertruppen eyed each other nervously – was the game up, they asked each other? The Germans could not disperse from their assembly areas and for more than thirty minutes they endured the shattering explosions which tore up the ground, showering men and machines in deadly scalding shrapnel and smoking clods of soil. When the bombardment stopped a flicker of unease ran through some German commanders, who worried that the barrage heralded a Soviet spoiling attack.

Zhukov, at Rokossovsky's HQ, recalled, 'We could hear and feel the hurricane-like fire and could not help conjuring up the terrible picture on the enemy's initial bridgehead, as he was suddenly hit by the whirlwind of counter-preparation fire.' However, he was subsequently very critical of this pre-emptive bombardment, despite authorising it, viewing it as a waste of ammunition. He acknowledged that they were firing in the dark and that the 'counter-preparation' plans had not been fully worked out. As a result, the Germans did not suffer heavy losses nor was Citadel greatly impeded. To compound matters, the Red Air Force's large pre-emptive strike at daybreak on the Luftwaffe's airfields around Kharkov was swiftly shot from the sky with the loss of 120 aircraft. Zhukov concluded that Rokossovsky and Vatutin had opened fire too soon and that they should have waited another forty minutes.

General Pukhov's 13th Army found itself on the receiving end of things when the German artillery returned fire at 0430 hrs. The German gunners ranged far and wide, zeroing in on strongpoints and gun pits which had been identified by aerial photography. They also sought to clear a way through the dense minefields before the ground forces had to navigate them. Thirty minutes later, screaming Stuka dive-bombers preceded the panzers and assault guns. Despite this deluge, when Citadel finally got underway it made little headway before being checked by the Soviet defences.

Soviet field telephones began ringing as spotters called in the positions of the panzers to their artillery and the dive-bombers of the Red Air Force. Within an hour of the German guns opening up, enemy infantry was reported advancing along the 13th Army's front and the right flank of the 70th Army. They blundered through anti-personnel mines across open ground toward the Soviet trench lines. Soviet infantry, issuing from their bunkers once the artillery slackened off, took up their firing positions gripping their rifles, sub-machine guns and machine guns as tightly as their hands could bear. They then poured fire into the Germans emerging from the ripening crops that were still standing after the bombardment.

The Central Front's strongest anti-tank defences were deployed on the northern shoulder of the bulge in the area held by the 70th, 13th and 48th Armies. Pukhov's 13th Army had thirty anti-tank guns per kilometre. The panzers and assault guns charged forward, but many commanders must have been torn between standing off and destroying as many Soviet tanks as possible and closing to escape the anti-tank mines, anti-tanks guns and heavy artillery (especially the howitzers) that were quickly turning the Kursk steppe into a panzer graveyard.

Soviet war correspondent, Vasily Grossman noted a change in Soviet strategy:

> From the point of view of artillery, the Kursk operation is more sophisticated than the Stalingrad one. In Stalingrad, the beast was beaten in his lair. In Kursk, the artillery shield resisted the enemy's attack and the artillery sword started crushing them during the advance.[2]

Model's six panzer divisions included sizeable numbers of the old Panzer Mk III and these, along with their self-propelled guns, had limited stand-off protection, which meant that it was unwise to linger in the killing grounds of the Soviet '*pakfront*' zones. The need to clear the Soviet minefields and the front-echelon weapons positions meant that only the 20th Panzer Division of the 47th Panzer Corps was involved in the initial assault.

They scored some success, pushing through the Soviet 15th Rifle Division's front-line trenches at 0900 hrs and fighting their way between Bobrik and Gnilets. The Soviet 321st Rifle Regiment was barged out of the way and Bobrik secured 3 miles behind Soviet lines. Many Soviet units, knowing exactly what to expect, held their ground resolutely. The Soviets did everything they could to stop the Germans from breaking through to the Kursk–Orel Highway.

'A battery commanded by Captain G.I. Igishev took the brunt of the attack and destroyed nineteen panzers during the day,' recalled Zhukov. 'All the men of the battery died heroically in battle, but did not let the Fascists pass.'[3]

While the Luftwaffe was not in a position to achieve air supremacy against the rejuvenated Red Air Force, it was vital that it gained local air superiority. This was important for two reasons: the Germans' lack of artillery meant that the vulnerable stukagruppen dive-bombers serving as flying artillery would have to be protected, and the Red Air Force would have to be kept off the massed and exposed panzer columns trundling across the open steppe. In the air, the air forces of both sides, as well as trying to support their ground forces, were soon locked in deadly aerial combat.

Oberfeldwebel Hans Krohn, a Stuka radio operator, said:

Our 'cannon aircraft' took a terrible toll of Soviet armour. We attacked at very low altitude … and my pilot opened fire at a distance of only 50 metres. Most of our attacks were made against the side of the tanks, because in that way they offered the largest targets. I know that some pilots attacked from behind because that was where the armour was weakest, but that also meant the target was so small that it was difficult to hit. By this time Soviet tank crews appeared to be well aware of the potency of our 'cannon planes'. Whenever we appeared, the tanks would start wild evasive manoeuvres. Occasionally we could see tank crews jump out of the hatches and abandon their tanks when we dived to attack them.[4]

On the 20th Panzer's left, the 6th Infantry Division thrust down the Oka Valley supported by the Tiger tanks of Heavy Panzer Battalion 505. The Soviet T-34s and anti-tank guns were unable to stop them taking the village of Butyrka. This exposed the Soviet 81st Rifle Division, which was busy trying to fend off the 292nd Infantry Division. The Germans' heavy Ferdinand tank destroyers ploughed through the Soviet lines with impunity, reaching Alexsandrovka, but lacking machine guns they soon found they could not deal with the Soviet infantry and fell foul of Soviet anti-tank teams.

The 86th Infantry Division reached Ponyri late that afternoon, while the 78th and 216th Infantry Divisions fought their way through the Soviet defences toward the road junction at Maloarkhangelsk with the support of Ferdinands. Model got just 6 miles before being stopped by the defences in front of Olkhovatka and Ponyri, losing 25,000 of his men, 200 panzers and 200 aircraft in the bloody process. The northern pincher had been halted.

To the south, Hausser's 2nd SS Panzer Corps struck toward Bykovka with 365 tanks and 195 assault guns. Confronting them were the Soviet 52nd Guards Rifle and the 375th Rifle Divisions. The SS took the town, while other units cut the Oboyan–Belgorod road, only to be obstructed by the Soviet 96th Tank Brigade. Similarly, a penetration was made on the right flank of the 375th Division, but the Germans could get no further. The strength of the Soviet defensive positions stopped the Germans breaking through north of Belgorod, which was to cause Hoth problems.

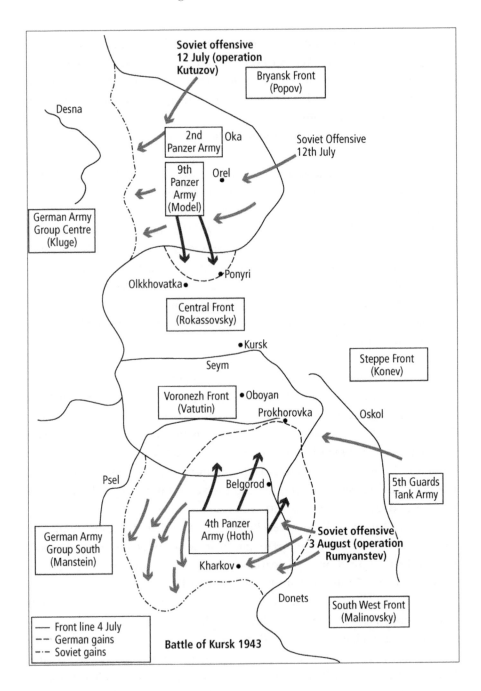

Soviet offensive 12 July (operation Kutuzov)

Bryansk Front (Popov)

Desna

2nd Panzer Army

Oka

Soviet Offensive 12th July

9th Panzer Army (Model)

Orel

German Army Group Centre (Kluge)

Olkkhovatka

Ponyri

Central Front (Rokassovsky)

Kursk

Seym

Steppe Front (Konev)

Voronezh Front (Vatutin)

Oboyan

Prokhorovka

Oskol

Psel

Belgorod

5th Guards Tank Army

German Army Group South (Manstein)

4th Panzer Army (Hoth)

Soviet offensive 3 August (operation Rumyanstev)

Kharkov

Donets

South West Front (Malinovsky)

—— Front line 4 July
- - - German gains
-·- Soviet gains

Battle of Kursk 1943

Operation Citadel, during the Battle of Kursk, 5 July 1943.

Colonel Ritgen with the 6th Panzer Division, part of Breith's 3rd Panzer Corps, remembered the depth and intensity of the Red Army's defences:

6th Panzer Division, as part of the southern pincher, penetrated 30km [19 miles] into the Russian salient during the first days of the fighting, exploiting a breach created by a neighbouring division. It was, however, slowed down badly by minefields. In this operation the gallant divisional commander, General von Huenersdorff, was fatally wounded – a serious loss for 6th Panzer.[5]

Hoth's forces managed 25 miles, losing 10,000 men and 350 panzers. Elements of the Steppe Front and the Voronezh Front's reserves were committed to halt him in front of Prokhorovka and Oboyan. Stavka was not slow to react, and during the night of 8/9 July they hastened the concentration of their strategic reserve in order to get Rotmistrov's 5th Tank Army and Zhadov's 5th Guards Army with 80,000 men to the Prokhorovka area.

On 10 July, the Germans broke through between Melikhovo and Sasnoye Station. By dusk on the 11th, panzers and armoured fighting vehicles were heading for Prokhorovka. On the Psel River facing part of the SS Panzer Corps, Zhadov had no armour, but at Prokhorovka, Rotmistrov massed some 800 tanks (although only 501 were T-34s, the rest comprised 264 largely useless T-70 light tanks and thirty-five British-supplied Churchill heavy tanks).

A bloody battle ensued at Prokhorovka on 12 July, when Hausser's panzers attacked Rotmistrov's positions. This led to a massive armoured brawl as unit commanders lost all control and the crews had to fend for themselves in the chaos. Around 1,200 tanks were involved in the swirling, highly confused battle. Soviet tank crews were fresh; but the exhausted Germans were not. In light of the superior firepower and killing range of the Panther and Tiger, the Soviet T-34 crews had to close on their enemies as quickly as possible. This was armoured warfare at its most brutal, with tanks slugging it out at point-blank range. According to one Soviet veteran, the tanks were as close as 10–15m. Once hit, many of the crews had little chance of bailing out and were splattered all over the insides of their tanks. Those who did try to escape their blazing tanks were mown down and their lifeless bodies left obscenely charred and shrivelled.

There were simply not enough Tigers and Panthers to halt the massed ranks of T-34s thrown at them. Likewise, to the north, the new impregnable Ferdinand tank destroyer, Hitler's other new secret weapon, proved mechanically unreliable and a vulnerable liability. Prokhorovka was a bloodbath, with more than 700 tanks knocked out on both sides.

Significantly, however, Rotmistrov remained in possession of the battlefield and Hausser's breakthrough had been contained. This victory cost Rotmistrov over 50 per cent of his command and Stalin, appalled by the 5th Guards Tank Army's destruction, ordered an investigation. For a brief moment it looked as if Rotmistrov might be sacked or worse. What was very evident was that despite their heavy casualties, the T-34 had held its own against the formidable Tiger and Panther. Rotmistrov was spared to fight another day.

Von Manstein claimed that those Red Army units facing his Army Group South lost 24,000 men captured, as well as losing 1,800 tanks, 267 field guns and 1,080 anti-tank guns. Nonetheless, Citadel had been fought to a bloody standstill and the troops were suddenly needed elsewhere. 'On 13 July, Field Marshals von Manstein and von Kluge were summoned to East Prussia,' recalls von Mellenthin, 'and Hitler informed them that Citadel must be called off immediately as the Allies had landed in Sicily.'[6]

However, the terrible bloodletting on the Eastern Front was far from over. While the battle of Prokhorovka was in full swing, to the north General V.D. Sokolovsky's Western Front and General M.M. Popov's Bryansk Front marshalled their troops ready to attack the exposed Orel salient. Their assault commenced in the early hours of 12 July.

Twelve days later, in his Order of the Day addressed to Generals Rokossovsky, Vatutin and Popov, Stalin stated:

> During the engagements from 5–23 July the enemy suffered the following losses: Officers and men killed, over 70,000; tanks destroyed or disabled, 2,900, self-propelled guns, 195; field guns, 844; planes destroyed, 1,392; and motor vehicles, over 5,000.
>
> I congratulate you and the troops under your command on the successful liquidation of the German Summer Offensive. I express my gratitude to all men, commanders and political workers of the troops under your command for their excellent operations.
>
> Immortal glory to the heroes who fell in the fight for the freedom and honour of our Motherland![7]

Colonel General S.M. Shtemenko recorded how the Red Army had withstood Hitler's massed power:

> On 5 July 1943 the defensive stage of the famous Battle of Kursk began with an enemy attack. Day and night, our troops beat back massive attacks of tanks, planes, and infantry, waging extremely bitter and bloody fights. The enemy's mountains of steel forged ahead, but after eighteen days of bitter fighting against our well-prepared defences, they only dented the Orel-Kursk sector and drove a wedge into the defences in the Belgorod-Kursk sector.[8]

Zhukov unleashed his massive counter-offensive, sweeping back the Germans' hard-won gains and pushing them out of their Orel and Kharkov salients. The first operation, 'Kutuzov' (Orel Strategic Counter-Offensive Operation), ran from 12 July–18 August. This capitalised on the Germans' shortcomings and further emphasised that the strategic and operational initiative had passed firmly over to the Red Army. Zhukov intended not only to liberate the Orel salient, but also ensnare as much of Model's 2nd Panzer Army (its previous commander, Rudolf Schmidt, had been sacked on 11 July) and the 9th Army, both of which formed part of von Kluge's Army Group Centre.

Sokolovsky mustered 211,458 troops, 745 tanks and self-propelled guns, and 4,285 guns and mortars, and Popov another 170,000 men, and over 350 tanks and self-propelled guns. The newly formed 3rd Guards Tank Army held in reserve had another 731 tanks. Rokossovsky also committed three of his armies.

It was intended that Sokolovsky's 3rd and 63rd Armies would push west from the Novosil area over the Susha River, cutting through the junction of the 2nd Panzer and 9th Armies to liberate Orel. This would pin the Germans down while the 3rd Guards Tank Army pushed through to exploit the situation further west. In the meantime, the West Front's 11th Guards Army was to attack south from the Belev area to smash the left shoulder of the German salient, which allowed the 4th Tank Army to press on and cut off the 2nd Panzer Army.

The Germans were not naive of Soviet intentions; photoreconnaissance and radio intercepts provided a clear picture of what the Red Army intended. However, Model simply did not have sufficient manpower to conduct any spoiling attacks, although this intelligence did enable his men to prepare in-depth defences. This was especially important for General Dr Rendulic's 35th Corps, which would have to bear the brunt of the 63rd Army's attack. In the event, the latter was only able to make slow progress toward Orel. To the north, the 11th Guards Army pushed the Germans back 16 miles in two days in the face of bitter resistance.

Operation Kutuzov overlapped with Operation Polkovodets Rumyantsev (Belgorod-Kharkov Strategic Offensive) from 3–23 August against the southern sector of the Kursk bulge. Despite Citadel being rebuffed, remarkably the Wehrmacht had not been sent reeling. Guy Sajer, serving with the Grossdeutschland Division, felt not all was lost:

> The situation was not yet entirely in their hands, and strong counter-attacks from our side often broke their frantic thrust. Belgorod, Kharkov and Stalino all feature prominently in any account of German counter-attacks. Sixty thousand troops took part in the battle of Belgorod. I was one of them. Eighteen thousand Hitlerjugend had also arrived from Silesian camps to receive their

baptism of fire in this unequal combat, in which a third of them lost their lives. [...] 500,000 Russians were jostled back by 60,000 Germans.[9]

As always, the fighting was visceral. 'Guts splattered across the rubble,' says Sajer, 'and sprayed from one dying man onto another; tightly riveted machines ripped like the belly of a cow which has just been sliced open, flaming and groaning.'[10]

Nonetheless, the Red Army pushed the Germans back, liberating both Belgorod and Kharkov. The success of these operations meant that German forces in Ukraine were obliged to withdraw behind the Dnepr and paved the way for the liberation of Kiev. At 0600 hrs on 5 August 1943, the 89th Guards Rifle and the 305th and 375th Rifle Divisions broke into the city of Belgorod.

The Soviet High Command was overjoyed at the liberation of both Orel and Belgorod, as Shtemenko noted:

> It was decided to proclaim [the] victories of our troops by solemn artillery salvoes in Moscow, to accompany every salvo with multicoloured fireworks, and to precede the salute by reading Stalin's official message over every radio station in the Soviet Union. [...]
>
> The first salute consisted of twelve salvoes from 124 guns. We figured it would also be that way in the future. But on 23 August, Kharkov, the second capital of the Ukraine, was taken, and we saw at once that one shouldn't treat all victories in an identical way. Kharkov had very great significance, and it was decided to give twenty salvoes from 224 guns in honour of its liberation.[11]

Events in Italy now took a hand, as Benito Mussolini had been ousted following the Western Allies' landing on Sicily. Von Kluge was ordered to evacuate the Orel salient. Despite the committal of the Soviet Central Front on the southern shoulder of the salient, the Germans were able to withdraw to the half-completed Hagen Line in front of Bryansk. However, there was to be little respite, for on 23 August Zhukov launched an offensive to push the Germans back from Nevel, south to the Black Sea, defended by Army Groups Centre, South and A.

Stalin's triumph at Kursk came at a terrible price. The Red Army experienced yet another savage mauling, losing almost four times the number of casualties and five times the number of tanks and self-propelled guns as the Germans. It was a hard-won victory, but a victory nonetheless. Casualties for the three Soviet fronts totalled 177,847 men and 1,614 tanks and self-propelled guns.

Hitler's summer offensive lasted just a week, but afterwards Stalin kept up the pressure for five weeks. For Hitler's generals, this showed what immense resources the reinvigorated Red Army could call on. German losses at Kursk were just short of 50,000 (Army Group South 29,102, and 9th Army, 20,720), while 1,612 panzers were damaged and 323 were irreparable losses. This was nothing in comparison to Stalingrad. Nonetheless, Kursk was a disaster for Hitler as it exhausted his last offensive strength on the Eastern Front. Worryingly for German morale, it was the first occasion a major offensive had been stopped before it achieved a sizeable breakthrough. From this point on, Hitler was on the strategic defensive on the Eastern Front. He should have held his ground and let his forces destroy the impending offensives by the Red Army, but he would not listen to Gehlen and the others.

Heinz Guderian wrote in his diary:

With the failure of *Zitadelle* we have suffered a decisive defeat. The armoured formations, re-formed and re-equipped with so much effort, had lost heavily in both men and equipment and would now be unemployable for a long time to come. It was problematical whether they could be rehabilitated in time to defend the Eastern Front ... Needless to say the Russians exploited their victory to the full. There were to be no more periods of quiet on the Eastern Front. From now on, the enemy was in undisputed possession of the initiative.[12]

If anyone was to blame for this situation it was Gehlen, his warning was simply too late. Citadel had been under preparation since mid-April and he had plenty of time to warn of the Soviet build-up around Kursk. Despite this appalling defeat at Kursk, Gehlen was remarkably self-congratulatory. A Soviet document was captured that identified all the German divisions that had gathered for Citadel except for one which, in Gehlen's mind, vindicated Branch 12's alarm. He wrote to his staff, saying:

The course of the fighting on the Eastern Front these last few days has once again confirmed precisely every detail of the enemy-Intelligence picture we produced ... The chief of staff expressed particular commendation for this a few days ago.[13]

He conveniently avoided the fact that the Wehrmacht had expended the last of its strategic offensive capability on the Eastern Front.

'The outstanding victory of our troops at Kursk demonstrated the growing power of the Soviet state and its armed forces,' wrote Zhukov, acknowledging a turning point in the war and a boost to the fortunes of the Red Army. 'The counter-offensive at Kursk involved larger forces than previous offensive operations. ... twenty-two full strength field armies, five tank armies and six air armies and large long-range bomber units participated.'[14]

Fearful of being outflanked, the bulk of the German forces in the Soviet Union fell back on the Dnepr River. West of Moscow, the Red Army from early August to the beginning of October struggled in a series of operations to push back the Wehrmacht and retake the city of Smolensk. These were conducted by the Kalinin and Western Fronts against Army Group Centre. Smolensk was liberated in late September at the cost of 450,000 casualties; German losses were assessed at around a quarter of a million. This finally removed Hitler's lingering threat to Moscow. He had lost his chance.

In the Caucasus, things also went Stalin's way. In his congratulatory Order of the Day sent to Colonel General Petrov and Vice Admiral Vladimirskiy on 16 September 1943, he declared:

Today, 16 September, our troops of the Northern Caucasus Front, in col-laboration with the ships and units of the Black Sea Fleet, as the result of a daring operation, by an attack on land and the landing of a force from the sea, after five days of fierce battles in the course of which the German 73rd Infantry Division, the German 4th and 101st Mountain Infantry Divisions, the Romanian 4th Mountain Infantry Division and the harbour defence force of the German Marines were routed, took by storm the important Black Sea port and town of Novorossiisk [Novorossiyk – just east of the Crimean Kerch Straits].[15]

The Red Army's relentless gains of 1943 were to continue into 1944 with the liberation of Sevastopol and the Crimea.

14

STALIN'S D-DAY

The New Year did not start well for Hitler, with the Red Army continuing to keep the Wehrmacht off balance. On 14 January 1944, the Leningrad, Volkhov and 2nd Baltic Fronts, supported by the Baltic Fleet, attacked Army Group North.

Soviet forces totalled a staggering 1.2 million men, 1,475 tanks and 21,600 field guns and mortars, while Field Marshal Georg von Küchler's Army Group North, consisting of the German 18th and 16th Armies, could field 741,000 men, 385 tanks and 10,070 field guns. Although well dug in, this did not prevent 35,000 Soviet partisans setting about Küchler's lines of communication, derailing trains and bringing down bridges.

The Red Army successfully drove Küchler's troops westward away from Leningrad. However, lifting the 900-day siege cost Stalin an appalling 313,953 casualties, including 76,886 dead, captured or missing. Küchler lost three divisions, leaving seventeen badly depleted units to hold the line. While he managed to stem the Soviet tide, to the south things did not go half so well.

At the end of 1943 the Red Army sought to liberate Ukraine, west of the Dnepr. The 1st, 2nd, 3rd and 4th Ukrainian Fronts massed 2.3 million men, 2,040 tanks and self-propelled guns, 28,800 field guns and mortars and 2,370 aircraft, to smash von Manstein's Army Group South and Kleist's Army Group A (they could muster some 1.7 million troops, with 2,200 panzers, 16,800 field guns and 1,460 aircraft). Once again, Soviet partisans (numbering 50,000) played a role in causing severe disruption behind enemy lines.

In the wake of the Germans taking Zhitomir and their attempts on Kiev, Stavka ordered the 1st Ukrainian Front to destroy the 4th Panzer Army with the Zhitomir-Berdichev offensive. For the attack, Vatutin's 1st Ukrainian Front massed sixty-three infantry divisions and three cavalry divisions plus six tank and two mechanised corps. These were organised into the 1st Guards, 13th, 18th,

27th, 38th, 40th and 60th Field Armies, and the 1st and 3rd Guards Tank Armies. It was another overwhelming show of force.

Vatutin's offensive commenced on 24 December 1943 and within six days had forced a breakthrough 187 miles wide and 62 miles deep. The breach south-west of Kiev drove the 4th Panzer Army back over 100 miles, exposing the German 8th Army's right flank, as it had a foothold on the southern banks of the Dnepr. It was not long before the Red Army was attempting to ensnare it. This was vital, as these forces sat astride the junction of the 1st and 2nd Ukrainian Fronts.

Called the Korsun–Shevchenkovsky salient by the Soviets (but also known as the Cherkassy pocket), according to their intelligence the 1st Panzer and 8th Armies had nine infantry, one panzer and one motorised division. To over-whelm them, the Red Army launched twenty-seven rifle divisions, four tank, one mechanised and one cavalry corps armed with 370 tanks and self-propelled guns and almost 4,000 guns and mortars on 24 January 1944.

The German High Command ordered a counter-attack, with the 3rd, 4th, 11th and 13th Panzer Divisions sent to the Novo–Mirgorod region. The 16th and 7th Panzer Divisions were also gathered in the Rizino area. However, the Red Army's second envelopment attempt succeeded on 3 February, when the 1st and 2nd Ukrainian Fronts linked up near Zvenigorodka, trapping 56,000 men in the Korsun (Cherkassy) pocket.

Desperately, Hitler attempted a two-pronged relief with the 1st Panzer Army's 3rd Panzer Corps driving from the south-west and the 8th Army's 47th Panzer Corps striking from the south. The 5th SS Panzer Division led the break-out on the 16th, only to run headlong into the Soviet 4th Guards and 27th Armies. The Soviets claimed the battle resulted in 55,000 German dead or wounded and 18,200 POWs, while the Germans maintained that 30,000 men escaped, with 20,000 killed and 8,000 captured.

After Vatutin was mortally wounded, Zhukov took charge of destroying von Manstein's Army Group South, aiming to trap the 1st and 4th Panzer Army, along with 200,000 men. He attacked on 4 March, covering 100 miles in a few days. Once the 1st Ukrainian Front reached the Tarnopol–Proskurov Line and the 2nd Ukrainian Front cleared Uman and forced the Southern Bug River near Dzhulinka, the 1st Panzer Army was indeed threatened with encirclement. On the route to Uman the Germans lost 200 panzers, 600 field guns and 12,000 lorries as they sought to flee.

In the Crimea, General Erwin Jänecke's 17th Army, cut off since the end of 1943 by the 4th Ukrainian and North Caucasian Fronts, faced a similar fate to that of the 6th Army at Stalingrad. Although protected by consid-erable defences, the situation for the German and Romanian defenders, totalling around 230,000 men, with 215 panzers, 3,600 guns and mortars and

148 aircraft, was not good. The 4th Ukrainian Front attacking from the north and the Separate Maritime Army from the east had an overwhelming force of 470,000 men, 559 tanks and self-propelled guns, nearly 6,000 field guns and mortars supported by 1,250 aircraft.

The Red Army's offensive to liberate the Crimea commenced in earnest on 8 April 1944. The fall of Kerch, three days later, sealed the fate of the defenders and once it was apparent that the northern Perekop defences could not hold, the Germans began to evacuate regardless of Hitler's ridiculous orders to stand fast.

Up until mid-May, the Romanian Navy evacuated almost 121,000 men across the Black Sea. Pushed back to Sevastopol, the Germans lost 12,221 men and their Romanian allies 17,652 plus nearly all their armour. The 17th Army held until 9 May and the Khersones bridgehead lasted until the 12th, when the last 3,000 troops were overwhelmed. In total, some 25,000 German troops surrendered that day.

Although half of the 17th Army escaped, 117,000 were killed, wounded or captured. The Germans lost 65,100 casualities and their Romanian allies lost 31,600; some 20,000 local Soviet 'volunteers' were also lost. Soviet casualties sustained while clearing the Crimea numbered some 84,800 men, 171 tanks, 521 pieces of artillery and 179 aircraft.

On 14 May, Alexander Werth flew to view liberated Crimea. He wrote:

In the plains around Sapun Ridge and along the road that runs to Sevastopol through the Valley of Inkerman, the air was filled with the stench of death. It came from the hundreds of horses still lying there, inflated and decaying at the roadside, and from the thousands of dead, many of whom had not been buried deep enough, or even not buried at all.[1]

On the killing fields of the Khersones Peninsula he also saw the ground was:

[...] ploughed up by thousands of shells and scorched by the fire of the Katyusha mortars.

Hundreds of German vehicles were still there, or were being carted away by Russian soldiers. The ground was littered with thousands of German helmets, rifles, bayonets, and other arms and ammunition. [...] Over the ground were also scattered thousands of pieces of paper – photographs, snapshots, passports, maps, private letters – and even a volume of Nietzsche carried to the end by some Nazi superman.[2]

Werth strolled around the grounds of the lighthouse where 750 SS troops had made their last stand. Amongst the bodies at the water's edge, he found the skeleton of a Soviet Black Sea sailor who had died there almost two years earlier. 'Around the lighthouse, the blue sea was calm, and perhaps not very far away some rafts were still drifting over the sea, with desperate men clinging to them.'[3]

Just under a month later, on 9 June 1944 Stalin launched a major offensive against Hitler's Finnish allies north of Leningrad, along the Karelian Isthmus and in the Lake Ladoga area. Although Finland commenced peace negotiations in February, Stalin still struck with 500,000 men, 800 tanks, 10,000 artillery pieces and 2,000 combat aircraft. The Finnish Army numbered just over half this, with 268,000 men supported by just 110 tanks, 1,900 guns and 248 combat aircraft.

Within just two days the Red Army pierced Finnish lines. With limited German aid, the Finns were able to halt the Soviets in early July, although they were forced back about 62 miles to approximately the same line they had held at the end of the Winter War. The exhausted Finns made peace with Stalin in August and Germans troops withdrew into northern Norway.

By 1944, Hitler's armed forces had just over 9 million men under arms, over half of which were in the army and Waffen-SS formed into 315 divisions: these comprised 258 infantry, thirty-four panzer, seventeen panzergrenadier and six parachute divisions. The bulk of his massive manpower were deployed fighting the Red Army – 3.1 million men organised into 179 divisions, including twenty-three panzer and seven panzergrenadier divisions. Hitler's East European allies supplied another 800,000 men deployed in forty-nine divisions of variable quality.

Instead of the thirteen armies (including four panzer) that had defended the Eastern Front at the end of 1943, by the summer of 1944 there were only ten armies (of which just two were panzer). Of these, one was Hungarian and two were German-Romanian and were of dubious fighting value. By June, Hitler had a total of about 150 combat worthy divisions deployed on the Eastern Front, compared to 144 division on all other theatres of operation, including those still in Germany. The rest were either refitting, had been written off or were redeployed.

Hitler and his generals were now anticipating a Soviet summer offensive on the Eastern Front, but they had no way of appreciating its vast scale. Thanks to Soviet deception efforts, the Germans anticipated another assault on Army Group North Ukraine and diverted increasingly scarce resources there.

Although originally intended to coincide with D-Day, Stalin wrote to Prime Minister Churchill and President Roosevelt on 6 June 1944 to inform them that his own massive D-Day had slipped:

> The summer offensive of the Soviet troops, to be launched in keeping with the agreement reached at the Tehran Conference will begin in mid-June in one of the vital sectors of the Front. The general offensive will deploy by

stages, through consecutive engagement of the armies in offensive operations. Between late June and the end of July the operations will turn into a general offensive of the Soviet troops.[4]

Throughout May and June, Hitler's intelligence had been misled by fake build-ups in the 3rd Ukrainian Front and 3rd Baltic Front areas, convincing him that Stalin's major attacks would take place in Ukraine or the Baltic States. Nonetheless, many of Hitler's commanders were uneasy about maintaining the 'Byelorussian Balcony', as the bulge in Army Group Centre's line was nicknamed. To no avail, Field Marshal Ernst Busch, commanding Army Group Centre, pleaded with Hitler to pull out of Byelorussia, or at least to 'shorten the line'.

Nikolai Belov, commanding a regiment in a Soviet Rifle Division, had gone stir crazy during the winter. He had been billeted in a log cabin and to pass the time had read a biography on Napoleon. In one of those quirks of fate, in April 1944 he had started a second book about a Georgian general killed at Borodino – his name was Bagration. By the summer, it was clear to him that the Red Army was about to launch a counter-offensive in Byelorussia. On 18 June, Belov wrote in his diary:

There are grounds for thinking that we'll go into the attack on 21 or 22 June, which happens to be the third anniversary of the war. It's interesting that 21 June is also four months since we crossed the Dnepr. For some reason I have been feeling physically poor lately, and my nerves are utterly shattered … we'll soon be in battle, and then I'll forget everything. The whole thing is unpleasant and pretty strange.[5]

From that point on, he did not have time to keep his diary.

On 19 June, Army Group Centre's Intelligence Summary completely missed the main objective of Stalin's Operation Bagration:

The enemy attacks to be expected on Army Group Centre's sector – on Bobruisk, Mogilev, Orsha and possibly south-west of Vitebsk – will be of more than local character. All in all the scale of ground and air forces suggests that the aim is to bring about the collapse of Army Group Centre's salient by penetrations on several sectors. On the other side the Red Army order of battle, so far as it is known or can be estimated, is not yet indicative of a deep objective like Minsk.[6]

This assessment was completely wrong. Holding Vitebsk and the land bridge between the Dvina and Dnepr rivers was a strategic mistake, Busch reasoned;

why not shorten Army Group Centre's front by 150 miles with a withdrawal to the Dnepr or Berezina, a move 45 miles westward? The Dvina-Drut or Berezina lines might have been more manageable. Indeed, the Niemen River would have made a better defensive line as it extends almost to the Pripyat Marshes, but Hitler would never have countenanced pulling his forces back 150 miles, let alone 45.

To make matters worse, the loss of armoured units to northern Ukraine and France meant that Army Group Centre was mainly an infantry force. Critically, it only had 553 of the 4,740 tanks and assault guns on the Eastern Front, and most of these were in fact assault guns. The bulk of the armour, forty panzers (including twenty-nine Tiger Is) and 246 StuG IIIs, were deployed with General von Tippelskirch's 4th Army defending Orsha.

On top of this, Busch had no real reserves except for the 14th Infantry Division, the weak 20th Panzer Division and the remains of Panzergrenadier Division Feldherrnhalle. Consequently, his command had little strategic depth and lacked punch. Overall the balance sheet favoured Stalin, with a three to one advantage in manpower, ten to one in tanks and self-propelled artillery, and eight to one in guns and mortars. The correlation of forces was such that Busch's troops would be overwhelmed if they did not conduct a swift fighting withdrawal.

Hitler steadfastly refused to accept the reality of the situation, and General Hans Jordan was far from happy with the problems facing Army Group Centre. On 22 June, he wrote in the 9th Army's war diary:

> Ninth Army stands on the eve of another great battle, unpredictable in extent and duration. One thing is certain: in the last few weeks the enemy has completed an assembly of the very greatest scale opposite the army, and the army is convinced that the assembly overshadows the concentration of forces off the north flank of Army Group North Ukraine.[7]

Jordan understood Stalin's intentions perfectly well, adding:

> The army has felt bound to point out repeatedly that it considers the massing of strength on its front to constitute the preparation for this year's main Soviet offensive, which will have as its objective the reconquest of Byelorussia.[8]

He and his men were directly in the firing line.

Stalin's armoured fist was immensely powerful. He massed 118 rifle divisions, eight tank and mechanised corps, six cavalry divisions, thirteen artillery divisions and fourteen air defence divisions. These forces (including support troops) numbered 1.7 million men, more than double that of Army Group Centre.

Most notably, for the opening stages of the offensive Stalin had 2,715 tanks and 1,355 assault guns, about six times the numbered deployed by Busch. Nothing could withstand such brute force.

Stalin's Operation Bagration commenced at 0500 hrs on 23 June with a barrage that lasted for over two hours and to a depth of nearly 4 miles. For fifteen minutes, Red Army gunners furiously poured hot metal onto the German positions to a depth of 2 miles; after that there was ninety minutes of fire directed at observed targets, artillery positions and weapons pits. There was also twenty minutes of general bombardment dropped onto the Germans' main line of resistance and their rear areas.

For the troops of Busch's Army Group Centre, the density of this was truly shocking. Stalin's forces brought to bear 24,000 guns and mortars along the 431-mile line. Up to 90 per cent of the artillery was deployed on the breakthrough sectors, which only represented up to 20 per cent of the overall width of the front under attack. This was to be no amphibious assault as in Normandy, but a massive armoured charge across the length and breadth of the Soviet Republic of Byelorussia (or White Russia). Opposite Busch were four Soviet fronts; this meant that over 40 per cent of the entire Red Army was to be committed to Bagration.

In the face of Soviet attack, Army Group Centre's diary recorded, somewhat disingenuously, 'The major attack by the enemy north-west of Vitebsk has taken us by compete surprise. Until now our intelligence services had not indicated any type of enemy concentration of this size.'[9]

Busch's northern wing was held by General Georg-Hans Reinhardt's 3rd Panzer Army with 6th, 53rd and 9th corps respectively. Despite being a panzer army, this formation had no panzer or panzergrenadier divisions and consisted entirely of infantry and weak Luftwaffe field divisions. Facing the 3rd Panzer Army were elements of General Ivan Chernyakovsky's 3rd Byelorussian Front and General Ivan Kh. Bagramyan's 1st Baltic Front.

Way to the south was General Walter Weiss' weak 2nd Army. Even though it was screened by the Pripyat Marshes, the 8th, 20th and 23rd Corps were reliant on a few security and training divisions trying to hold the southern shoulder of the 'Byelorussian Balcony', as well as containing the Soviet partisans. Their operational effectiveness against regular Red Army formations was highly dubious and was simply a matter of expediency in the face of Hitler's growing manpower shortages.

General Hans Jordan's 9th Army was holding the Bobruisk area, with the 50th, 41st Panzer and 35th Corps running roughly south to north. The 41st Panzer Corps had no panzer divisions and the only real armoured unit was that of the 20th Panzer Division deployed at Bobruisk. Facing them were the armies of General Konstantin K. Rokossovsky's 1st Byelorussian Front.

Beyond these forces lay the German 4th Army with 12th Corps south of Mogilev, and 39th and 27th Corps running northward between Mogilev and Orsha. Again, the 39th Panzer Corps had no armoured divisions, although the other two corps could muster the 19th and 25th Panzergrenadier Divisions. Opposite these troops were General Georgi F. Zaharov's 2nd and Chernyakovsky's 3rd Byelorussian Fronts.

Unfortunately, the resulting smoke and early morning fog on 23 June greatly hampered the supporting air attacks by the Red Air Force. Only Chernyakovsky enjoyed clear weather, allowing his bombers to carry out 160 sorties. The ground-attack Shturmoviks had to wait until the artillery and rocket launchers had finished their work. Afterwards, the Soviet infantry surged forward to seize tactical ground that could be exploited as a springboard for the impending tank breakthrough.

Bagramyan, after rapidly breaking through the German defences as early as 24 June, crossed the Western Dvina at Beshenkovichi and established bridge-heads. The 43rd Army's 60th Infantry Corps reached Gnezdilovichi, west of Vitebsk, just 3–6 miles from Chernyakovsky's 39th Army's 5th Guards Corps pressing from the opposite direction, thereby threatening the two Luftwaffe field divisions exposed in the bugle in the German line west of Vitebsk. By mid-afternoon Busch had informed Army High Command that the situation around Vitebsk looked precarious and Reinhardt's 3rd Panzer did not have the ability to restore the situation.

By the end of 23 June, Hitler had still not woken up to the fact that this was Stalin's main assault on the Eastern Front. General Heidkämper, Reinhardt's chief of staff, was dismayed at the rapidity of the Red Army advances and that day he and Reinhardt were involved in the first of a series of heated meetings with Busch in Minsk, where they demanded the rapid evacuation of Vitebsk. Busch's response was an unequivocal 'no', nor would he permit the 3rd Panzer Army's reserves to be deployed until he got permission from Army High Command.

By the evening of 23–24 June, General P.F. Malyshev's 4th Shock Army had turned General Rolf Wuthmann's 9th Corps' front line, and in places had pierced the Tiger Line, which formed the second belt of defences.

The greatest danger, however, was to the north of Vitebsk, where General I.M. Chistyakov's 6th Guards Army was on the brink of cutting off General Friedrich Gollwitzer's 53rd Corps in the city from Wuthmann. To the dismay of the defenders of Vitebsk, at 0245 hrs Wuthmann was instructed to fight his way back from the Tiger Line to the defences west of the Dvina. By midday, the Red Army had reached the river and it was apparent to General Reinhardt that the Soviets were intent on cutting Vitebsk off and that there was little to keep the 6th Guards Army and 43rd Army from linking up to the west.

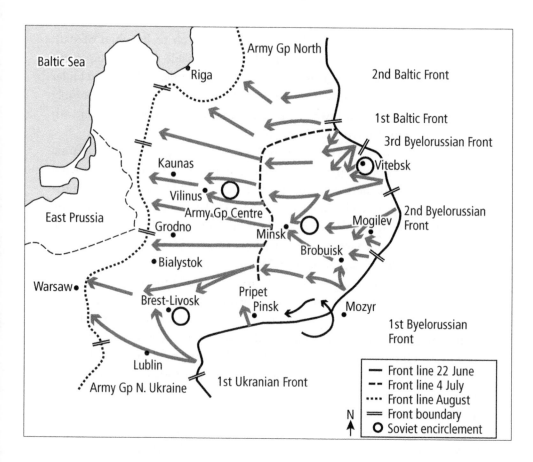

Operation Bagration, 22 June–19 August 1944.

Minutes later, Reinhardt's HQ received a radio message from Gollwitzer – the road west from Vitebsk was under immediate threat from enemy forces. This was relayed to Busch with another plea to withdraw. Within the hour, Busch was onto Hitler's HQ only to be told that Vitebsk must be held and if the road was cut it was to be reopened by counter-attack. Busch, knowing full well that they would be too late, plucked up courage and phoned Hitler personally that evening. Whatever argument Busch offered, Hitler was adamant that Gollwitzer's corps would remain in Vitebsk.

Busch began planning counter-offensives as if it were the good old days, although Hitler did not make it apparent where the forces for such an operation would come from. Pathetically, Hitler ordered the other army groups each to send a single division to help Busch. In the event, four divisions were transferred, but even if they had got there in time they would have been unable to affect the impending battle.

'What can I do? What can I do?' lamented Busch to his chief of staff, Lieutenant General Hans Krebs.[10] Clearly he was unable or unwilling to put his career on the line to safeguard his men. It mattered little, as Busch, and Hitler for that matter, had lost the limited window of opportunity in which to possibly retrieve the situation. Meanwhile, the rest of the 3rd Panzer Army, 9th and 6th Corps were being driven away from Vitebsk.

General Gollwitzer was determined that his 53rd Corps would not become trapped, and sensibly prepared to conduct a fighting withdrawal. He ordered Generalleutnant Robert Pistorius' 4th Luftwaffe Field Division to the south-west ready to spearhead a break-out. While Hitler refused to authorise any retreat, Busch told Gollwitzer to use both his Luftwaffe divisions to prepare two break-outs while Generalleutnant Alfons Hitter's 206th and Generalmajor Claus Müller-Bulow's 246th Infantry Divisions defended Vitebsk.

Reinhardt and Heidkämper paced the room in frustration as alarming situation reports poured in. Then unexpectedly, two whole hours later at 1830 hrs, 3rd Panzer received a radio message from Hitler instructing that 53rd Corps should fight its way to the Tiger Line, but one division should be nominated to hold the fortress. Hitter was to stay behind to cover the withdrawal. However, because of all this dithering, Pistorius was now encircled near Ostrovno. Heidkämper was far from happy, what logic was this? If a whole corps could not hold, what was the point of sacrificing a single division?

By early afternoon of 25 June, Bagramyan's 1st Tank Corps under General Butkov had reached the Dvina and taken a damaged bridge. In Chernyakovsky's sector, Lyudnikov's 39th Army was also pushing on the river and, supported by some elements of the 43rd, was assigned the task of destroying the German units trapped at Vitebsk. The Germans tried to break through the Soviet cordon, launching twenty-five counter-attacks on the 25th and a similar number the following day, but without success.

Busch asked Hitler for permission to try and save Hitter's 206th Infantry. Hitler ridiculously ordered that a staff officer be dropped into Vitebsk to remind Gollwitzer of his instructions. Reinhardt was furious and phoned Busch, 'Tell the Führer that if he stands by this order, there is only one officer in the 3rd Panzer Army that can carry it out, and that is the commander. I am ready to execute this order!' All this mattered little, as Hitter was now trapped and the two other divisions were isolated to the south-west.

Gollwitzer was in a hopeless position by the evening of 26 June and, defying orders, he split his forces up with instructions to try and head west. His 53rd Corps' last message was sent out at 0345 hrs to Reinhardt requesting air support and the location of the nearest German units. Gollwitzer and his remaining men got a dozen miles before being surrounded again. Thus, between the second and fourth days of Bagration, Hitler recklessly threw away his single strongest position on the whole of the Fatherland Line.

Those men who did escape fell prey to bandit country full of Soviet partisans hell-bent on revenge and with little interest in taking prisoners. The Soviets and the Germans argued over the details, with Gollwitzer claiming that his command lost 5,000 killed and 22,000 captured and the Soviets contesting that 20,000 Germans were killed and 10,000 captured.

To the south, Soviet inroads against the 4th Army were being made and they were aiming for the Moscow–Minsk Highway that also linked Smolensk with Orsha. This region was defended by General Paul Völckers' 27th Corps, consisting of Generalleutnant Paul Schürmann's 25th Panzergrenadier Division, Generalleutnant Hans Traut's 78th Sturm (Assault) Division and Generalleutnant Albrecht Wüstenhagen's 260th Infantry Division. Traut's men were used to and expecting Soviet bombardment, but the ferocity of the shelling on 23 June must have stunned even them. Minefields and barbed wire belts were obliterated, sandbags were torn asunder and scattered, weapon pits and trenches vanished. Any weapons caught on the surface soon became so many twisted, useless pieces of steel.

The plan was that General K.N. Galitskiy's 11th Guards would overwhelm the German defences along the Moscow–Minsk Highway, which would permit Rotmistrov's 5th Guards Tank Army to deploy across the terrain either side. Although the 11th Guards struggled against the determined resistance from Traut, the 1st Guards Rifle Division pushed between him and the 256th Infantry to the north. Galitskiy then pushed Burdenyniy's 2nd Guards Tanks Corps through this gap along a railway line.

The Germans counter-attacked south of Lake Orekhi on 24 June, and failed. However, the hold-up with the 11th Guards Army meant that Rotmistrov was redirected to the 5th Army's sector. With Traut's men being slowly overwhelmed, General von Tippelskirch knew that 27th Corps must withdraw to the Dnepr. A sense of panic began to overwhelm those in Orsha. Defying orders, Tippelskirch allowed some units to fall back, but it was too late. Burdenyniy's tanks swept north of the city toward the end of 26 June, and his T-34s rolling to the west caught a German train full of wounded being evacuated from Orsha and blew it from the rails. That night, the 11th Guards and 31st Armies overran the city.

Zakharov's offensive opened with Grishin's attack north of Mogilev, supported by General K.A. Vershinin's 4th Air Army. His men began crossing the Dnepr on 26 June. To the south, General I.V. Boldin's 50th Army also thrust toward Mogilev. East of the city, the 33rd and 49th Armies hit the 337th Infantry Division and broke through on the Ryassna–Mogilev road. Once the first and second German trench lines were breached, Soviet armour poured into the rear area of Weidling's 39th Panzer Corps.

General von Tippelskirch, acting as 4th Army's commander while Heinrici was on sick leave, recommended a withdrawal behind the Dnepr, but Busch said no. To plug the gap east of Mogilev, von Tippelskirch had little choice but to throw in the recently arrived Panzergrenadier Division Feldherrnhalle under Generalmajor Friedrich-Carl von Steinkeller. He was to join the battle in 39th Panzer Corps' sector. The panzergrenadiers were swamped, and just three days later von Steinkeller was forced back across the Dnepr with the survivors of his division, only to be taken by the Red Army near the Berezina.

By 25 June, von Tippelskirch was in a fraught situation; his 39th Panzer Corps had been overwhelmed and the armies to the north and south – 3rd Panzer and 9th – were falling apart. Martinek was killed and replaced by General Otto Scheunemann, who tried to lead the 39th Panzer Corps in a westward break-out attempt. He was also killed and the corps disintegrated under the Soviet onslaught. Two days later, General Bamler assumed command of Mogilev from General Erdmannsdorf, just in time to be taken prisoner along with 3,000 troops, all that remained of the 8,000-strong garrison.

To the south Bobruisk, held by General Adolf Harmann, was protected by the Drut River and its marshy flood plain and then the Berezina River. Just as the 3rd Byelorussian Front was pressing on Minsk from the north, Rokossovsky's 1st Byelorussian Front was striking from the south. His front went into action on 24 June in the direction of Bobruisk. Jordan's 9th Army, although suffering heavy casualties, held off his attacks.

General Jordan sought and received Busch's permission to commit the 20th Panzer Division to try and stem the Soviet tide, but it could muster just seventy-one Panzer Mk IVs. At this moment, Batov's 65th Army broke through on the southern approaches to Bobruisk and Rokossovsky committed the 1st Guards Tank Corps to exploit the breach. Perhaps panicking, Jordan ordered 20th Panzer to retrace its steps and head south, bumping into the Soviets near Sloboda south of Bobruisk. Now, not only was Bobruisk under threat but also those German divisions still east of the Berezina. By 26 June, 20th Panzer had been driven back to the city with the Soviet 9th Tank Corps bearing down on it from the east and the Soviet 1st Guards Tank Corps from the south. The 1st Guards Tank Corps cut the roads from Bobruisk to the north and north-west on the night of 26/27 June.

Only on 28 June did Busch authorise the 4th Army to retreat behind the Berezina, but von Tippelskirch was already there, having lost 130,000 of his 165,000 men. In the meantime, Rokossovsky's 1st Byelorussian Front smashed through the 9th Army's front while Jordan dithered for twenty-four hours over committing his reserve, the 20th Panzer Division.

By the morning of 27 June, General B.S. Bakarov's 9th Tank Corps had secured the Berezina crossings. Rokossovsky, sensing the time was right, committed the 1st Guards Tank Corps and 1st Mechanised Corps from Batov's 65th Army, sending them toward Baranovichi, south-west of Minsk. Rokossovsky's 1st Byelorussian Front trapped a sizeable number of German troops east of Bobruisk. Any withdrawal or break-out attempt had now been left far too late.

The Red Air Force's 16th Air Army launched 526 aircraft, 400 of them bombers, against the trapped Germans, dropping 12,000 bombs in just under an hour and adding to the conflagration created by the Germans who had torched their supply dumps and stores. In desperation, the Germans scattered under this air assault. Soldiers fled in panic, and panzers and trucks swerved off the roads in a desperate bid to escape the bombs only to get stuck in the mud. Those men trying to swim the Berezina were gunned down by the Soviets advancing along the western banks.

Attempts by General Kurt-Jürgen Freiherr von Lützow's 35th Corps to break out to the north spearheaded by 150 panzers and self-propelled guns were smashed on the evening of 27 June. They ran headlong into General Teremov's 108th Rifle Division. Confusion seemed to reign with 41st Panzer Corps, as General Edmund Hoffmeister of the 383rd Infantry Division was temporarily in command. He was given permission to make a run for it, although General Hamann, the Bobruisk city commandant, drew the short straw as he and a division were instructed to act as rear guard. Also, 3,500 wounded were to be left behind. Some 5,000 men made a dash for it at 2300 hrs on 28 June.

The tanks of 20th Panzer led the break-out north-west along the western bank of the Berezina, with the rear guard instructed to hold until 0200 hrs on 29 June. The panzers and panzergrenadiers soon found themselves under attack by T-34s and by the Red Air Force. The survivors managed to cut their way through, however they still had to cover 12 miles to reach the Svisloch River and 12th Panzer.

A panzergrenadier battalion from 12th Panzer, supported by a company of tanks under Major Blanchbois, attempted unsuccessfully to go to the rescue but could not get over the Svisloch north-west of Bobruisk, as the Soviets held the only local bridge. However, many German troops made a swim for it and up to 20,000 'Bobruiskers' were saved. German wounded remained in Bobruisk, along with General Hamann who bravely stayed with them. By 2 July the Soviets claimed to have captured 32,000 German troops in and around the city and killed another 16,000.

General Jordan's 9th Army front was in tatters and Busch flew to the Berghof late on 26 June to try to get Hitler to rescind his hold-fast orders. Jordan, who accompanied Busch, found himself relieved on the 27th. Busch suffered the same fate the following day. Field Marshal Walter Model, commander of Army Group North Ukraine, was appointed to replace Busch and instructed to fly to Minsk to try and retrieve the situation immediately.

Effectively, the fall of defensive lines Vitebsk, Orsha, Mogilev and Bobruisk meant that it was all over for Army Group Centre. The entire defensive system in the central zone had collapsed. The trail of destruction was truly appalling and Model must have looked on in despair as the reports came in detailing the toll. By 30 June, the first phase of the Battle of Byelorussia was over; according to the Soviets, they killed 132,000 Germans and took another 66,000 prisoners, as well as capturing or destroying 940 tanks, over 5,000 guns and about 30,000 motor vehicles. The military historian Basil Liddell Hart noted:

> This great pincer movement bore a striking resemblance to the one which the Germans had executed three years earlier [namely Barbarossa], in the opposite direction. As in that case, only a proportion of the enveloped forces succeeded in slipping out the trap.[11]

General M.F. Panov's 1st Guards Tank Corps from the 1st Byelorussian Front followed the armour of the 3rd Byelorussian Front to Minsk from the south-east. The German 4th Army now found itself being squeezed by seven tank, motorised and cavalry corps. In the meantime, other troops of the 1st Byelorussian Front were chasing the Germans toward Pukhovichi-Minsk and Slutsk-Baranovichi.

Minsk was held by mixture of units, including elements of the 5th Panzer. The defenders' priority, regardless of Hitler's grand designs, was to get the wounded and administrative staff out and to hold the railway open for as long as possible. The situation in the city was desperate, especially as it was full of non-combatant rear-echelon staff and demoralised stragglers. Minsk was liberated by the evening of 3 July, and the people danced in the streets of rubble with tears in their eyes as they welcomed the Red Army with flowers.

'In Russia there has been a major breakthrough in the centre and a rush of unclear movements,' wrote Iosif Hechter, on 4 July. 'Vitebsk, Orsha, Mogilev, and Bobruisk have fallen one after the other. Yesterday Minsk. Today Polotsk. In Normandy things have not moved much since the fall of Cherbourg.'[12] In France, the Allies would not liberate Paris until late August.

Lieutenant General Otto Drescher, commander of the 267th Infantry Division which had acted as rear guard for forces trapped in one of two Minsk pockets, called on his men to save themselves on 5 July:

> During this battle the enemy succeeded in encircling our troops. This encirclement must be broken and we must fight our way to freedom and to our

homeland. If we are to see our homeland and families again, we must fight. I want no one to doubt that the way will be difficult and great sacrifice will be required. Whoever prefers the dishonourable fate of captivity will be subjected to the habitual cruelty of the Bolshevik murderers. I have no doubt that the choice will not be difficult.[13]

In the far south, Konev's powerful 1st Ukrainian Front, numbering over a million men, equipped with 1,600 tanks and assault guns, 14,000 guns and mortars and 2,806 combat aircraft, was poised to launch another attack. His intended target was Army Group North Ukraine, which consisted of 900,000 men with 900 panzers and assault guns, 6,300 field guns and mortars, and 700 aircraft.

In the north beyond Konev's Front lay units of Rokossovsky's 1st Byelorussian Front that had not fought in Bagration, and which were to attack 56th Panzer Corps. Konev's 3rd Guards and 13th Armies, and 1st Guards Tank Army, and General V.K. Baranov's mechanised cavalry corps were instructed to advance on Rava-Russkaya and the 4th Panzer Army north of Lvov. His 60th and 38th Armies, plus the 3rd Guards and 4th tank Armies and General S.V. Sokolov's mechanised cavalry group were to cut through the 1st Panzer Army. Further south, the 1st Guards and 18th Armies, followed by 5th Guards Army, were to attack the Hungarian 1st Army.

Konev's offensive commenced on 13 July 1944, with General V.N. Gordov's 3rd Guards Army and General N.P. Pukhov's 13th Army attacking toward Soka, Radekhov, Rava-Russkaya and Lublin respectively. This was followed the next day by the main attack, with 38th and 60th Armies toward Lvov via Zolochev. By the evening of the 15th, the Rava-Russkaya attack had pushed 9 miles, with Baronov's mechanised cavalry corps and General M.Y. Katukov's 1st Guards Tank Army following up on the 16th and 17th heading toward Yaroslav and behind Brody.

Five days after the offensive started, Konev's forces had cut a breach in the German defences 156 miles wide by 60–90 miles deep and routed the 4th Panzer Army and the 17th Army. At nightfall on 18 July he surrounded 45,000 Germans near Brody. They held out for four desperate days and lost 30,000 killed and 15,000 captured, as well as sixty-eight panzers, 500 guns and 3,500 lorries.

Lvov was finally liberated on 27 July. About half of the 40,000 German troops in and around the city were killed or captured. In the past month, the Soviets claimed that German losses stood at 381,000 dead, 158,000 captured, 2,735 tanks and assault guns, 8,702 guns and 57,000 motor vehicles. Army Group Centre had been completely smashed.

Zeitzler urged Hitler to withdraw Army Group North from the Baltic States before it was encircled. Hitler refused and a row ensued. Guderian said:

Zeitzler had on five occasions offered to resign his appointment. Such behaviour was wrong in wartime, and should be no more permissible to generals in authoritative positions than it was to soldiers in the field.[14]

After falling out once too often, Hitler finally replaced Zeitzler with Guderian at the end of July 1944.

By the end of August, the Red Army had liberated Byelorussia and over three-quarters of Lithuania, driven the Wehrmacht from Ukraine and begun liberating Poland. However, by October Bagration's momentum had ended. With the 1st Byelorussian Front still to liberate Warsaw, the 2nd and 3rd Byelorussian Fronts had yet to crush the East Prussian citadel of Konigsberg.

In the very far north the Red Army's Karelian Front, with 97,000 troops, attacked the 56,000-strong German 19th Mountain Corps west of Murmansk on 7 October 1944. The Soviet 14th Army defeated them in the three-phased, twenty-four-day Petsamo-Kirkenes Operation. However, although the Soviet 14th Army failed to destroy the corps as 18,000 men escaped, it inflicted over 9,000 casualties at a cost of 16,000 men.

In the meantime, the Soviets reached the Baltic near Memel on 10 October, trapping Army Group North. Approximately 200,000 German troops (roughly twenty-six divisions) were to remain isolated in Latvia for the rest of the war in the vast Courland pocket. The Soviets lost approximately 390,000 casualties, 2,700 tanks, 1,120 piece of artillery and 720 aircraft in trying to overrun it. By the time the renamed Army Group Courland surrendered on 7 May 1945, it was the only major German formation left intact.

Following Memel, Stavka ordered Chernyakovsky to strike into the heart of Prussia along the Gumbinnen–Konigsberg axis. Colonel General N.I. Krylov's 5th and Colonel General Galitskiy's 11th Guards Armies were tasked with piercing German defences, followed up by the 2nd Guards Tank Corps and the 28th Army. On the flanks, the Soviet 31st and 39th Armies were to provide support. The attack was launched on 16 October and four days later, after bitter fighting to overcome strong German defences, the 11th and 2nd Guards reached Gumbinnen. On 21 October Lieutenant General Luchinsky's 28th Army was committed to the battle, but the offensive ground to a halt in the Stallupinen defensive region. The fighting dragged on until 27 October in the face of German panzer reinforcements.

Bagration was the worst defeat ever inflicted on the Wehrmacht on the Eastern Front and resulted in the loss of 670,000 men. Stalingrad and Kursk came nowhere near this magnitude of defeat. The Allies took two and a half months to defeat Army Group B in Normandy – on the Eastern Front, Army Group Centre had been destroyed in just two weeks. It was decimated, with 300,000 killed,

120,000 captured and 250,000 wounded. Added to the other losses incurred by Army Group North Ukraine, Hitler lost at least fifty-four irreplaceable divisions. The summer of 1944 was a complete and utter catastrophe for the Führer.

15

HITLER'S LAST TRIUMPH

In just five weeks of bitter fighting during the summer of 1944, Rokossovsky's troops stormed over 450 miles and were within reach of Warsaw. The Polish capital looked a tempting prize for Stalin as a culmination of Operation Bagration's remarkable success, but his summer offensive was beginning to lose momentum. Rokossovsky's 1st Byelorussian Front was at the very limit of its supply lines; ammunition and rations were exhausted, as were his men.

Rokossovsky, at this stage, enjoyed a 3:1 superiority in infantry and 5:1 in armour and artillery. He had at his disposal nine armies: one tank army, two tank corps, three cavalry corps, one motorised corps and two air armies. Against this, Field Marshal Walter Model's 2nd Army could muster barely five under-strength panzer divisions and one infantry division, while the battered 9th Army had just two divisions and two brigades of infantry.

In many ways, Hitler's defence of Warsaw echoed that of Minsk. The eastern approaches of the Polish capital were protected by a 50-mile ring of strongpoints. The only difference was that, this time, Model had sufficient mobile reserves with which to parry Rokossovsky's armoured thrusts. He had gathered his wits and, more importantly, sufficient men with which to thwart Rokossovsky's oncoming tide. Model's defences coalesced around his panzer divisions with around 450 tanks and self-propelled guns. Over the next week, things would start to go badly wrong for Rokossovsky and his men would experience their first major setback.

Rokossovsky's Lublin–Brest Offensive was conducted from 18 July to 2 August 1944 as a follow-up to Bagration and to support General I.S. Konev's Lvov–Sandomierz Offensive by tying down German forces in central eastern Poland. It culminated in the major tank Battle of Radzymin. To the north of Konev's 1st Ukrainian Front, Rokossovsky's 8th Guards, 47th and 69th Armies supported by the 2nd Tank Army, and the Polish 1st Army struck from the Kovel area toward Lublin and Warsaw, thereby making Army Group North Ukraine's position untenable.

It seemed appropriate to Stalin that eastern Poland should be liberated as part of Byelorussia, as that is how Hitler had treated it. For administrative purposes, parts of German-occupied Poland had been lumped in with western Byelorussia. When Hitler divided prostrate Poland with Stalin in 1939, he also annexed the region south-west of East Prussia (Wartheland) to the Reich, while the Reichkommissariate of '*Ostland*' (an area incorporating Minsk and the Baltic States) and 'Ukraine' governed parts of eastern Poland, and the 'rump' in the middle was run as the *Generalgouvernement*.

In mid-1944 north of Warsaw, Model turned to Heinrich Himmler's Waffen-SS for assistance in stabilising the front. The remnants of the 1st SS and 2nd SS Panzer Divisions had been shipped west after their mauling in the Kamenets–Podolsk pocket to re-equip and prepare for the anticipated Anglo-American landings in France. However, the tough 3rd SS and 5th SS Panzer Divisions remained in Romania and Poland rearming.

The 3rd SS was notified to move north as early as 25 June, but the disruption to the rail networks and roads meant that it took two weeks to get to north-eastern Poland. Arriving on 7 July, it found the Red Amy was already striking toward the Polish city of Grodno, threatening the southern flank of Army Group Centre's 4th Army and the northern flank of the 2nd Army.

Deployed to Grodno, the 3rd SS were given the task of creating a defensive line for the 4th Army to retire behind. Spectacularly, the division held off 400 Soviet tanks for eleven days before withdrawing south-west toward Warsaw. Joined by the Hermann Göring Panzer Division at Siedlce, 50 miles east of the Polish capital, they held the Red Army for almost a week from 24 July, keeping open an escape corridor for the 2nd Army as it fled toward the Vistula. Three days later, the Red Army threw almost 500 tanks to the south and by 29 July it was at the very suburbs of Warsaw.

The 5th SS arrived in western Warsaw on 27 July and trundled through the troubled city to take up positions to the east. The next day, Stalin ordered Rokossovsky to occupy Praga, Warsaw's suburbs on the eastern bank of the Vistula, during 5–8 August, and to establish a number of bridgeheads over the river to the south of the city.

As instructed, the Soviet 2nd Tank Army and 8th Tank Corps attacked westward along the Warsaw–Lublin road toward Praga. About 40 miles south-east of Warsaw, in the Garwolin area, the 2nd Tank was opposed by two advanced battalions of Genera Fritz Franek's 10,800-strong 73rd Infantry Division. Holding the north bank of the Swidra River, they were backed up by the Hermann Göring Panzer Division 12 miles east of Praga.

In addition, four panzer divisions (3rd SS, 5th SS, 4th and 19th Panzer) which were poised to counter-attack now defended the approaches to the Polish capital. The men of 19th Panzer were veterans of the Eastern Front, having fought on the central and southern sectors from June 1941 to June 1944, before being shipped to the Netherlands for a refit. Hasso Krappe, an officer with 19th Panzer, recalled the fighting around Warsaw, 'Over the next two weeks the battles centred on the region north of Warsaw [between the Bug, Narev and Vistula], and on the Varka, which has gone down in military history as the "Magnushev Bridgehead".'

Franek's division had endured a rough time during its career, having taken part in the invasions of Poland, the Low Countries, France and Greece before entering the Soviet Union via Romania. It fought at Nikolayev, Cherson, Sevastopol and the Kuban bridgehead. Suffering heavy losses near Melitopol, the 73rd Infantry was withdrawn only to be trapped by the Red Army in Sevastopol in May 1944 and re-formed in June in Hungary under Franek.

Franek's men and the Hermann Göring bore the brunt of the powerful attacks launched by two Soviet Tank Corps. Garwolin was partially captured during the night of 27/28 July and the 73rd fell back. Despite the presence of elements of 19th Panzer and the Hermann Göring, by noon on 29 July the Soviet 8th Tank Corps had secured Kołbiel and Siennica. About 26 miles from Warsaw at Minsk Mazowiecki, Lieutenant General N.D. Vedeneev's 3rd Tank Corps broke the German defences, and at Zielonka, General Franek and some of his staff were captured.

Brest-Litovsk fell to Rokossovsky on 28 July and with his troops at Garwolin, three German divisions tried to escape toward Siedlce, south-east of Warsaw. They were surrounded between Biała and the river and crushed, with 15,000 killed and just 2,000 captured. In Moscow, Stalin and his commanders were very pleased with Rokossovsky's efforts and on 29 July he was nominated a Marshal of the Soviet Union.

Captured German documents showed that the 5th SS Reconnaissance Unit was deployed near Minsk Mazowiecki; units of the Hermann Göring and the 73rd Infantry were holding the Cechowa and Otwock sector of Warsaw's outer defences; 19th Panzer was defending the approaches to Praga and the 3rd SS were in the Okuniew and Pustelnik suburban areas.

When the 2nd Tank Army's 16th Tank Corps struck toward Otwock along the Lublin road, the 19th Panzer counter-attacked with forty panzers and an infantry regiment but were unable to hold, and by the evening the Soviets were a mere 15 miles from Warsaw. They were now poised to assault the key defences of Okuniew. The 8th Tank Corps opened the attack, only to be stalled by determined German air and artillery fire.

In the meantime Vedeneev, bypassing German defences, drove them from Wołomin and Radzymin, just 12 miles north-east of Warsaw, where he took up defensive positions along the Dluga River. Having outstretched his supply lines and outrun the rest of the Soviet 2nd Tank Army, Vedeneev was in a dangerously exposed position. The 39th Panzer Corps was in the area and the panzer divisions were coming together in the direction of Radzymin-Wołomin.

Rokossovsky's forces were quick to react to this threat and attempted to alleviate the pressure on Vedeneev with a diversionary attack. At dawn on 31 July, followed by heavy air and artillery bombardment, the Soviet 8th Tank Corps threw themselves at the Germans who fell back toward Okuniew. The 5th SS counter-attacked in a westerly direction with fifty panzers from Stanislawów, in an effort to link up with the Hermann Göring and 19th Panzer, who were fighting a tank battle with the Soviets at Okuniew and Ossow.

The 5th SS were repulsed and on the evening of 31 July the Soviets took Okuniew, but could not budge the enemy from their strongpoint at Osos. North of the Soviet 8th Tank Corps, the 3rd Tank remained unsupported and, like the 16th Corps, endured a day of heavy attacks from German armour, artillery and infantry. The commander of the Soviet 2nd Army was in an impossible position; his units were enduring heavy casualties; he was short of supplies and his rear was under threat.

Rokossovsky simply could not fulfil his orders to break though the German defences and enter Praga by 8 August – it was simply not possible. On 1 August, at 1610 hrs he ordered the attack to be broken off just as Model launched his major counter-attack. On 2 August, all Red Army forces that were assaulting Warsaw were redirected. The 28th, 47th and 65th Armies were sent northwards to seize the undefended town of Wyszków and the Liwiec River Line. Crucially, this left the 2nd Tank Army without infantry support. This situation was compounded when the 69th Army was ordered to halt while the 8th Guards Army under Vasily Chuikov ceased the assault, to await a German attack from the direction of Garwolin.

Model began to probe the weak spot in Rokossovsky's line between Praga and Siedlce. His intention was to hit the Soviets in the flank and the rear, and soon, to the north-east of Warsaw, the 39th Panzer Corps was counter-attacking the 3rd Tank Corps and forcing it back to Wołomin. The 3rd SS, Hermann Göring and 4th and 19th Panzer Divisions struck south into the exposed Soviet columns.

The Hermann Göring's 1st Armoured Paratroop Regiment launched their attack from Praga toward Wołomin on 31 July, heralding the much larger effort to halt the Red Army in its steps before Warsaw. From the south-west, along the Warsaw–Wyszków road attacking toward Radzymin, came the 19th Panzer, while from Wyszków the 4th Panzer acted in support.

The next day, from Węgrów pushing toward Wołomin, came the panzers of the 5th SS. At the same time the 3rd SS was launched into the fray from Siedlce toward Stanislawów with the intention of trapping those Soviet units on the north-eastern bank of the Dluga. General Nikolaus von Vormann, appointed by Guderian to command the 9th Army and bringing up reinforcements from the 2nd Army's reserves, also launched a counter-attack. Using men of the 5th SS and 3rd SS attacking from the forests to the east of Michałów, he drove the Soviet 8th Tank Corps from Okuniew at 2100 hrs on 1 August and linked up with 39th Panzer Corps from the west.

By 2 August, the 19th followed by 4th Panzer were in Radzymin and the Soviet 3rd Tank Corps was thrown back toward Wołomin. The following day, the Hermann Göring Panzer Division rolled into Wołomin. Pressed into the area of Wołomin, Vedeneev was completely trapped. Attempts by the 8th Guards Tank Corps and the 16th Tank Corps to reach him failed with the former suffering serious casualties in the attempt.

After a week of heavy fighting, the Soviet 3rd Tank Corps was surrounded; 3,000 men were killed and another 6,000 captured. The Red Army also lost 425 of the 808 tanks and self-propelled guns they had begun the battle with on 18 July. By noon on 5 August the Germans had ceased their counter-attack and the battle for the Praga approaches had come to an end. Two German divisions had to be transferred south to deal with the Soviet threat there.

Vedeneev's corps was destroyed and the 8th Guards Tank Corps and the 16th Tank Corps had taken heavy losses. The exhausted Soviet 2nd Tank Army handed over its positions and withdrew to lick its wounds.

Post-war Communist propagandists cited the Battle of Radzymin as evidence that the German counter-attack prevented the Red Army from helping the Warsaw Uprising. Stalin clearly did not hold Vedeneev responsible. He remained in charge and the 3rd Tank Corps was honoured by being designated the 9th Guards Tank Corps in November 1944. It was not until 25 August that Rokossovsky would inform Stalin that he was ready to have another go at Warsaw.

After such heavy fighting north-east of the Polish capital, it is easy to see why Stalin saw the Polish Home Army's Warsaw Rising as of little consequence to the overall strategic scheme of things. General Tadeusz Bór-Komorowsky, commander of the underground Polish Home Army, ordered his men to rise up against the German occupation of Warsaw on 1 August. Two days later, Stanislaus Mikołajczyk, who had been appointed prime minister by the exiled Polish government in London, gained an audience with Stalin in the hope of getting help for the Warsaw Rising. Stalin showed little faith in the Home Army's fighting capabilities:

What is an army without artillery, tanks and an air force? They are even short of riles. In modern warfare such an army is of little use. They are small partisan units, not a regular army. I was told that the Polish government has ordered these units to drive the Germans out of Warsaw. I wonder how they could possibly do this, their forces are not up to that task.[1]

Rokossovsky was ordered to go over to the defensive and watched the Germans systemically crush the Poles for two whole months. Likewise, the Red Air Force, which was just 100 miles away, did very little. At Kraków, the capital of the *Generalgouvernement*, the Wehrmacht garrison was 30,000 strong, twice that of Warsaw, which had a much bigger population. In addition, there were some 10,000 armed German administrators in the city. As a result, there was no secondary Home Army rising in Kraków.

Just 12.5 miles south of Warsaw, Chuikov's 8th Guards Army crossed the Vistula on 1 August at Magnuszew. He held onto his tiny bridgehead despite determined counter-attacks. By the 8th, the bridgehead contained three Soviet corps. Holding the northern shoulder of the bridgehead and preventing the Soviets from expanding it was a Volksgrenadier Brigade and a battalion of panzers, while to the south were the 17th Infantry Division.

General Zygmunt Berling's Soviet-trained Polish 1st Army had reinforced Rokossovsky during the spring of 1944. This was, in fact, the second Polish army to be formed in the Soviet Union and was the military wing of the so-called Union of Polish Patriots, which had come into being with Stalin's approval in 1943. The earlier army of General Władysław Anders had managed to slip Stalin's grasp in 1942, getting itself redeployed to fight with the British in the Middle East and Italy.

Berling was ordered to cross the Vistula at Puławy on 31 July on a wide front to support other elements of the Soviet 69th and 8th Guards Armies crossing near Magnuszew. Two Polish divisions gained the west bank on 1 and 2 August, but by the 4th they had suffered 1,000 casualties and were ordered to withdraw. They were then assigned to protect the northern part of the Magnuszew bridgehead.

When Berling joined Rokossovsky he had 104,000 men under arms, comprising five infantry divisions, a tank brigade, four artillery brigades and an air wing. Many recruits who were former POWs from 1939 saw it as a way of getting home, although Stalin kept them on a tight political leash. Berling, like Rokossovsky, was a career soldier having served with the Austrian and Polish armies. The fact that Stalin had spared him and that he had not stayed with Anders made him appear a turncoat to many of his countrymen. Berling was also given the onerous task of endorsing Stalin's lie that Hitler had perpetrated the massacre of Polish officers in Katyn Forest.

When Poland was partitioned by Stalin and Hitler under the Non-Aggression Pact, 130,000 Polish officers and men immediately fell into the hands of the Red Army (although, in total, some 250,000 soldiers were eventually moved into the Soviet Union as POWs). Stalin had a long memory and a score to settle with the Poles (in 1920 they had defeated the Red Army), and he also wanted to destroy the basis for any future opposition to the Soviet occupation of eastern Poland, which would act as a buffer against post-war Germany. Stalin had acted swiftly and brutally.

He rounded up every Polish officer in his part of pre-war Poland (now the western Ukraine and western Belorussia) and in early 1940 he ruthlessly organised their slaughter. In April–May 1940, 15,000 Polish officers and police-men were evacuated from camps at Kozielsk, Starobielsk and Ostachkov and turned over to the NKVD in the Smolensk, Kharkov and Kalinin regions. With Hitler's invasion of the Soviet Union, the Polish government in exile signed an agreement with Moscow – the provisions included raising a Polish army in the Soviet Union. However, of the 15,000 Polish officers held by the Soviets, only 350–400 reported for duty. Like the *kulaks* and Red Army officers before them, the Polish officer class had been ruthlessly butchered.

Stalin's duplicity in his treatment of Poland and the Polish Army knew no bounds. In December 1941, Generals Wladyslaw Sikorski and Anders plus the Polish ambassador met with Stalin to discuss the whereabouts of approxi-mately 4,000 named Polish officers who had been deported to Soviet prisons and labour camps. Stalin initially claimed rather disingenuously that they had escaped to Manchuria. He then changed tack, suggesting they had been released, adding, 'I want you to know that the Soviet government has not the slightest reason to retain even one Pole'.[2] What he meant was 'even one *living* Pole'.

Hitler announced that he had found the mass grave of up to 4,000 Polish officers in the forest of Katyn, near Smolensk, in April 1943. The Germans continued to dig, unearthing an estimated 10,000 bodies, and Hitler set up a Committee of Inquiry which 'proved' the Poles had been shot in 1940 by Stalin's NKVD. The Soviets dismissed the claim as propaganda, calling it 'revolting and slanderous fabrications'.[3]

Hitler's discovery had strained Soviet–Polish relations even further, allowing Stalin to undermine the validity of the Polish government in exile in London as a prelude to establishing a Communist government in Warsaw. As far as Stalin was concerned, Poland came within his sphere of influence and he had every intention of it remaining so. On retaking Smolensk, Stalin set up his own com-mission which stated categorically that the men had been killed in 1941 while road-building for the Germans.

On the morning of 2 August 1944, Rokossovsky went to view the Polish capital and got a good indication of the Polish Home Army's efforts, recalling:

Together with a group of officers I was visiting the 2nd Tank Army, which was fighting on that sector of the front. From our observation point, which had been set up at the top of a tall factory chimney, we could see Warsaw. The city was covered in clouds of smoke. Here and there houses were burning. Bombs and shells were exploding. Everything indicated that a battle was in progress.[4]

Why did Rokossovsky not try for a bridgehead at Warsaw if the Red Army had established footholds at Magnuszew, Puławy and on the upper Vistula near Sandomierz? To have done so would have been far tougher than in the Radom region, way to the south. Sandomierz had cost them dearly, plus Stalin saw Warsaw as anchoring the Germans' line on the Narev and Bobr and, in turn, East Prussia and knew they would fight bitterly to defend this. Without the Baltic States secured, Hitler could strike from East Prussia against the flank and rear of the Red Army once it was advancing beyond the Vistula.

Also, by now Rokossovsky was facing twenty-two enemy divisions, this included four security divisions in the Warsaw suburbs, three Hungarian divisions on the Vistula, south of Warsaw, and the remains of six or seven divisions which had escaped from the chaos of Belostok and Brest-Lotovsk. At least eight divisions were identified fighting to the north of Siedlce, amongst them two panzer and three SS panzer or panzergrenadier divisions. Stalin was waiting in the wings with his own Polish government and armed forces.

Marshal Zhukov blamed Polish leader Bor-Komorowski for a lack of co-operation with the Red Army:

As was established later, neither the command of the Front [Rokossovsky] nor that of Poland's 1st Army [Berling] had been informed in advance by Bor-Komorowski, the leader of the uprising, about forthcoming events in Warsaw. Nor did he make any attempt to co-ordinate the insurgents' actions with those of the 1st Byelorussian Front. The Soviet Command learned about the uprising after the event from local residents who had crossed the Vistula. The Stavka had not been informed in advance either.[5]

In light of Rokossovsky's efforts to the north-east and south-east of Warsaw in the face of the tough Waffen-SS, this is largely true.

In Warsaw, General Reiner Stahel's 12,000-strong garrison included 5,000 regular troops, 4,000 Luftwaffe personnel (over a quarter of whom were manning the air defences) and the 2,000-strong Warsaw security regiment. Wehrmacht forces in the immediate area numbered up to 16,000 men, with another 90,000 further afield. Army Group Centre was to have a limited role in fighting the Warsaw Rising. General Vormann, commanding the 9th Army, sent 1,000 men to Praga to help hold the Poniatowski Bridge. An additional three battalions were also sent to help to assist the Hermann Göring Division in clearing a way through the city to the Kierbedz Bridge.

With the Wehrmacht fully tied up fending off Soviet attacks, it was left to the reviled SS to stamp out the Polish rising, involving military police units and SS troops under SS-Standartenführer Paul Geibel supported by factory and rail guards. Geibel also managed to scrounge four Tiger tanks, a Panther tank, four medium tanks and an assault gun off the 5th SS to strengthen his forces. A motley battle group under SS-Gruppenführer Heinz Reinefarth, supported by thirty-seven assault guns and a company of heavy tanks, was also assembled to crush the Polish Home Army in Warsaw.

SS reinforcements included SS-Brigadeführer Bratislav Kaminski's hated Russian National Liberation Army Brigade. Kaminski supported SS-Oberführer Oskar Dirlewanger's Anti-Partisan Brigade. This consisted of two battalions of criminals, three battalions of former Soviet POWs, two companies of gendarmes, a police platoon and an artillery battery. Additionally, Colonel Wilhelm Schmidt supplied men drawn from his 603rd Regiment and a grenadier and police battalion.

All the forces in Warsaw were placed under SS-Obergruppenführer Erich von dem Bach-Zelewski, who had been overseeing the construction of defences on the Vistula near Gdańsk. He was the nemesis of partisan forces in the east. Von dem Bach-Zelewski was soon to find that both Kaminski and Dirlewanger's men were atrociously disciplined. Their brutality in Warsaw was to horrify even the battle-hardened SS, and von dem Bach-Zelewski thought they were the lowest of the low, remarking, 'The fighting value of these Cossacks was, as usual in such a collection of people without a fatherland, very poor. They had a great liking for alcohol and other excesses and had no interest in military discipline.'[6]

On 5 August 1944, Dirlewanger and Kaminski's troops counter-attacked the brave Polish Home Army. For two days, they ran amok. After the war, the German officers involved disingenuously laid the blame firmly on the shoulders of Kaminski and Dirlewanger.

On 19 August the Polish Home Army's efforts to fight its way through to those forces trapped in the Old Town came to nothing and it was clear they would have to be evacuated to the city centre and Żoliborz district. About 2,500 fighters withdrew via the sewers, leaving behind their badly wounded. It was now only a matter of time before the SS crushed resistance in the city centre and cleared resistance between the Poniatowski and Kierbedz Bridges.

To ward off a wider encircling movement by the Red Army to the north, Model deployed the 4th SS Panzer Corps with the 3rd SS and 5th SS moving into blocking positions. From 14 August, the Soviets attacked for a week but the SS successfully held off fifteen rifle divisions and two tank corps. Also in mid-August, Model relinquished his command of Army Group Centre and hastened to France to take charge from Günther von Kluge in a vain attempt to avert the unfolding German defeat in Normandy.

Stalin's great offensive that had commenced in Byelorussia on 23 June 1944 had all but ended by 29 August. By the 26th, the 3rd SS had been forced back to Praga, but a counter-attack by them on 11 September thwarted another attempt to link up with the Polish Home Army. It was the 3rd SS and 5th SS who had the dubious honour, along with Stalin, of consigning Warsaw to two months of bloody agony.

From 13 September, the Red Air Force spent two weeks conducting 2,000 supply sorties to the insurgents. The supplies were modest, including 505 anti-tank rifles, nearly 1,500 sub-machine guns and 130 tons of food, medicine and explosives. By the time Berling's Polish 1st Army was committed for the battle for Praga, time was running out, with Żoliborz under attack by elements of the 25th Panzer Division and just 400 insurgents left holding a narrow strip of the river.

Berling recklessly threw his men over the river at Czerniaków, but tragically could make no headway against determined German resistance. He landed three groups on the banks of the Czerniaków and Powiśle areas and made contacts with Home Army forces on the night of 14/15 September. His men on the eastern shore attempted several more landings over the next four days, but during 15–23 September those who had got over suffered heavy casualties and lost their boats and river-crossing equipment.

On 22 September, Berling's men were ordered back across the Vistula for a second time. There was hardly any Red Army support and out of the 3,000 men who made it across just 900 got back to the eastern shores, two-thirds of whom were seriously wounded. In total, Berling's Polish 1st Army losses amounted to 5,660 killed, missing or wounded, trying to aid the Warsaw Uprising.

After sixty-two days of fighting, and having lost 15,000 dead and 25,000 wounded, the Polish Home Army surrendered in Warsaw on 2 October. Up to 200,000 civilians had been killed in the needless orgy of destruction. After the surrender, 15,000 members of the Home Army were disarmed and sent to POW camps in Germany, while up to 6,000 fighters slipped back into the population with the intention of continuing the fight. However, the vengeful Himmler expelled the rest of the civilian population and ordered the city be flattened.

Crushing the Poles had been a pointless exercise which cost Hitler 10,000 dead, 9,000 wounded and 7,000 missing. It was clear from the fatalities out-numbering the wounded that no quarter had been given. However, German morale was given a much-needed boost, which had them believing their feat of arms, rather than Stalin, had halted Rokossovsky at the very gates of Warsaw.

Rokossovsky would not occupy the Polish capital for another six weeks, leaving Hitler triumphant before Warsaw. It was to be his last real victory of the war.

At the height of the fighting on the Eastern Front in 1944, 63 per cent of Hitler's divisions and 70 per cent of his manpower were tied up fighting Stalin's Red Army. It also accounted for 57 per cent of all his panzers and assault guns, 71 per cent of all guns and mortars and 51 per cent of all operational aircraft. The other two active fronts in France and Italy accounted for just 30–35 per cent of Hitler's total combat strength.

Despite holding the Red Army before Warsaw and crushing the Polish rising, it was hard to see how Hitler's Wehrmacht could survive the twin calamities of Byelorussia and Normandy. The enormous loss of manpower urgently needed addressing. While German industry worked wonders reconstituting the shattered panzer formations thanks to Albert Speer's weapons factories, new infantry divisions were also desperately required. In autumn 1944, Hitler ordered the creation of almost eighty Volksgrenadier divisions. These had fewer infantry battalions and heavy weapons than regular infantry divisions, but issuing them with more sub-machine guns and assault rifles than usual compensated for this.

Initially thirty-five skeleton divisions were refitted and another fifteen new ones created. To the OKW's displeasure, for propaganda purposes Hitler insisted on naming them *Volksgrenadiers* (People's Grenadiers) and placing them under the auspices of the SS. The German Replacement Army was soon gathering men from disbanded army units and convalescing in hospitals, as well as surplus Luftwaffe and Kriegsmarine personnel. Old men and teenagers previously considered unsuitable were also rapidly conscripted.

There was constant competition between the army, Waffen-SS and Luftwaffe for resources that created a wholly unnecessary duplication of effort. The OKW would have preferred that all available men were used as combat replacements for existing army units, rather than creating new ones. The army had struggled to gain control of Göring's twenty-two weak Luftwaffe field divisions in late 1943. By which time the damage was done, as they were standing units and the men could not be transferred. Himmler's Waffen-SS controlled another thirty-eight elite divisions, which operated outside the army's chain of command.

The creation of the Volksgrenadier units caused Allied intelligence some confusion, as Hitler's home guard was known as the Volkssturm. This resulted in the firepower of the Volksgrenadier divisions being greatly underestimated. They were sent to fight on both the Eastern and Western Fronts. However, fifteen divisions were assigned to Hitler's Ardennes Offensive. Guderian would rather have seen them and the re-formed panzer divisions all sent east to hold the Oder, but it was not to be.

AXIS TURNCOATS

Hitler ultimately treated most of his Axis allies with contempt. While he courted Antonescu and Horthy until the end, he never really trusted Mussolini and his inept military. By the end of May 1941, talks with the General Staffs of Finland, Hungary and Romania ensured that they were fully committed to supporting Barbarossa.

In contrast, Hitler chose to keep his principal ally, Mussolini, in the dark. The Italian government did not learn of Hitler's invasion of the Soviet Union until thirty minutes after it had begun. His message to the Italian leader said Libya was out of danger until the autumn and that he had been distracted from the war with England because 'all available Russian forces are at our border'.[1] He also said he would not need Italian troops in the Soviet Union. Neither of which was true.

Furthermore, Hitler deluded himself and the Italian dictator that it would be a short and manageable war. 'Even if I should be obliged at the end of the year to leave sixty or seventy divisions in Russia,' he said, 'that is only a fraction of the forces I am now continually using on the Eastern Front.'[2] Ironically, Mussolini's support for Hitler was to vastly outweigh the help he gained in Albania, Libya and Sicily.

After the Wehrmacht suffered its series of defeats at Stalingrad and Kursk, Hitler began to fret about the loyalty of his exhausted Axis allies. He was particularly furious at the collapse of his inadequate allies at Stalingrad and lost all confidence in their fighting capabilities. The average citizen in the East European capitals had no idea what was happening at the front as Hitler controlled the news. In Bucharest, an intrigued Iosif Hechter noted on 22 December 1942:

The official German communiqué issued yesterday evening contains an unusual passage: On the middle Don, the enemy has been attacking for several days with a very powerful concentration of armour, and has managed to penetrate the local defensive front. This breakthrough cost huge Bolshevik casualties. […] German combat divisions took up prepared positions to their rear.[3]

Although the report implied some sort of retreat, it gave no impression of the scale of the Red Army's advances or the implications. While the Romanian and Italian military enjoyed reasonably good relations with their German counterparts, understandably they felt they had been abandoned by Hitler at Stalingrad. He left two whole Romanian armies out on a limb and had done nothing to save them from destruction.

Reporter Henry Shapiro wrote:

Except for small groups of [Fascist] Iron Guard men, who here and there, put up a stiff fight, the Romanian soldiers were sick and tired of the war; the prisoners I saw all said roughly the same thing – that this was Hitler's war, and that the Romanians had nothing to do on the Don.[4]

All trust with the Wehrmacht had been lost at Stalingrad. The German Army now considered the Romanians cowards. One German staff officer said, '[They] want only to save their own lives. Nothing else means a thing.'[5] Another recorded:

They all had an expression of horror which seemed to be frozen on their faces. You would have thought the very devil was snapping at their heels. They had thrown everything away as they made their escape. And as they ran for it they added to the number of withdrawing troops, which was huge enough without them.[6]

In turn, Antonescu, Horthy and Mussolini held the Führer increasingly responsible for their losses. German intelligence collection was far more sophisticated than their modest efforts so they were reliant on Hitler for the bigger picture. Horthy had presided over the worst military disaster ever inflicted upon the Hungarian Army and was swift to accuse Hitler of abandoning his men to their fate. The admiral ordered the remains of the 2nd Army home in March; both Romanian armies were also taken out of the line. Eventually, to shore up his defence in the Balkans and on the Eastern Front Hitler was obliged to first occupy northern Italy and then Hungary as they sought to defect.

The Germans were not happy with Horthy's actions. 'After the withdrawal of their army from the battlefront,' complained von Manstein, 'the Hungarians had left only a few divisions behind in the Ukraine. It was expressly laid down that these forces should not become involved in any fighting with the Soviets.'[7]

Only Tiso's Slovak Mobile Division performed well, helping cover the German withdrawal from the Caucasus.

Antonescu was much more accommodating. His forces which were with the German 17th Army in the Kuban bridgehead remained put and other forces were made available for coastal defence on the Sea of Azov. The remnants of the Romanian 1st Tank Division and their cavalry divisions were regrouped for refitting. To make good Antonescu's losses, Hitler sent just eighty-five panzers and assault guns. First to arrive were elderly Czech light tanks, which were delivered in March 1943 and used to re-equip the 1st Tank Regiment.

Throughout 1942, Bulgaria's King Boris was thoroughly alarmed by Hitler's weapons deliveries to neutral Turkey, so as a counterweight Hitler agreed to equip ten Bulgarian infantry divisions, one cavalry division and two armoured brigades. Hitler supplied Boris with panzers and assault guns in July 1943, a move he was later to regret.

While Antonescu, Horthy, Mussolini and Tiso all provided troops, to Hitler's displeasure Boris stubbornly continued to refuse to declare war on Stalin or send any help. As a result, Boris was summoned to see Hitler at Rastenburg in August 1943; but he did not give in, citing his country's historic friendship with Russia and the threat posed by neutral Turkey. Shortly afterwards, Boris died of an apparent heart attack. Some muttered that he was poisoned on Hitler's instructions. Successive prime ministers now tried desperately to extricate Bulgaria from its corrosive relationship with Hitler.

The Bulgarians officially designated their fledgling armoured regiment the 1st Armoured Brigade in October 1943. Some armour was despatched to support the army in central Bulgaria, fighting the growing Bulgarian partisan movement, and a few others were assigned to the Bulgarian formations in Serbia to help fight the troublesome Yugoslav partisans.

By the spring of 1943, after the defeat of the Axis forces in Tunisia, Mussolini was facing further disaster with the Allies poised to attack Sicily. At this stage, Mussolini was incapable of defending his homeland, let alone Sicily; he had lost 200,000 men killed or captured in North Africa and his quarter of a million-strong force on the Eastern Front had disintegrated. He had another half a million men bogged down in the Balkans fruitlessly fighting Albanian and Yugoslav partisans. By the summer, a thoroughly dispirited Mussolini withdrew the remnants of his ill-advised expedition to the Soviet Union. Hitler was not sorry to see them go, nor were his generals.

The Allied invasion of Sicily triggered Mussolini's fall from power and the Italian armistice on 9 September 1943 resulted in Hitler seizing control of his former ally. After being rescued from house arrest, the disillusioned Mussolini became the puppet ruler of his German-occupied homeland. His remaining armed forces totalled just over half a million men and were only ever employed against the Italian resistance; the German Army successfully shouldered the burden of resisting the Allies' advance in Italy.

In mid-1943, Horthy reconstituted his battered Hungarian 1st Armoured Division and created a second. Both were organised along German lines, but equipped with Hungarian-built medium tanks. In addition, eight assault artillery battalions were also created, which were to have been equipped with Hungarian assault guns. However, there were only enough of these to arm two battalions, so the rest employed German-built assault guns. Between 1942–44 Hitler was obliged to supply Horthy with almost 400 German-built tanks to try and prop up his army.

Sensing that Horthy was losing the stomach for the fight, on 19 March 1944 Hitler occupied another former ally. He initially proposed garrisoning Budapest with Romanian and Slovak troops, but such nonsense would have created immediate internecine war amongst the Axis allies. German troops drove from Vienna, and Budapest's surrounding airfields were seized by German paratroops. Publicly Horthy remained compliant, while privately trying to distance himself from Hitler.

By then, von Manstein was lamenting that 'the scale and quality of the Hungarians weapons did not meet the requirements of warfare against Soviet armoured units'.[8] He was horrified that, by this stage of the war, the Hungarian chief of staff and commander of the Hungarian 1st Army had the cheek to complain about their lack of preparedness and lack of anti-tank weapons. Von Manstein wanted to know just how they had been spending their time!

While planning for Operation Bagration, Stalin had kept the pressure up on Hitler's wavering allies. In April 1944, the war came to the streets of Bucharest, Hechter remembered:

> Four days after the bombing, the city is in the grip of madness. [...] Everyone is fleeing or wants to flee. [...] Half the city is without electricity. There is no water supply. The radiators do not work. [...] The number of dead is not known. [...] Rosetti said 4,200 – but that isn't certain either.[9]

Only now did Hitler despatch any significant numbers of tanks to Antonescu's army, consisting of several hundred panzers and assault guns. Although Antonescu remained committed to the Führer's cause, reorganising and re-equipping the Romanian Army was a painfully slow process. The Romanian 1st Tank Division was re-established along German panzer division lines in April; equipped with German tanks, it returned to the Eastern Front and continued to resist the Red Army. It had been intended that the Romanian 8th Cavalry Division become a motorised unit, but in July 1944 it was decided to use it to create Romania's 2nd Armoured Division, but this was not completed before Romania defected to Stalin.

Antonescu was loyal to Hitler to the last and refused to believe that the days of his regime were numbered. He met with Hitler, Keitel and Guderian at the Wolfsschanze at Rastenburg on 5 August 1944. 'Antonescu had appeared to us quite au fait with the information from the front,' noted Guderian's adjutant, Major von Loringhoven, 'but he was deluding himself in his evaluation of the situation inside Romania when he assured us of the unconditional loyalty of his people, and of his own army to the German Reich.'[10]

King Michael and the Romanian Army had other ideas when it came to safeguarding their country. Several weeks later, King Michael, sick of the war, had Antonescu arrested and his entire government dismissed. Within a few weeks an armistice was signed with Stalin. The German instructors training the Romanian 4th Armoured Regiment seized the panzers supplied by Hitler and used them to help cover their withdrawal from Romania. Even before the fall of Antonescu, once-loyal Romanian troops blocked the Danube bridges to Hitler. Almost all of the resurrected German 6th Army and part of the 8th, some sixteen divisions in total, were forced to surrender to the Soviets. The rest fled over the Carpathians to fight on in Hungary. Bucharest lay open, as did the rear of Hitler's Balkan front.

General Guderian and his colleagues were dismayed at Romania's actions:

On 20 August 1944, the Russians launched their attack against Army Group South Ukraine. This was successful against those sectors that were held by Romanian troops. But that was not all; the Romanians deserted in large numbers to the enemy and turned their guns against their allies of yesterday. Neither the German troops nor their leaders had reckoned on such treachery.[11]

Once the Romanians had closed the Danube, thousands of Germans were trapped. 'These German soldiers,' adds Guderian, 'fought valiantly and to the bitter end; their military honour unsullied. They were in no way responsible for their sad fate.'[12]

In Bucharest, Iosif Hechter recorded in his journal, on 21 August, with some apprehension:

The Soviet offensive in Moldavia and Bessarabia has been underway for two days. Apparently Iași has fallen.

The war is coming toward us. It is not the war that has weighed us down for five years like a moral drama, now it is a physical war. Great turnarounds can occur at any hour or minute. Again our lives are on the line.[13]

He worried that Hitler might seek to occupy Romania, 'Capitulation means (who knows!) a repressive German response, in the style of northern Italy.'[14] Hitler did not have the manpower or the time for such an enterprise.

During 20–29 August, the Red Army thrust into eastern Romania, with the 2nd and 3rd Ukrainian Fronts' Jassy–Kishinev Offensive. The denuded Army Group South Ukraine only had three armoured units consisting of the 13th Panzer and 10th Panzergrenadier Divisions and the Romanian 1st Armoured Division. Within three days, 13th Panzer had all but collapsed. Army Group South Ukraine was overwhelmed and the German 6th Army was surrounded; losses amounted to about 200,000 men, eighty-three tanks and assault guns, 108 guns and 111 aircraft.

The revitalised Romanian 3rd and 4th Armies' loyally fighting alongside the Germans suffered 8,305 killed, 24,989 wounded and 153,883 missing and captured (up to 40,000 of whom died while held in Moldava). The Red Army lost 13,197 killed and 53,933 sick and wounded. With the Red Army deep inside their country, the Romanians had little choice but change sides. The Romanian Army attacked Hitler's units guarding the important Ploesti oilfields and in total took 50,000 German prisoners, who were handed over to the Red Army. The fall of Antonescu and the loss of Romania was a serious blow to Hitler, particularly access to its vital oilfields.

In the west, things had gone just as badly for Hitler following the Allies' liberation of France. By the end of August 1944 his armies had lost forty-three divisions (thirty-five infantry and eight panzer divisions), sustaining a total loss of 450,000 men, as well as most of their equipment consisting of 1,500 tanks, 3,500 pieces of artillery and 20,000 vehicles. Only in Italy were his armed forces keeping the Allies at bay following the landings there in 1943, although this secondary theatre of operations was a constant drain on his resources. The loss of Rome in June had cost Hitler about 30,000 troops.

Hungary was not to be spared by Stalin either. After Friessner's Army Group South Ukraine blunted Stalin's Belgrade Strategic Offensive Operation, the Red Army turned its attentions toward Budapest by striking from the Arad area. In the meantime, Hechter recorded on 29 August, 'How shall I begin? Where shall I begin? The Russians are in Bucharest.'[15] Two days later, he noted:

A parade of Soviet heavy tanks on Bulevardul Carol, beneath the windows of the house where we have taken refuge. It is an imposing sight. Those tired, dusty, rather badly dressed men are conquering the world. They're not much to look at – but they are conquering the world.

Afterwards a long column of trucks full of Romanian soldiers: former prisoners of war in Russia, now armed and equipped and fighting in the Red

Army. They are young and happy, with excellent equipment. You can see they are not coming from battle. They are a parade unit, probably kept in waiting for the entry into Bucharest.[16]

Inspired by the Romanians, the Slovaks were premature in trying to throw off Hitler on 23 August. Despite being loyal allies on the Eastern Front, the Slovaks, under Defence Minister General Catlos, and part of the Slovak Army, under General Golian, rebelled at Neusohl in the Carpathians against Premier Tiso and Hitler. For the Führer, this was another potential disaster as it not only threatened the vital tank factories in neighbouring Bohemia and Moravia, but also blocked the retreat of the defeated German 8th Army.

Hitler had no troops available and an improvised armoured unit had to be cobbled together from the various SS training schools in Bohemia and Moravia. The unfortunate Slovaks had no tanks or anti-tank guns with which to resist the panzers, as their remaining armour had been lost with the Slovak Mobile Division on the Eastern Front. Hitler moved quickly to disarm the Slovak Army's two regular army infantry divisions and many Slovak soldiers fled to central Slovakia to join the partisans. Czechoslovak airborne forces flown in by Stalin also joined them. Unfortunately, Neusohl (the centre of the rising) could not be held without heavy weapons and fell by the end of the month to the German armour. The arrival of elements of two SS divisions sealed the fate of the remaining rebels. The Slovak people would have to wait until the spring for the arrival of the Red Army before they would taste freedom.

When Romania swapped sides, Bulgaria was already secretly negotiating with Stalin. In addition to its commitments in Greece and Yugoslavia, the Bulgarian Army found itself countering a growing partisan movement at home.

As Bulgarian loyalty was suspect, Hitler switched further shipments of panzers en route to German troops in Yugoslavia. He also secretly planned to disable Bulgaria's existing panzers and assault guns. At the end of August 1944 Guderian, accompanied by Loringhoven, flew to Budapest with a letter from Hitler to Admiral Horthy. 'The admiral had received him courteously,' recalled Loringhoven, 'but had given him the impression of being on the verge of terminating his alliance with Germany.'[17] General Vörös, Chief of the Hungarian Staff, was especially friendly and assured them of the Hungarian Army's loyalty while secretly planning his defection to Stalin.

Romania's defection had exposed Hungary's southern frontier. Desperately trying to stem the Soviet and Romanian forces pushing from the east, the Hungarians succeeded in briefly giving the Soviets a bloody nose at Arad on the River Lipova. The Battle of Arad, fought in September 1944, was the last independent action of the war by the battered Hungarian Army and one of the very few successes achieved by its limited armoured forces. The Hungarian 4th Corps, spearheaded by its 1st Armoured Division and supporting a German offensive, had attacked the Romanian town. Ironically, this fighting took place against one of Hitler's former Axis allies.

Although Arad fell on 13 September, the Hungarians soon found themselves caught up in a violent six-day battle with the Romanian Army, which enjoyed significant air support and succeeded in destroying twenty-three Hungarian tanks. After the arrival of Stalin's Red Army, a joint Soviet-Romanian counter-attack was launched, throwing the invaders out.

The outclassed Hungarians, lacking air support, were forced to evacuate Arad just a week after capturing it. They claimed to have destroyed sixty-seven Soviet tanks at the cost of eight German-supplied assault guns and a further twenty-two damaged. German-supplied panzers of the Romanian 2nd Armoured Regiment then fought alongside the Red Army in Hungary and ended up in Czechoslovakia. By the end of 1944, the Hungarian 1st Army had withdrawn into Slovakia and the 2nd Army had been disbanded.

In the meantime, Stalin declared war on Bulgaria on 5 September and commenced hostilities three days later. The Bulgarians sought to save themselves by declaring war on Germany, but pushing through Romania, the Red Army thrust into Bulgaria north of Varna and veered west. The Soviet motorised columns outstripped their infantry and met no resistance, arriving in Sofia on 15 September. Hitler acted quickly to deal with his turncoat allies deployed in Serbia and Macedonia, ordering the disarming of the Bulgarian 1st Army. Only their 5th Army offered short-lived resistance. German instructors from the combat school at Niš in Serbia were put on alert to move to the German training camp at Plovdiv in Bulgaria, from where they would act against the Bulgarian panzers.

Instead, a column consisting of sixty-two panzers and other armoured fighting vehicles from the Bulgarian 1st Armoured Brigade, moved to block the Sofia–Niš road, outside Sofia, and local German forces were arrested. Bulgarian troops were then withdrawn from Greece ready for an inevitable Soviet attack on Hitler's forces in Yugoslavia. At the same time, Hitler's forces in Yugoslavia found themselves attacked by panzers manned by German-trained Bulgarian tank crews. Supporting the Red Army, the 1st, 2nd and 4th Bulgarian Armies were launched into Yugoslavia on 28 September 1944.

The Bulgarian 1st Armoured Brigade went into action against its former allies on 8 October, when sixty tanks were thrown against Hitler's occupation forces. Twenty-one Bulgarian tanks recaptured Vlasotince, driving the German defenders out. At Bela Palanka the Germans found themselves under attack by panzers on 12 October, but the Bulgarians ran into well-prepared defences, including 88mm anti-aircraft guns, and lost five.

It was clear that Hitler's East European allies were abandoning him like rats from a sinking ship. At the end of November, the Bulgarian panzers were in Pristina and Kosovska Mitrovica marking the end of operations in Yugoslavia. Elements of the brigade subsequently fought with the Bulgarian 1st Army and the Soviets in Hungary.

On 6 October 1944, Marshal Rodion Malinovsky's 2nd Ukrainian Front set about the remains of Friessner's Army Group South Ukraine, attacking General Maximilian Fretter-Pico's German 6th Army and the Hungarian 7th Corps. His target was Debrecen and the Tisza in Hungary. Within four days Malinovsky was over the river and within 45 miles of Budapest.

Friessner was instructed to smash the 27th Army and Soviet 6th Guards Tank Army and to retake two vital passes in the southern Carpathians to cut Malinovsky's lines of communication. Hungarian counter-attacks against the Mindszent bridgehead required the Soviets to rely on Romanian reinforcements, which came under attack from Hungarian and German troops. The Romanian 4th Division was surrounded and forced to surrender on the 20 October and the 2nd Romanian Division was driven back across the river.

The bridgehead at Alpar, however, was not dislodged. On 11 October, the 4th Guards Cavalry Corps, part of Cavalry Mechanised Group Pliyev, had reached Debrecen, and nine days later Romanian troops captured the town. However, on 23 October a German counter-attack striking east and west surrounded Pliyev, forcing his men to abandon all their weapons and flee to Soviet lines five days later.

Having blunted the Soviet advance, the Germans and Hungarians lost up to 35,000 killed or missing as well as 500 tanks and 1,656 guns and mortars. Some 20,000–40,000 Axis troops were captured. The Red Army sustained 11,900 dead and 6,662 missing, as well as 358 tanks knocked out.

On 15 October Hungarian radio announced Horthy had requested an armistice with the Soviet Union, Britain and America. Fortunately for Hitler, Major General Iván Hindy, commander of the Hungarian Army 1st Corps, ensued that Budapest was not immediately lost to the Axis cause. Hindy was alarmed at the prospect of the Soviets capturing the capital and took matters into his own hands. When his commander, Lieutenant General Aggteleky, ordered him to stop German units from occupying the citadel and Sashegy Hill in Buda, he promptly arrested Aggteleky.

Hindy gathered his officers and made his allegiance clear:

A conspiracy against our German comrades is being prepared here. [...]
Unfortunately the Regent is being influenced by cliques of Jewish agents
and defeatists and is not prepared to dissociate himself from these criminal

cliques. The radio proclamation is treason. It is possible the regent doesn't even know about it, otherwise it would have been read out by him and not by a common newsreader. To prevent this treason I had to take over the command. I expect the officers of the army corps to support me.[18]

The following day, Hitler carried out Operation *Panzerfaust*. German troops seized Buda Castle in Budapest and Horthy was kidnapped. General Béla Miklós von Dalnoki, commander of the Hungarian 1st Army, after telling his countrymen to treat the Germans as foes, defected to the Soviets. Colonel General Lajos Verres, commander of the Hungarian 2nd Army, was arrested by the Germans before he could act. Hindy's actions enabled Hitler to take control of some 55,000 loyalist Hungarian troops in the Budapest area, although only about 15,000 of these were deployable as infantry.

The 2nd Ukrainian Front renewed its attempt on Budapest on 29 October and had secured the southern approaches to the city by 2 November, but could get no further. A frontal attack on the city from the east was also fended off. The Soviets launched a fresh assault on 5 December aiming to trap the city in a pincher movement. The Soviet 7th Guards and 6th Guards Tank Armies and Pliyev's mechanised cavalry group struck from the north-east while the 46th Army attacked from the south-west. Four days later, they had got as far as Šahy and the Danube to the north of the city. While the 46th got across the river, it was at great cost and it could still not get through the defences to the south-west.

On 12 December 1944, the 2nd and 3rd Ukrainian fronts were instructed to take Budapest. The 2nd Ukrainian Front on the left was to attack from Šahy, southward to the Danube north of Esztergom, which would cut off any German retreat to the north-west. The 3rd Ukrainian Front was directed to move northward from Lake Velencei and link up with the 2nd Ukrainian Front near Esztergom. This offensive commenced on 20 December and within six days the two fronts had met, encircling the Hungarian capital. Hitler's last ally was now knocked out of the war. The Wehrmacht was on its own.

17

FINAL STAND

Hitler's intelligence was well informed of Stalin's intentions for early 1945. Stalin had mobilised every last resource at his disposal. His priorities were to occupy East Prussia and defeat the remaining German forces in Poland, Czechoslovakia, Hungary and Austria. The Warsaw–Berlin line of attack was to constitute his main effort. Simple mathematics meant that Hitler's Third Reich was completely doomed.

According to General Heinz Guderian, now chief of the General Staff:

We calculated that the attack would begin on 12 January. The Russians' superiority to us was 11:1 in infantry, 7:1 in tanks, 20:1 in guns. An evaluation of the enemy's total strength gave him a superiority of approximately 15:1 on the ground and 20:1 in the air, and this estimate did not err on the side of exaggeration. [...]

I was faced with the problem of whether in fact what was now demanded of our soldiers was humanly feasible.[1]

Guderian says that he had every confidence in the intelligence and assessments of the Foreign Armies East Department: 'I had known its head, General Gehlen, and his colleagues' methods and results for long enough to be able to judge their efficacy. General Gehlen's estimates of the enemy were, in due course, proved correct.'[2]

By January 1945, Hitler had twice as many divisions under arms as in May 1940. On paper, he had 260, of which ten divisions were in Yugoslavia; seventeen in Scandinavia; twenty-four in Italy and seventy-six in the west. In the remnant of German-occupied Hungary, twenty-eight divisions were futilely clinging on to Budapest. To ward off a Red Army push across the northern plains to Germany's eastern industrial heartland of Silesia, Saxony and then Berlin itself there were just seventy-five under-strength divisions. Once reinforcements were despatched to beleaguered Budapest, Hitler could muster just twelve and a half divisions in reserve to assist a front stretching over 750 miles. In the west, Hitler would not be distracted eastwards, instead he pressed on with his Ardennes counter-offensive and launched another futile offensive in the northern Alsace.

Guderian visited Hitler, Keitel and Jodl on 24 December 1944 to get them to transfer troops to the east, where Stalin's preparations for his offensive in the New Year were all too evident. Hitler rejected Guderian's requests and concerns, claiming that Stalin was bluffing. The Führer and Jodl insisted priority be given to the west. Guderian had to make do with what he had deployed in the east. He knew that it would not be enough to stop Stalin's anticipated Vistula–Oder Offensive. There could be no denying the situation on the Eastern Front was now extremely grim.

Instead of reinforcing the crumbling Eastern Front, the rejuvenated and re-equipped forces that had been so masterfully assembled in late 1944 were thrown away in the Ardennes and Alsace. Hitler gathered his commanders on 28 December 1944 and gave them a dressing down for their pessimism. Once again, he was delusional in believing times had not changed:

> Gentlemen, I have been in this business for eleven years and during those eleven years I have never heard anybody report that everything was completely ready. Our situation is not different from that of the Russians in 1941 and 1942 when, despite their most unfavourable situation, they manoeuvred us slowly back by single offensive blows along the extended front on which we had passed over to the defensive.[3]

Hitler withdrew his FHQ to the Führer bunker under the Reich Chancellery in Berlin, in January 1945. Secretary Christa Schroeder witnessed her boss's deteriorating health:

> At six in the morning, when Hitler received us after the nightly situation conference, he would usually be lying exhausted on the little sofa. His physical decline made daily advances despite his desperate attempts to hold himself together. [...] He was almost permanently emotional and his talk was increasingly the monotonous repetition of the same stories.[4]

Hitler was failing fast, thanks to the enormous pressure he was under and ill-advised medicines being administered by his personal physician. Guderian recalled, 'It was no longer simply his left hand, but the whole left side of his body that trembled. [...] He walked awkwardly, stooped more than ever, and his gestures were both jerky and slow.'[5] When Guderian tried to highlight the realities facing the Eastern Front in a conference with Hitler on 9 January 1945, he was given the usual hysterical tirade. 'He had,' explained Guderian, 'a special picture of the world, and every fact had to be fitted into that fancied picture. As he believed, so the world must be: but in fact, it was a picture of another world.'[6]

Captain Gerhardt Boldt, who served first as Guderian's aide-de-camp and then General Kreb's (the last chief of the Army General Staff), was also aghast at the condition of Hitler:

> His head was slightly wobbling. His left arm hung slackly and his hand trembled a good deal. There was an indescribable flickering glow in his eyes, creating a fearsome and wholly unnatural effect. His face and the parts around his eyes gave the impression of total exhaustion. All his movements were those of a senile man.[7]

During the beginning of 1945 the Red Army maintained its relentless pressure on the Wehrmacht, with major offensives in Poland, Silesia, Pomerania and Prussia. These were, in part, driven by Stalin's desire to secure his flanks from the threat of German counter-attack before driving on to Berlin.

Stalin launched his Vistula–Oder Offensive Operation as predicted, which took the Red Army from the Vistula in Poland to the Oder, east of Berlin. The 2 million men of Zhukov's 1st Byelorussian Front and Konev's 1st Ukrainian Front, supported by 4,529 tanks and 2,513 assault guns, simply overwhelmed the 400,000 troops of Army Group A (consisting of the 4th Panzer Army, and the 9th and 17th Armies) with 1,150 tanks and 4,100 artillery pieces.

Guderian recalled the fall of Stalin's sledgehammer in the early New Year:

> So on 12 January the first blow fell at Baranov [south of Warsaw]. Fourteen rifle divisions, two independent tank corps and elements of another army were committed. The mass of the Russian tanks assembled in this area was apparently held back during the first day, since the enemy wished to decide, according to the results of the initial attack, in which direction he could best advance. The Russians had a superabundance of equipment and could afford such tactics.
>
> The enemy's attack succeeded and he penetrated far into the German defences.
>
> On this day a great convergence of Russian offensive force was observed moving into the bridgeheads over the Vistula farther to the north at Pulavy and Magnuszev. Thousands of vehicles were counted. Here, too, the attack was obviously about to start. It was the same story to the north of Warsaw and in East Prussia.[8]

After twenty-three days, the Zhukov and Konev, supported by the 2nd Byelorussian and 4th Ukrainian Fronts, tore open a breach 625 miles wide by 375 miles deep and swept across the Oder. Zhukov's 1st Byelorussian Front secured a bridgehead a Kuestrin, just 35 miles from Berlin. It was only a matter of time now for Hitler and his generals.

At the same time, Stalin and his generals conducted the East Prussia Offensive Operation on 13 January 1945, which represented the Red Army's renewed effort to subdue the region following its unsuccessful attempts in late 1944. This was carried out by Chernyakovsky's 3rd Byelorussian Front thrusting west toward Königsberg against the 3rd Panzer Army and 4th Army, part of Army Group Centre under General Georg-Hans Reinhardt. From the north, Bagramyan's 1st Baltic Front attacked the 3rd Panzer Army and to the south Rokossovsky's 2nd Byelorussian Front initially attacked north-west to the Vistula through the German 2nd Army, sealing off East Prussia. By 2 February, Hitler's forces had suffered 1.4 million casualties comprising 377,000 killed, 334,000 wounded and 292,000 missing. The Red Army sustained 193,125 casualties, including 43,251 killed and missing.

The German 4th Army withdrew toward the German 2nd Army at Elbing, but found its way barred by the Soviet 48th Army. An initial German breakthrough was quickly sealed. The bulk of the 4th Army was surrounded on the shore of the Vistula Lagoon in the Heiligenbeil Pocket, which was not finally subdued until 29 March 1945. According to Soviet sources, some 93,000 German troops were killed and 46,449 taken prisoner. The remains of the 3rd Panzer Army were trapped in the city of Königsberg, holding out until 9 April. This offensive cost Stalin 126,464 killed and missing, along with a further 458,314 sick and wounded by 9 May.

In the meantime, Budapest was cut off by the Red Army on 26 December 1944, once the Budapest–Vienna road was secured. This trapped 33,000 German and 37,000 Hungarian troops, along with over 800,000 civilians. Refusing any withdrawal, Hitler declared '*Festung Budapest* (Fortress Budapest)', which was to be held to the last. The 9th SS Corps (consisting of the 8th SS and 22nd SS Cavalry Divisions) were inside the city while the 18th SS Panzergrenadier Division was forced to retreat. Budapest's mixed German-Hungarian garrison also included the Hungarian 1st Armoured, 10th Mixed and 12th Reserve Divisions, as well as several armoured car and assault artillery battalions.

Hitler blindly persisted until the end of the war with his fortress mentality. His rationale was that reinforcements would cut their way through to a strongpoint, which could then be used as a springboard for a counter-offensive. In the early years of the war this strategy often worked well, but by this stage the Wehrmacht simply did not have the resources to indulge in such luxuries. In an effort to raise the siege of Budapest, the 4th SS Panzer Corps comprising the 3rd and 5th SS Panzer Divisions was diverted from Warsaw. They did have some opportunity of breaking through, as initially they had 70 per cent more troops and 140 per cent more armour than the Soviet 4th Guards Army holding the outer ring; although the Soviets did enjoy a three to one superiority in artillery.

General Kurt Dittmar was dismayed at Hitler's fixation with holding Hungary and Budapest. Three of the best-equipped panzer divisions were diverted away from the defence of the Vistula, 'the reserves that had been held ready to meet the threat were taken away at the critical moment and despatched to the relief of Budapest,' noted Dittmar.[9]

Operation Konrad I was launched on 1 January 1945, which saw the 4th SS Panzer Corps strike from Tata, north of Budapest. Attacks were also conducted to the west. Martin Steiger, commander of the 3rd SS Panzer Division's tank regiment, was in the thick of the bitter fighting trying to reach Budapest. 'The attack began on 1 January 1945, at 6 p.m., without preparatory artillery fire,' Steiger recounts, 'Enemy tanks of the Type T-34/85 sat in the farms in town [Dunaalmás] and fired at our point vehicles from only five metres away.'[10] Every step of the way his men met determined resistance.

The Soviet 6th Guards Army thwarted the first attempt, which launched from Komarno and initially pushed the Soviets back along the right bank of the Danube. The 6th Guards were ordered to march down the left bank to Komarno, thereby compromising the Germans' flank and rear. The Soviets deployed four extra divisions and the German counter-attack was halted at Bicske and by 12 January they were forced to withdraw having got to within 15 miles of the city. Desperate to open an air bridge to Budapest, Hitler tried to recapture Budapest Airport.

Operation Konrad II was launched from Esztergom, but again was halted just short of its objective. Konrad III, the last part of the operation, commenced on 17 January with 4th SS Panzer Corps and 3rd Panzer Corps attacking from the south, with the aim of trapping ten Soviet divisions. Again, this operation failed.

During the second counter-attack, 100 panzers supported by two regiments of motorised infantry tried to punch through the Soviet 5th Guards Airborne Division. Eighteen panzers broke through, only to run into a Soviet anti-tank regiment, which accounted for half the tanks. The Soviet 34th Guards Division also held fast despite everything that was thrown at them.

Also on 17 January, Hitler reluctantly agreed that the garrison could abandon low-lying Pest, in order to hold the hillier Buda. The garrison and the civilian population fled across the five Danube bridges, until the Germans brought them down the following day in the face of Hungarian objections.

The SS ensconced themselves in the citadel on Gellért Hill, while other units defended the city cemetery and Margaret Island. Soviet plans were distracted on 20 January by a renewed German relief effort which was attempted to the south of the city. Karl-Heinz Lichte was with the 5th SS Panzer Division Viking when their attack was thwarted. He recalls the battle, 'A number of "Josef Stalin" tanks were spotted.'' The numerically vastly superior enemy bypassed us and attacked our flank. Then, the first of our Panzers was knocked out.' Their commander was killed and Lichte ordered a withdrawal. 'At the same time I grasped a smoke grenade,' he recalls, 'pulled and threw it to obstruct the enemy field of vision of our withdrawal. That very moment, there was an immense bang. I saw a bright flash, then darkness.'

Martin Steiger continues:

Counter-attacks began, and our attack had to be stopped. […] The expected enemy tank attack deep into our flanks took place on 29 January from Vertes Aska. It started a huge tank battle near Pettend. Some 200 enemy tanks were knocked out.

The enemy attacks increased on 30 January. We could no longer hold our positions and withdrew westward on both sides of the Valencze Lake.[12]

This third counter-attack, launched from north of Lake Balaton, proved to be the most threatening. The Germans quickly got to the Danube near Dunapentele on the western bank of the river and cut the 3rd Ukrainian Front in two. To counter this, reinforcements had to be transferred from the 2nd Ukrainian Front. From these, two combat groups were formed and they counter-attacked north and south of the German breakthrough on 27 January. Ten days later, they had restored the outer ring around Budapest.

Toward the end of January, garrison commander General Pfeffer-Wildenbruch signalled:

The battle of Castle Hill has begun … Forming a main battle line in the jumble of houses on Castle Hill is an illusion. […] All day there have been extremely heavy air attacks on the Castle and the fighting troops. […] The plight of 300,000 Hungarian inhabitants cooped up in the smallest possible space is terrible. No building is intact. Losses due to enemy action are enormous.[13]

By the end of the first week of February, the exhausted Hungarian defenders could endure no more. Colonel Lajos Lehoczky, the last commander of the Hungarian 10th Infantry Division, reported to Colonel General Schmidhuber, commanding the 13th Panzer Division:

The sufferings and deprivations of the civilian population are even greater than those of the garrison and from this moment the historical responsibility will rest with the commander of the Hungarian Army corps, Colonel General Hindy. […]

I can see no other way out of the conclusive and catastrophic disintegration than the issuing of a general order for the unified cessation of hostilities.[14]

General Balck, commander of the 4th Army seeking to trap ten Soviet divisions north of Lake Balaton, called the 4th SS to his assistance, but stiff Soviet resistance also thwarted this effort. The diversion sealed the fate of Budapest's garrison. It took Soviet troops two days to capture the city's southern railway station on 10 February, and this allowed them to push up to the Castle Hill.

Jenő Sulyánsky, a 15-year-old Hungarian cadet, recalled:

During the night and morning a huge battle raged, particularly near Lenke Square. Burnt-out tanks, lorries, bodies everywhere. […] Not far from us in Horthy Miklós Road, a retreating German military lorry had received a direct hit and was on fire. In and around it were bodies of German soldiers, partly or entirely charred.[15]

The defenders of Gellért Hill successfully repulsed several Soviet attacks until 11 February when a three-pronged assault seized the feature. Soviet artillery was quickly moved on to the hill, which enabled them to dominate the entire city. The garrison continued to refuse to surrender.

That night, 28,000 German and Hungarian soldiers attempted to escape Castle Hill. General Pfeffer-Wildenbruch fled through the sewers, only to emerge into the midst of the Red Army. Everywhere his fleeing men were mown down and massacred, only 800 men reached German lines. The vengeful Soviets annihilated both the SS divisions in the city. During the failed breakout, General Joachim Rumohr, commander the 8th SS Cavalry Division, was wounded and took his own life rather than face capture; just 170 of his men got away.

Taking Budapest cost Stalin 80,000–160,000 dead and 240,056 wounded and sick. The German and Hungarian armies lost up to 150,000 killed, wounded and captured, while 40,000 civilians perished. Eighty per cent of the city lay in ruins. The Red Army anticipated a trouble-free push through the rest of Hungary to the Austrian capital, Vienna.

However, Hitler planned otherwise. In total, ten panzer and five infantry divisions were to launch a counter-offensive dubbed Operation *Frühlingserwachen* (Spring Awakening), between Lake Balaton and Lake Velencze, splitting Marshal

Tolbukhin's 3rd Ukrainian Front in two. Hitler was convinced if the Soviets were caught by surprise it would be their undoing. To this end, secrecy was taken to extremes and reconnaissance of the attack routes was forbidden, lest it tip the Soviets off.

Not only was his last-ditch offensive relying on surprise, but also the weather to carry it through. It would take a severe frost to ensure the marshy ground around Lake Balaton would take the weight of the panzers, especially the massive King Tiger.

Under Army Group South's direction, the 6th SS Panzer Army and 6th Army, supported by the Hungarian 3rd Army, were to attack between the lakes, while the 4th SS Panzer Corps held the Margarethe defences around Lake Balaton itself. The German 8th Army north of Budapest was also to remain on the defensive. At the same time, Army Group South's 2nd Panzer Army, equipped only with assault guns, would employ its four infantry divisions to attack in an easterly direction south of Lake Balaton. This was to be co-ordinated with a supplementary attack by General Löhr's Army Group E in Yugoslavia, which was to launch three divisions from the direction of the Drava to link up with the 6th SS Panzer Army.

In theory, this pincher attack would crush Marshal Tolbukhin's 3rd Ukrainian Front. This consisted of five Soviet Field Armies, 4th Guards, 26th, 27th and 57th, plus former German allies, the 1st Bulgarian Army, supported by the Soviet 17th Air Army. The Soviet 9th Guards Army formed the reserve southeast of Budapest.

To the north, Marshal Malinovsky's 2nd Ukrainian Front stretched from Zvolen to the River Hron (a northern tributary of the Danube), in Hungary. The Soviets received intelligence from the British Military Mission on 12 February, just as Budapest was liberated, that 6th SS Panzer Army had moved east from the Western Front following the aborted Ardennes Offensive.

On 17 February Malinovsky and Tolbukhin were directed to prepare their own counter-offensive which would destroy the German's Army Group South, drive them from Hungary, deprive them of the Nagykanizsa oilfields, occupy Vienna and threaten southern Germany. This move would also threaten to cut off German forces operating in Yugoslavia and Italy. Stavka ordered the offensive to open on 15 March, but little did they know that Hitler was about to pre-empt them.

In total, the German-Hungarian force destined to assault Tolbukhin's troops amounted to thirty-one divisions, eleven of them armoured plus other supporting formations, numbering 431,000 men, 5,630 guns and mortars, 877 tanks and assault guns, supported by 850 aircraft. The main strike force accounted for almost 150,000 men, 807 tanks and assault guns, and over 3,000 guns and mortars. This was a remarkable achievement considering the catalogue of defeats the Third Reich had suffered since 1943 and in light of the fact that the war would be over within two months.

The 6th SS Panzer Army fielded six panzer divisions, two infantry and two cavalry divisions, as well as two heavy tank battalions. The 6th Army had five panzer and three infantry divisions, and the 3rd Hungarian Army had one tank division, two infantry and a cavalry division. On paper, the 6th SS Panzer Army was a formidable formation that included four veteran SS panzer divisions, with the 1st and 12th grouped into the 1st SS Panzer Corps and the 2nd and 9th formed into the 2nd SS Panzer Corps. However, these forces had been spent during Hitler's Ardennes Offensive, which had failed to seize Antwerp. The Hungarian 2nd Armoured Division, equipped with Hungarian-built Turan medium tanks, was considered inadequate for offensive operations and only a single Hungarian infantry division was placed under General 'Sepp' Dietrich's command. Since Stalingrad, the Germans had little or no faith in their dwindling East European allies.

Hitler had a 2:1 superiority in tanks, and Stalin's forces in Hungary were weak in armour, which meant anti-tank guns would be their main defence against the panzer force about to be thrown at them. However, the area chosen for the attack between the River Danube and northern end of Lake Balaton was crisscrossed by canals and ditches and was unsuitable for the panzers. Tolbukhin was ordered to hold the Germans, while the Red Army prepared its own offensive. His men established three main defensive lines of considerable depth.

Soviet suspicions regarding the direction of the Hitler's attempts to stop them were confirmed on 2 March, when Hungarian deserters told their captors of a German attack due in three days' time in the Balaton-Velencze sector. Now fully prepared, Tolbukhin sat back and awaited the German offensive.

On the morning of 6 March 1945, after a thirty-minute artillery bombardment supported by air attacks the 6th SS Panzer and 6th Army crashed into the Soviet defences. As planned, the Germans launched a furious three-pronged attack with the 6th SS Panzer Army striking in a south-easterly direction, between Lakes Velencze and Balaton. The 2nd Panzer Army struck eastward in the direction of Kaposvar, while Army Group E attacked north-east from the right bank of the Drava with the aim of uniting with the 6th SS Panzer Army.

General 'Sepp' Dietrich described the 6th Panzer Army's role as follows:

My left flank [2nd SS Panzer Corps] had no success worth mentioning. The emplacements along the western bank of the Danube, the hard, strong enemy, and the marshy terrain, impassable for tanks, prevented our advancing and attaining our goal. The attacked was bogged down at Sarosd and Sar-Keresztur.

The centre [1st Panzer Corps and the cavalry divisions] reported good success, yet when tanks were employed to exploit the initial success, the terrain proved completely impassable. The terrain, which was supposed to be frozen hard, and which General von Wöhler had maintained as passable, was wet and marshy. For reasons of camouflage, I had been forbidden to make an earlier terrain reconnaissance. Now 132 tanks were sunk in the mud and fifteen King Tigers were sunk up to their turrets, so that the attack could be maintained only by infantry. Considerable losses of men followed.[16]

His panzers ran headlong into the defences of the Soviet 26th Army and part of the 1st Guards' Fortified Area (part of the 4th Guards Army). In response, the Soviets pounded them with artillery and air attacks. ... The 1st SS Panzer Corps managed to push through Soviet defences to a depth of 25 miles, but the 2nd SS Panzer Corps struggled forward just 5 miles.

Two days after Hitler's Spring Awakening opened, the 2nd SS Panzer Division reinforced the offensive with 250 tanks, followed by the 9th SS the next day. The Red Army now found itself under attack by almost 600 panzers. Nevertheless, the Germans were rapidly running out of time and resources. Hitler, however, refused all Dietrich's requests to halt Spring Awakening.

In a final desperate push for the Danube, the 6th Panzer Division with 200 tanks and self-propelled guns, Spring Awakening's last reserves, were committed on 14 March. They managed to force their way to the Soviet rear defence lines, but no further. Although the Soviet 9th Guards Army was moved south-west of Budapest, Tolbukhin was under strict instructions not to employ it in his defensive operations. It was to be held ready for the Soviets' counter-blow.

Elsewhere, Hitler's master plan was coming unstuck. The 2nd Panzer Army's attack launched east of Nagykanizsa was broken up by concentrated Soviet artillery fire. Similarly, Army Group E, which attacked the 1st Bulgarian Army and 3rd Yugoslav Army on the night of 6/7 March, was soon driven back across the Drava by massed Soviet artillery. Tolbukhin, lacking armour, was reinforced by the 406 tanks and self-propelled guns of the Soviet 6th Guards Army. On 16 March, Stalin launched his counter-offensive stroke west of Budapest hitting General Balck's 6th Army and the Hungarian 3rd Army north of Lake Velencze. Motorised infantry rolled through a breach, which 12th SS Panzer Division tried to block, and the Red Army swept south-west toward Balaton.

The Soviets sought to encircle the 6th SS Panzer Army and 6th Army. In a repeat of the disaster at Stalingrad, Hitler's forces were once again let down by their Eastern Front allies. The inadequately equipped Hungarians on 2nd SS Panzer Corps' left flank defected, with inevitable results. The skeletal Hungarian 3rd Army withdrew west, losing the 1st Hussar Division near Budapest. Under pressure, the 1st SS Panzer Division gave ground exposing Balck's flank. Six days later, the 6th SS Panzer was trapped south of Szekesfehervar and barely managed to get away.

By 25 March, Malinovsky had torn a 60-mile-wide gap in the German defences and penetrated more than 20 miles. He then prepared to strike toward Bratislava. The 6th SS Panzer Army and 6th Army took up positions on the Raab River, south of the Austrian capital, and on Lake Neusiedl against Tolbukhin's troops. Three days later, the Red Army was over the river. The Soviets pressed home their attack, pushing toward Papa and Gyor and by 2 April had reached Lake Neusiedl on the border between Hungary and Austria.

After the dismal failure of Spring Awakening, a Soviet attack into Austria was inevitable. A question mark remained over its status amongst the allies, so Stalin was keen to grab his share. Although Stalin was ready to attack Berlin, the ultimate strategic prize as early as February, he decided it prudent to secure his flanks to the north and south where sizeable German forces remained a possible threat. He also deemed Austria a useful pawn in the inevitable horse-trading that would take place over post-war boundaries. Spring Awakening had cost Dietrich 40,000 men, over 500 tanks and assault guns, and 300 guns. Using the excuse of defending Vienna, he retrieved his surviving forces.

At the end of March the Red Army forced the Hron and Nitra rivers, swept into Sopron and Nagykanizsa and crossed the boundary between prostrate Hungary and Austria. This placed Tolbukhin's 3rd Ukrainian Front in position to strike at the Austrian capital. The only thing that stood in his way was the 2nd SS Panzer Corps. Vienna had been under aerial attack by the British and American bomber fleets for a year by March 1945. These had dropped 80,000 tons of bombs, killed 30,000 people and levelled 12,000 buildings, which had left 270,000 people homeless. On 12 March it had been struck by 747 bombers.

General Dietrich knew that keeping the Red Army out of Vienna was a tall order:

> My orders were to get four divisions as fast as possible for the hitherto unprepared defence of the city. We had to defend in, but not in front of Vienna. The city still had 3,000,000 inhabitants, and no water or supplies for the civilians, but these conditions were not even discussed. General von Buenau was appointed Battle Commander of Vienna, and arrived without bringing any troops for the defence.[17]

Stalin's Vienna Offensive opened on 2 April and lasted just under two weeks. The Red Army quickly overran Wiener Neustadt, Eisenstaedt, Neunkirchen, Gloggnitz, Baden and Bratislava. That day, the Germans denied Vienna had been declared an open city, thereby condemning it to bloody street fighting. Once the 3rd Ukrainian Front had surrounded Vienna, the Soviet 4th Guards, 6th Guards Tank, 9th Guards and 46th Armies were thrown against the city's defences. By 9 April they had reached the city centre, and two days later the 4th Guards attacked across the Danube canals, while other forces moved to secure the Reichsbrücke Bridge. The fierce battle cost the Germans 19,000 dead and the Soviets 18,000 and the city capitulated on 13 April. The city was overrun, with the loss of 125,000 prisoners.

Stalin then shifted this attention to Czechoslovakia. His Prague Offensive was his last assault of the war and was conducted after Berlin had been overwhelmed and Germany had surrendered. The war had first come to Prague on 14 February 1945, when the American Air Force bombed the city, killing 701 inhabitants, destroying 100 buildings and damaging another 200.

Fought from 6–11 May, the Prague Offensive culminated in the liberation of the city. Army Group Centre, which had been at the very heart of Operation Barbarossa and Hitler's dream of capturing Moscow, fought to the very last. It did not surrender until nine days after the Red Army had captured Berlin and three whole days after Victory in Europe Day.

This final major offensive was conducted by Konev's 1st, Rodion Malinovsky's 2nd and Andrei Yeremenko's 4th Ukrainian fronts. Konev's troops, although exhausted after their efforts against Berlin, were directed south to help secure Prague. Soviet forces amounted to over 2 million men; they were supported by the Czech 1st Corps, the Polish 2nd Army and the Romanian 1st and 4th Armies. Hitler's old allies now had new masters.

Field Marshal Ferdinand Schörhner's battered Army Group Centre comprised the 1st and 4th Panzer Armies and the 7th and 17th Armies – in all, about 900,000 men. They were supported by the miserable remnants of Army Group South, now known as Army Group Ostmark.

General Alfred Jodl, chief of staff of the German armed forces (OKW), surrendered to the Western Allies on 7 May. Two days later, the Red Army rolled into Prague, but elements of Army Group Centre needlessly held out until 11 May. Once the Soviets had linked up with the Americans, Army Group Centre was surrounded, making any further resistance a futile exercise as there could be no escape westward. Even though these were the dying days of the war in the east, Army Group Centre still had fight left in it. This last, and in many ways, futile operation by the Red Army cost them 52,498 casualties, 11,997 killed and 40,501 wounded and sick, 373 tanks, 1,006 artillery pieces and eighty aircraft.

18

MADMEN IN BERLIN

By early 1945 Hitler had completely exhausted Germany's available manpower and Stalin's vastly superior numbers were relentlessly overwhelming his country's defences. Nonetheless, the German Army continued to inflict heavy losses on the advancing Red Army.

Hitler decided to bolster the army with his version of 'Dad's Army', optimistically dubbed the Volkssturm (People's Storm). Every German city was to become a fortress and the inhabitants drafted into this People's Militia. Hitler demanded 6 million new recruits. While the Volksgrenadier divisions performed quite well and were reasonably trained and equipped, the Volkssturm were at the other end of the spectrum. The SS had already taken the older teenage members of the Hitler Youth and Reich Labour Service as a military manpower reserve to replace its combat losses. This had resulted in the creation of three very effective Waffen-SS panzer divisions. Likewise, the Volksgrenadiers had taken the last of the teenagers and men deemed too old to fight. Now the Hitler Youth resorted to recruiting 12-year-olds who were enrolled into the Volkssturm, along with men deemed medically unfit or simply too frail.

In contrast to the Ruhr in the west which had been bombed incessantly, Silesia was the only German industrial area that had escaped a major mauling from air attack. Stalin's Lower Silesian Offensive Operation, commencing on 8 February 1945, was designed to clear Lower Silesia and take the provincial capital, Breslau. It followed the Vistula–Oder Offensive, and having driven Hitler's Army Group A from Poland, liberating Krakow and taking bridgeheads over the Oder River, Konev now planned to break out of the Steinau and Ohlau bridgeheads.

To defend the vital industrial resources of Upper Silesia, Hitler would have needed a minimum of twelve divisions. East of the Oder and south of Breslau, the main strength of the German 17th Army lay around Beuthen and Hindenburg.

However, Soviet penetrations at Tanowitz to the north and Sosnowitz to the south threatened to encircle elements of this army.

On 20 January, General von Edelsheim's 48th Panzer Corps could only muster the remains of the 68th and 304th Infantry Divisions supported by some assault guns. The 97th Jäger Division and the 712th Infantry Division only had half their combat units in Upper Silesia, while the 75th Infantry Division was holding a position north-west of Krakow. Elements of two Panzer divisions (8th and 20th) were en route but it was doubtful they would arrive in time. On 29 January, the 344th Infantry Division received orders to hold a position west of the Oder between Ratibor and Cosel once the Soviets had established a bridgehead over the river between the two. Weak elements of the 8th and 20th Panzer Divisions also launched a series of desperate counter-attacks.

By this point, with East Prussia overrun except for Königsberg, Silesia penetrated and the Soviets in Germany, Hitler decreed that it was time for Germany's Home Guard to act. On 28 January, he declared:

> Experience in the East has shown that the Volkssturm emergency and reserve units have little fighting value when left to themselves, and can be quickly destroyed. The fighting value of these units, which are for the most part strong in numbers but weak in the armaments required for modern battle, is immeasurably higher when they go into action with troops of the regular army in the field.
>
> I therefore order: where Volkssturm … are available, together with regular units, in any battle sector, mixed battle groups [brigades] will be formed under unified command, so as to give the Volkssturm … stiffening and support.[1]

This would have been farcical if it had not been so tragic. The last thing regular army units wanted was old men and frightened young boys drawn from the Hitler Youth under their wing. The conscripts' lack of experience and poor training was prone not only to get themselves killed but everyone around them.

German soldier, Guy Sajer, witnessed how Hitler had slaughtered whole generations on the Eastern Front and resorted to mobilising pensioners and school children to fight the Red Army:

> While we waited, we watched a crowd of men, part of a new Volkssturm battalion, swarm into the factory courtyard. [...] Some of these troops with Mausers on their shoulders must have been at least sixty or sixty-five … now we were looking literally at children marching beside these feeble old men. [...] They had been hastily dressed in worn uniforms cut for men, and they

were carrying guns which were often as big as they were. [...] Not one of them could have imagined the impossible ordeal which lay ahead.[2]

On 5 February 1945, General Otto Lasch was appointed Fortress Commander of Königsberg. He had a thankless task with his weak garrison consisting of four under-strength divisions, with few willing recruits for the Waffen-SS or Volkssturm. More defences were prepared, with the main line anchored on twelve outer forts of the city. The inner defences were also anchored on ancient forts built in the mid-nineteenth century. The bombed remains of the old royal castle located above the Pregel River were also fortified.

By the end of the first week of February, in Middle and Lower Silesia the Germans' Oder defence had collapsed and the Red Army was beyond the left flank of the Upper Silesian Front. On the night of 12/13 February, Soviet troops came together in the Tinz-Domslau area between Lohe and Weistritz, encircling Breslau. About 200,000 civilians and 40,000 troops were trapped.

The key point in this offensive occurred on 13 February, when the 19th Panzer Division in the Kostomloty area held open the autobahn to enable two infantry divisions to escape from Breslau. That night, the 7th Guards Tank Corps succeeded in sealing off the rest of the garrison. By 15 February, Soviet forces from the two bridgeheads had surrounded Breslau, while 3rd Guards Tank Army had completely closed the gap to the west.

Striking from Greiffenberg, 8th Panzer made a surprise attack on 18 February against the southern wing of the Soviets advancing from Löwenburg to Lauban. Although they slowed them, eight days later there was heavy fighting in Lauban and on 28 February it fell to the Soviet 3rd Guards Tank Army, allowing them to prepare to move on Görlitz and Dresden.

The Germans prepared a counter-attack. The divisions and *kampfgruppen* from General Decker's 39th and Kirchner's 57th Panzer Corps, under the direction of Nehring's 24th Panzer Corps, moved into position on the night of 1/2 March. The main strike force was made up of elements of the 8th, 16th and 17th Panzer Divisions. General Hax of 8th Panzer recalled, 'We succeeded in hitting the enemy on their southern flank, between Löwenburg and Lauban, and thereby decisively halting the enemy advance on Görlitz.'[3] On the first day of the attack, 17th Panzer destroyed eighty Soviet tanks and 8th Panzer accounted for a total of 150.

With Hitler desperately throwing reinforcements into the battle, Konev brought the offensive phase of operations to a close sixteen days after his start, having secured a small bridgehead across the Neisse near Forst. This defined the start lines in that sector for the Berlin Offensive later in the year.

It was not until early March that Hitler attempted to relieve Breslau, gathering seven divisions including four panzer divisions in the Görlitz area. On 3 March they attacked the weak 3rd Guards Tank Army, but after fierce fighting the German attack was halted with both sides suffering heavy casualties. During the siege, which lasted until 6 May, the Soviet forces inflicted approximately 29,000 civilian and military casualties and took more than 40,000 prisoners. Securing Breslau cost them 8,000 casualties.

A despairing Guderian recalled the worsening situation:

Finland declared war on Germany on 3 March.

On this day German troops attacked in the area of Lauban, in Silesia, in order to recapture the sole rail-line east of the Riesengebirge between Berlin and Silesia. The attack was successful until 8 March but had only local significance.

On 4 March the Russians reached the Baltic between Köslin and Kolberg. All outer Pomerania was now lost to us.[4]

Guderian also noted, 'The behaviour of the Russians in the occupied German provinces was indescribably atrocious.'[5] Thousands of women and children suffered at the hands of rapacious Soviet soldiers; Stalin's men had little regard for the rule of law.

The East Pomeranian Strategic Offensive Operation, which opened on 24 February, was designed to clear Hitler's forces from East Pomerania and East Prussia. The Red Army and Polish 1st Army fought to overcome resistance from the Baltic seaport of Kolberg, held by 10,000 German troops, during 4–18 March. Designated a fortress, it formed a vital link between Pomerania and Prussia. It was hoped it would distract Stalin away from Berlin while the capital's defences were strengthened.

The battle to overcome Kolberg cost the Poles about 1,000 dead and 3,000 wounded, but some 40,000 German troops were successfully evacuated from the port as part of Operation Hannibal. Danzig fell on 28 March, and the survivors from the German 2nd Army fell back into the Vistula delta north-east of the city. The following month, over a quarter of a million people were evacuated from this area. The East Pomeranian Offensive cost Stalin 225,692 casualties.

During March the Red Army sought to clear the rest of Silesia, with the Upper Silesian Offensive operation conducted from 15–31 March 1945. Konev launched his main assault with the 4th Tank Army piercing the German lines west of Oppeln and heading southward for Neustadt. South-east of Oppeln, the 59th and 60th Armies also broke through the German defences, swinging westwards to link up with the 4th Tank Army. The 1st Panzer Army's 11th Corps, holding the lines near Oppeln, was threatened with encirclement.

By 22 March the Soviet 59th and 21st Armies had crushed the Oppeln 'cauldron', claiming to have killed 15,000 Germans and captured a further 15,000.

This offensive stabilised Konev's left flank in preparation for the advance on Berlin and removed the threat from Army Group Centre. In total, the Red Army claimed to have killed 40,000 troops and captured another 14,000 at a cost of 66,801 casualties during the Upper Silesian Campaign.

By this stage of the war, there was no hiding intelligence chief Reinhard Gehlen's pessimism:

> In what was to prove my last intelligence digest, early in April, I indicated that the impending loss of Königsberg, capital of East Prussia, would release fresh Russian strength against us, and that the same was true for Vienna. Massive troop reinforcements were pouring into the area between Küstrin and Frankfurt on Oder for the final assault on Berlin. [...] Hitler dismissed it as 'absolutely idiotic' and defeatist, and on 9 April I was relived of my position as head of Foreign Armies East.[6]

Hitler simply did not want to face up to the reality of the situation and lived in a perpetual state of denial. The Red Army and Red Air Force continued to pound 'fortress' Königsberg into rubble. On 7 April, 246 bombers hit the city while artillery and rocket launchers kept up a deadly barrage. Up to 35,000 troops, 15,000 foreign workers and 100,000 civilians remained trapped.

The Red Army crossed the Pregel on 8 April, cutting off central Königsberg. General Lasch recalled:

> Local knowledge ceased to be of any help in the inferno, which had once been the city of Königsberg. Ghostly lunar landscapes had come into being in place of the great avenues which used to lead through the city. Paths could be reconnoitred and just an hour later they were impassable.[7]

Terrified civilians gathered on the old Pillau Road in a desperate bid to escape the 'inferno' were promptly massacred by Soviet fire. Lasch had little option but to surrender the following day. Hitler's response was predictable. In Berlin, the daily news bulletin announced:

> Königsberg Fortress was handed over to the Russians by General of Infantry Lasch. Despite this, parts of the loyal garrison have continued to resist. For surrendering to the enemy, General of Infantry Lasch has been condemned to death by hanging. His family has been arrested.[8]

In Königsberg the Red Army went on a drinking, killing, looting and raping spree.

'There is nobody less popular than a prophet of misfortune whose predictions have been proved true in every detail,' said Gehlen, in response to his dismissal.[9] He recalled:

> On 12 April, my colleagues insisted on holding a small farewell party for me, to mark my departure from Foreign Armies East; three years had passed since I had taken the branch over and started to build it up. It was a gloomy celebration, for nobody knew what now lay ahead.[10]

Zhukov arrived in Moscow on 29 March to discuss with Stalin the coming assault on Berlin. Zhukov's intelligence indicated that Hitler had four armies in the region with no less than ninety divisions, including fourteen panzer and motorised, plus thirty-seven separate regiments and ninety-eight separate battalions. Later, it was established by the Soviets that Hitler had 1 million men, with 10,400 artillery pieces and mortars, 1,500 tanks and assault guns, 3,500 combat aircraft, and an additional 200,000-strong garrison was being formed. In fact, none of the German units had anywhere near their established strength, nor were they fully equipped; ammunition, rations and morale were in short supply.

In the west, on 1 April Field Marshal Model's Army Group was trapped in the Ruhr, and within three weeks would lay down their arms. On 15 April 1945, Hitler issued his last Führer Order, warning Germany of the fate that awaited their women and exhorting everyone to fight to the last:

> We have foreseen this thrust, and since last January have done everything possible to construct a strong front. The enemy will be greeted by massive artillery fire. Gaps in our infantry have been made good by countless new units. Our front is being strengthened by emergency units, newly raised units, and by the Volkssturm. [...]
>
> Form yourselves into a sworn brotherhood, to defend, not the empty conception of a Fatherland, but your homes, your wives, your children, and, with them, our future. In these hours, the whole German people looks to you, my fighters in the East, and only hope that, thanks to your resolution and fanaticism, thanks to your weapons, and under your leadership, the Bolshevik assault will be choked in a blood bath.[11]

Germany had given all it could in the name of sacrifice on the Eastern Front, now the enemy was at the very gates of Berlin. Hitler's war in the east had come home to roost in an orgy of wanton destruction and revenge. The Red Army were behaving like marauding beasts, but what more could have been expected after the atrocities committed by the Germans across the Soviet Union?

Berliners were thoroughly war weary and exhausted. It had been intended to have 100,000 workers preparing Berlin's defences, but in fact only about 30,000 were ever mobilised. Colonel Hans Refior, chief of staff to Berlin's comman-dant, noted, 'Berlin gardeners apparently considered the digging of their potato plots more important than the digging of tank traps'.[12]

It was clear that Berlin's outer defences would never be ready in time, nor was there the manpower to effectively defend the city. It was calculated that 200,000 experienced troops would be needed to hold the city's 320 square miles. Instead, the bulk of the garrison consisted of 60,000 untrained Volkssturm. They lacked weapons, ammunition, vehicles and radios. Berlin's commander, Major General Helmuth Reymann was soon informed he would get no help from the German armies desperately trying to hold the Oder.

Lieutenant General Eberhard Kinzel was serving as deputy chief of staff of Army Group Vistula, under Heinrich Himmler, when Colonel General Gotthard Heinrici took charge in March 1945. Promoted to chief of staff, Kinzel was present when Heinrici was informed that not only had he responsibility for holding the Oder but also defending Berlin. Heinrici's response was that this was 'absurd' and he refused.

In one of the final ironies of the war on the Eastern Front, it was now very evident that Hitler did not have enough troops to defend the Oder and his capital. Army Group Vistula, comprising Manteuffel's 3rd Panzer Army in the north and Busse's 9th Army in the south, could muster 480,000 troops with practically no reserves. Intelligence indicated that the Red Army might have up to 3 million men facing them.

Kinzel must have felt that the proverbial chickens had come home to roost. His early warnings about Stalin having up to sixty fresh divisions had been ignored, and now three years on the Wehrmacht had been completely overwhelmed all along the Eastern Front. It did not matter how many Soviet soldiers they killed, how many tanks they destroyed or aircraft they shot down, the vengeful Red Army just kept coming. He had witnessed at first hand the price of underestimating Soviet reserves when he had served with 29th Corps, which formed part of Field Marshal Paulus' fated 6th Army, so spectacularly destroyed at Stalingrad. Luckily for Kinzel, 29th Corps had avoided being encircled and he had survived to take part in the last-ditch defence of Berlin.

It fell to Kinzel to deliver the bad news regarding Heinrici's decision to Colonel Hans Refior. The latter said that neither the OKH nor OKW would take responsibility for the defence of Berlin. Kinzel explained that Heinrici had his hands full on the Oder and was very apologetic, blaming Hitler and saying, 'As far as I am personally concerned, those madmen in Berlin can fry in their own juice'.[13] Such sentiments were punishable by a firing squad. Once again, Kinzel's honesty got him sacked and he was replaced on 21 April.

Heinrici felt the appointment of Major General Thilo von Trotha, a Hitler favourite, was a deliberate ploy to try and influence his decisions – something Kinzel had not done. To the very end, Hitler would cling to the delusion that Army Group Vistula would come to Berlin's rescue. Kinzel was sent off to be chief of staff to Field Marshal Busch, commanding Army Group North-West, who was trying to fend off Montgomery. Although in disgrace, Busch, who had presided over the final nail in the Nazi coffin with the destruction of Army Group Centre the previous summer, had been summoned by Hitler in March 1945. Like Heinrici, he had an impossible task.

Berliners refused to give in, even though defeat was staring them in the face. Erich Kempka, Hitler's personal chauffeur, was amazed at their resilience:

> The Russians were closing the noose around Berlin ever tighter. The battle for the Reich capital became fiercer. The trams, underground and surface railway systems continued to operate, though naturally not all. Where there was still electric current and an intact track, the employees, men and women, did their duty like soldiers. Even a large number of factories kept working. The men and women of Berlin went to work under Russian artillery fire. Under the deluge of shells, Berliners held firm and calm just as they did under the heavy bombing. Until the last Berlin tram stopped running, every inhabitant of the Reich capital made a superhuman effort.[14]

The Red Army's assault on the Seelow Heights, effectively the gates of Berlin, commenced on 16 April. It opened with the usual massive Soviet bombardment using shells, rockets and bombs. The Oder was breached before dawn by the 1st Byelorussian Front, while the 1st Ukrainian Front barged across the Neisse.

From the very beginning it was a one-sided affair. In total, for the Berlin offensive the Soviet 1st and 2nd Byelorussian and 1st Ukrainian Fronts fielded 2.5 million troops, equipped with some 6,250 tanks, 41,600 artillery pieces and mortars, as well as 3,255 truck-mounted Katyusha rocket launchers and 7,500 aircraft. Zhukov was able to hurl almost 1 million men of the 1st Belorussian Front (including 78,556 soldiers of the 1st Polish Army), at the Germans' defensive positions on the Seelow Heights.

In their path lay about 100,000 German soldiers of General Theodor Busse's 9th Army, which formed part of Heinrici's Army Group Vistula. He defended the front from the Finow Canal to Guben, which encompassed the fortified Seelow Heights. In total, Busse had fourteen divisions with 512 tanks, 344 artillery pieces and 300 anti-aircraft guns. Further south, the front was held by the weak 4th Panzer Army, tasked with fending off Konev's 1st Ukrainian Front.

Colonel General Mikhail Katukov, commander of the Soviet 1st Guards Tank Army, was ordered by Zhukov to bludgeon his way through Busse's defences. However, the 65th Guards Tank Brigade found the going tough. 'Those Hitlerite devils!' exclaimed Katukov, when he was told of the hold-up, 'I have never seen such resistance in the whole course of the war.' He then informed those around him that he was going to find out 'what the hell is holding things up'.[15] He needed to take the Heights by morning to allow Zhukov's break-out.

General Helmuth Weidling, commanding the 56th Panzer Corps, recalled the sheer weight of the Soviet attack:

> On 16 April, in the first hours of the offensive the Russians broke through on the right flank of the 101st Army Corps on the sector of Division Berlin, thereby threatening the left flank of the 56th Panzer Corps. In the second half of the day Russian tanks broke through on the sector of the 303rd Infantry Division, part of the SS 11th Panzer Corps, and threatened to attack units of Division Müncheberg from the flank. At the same time the Russians exerted strong pressure on the front of the sector occupied by my corps. In the early hours on 17 April units of my corps, suffering heavy losses, were forced to retreat to the Heights east of Seelow.[16]

Despite stubborn German resistance, Katukov gained a foothold on the Heights. Lieutenant General Nikolai N. Popiel remembered that just before midnight 'the first three houses in the northern suburbs of the town of Seelow had been captured. [...] It was a bitter operation.'[17] The defenders did not give in. 'The Germans didn't even have to aim,' Popiel adds, 'They just fired over open sights.'[18] Not until the night of 17/18 April were the Seelow Heights finally cleared.

Busse's defences weathered the preliminary attacks and then spent twenty-four hours enduring the full force of Zhukov's assault. In the Seelow area, they knocked out over 150 Soviet tanks and shot down 132 planes, but it was not enough. In just three days the 1st Belorussian Front had smashed through the final defences of the Seelow Heights, leaving little in the way of effective defence between the Soviets and Berlin.

Reporter Vasily Grossman was with the Red Army on the road to Berlin, recording, 'The highway leading to Berlin. Crowds of liberated people. [...] and the police riff-raff, who had run away as far as Berlin ... People say Vlasov has taken part in the last battles in Berlin with his men.'[19] Vlasov, though, was to meet his fate in Prague not Berlin.

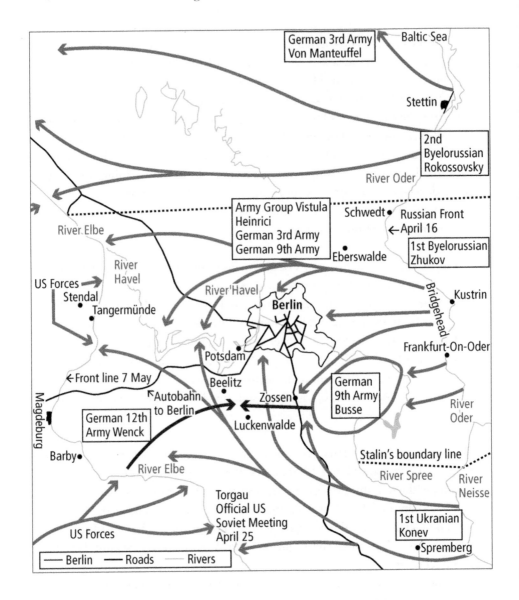

The Battle for Berlin, 16 April–1 May 1945.

On 18 April, General Reymann was instructed that 'all forces available, including Volkssturm, had been requested by the 9th Army to hold second line positions'.[20] His already inadequate garrison was denuded to man the outer defences alongside Busse's withdrawing men. Reichminister Dr Josef Goebbels, Berlin's Gauleiter and self-appointed defender, personally confirmed this order. Ten battalions of Volkssturm and an anti-aircraft defence regiment marched east. Bitterly, Reymann said, 'Tell Goebbels that it is no longer possible to defend the Reich capital. The inhabitants are defenceless.'[21]

Part of Zhukov's 1st Belorussian Front, striking south, and elements of 1st Ukrainian Front, which had broken through and turned north, surrounded the survivors from the 9th Army and 4th Panzer Army. Konev's other armies raced west toward the Americans on the Elbe.

By the end of 19 April, the Eastern Front as defined by the Seelow Heights no longer existed. The front line had completely collapsed. The defenders lost some 11,000 killed, while the Red Army suffered 30,000 dead. All that remained to hold Berlin itself were about 45,000 ill-equipped troops.

19

HITLER YOUTH

After the Seelow fortifications had been breached, the Führer's birthday was understandably an extremely sober affair. Christa Schroeder wrote:

> On Hitler's fifty-sixth birthday on 20 April 1945 Berlin was surrounded, and the first Russian tanks reached the outskirts. We could hear the thunder of field guns from the Reich Chancellery. The chorus of congratulations from personal staff and the military that morning were very restrained in comparison to earlier years.[1]

Immediately after his birthday, Hitler gave the order for his personal staff to be sent to safety, including Christa Schroeder:

> It was a macabre drive through the night past burning houses, smouldering heaps of rubble, ruins and smoke, and Volkssturm men hastily erecting street barricades. In the middle distance we could hear the thunder of Soviet artillery.[2]

That very day, Berlin was assaulted from the south-east by General Berzarin's 5th Shock Army and General Katukov's 1st Guards Tank Army. Zhukov wrote:

> At 1.50 p.m. on 20 April, the long-range artillery of the 79th Rifle Corps of the 3rd Assault Army commanded by Colonel General V.I. Kuznetsov was the first to open fire on Berlin, thereby starting the historic storming of the German capital. On 21 April units of the 3rd Assault, 2nd Guards Tank, and 47th Armies entered the outskirts of Berlin and began the struggle in the city.
>
> The struggle in Berlin approached its climax. We all wanted to finish off the enemy's grouping of forces in Berlin by 1 May in order to make the holiday

for the Soviet people even more joyous. But the enemy, although he was in the last agony, continued to cling to every house, to every cellar, and to every roof. Nevertheless, Soviet troops took block after block, house after house.[3]

Nothing could withstand Zhukov's steamroller as it barged its way through the shattered city. Despite the bitter street fighting, the defenders were driven back into ever-shrinking pockets of isolated resistance. General Weidling later told his captors:

> 20 April was the hardest day for my Corps and probably for all the German troops. They had suffered tremendous losses in previous fighting; they were worn down and exhausted, and were no longer able to resist the tremendous thrust of the superior Russian forces.[4]

During the day, Hitler ventured to the surface to decorate a group of orphans from Breslau or Dresden who had come to the capital to fight for the Hitler Youth. This event was captured on newsreel and presented a melancholy spectacle. The city was bombed all day and into the early hours of the next. It was now only a matter of time before the Red Army entered the city centre.

In the wake of Hitler's half-hearted birthday celebrations, the slaughter on the Eastern Front was in its last death throws. The final battle had begun. Erich Kempka, Hitler's chauffeur, says:

> We received the first warning signals early on the morning of 21 April. The Reich capital fell under heavy artillery bombardment. We could hear the explosions. They rolled nearer like thundering surf. [...] Already the Soviet shelling was hitting the government district. New craters appeared in the Reich Chancellery garden. Splinters whirred around; windowpanes shattered. The air filled with dust and smoke.[5]

Hitler's senior entourage pleaded with him to escape the Red Army's cordon and fly to the safety of the Berghof at Obersalzburg, but he would not leave the capital. On 22 April Hitler, in conference with Keitel, Jodl and Goebbels, agreed that Berlin would fall if reinforcements were not immediately summoned from somewhere. The only place this was possible was from the Elbe. It was decided that General Walther Wenck's 12th Army would leave a rear guard to hold the Americans and attack the Red Army surrounding the capital from the south.

Keitel and Jodl were despatched with instructions to oversee this proposed counter-attack. However, all this was simply too little, too late. Staring at his maps, Hitler failed to grasp that the exhausted armies deployed around

Berlin were themselves under siege and on the verge of collapse. On paper Wenck's army consisted of seven panzer, panzergrenadier and infantry divisions, but these amounted to just three weak infantry divisions with no tanks or fighter cover.

To the north-east of Berlin, the Army Group Steiner was also ordered to break through. It was barely of corps strength, consisting of units from three disparate divisions with few heavy weapons. Its commander, SS Major General Felix Steiner, could muster at most 11,000 men with less than fifty panzers, half of which had no fuel. He declined to obey orders, arguing:

> I had nothing with which to attack. The three divisions in reserve at Schorfheide had already been swallowed up attempting to stop the Russian juggernaut rolling westwards. Two new divisions that Army Group Vistula had promised never arrived. [...] The plan of attack was based on facts that had no basis in reality, but only in the fantasies of the Chancellery.[6]

The 5,000 reinforcements Steiner received, in the shape of Luftwaffe ground personnel and Hitler Youth, he refused to commit to the fighting on the grounds it would be irresponsible. 'I refused,' declared Steiner, 'to use the indescribable bands of soldiers which had been so hurriedly assembled; I did not want to lose a single man in an enterprise which was doomed to crushing disaster from the beginning.'[7]

When Heinrici heard of this mad scheme, he backed Steiner's decision not to co-operate. Even Jodl could not get Steiner to move. When a weary Heinrici pressed him as to why he was not attacking, an exasperated Steiner replied, 'It's very simple, I just don't have the troops. I don't have the slightest chance of succeeding'.[8]

Hitler imagined that Steiner's forces could swing across the top of the capital and south-westward to Spandau and the bridges over the Havel. Steiner could then link up with those forces advancing from the south. In principle, this was a sound plan, but in practice it was impossible.

Keitel found Wenck's HQ about 37 miles east of Magdeburg at Alte Hölle. Wenck was not pleased to see the head of the OKW, who immediately demanded, 'Liberate Berlin! Turn all your available forces around. Link up with the 9th Army. Get the Führer out. Wenck, you're the only one who can save Germany!'[9] While Steiner openly defied the Führer, Wenck was a little more circumspect and said what Keitel wanted to hear. Once Keitel had gone, Wenck looked at his situation maps and knew it was a fool's errand. He had no intention of going to Berlin; his greatest duty lay to the east and Busse's men. He intended to cut an escape corridor for them.

Wenck called Colonel Günther Reichhelm, his chief of staff, and the others together:

> Now, here's how we will actually do it. We will drive as close to Berlin as we can, but we will not give up our positions on the Elbe. With our flanks on the river we keep open a channel of escape to the west. It would be nonsense to drive toward Berlin only to be encircled by the Russians. We will try to link up with the 9th Army, and then let's get out every soldier and civilian who can make it west.[10]

After telling his staff that he was going to disobey orders, Wenck said, 'The fate of a single individual is no longer of any significance'.[11] Just for appearances sake, Wenck ordered his weak 20th Corps to attack toward Potsdam, which lay south-west of the capital. The rest of his army was to strike toward Busse. Wenck knew it was a desperate race against time. Once his troops had exhausted their ammunition and fuel it would all be over. The Red Army had overrun most of the Wehrmacht's depots and the Red Air Force dominated the skies, so there was no chance of re-supply.

Hitler and his staff were detached from reality in the dank gloom of the Führerbunker and had very little detailed or accurate information from the outside world. The OKW kept moving headquarters and many of Hitler's radio operators deserted. Staff Officer Major von Loringhoven took desperate measures:

> To obtain intelligence ... I had the idea of intercepting radio messages from Reuters in London ... We found ourselves in a grotesque position whereby any situation report given to Hitler was based largely on information derived from an enemy radio.[12]

A futile counter-attack by Weidling's 56th Panzer Corps was brushed aside and by the evening of 24 April the Soviets reached the Berlin S-Bahn ring railway on the north side of the Teltow Canal. This placed them just to the east of Tempelhof Airport. A few days earlier, Weidling had gone from being accused of cowardice to commander of the Berlin Defence Area. His predecessor, General Reymann, was dismissed for 'defeatism'.

Although the Red Army was closing in, Marshal Konev recalled the strong defences along the northern bank of the Teltow Canal:

> Imagine this deep, wide moat filled with water and lined with steep concrete walls. On the 12km long canal sector reached by Rybalko's tanks [3rd Tank Army], the Germans had herded together everyone they could lay their hands

on – some 15,000 men. A density of 1,200 men per kilometre is a very high figure, I must say, for fighting within a city. Besides that, they had more than 250 guns and mortars, 130 tanks and armoured carriers, and more than 5,000 machine guns. They also had an unlimited quantity of Faustpatronen [hand held anti-tank weapons].[13]

On 26 April, General Chuikov's 8th Guards Army and Katukov's 1st Guards Tank Army fought their way through the southern suburbs and attacked Tempelhof Airport, just inside the S-Bahn defensive ring. Chuikov, defender of Stalingrad, had an old score to settle with his enemy. All around him, Hitler's shattered capital now looked like Stalingrad. Berlin's defenders were steadily reduced to a pocket running about 10 miles east to west and 3.5 miles at its widest.

Vasily Grossman saw the disgusting horror of it all as the Reich convulsed in its final death throes, witnessing 'corpses squashed by tanks, squeezed out like tubes. Almost all of them are clutching grenades and sub-machine guns in their hands.'[14] These last desperate acts of resistance were futile, but continued to the very end. On the night of 26/27 April, the Soviets commenced shelling the Reich Chancellery building, where Hitler was still sheltering in the adjacent bunker built in the gardens. The Red Army was less than a mile away from its final destination.

For a very brief moment, hope flickered amongst those in the bunker who were ignorant of military matters. 'On 27 April, toward midday, I had the OKW on the telephone,' said Loringhoven. 'Wenck had reached Ferch, a village some dozen kilometres from Potsdam and twenty kilometres south-west of Berlin.'[15] Loringhoven knew Wenck would not get through; his forces comprised Hitler Youth and 'a hotchpotch of miscellaneous troops without any cohesion, randomly assembled from new recruits picked up in the streets'.[16]

The next day Hitler was still vainly waiting for Wenck's 12th Army to come to the relief of Berlin. He radioed Field Marshal Keitel, 'I expect the relief of Berlin. What is Heinrici's army [group] doing? Where is Wenck? What is happening to the 9th Army? When will Wenck and 9th Army join us?'[17] The truth was that the 12th and 9th Armies were fighting for their very lives and the remains of Heinrici's Army Group was desperately withdrawing west to avoid falling into the hands of the vengeful Red Army. 'By evening,' recalled Loringhoven, 'the intelligence left no doubt that the attack had failed.'[18]

In 1941, Hitler had refused to believe that he was outnumbered and he still clung to this delusional view to the bitter end. Likewise, the Nazi propaganda machine refused to acknowledge that the Third Reich was lost. German radio announced, 'In their attack to liberate Berlin, the young divisions of Wenck's army have reached the region south of Ferch.'[19] The Propaganda Ministry also produced leaflets declaring, 'Soldiers of the Wenck Army, we Berliners know that you have reached Potsdam. Hurry! Help us!'[20] They were 'accidentally' dropped throughout the capital to delude Berliners into believing that help was coming. Those leaflets issued to Wenck were incinerated on his orders, as he had no intention of resorting to moral blackmail. It was a cruel and needless trick, but by this stage the Nazi regime had lost all reason.

Wenck was understandably flabbergasted at this flagrant breach of operational security by the Propaganda Ministry. The Red Army was monitoring German broadcasts and would now concentrate their resources in stopping the 12th Army. 'We won't be able to move a single step farther tomorrow!' he said to Colonel Reichhelm.[21]

'In the bunker, a few had soon begun crying treason,' recalled Loringhoven, after hearing the broadcast, 'If the Russians had not guessed it already, Wenck's objective seemed obvious.'[22]

Just as Berlin was about to fall, another massive and futile battle was being fought to the south. According to Konev, around 200,000 German soldiers with Busse's 9th Army were surrounded during the Battle of Halbe, south-east of Berlin. Twice during the desperate struggle, they tried breaking through the Soviet encirclement of the Spree Forest, although on both occasions they were stopped with heavy losses. On the third attempt, 25,000 men from the Halbe pocket managed to successfully reach Wenck's forces in the Beelitz area, south-west of Berlin.

Wenck had reached the exhausted Busse at the eleventh hour. 'The men of the 9th were so tired, so worn out, in such terrible shape that it was unbelievable,' he recalled in dismay.[23] From the throng staggered a grubby unshaven general. 'Thank God you're here,' said Wenck, shaking Busse by the hand. Konev claimed that only 3,000–4,000 enemy troops ever got through. He was not very impressed with the performance of Wenck's troops, 'But the 9th Army, in breaking out of the ring, fought boldly, to the death. And it was precisely the determined nature of its actions that gave us such a lot of trouble in those last days of the war.'[24]

In fact, Busse had become trapped in the Spree Forest with about 80,000 men and made a complete mess of co-ordinating the break-out. Afterwards, the remnants of both the 9th and 12th Armies then fought their way to the Elbe to surrender to the Americans. In Hitler's imagination, he still thought that once Busse had linked up with Wenck their forces would come to the assistance of the beleaguered Berlin garrison – it was complete fantasy. In liquidating the Halbe pocket, the Red Army claimed to have captured 120,000 Germans and killed another 60,000. Hitler could have prevented this slaughter if he had authorised the 9th Army to withdraw west sooner. Busse, for his part, dithered too long.

The Führer's grand delusion that Wenck was coming to Berlin's rescue was to consign the last of his faithful Hitler Youth to a miserable fate. In Hitler's fevered mind, these schoolboys were panzer killers. Issued with bicycles, rifles and the German version of the bazooka called the *Panzerfaust*, they would stop Zhukov's tanks dead in their tracks. It was all nonsense, of course. The so-called Hitler Youth Division, created to conduct anti-tank warfare, only existed on paper.

There was an obscene grotesqueness in mobilising school children to defend Germany's cities. Over 1,000 of these boy soldiers were deployed in the capital and the bulk of them were instructed to hold the approaches from the Wannsee bridgehead to the south-west, ready for the arrival of Wenck.

Clinging on to Wannsee Island in the Havel River were some 20,000 German troops consisting of regulars, Hitler Youth and Volkssturm. To the west of Berlin at Pichelsdorf, a battalion of teenagers were assigned the bridge at the northern end of Havel Lake. Just to the north of them, Hitler Youth also held the Charlottenbrücke over the Havel to Spandau. They were ordered to hold these bridges at all costs.

'You cannot sacrifice these children for a cause that is already lost!' cried General Weidling in a fury. 'I demand that the order sending these children into battle be rescinded.'[25] His horror did no good, and the boy solders were not pulled out of the line. Just to the east of Wannsee at Zehlendorf, the Hitler Youth and Volkssturm units were swiftly massacred as Soviet tanks fired on everything that moved – and everything that did not. Likewise, the Charlottenbrücke became the scene of the most appalling bloodbath as people sought to escape across it. Some 400 12–15-year-olds defending the southern district of Schöneberg were also quickly trapped and wiped out. There is no way the architects of Operation Barbarossa could have ever envisaged that their country would be reduced to this.

Across Berlin, the Red Army perpetrated terrible atrocities. Konev and Zhukov assaulted Berlin with a hotchpotch of Soviet nationalities drafted from every distant republic of the Soviet Union. By this stage of the war, Stalin had almost exhausted his manpower reserves. Not only did they include Russians, Byelorussians and Ukrainians, but also Armenians, Azerbaijanis, Bashkirs, Georgians, Irkutsks, Karelians, Kazakhs, Mordvins, Mongols, Tartars, Uzbeks and, of course, Cossacks. Most of those from the Far East and Central Asia had never been in Europe before. Russian and Ukrainian officers could often not communicate with their own troops, as there were so many different languages and dialects.

Understandably, this was not conducive to good discipline at the height of the fighting. Once in Berlin these men raped and pillaged their way to final victory. In response to complaints about their behaviour, Stalin was dismissive, 'Can't you understand it if a soldier who has crossed thousands of kilometres through blood and fire has fun with a woman or takes a trifle?'[26] No matter her age, no female was safe.

While Busse, Steiner and Wenck outside Berlin were able to defy the Führer, SS General Wilhelm Mohnke was in the unenviable position of being the very last combat general under the immediate control of Hitler. The Führer had gone from the height of his power, commanding hundreds of divisions with millions of men under arms, to a single general with just 2,000 troops.

Defending the central government district, encompassing the old Reichstag and the Reich Chancellery, Mohnke managed to give Hitler one final fleeting victory. On 27 April, just as Loringhoven was taking the call that Wenck was almost at Potsdam, the Red Army attacked the government 'citadel'. Its tanks, caught in the rubble-strewn streets, were sitting ducks for Mohnke's regular troops, Hitler Youth and Volkssturm armed with *Panzerfausts*. He recounted:

> The Russians had brilliant tank commanders who had learned their business against us out on the steppes and in the open country. Even in city fighting, for example, in Stalingrad or Warsaw, they had never come up against hostile, armed civilians. They realised their mistake only belatedly, after they had lost hundreds of tanks. On the Potsdamer Platz, after that first frontal assault, they got smarter. They simply pulled back and plastered us with artillery. Of which they had a plentitude. They never tried to storm our position again.[27]

By 30 April there were around 10,000 German soldiers trapped in the city centre. About half of these were holding the Zoological Gardens. Weidling's orders were simple – fight to the last man. However, only the SS units in the central Reichstag district were likely to obey this instruction. Alongside them, Colonel Miguel Ezquerra (a former Spanish Blue Division Captain) commanded three Spanish companies as well as Belgian and French SS survivors. His Ezquerra Unit were prepared to fight to the last against the Soviets, although Ezquerra himself managed to escape after being captured.

At 1425 hrs, units of the Soviet 79th Rifle Corps, from Kuznetsov's 3rd Shock Army, stormed into the main part of the Reichstag building. It took a tank brigade and two rifle divisions a day and a half of heavy fighting to overwhelm Mohnke's remaining SS troops defending the Reichstag district. Because of continued fierce resistance, a second assault was launched at 1800 hrs and the victory flag was finally hoisted over the Reichstag at 2150 hrs. That day, Hitler took his own life.

Despite Hitler's death, the madness in Berlin did not end immediately. Shortly afterwards, the German High Command issued a secret announcement which was intercepted by British intelligence:

On 30/4 the Führer died in the heroic battle for Germany in Berlin with his men. According to his orders, Grand Admiral Karl Doenitz has become his successor. The Grand Admiral's Order of the Day will follow. The battle for our people is being carried on.[28]

There was no mention of Hitler's suicide or surrender. There was nothing heroic about the Führer's death and he had not died with his men.

On the night of 1/2 May, some of the surviving garrison attempted to escape, including twenty armoured vehicles which sped north-west until intercepted by Soviet tanks. This led to unfounded speculation that they were carrying senior Nazi officials, including Hitler. That morning, General Weidling finally surrendered to Chuikov and broadcast a radio message for the garrison to cease all resistance. Grossman was ecstatic about Germany's surrender, but even he, a hardened reporter, could not miss the suffering:

2 May. The Day of Berlin's capitulation. It's difficult to describe it. A monstrous concentration of impressions. Fire and fires, smoke, smoke, smoke. Enormous crowds of prisoners. Their faces are full of drama. In many faces there's sadness, not only personal suffering, but also suffering of a citizen. This overcast, cold and rainy day is undoubtedly the day of Germany's ruin.[29]

Doenitz, at Flensburg near the Danish border, was determined to surrender to the British first. The following day, Field Marshal Keitel, with Doenitz's authority, contacted Field Marshal Montgomery. Keitel wanted to surrender to him the three armies that were frantically withdrawing between Berlin and Rostock in front of the advancing Red Army. Montgomery was adamant that they would have to surrender to the Soviets. Keitel's representatives were alarmed at what might happen to these forces and the civilians under their protection.

'I said the Germans should have thought of all these things before they began the war,' recalled Montgomery, 'and particularly before they attacked the Russians in June 1941.'[30] Lecturing them on the horrors of Coventry and Belsen concentration camp, Monty expressed no sympathy for the fate of German soldiers or civilians at the hands of the Red Army.

General Kinzel was part of the military delegation that formally surrendered to Montgomery on Lüneberg Heath on 4 May. Kinzel stood out physically and professionally and immediately impressed Allied officers and reporters. 'He was a magnificent looking officer about 6' 5", in his late 40s,' recalled Monty's Canadian liaison officer, Lieutenant Colonel Trumbull Warren, 'complete with monocle – a real professional Prussian.'[31] War correspondent R.W. Thompson remembered, 'General Kinzel, thick-set, tall, monocled ...'[32]

Along with four other German officers, Kinzel's name was on the surrender document acting on behalf of the Wehrmacht in north-west Europe. This was the final humiliation. Even Monty was impressed by him and said, 'Kinzel is a very able and very highly trained staff officer and I shall keep him at my Tac[tical] HQ with a team of German liaison officers to work between myself and Busch.'[33] Monty's chief of staff, General Freddie de Guingand, was equally affected, 'He was undoubtedly a most efficient staff officer, and one could not help being impressed by his attitude and quickness'.[34] However, broken by his experiences, Kinzel and his girlfriend, Erika von Ashcoff, took their own lives shortly afterwards. Montgomery noted, 'Of the four Germans who arrived at my Tac[tical] Headquarters ... on 3rd of May ... three died violent deaths. Von Friedeburg poisoned himself. Kinzel shot himself, and Freidel was killed in a motor accident.'[35]

General Jodl, the German chief of staff, formally surrendered to the Americans in the French city of Reims on the morning of 7 May. The following day, Field Marshal Keitel presented himself at Zhukov's Berlin headquarters and very reluctantly surrendered to the Soviets. The bloody slaughter on the Eastern Front was at an end – the unconditional surrender of Nazi Germany had been achieved at colossal cost to the Red Army. Zhukov concluded:

> The fall of Berlin and the link-up between the Soviet Army and the troops of our allies led to the final collapse of Nazi Germany and its armed forces. The disorganised German Army was no longer capable of resistance. Everywhere in Italy and Western Europe, German troops began to capitulate. On 8 May representatives of the German command signed the Act of Unconditional Surrender, thus acknowledging their total defeat.[36]

The people of Moscow celebrated and saluted the victorious Red Army and Navy the following day with thirty thunderous salvoes by 1,000 guns. Also on 9 May, Doenitz signalled the Wehrmacht, 'From midnight the guns have been silent on all fronts'. He then acknowledged what Hitler would not, 'The German armed forces have been overcome, finally, by a superior force'.[37] Kinzel and Gehlen had been proved right.

However, Army Group Centre, for so long implacable foes of the Red Army, fought on in Czechoslovakia until 11 May. The remaining German armies laid down their arms, and by 13 May the Red Army had rounded up 189,000 German troops in the Kurland Peninsula and almost 75,000 men in the Vistula estuary and north-east of Gdynia. The Danish island of Bornholm yielded another 12,000 prisoners. Way to the south-west, the Red Army took 780,622 prisoners and by 19 May final resistance by units of Army Group Centre had been mopped up. Under the terms of the unconditional surrender, from 9–7 May, 1,390,978 German officers and men surrendered to the Red Army.

A triumphant Stalin made his victory address on 9 May 1945, stating:

> Three years ago Hitler publicly stated that his aims included the dismember-ment of the Soviet Union and the wresting of the Caucasus, the Ukraine, Byelorussia, the Baltic and other regions from it. He declared bluntly: 'We will destroy Russia, so that she will never be able to rise again.' This happened three years ago. However, Hitler's crazy ideas were not fated to succeed. The course of the war scattered them to the winds. In actual fact, something directly opposite to the Hitlerites' ravings has taken place. Germany has been utterly defeated.
>
> [...] Glory to our heroic Red Army which upheld the independence of our Motherland and won victory over the enemy![38]

The slaughter on the Eastern Front was at an end.

20

STALIN'S VENGEANCE

While Stalin strove to crush Hitler's forces and those of his Axis allies, he also moved to ensure his own security at home. His totalitarian Communist regime was not universally popular, particularly in Ukraine and amongst the other non-Russian members of the Soviet Empire. Operation Barbarossa had opened many old wounds from the days of the Revolution and the Civil War. Many Soviet citizens saw the invading Germans as potential liberators and it has been estimated that as many as 1.5 million men assisted Hitler's war effort: the equivalent of three whole army groups. The Germans recruited auxiliaries, general service personnel and Eastern Troops (or *Osttruppen*), mainly non-Russians, Balts, Ukrainians, Cossacks and Central Asians. The Cossacks, in particular, proved some of Hitler's most loyal volunteers.

While the Soviet Union was made up of many diverse peoples and races, in 1941 the dominant groups were the Slavic Russians, Byelorussians and Ukrainians. Notably, the 10th Reserve Army, which was created to help defend Moscow after the Nazi invasion, was 90 per cent Russian; the only other significant group were the Ukrainians, who made up about 4 per cent. Neither nationality was considered worthy of serving in the Wehrmacht.

However, the defection of Russian General Andrei A. Vlasov was a great embarrassment to Khrushchev, as he had selected Vlasov to command the 37th Army created to defend Kiev. In his defence, Khrushchev liked to point out that Stalin had even considered putting Vlasov in command of the Stalingrad Front!

Vlasov was from a new generation of Soviet commanders who showed great skill and personal courage in the face of the Wehrmacht. Nonetheless, he was sickened by the culture of brutality and corruption that surrounded Stalin and prevailed in the Red Army. In his memoirs, Khrushchev recalled the betrayal with faux puzzlement:

Naturally the Vlasov affair was a bitter pill to swallow – for me as well as Stalin. It was difficult to understand how one man who displayed such devotion, bravery, and skill and who had earned such respect, could betray his country. Vlasov must have had a very unstable character to let himself be recruited as an agent by the Germans. He was supposed to be a Communist … In civilian life he'd been a teacher. Apparently he wasn't a bad fellow. […] Of course it's possible he was just following mercenary motives when he became a soldier.[1]

Vlasov was a Civil War veteran who had risen through the ranks to become a divisional, corps and then army commander. He was no doubt bitter about how his 2nd Shock Army had been abandoned in June 1942 following the failed attempt to relieve Leningrad. This event precipitated his capture. Vlasov and the other officers who defected with him all feared the power and influence the NKVD exerted over the Red Army.

Hitler was chronically short of manpower during the Second World War, something that cost him dearly. Even at the end, German military industry churned out more armaments than the German armed forces could deploy. Hitler was to recruit more than 3 million foreign troops to help prop up the Nazi cause, particularly on the Eastern Front. By 1940, victorious Germany had already begun raising police and volunteer units all over occupied Europe. Most of these forces were indistinguishable from the Germans, except for the national arms shields on their uniforms.

Hitler received varying support from over fifteen European states, with tens of thousands of foreign nationals volunteering to fight within the ranks of the Wehrmacht or Waffen-SS. Most volunteers allied themselves with Hitler, either out of nationalist self-interest or from a desire to fight Soviet Communism. Some units were to prove more reliable than others and when things started to go badly for Hitler the politically reliable volunteers were absorbed into the Nazi elite Waffen-SS, forming their own weak national divisions.

German rear-area *Sicherungsdivision* (security divisions) were rapidly authorised to raise squadrons of Cossacks, and in April 1942 Hitler expanded this programme. On the Eastern Front, the Germans used so-called Cossack sections attached to regular German divisions to conduct brutal anti-partisan and rear suppression operations. In fact, many were Ukrainians and Russians, but as Hitler would not tolerate Slavs in German uniform they were designated 'Cossacks' for political convenience. Only Kononow's Cossack Unit was allowed to operate independently in Byelorussia with Army Group Centre. Although, in 1942, Regiment Von Jungschutz was committed in Army Group South's Atschikulak region, and Regiment Platow (raised in November 1942) was committed to the Caucasus.

Field Marshal von Manstein, commander of Army Group Don during the Stalingrad campaign, selected Novocherkassk, the old Don Cossack capital, as his headquarters. There, von Manstein was guarded by Don Cossacks and his aide-de-camp recalled that they stuck out their chests and stood to attention as if for 'His Imperial Majesty the Tsar himself'. During their counter-attacks, the Soviet North Caucasus Front, including the 5th Don Cavalry Corps, pushed the German Army Group A back northward toward Rostov and Novocherkassk.

At Novogroduk in Byelorussia, former Red Army Major Timofey Domanov took command of a 10,000-strong Cossack militia supporting the Germans. There, he was joined by numbers of White Russian émigrés, including former Don Cossack leader General Peter Krasnov and former Kuban Cossack leader, General Vyacheslav Namenko. This force, however, was little more than a para-military defence corps.

Although Hitler had a well-defined racial hatred for Russian Slavs and was determined to crush their nationalism, native Russians still ended up being recruited into the Wehrmacht. This was done on a rather ad hoc basis, which led to a number of uncentralised 'armies' that included Cossack troops. The brigade-strength Russian National Liberation Army (*Russkaia Osvoboditelnania Norodnaia Armiia* – RONA) was formed in 1942 and included Ukrainian Cossacks in its ranks. It is better known as the infamous Kaminski Brigade, which was later designated the 29th SS Grenadier Division, totalling about 6,000 men. Likewise, Russians of brigade strength formed the 30th SS Grenadier Division, which was used in France for security duties.

Also raised in 1942 was the short-lived Russian Peoples National Army (*Russkaia Natsionalnaia Norodnaia Armiia* – RNNA), again only of brigade strength. By 1943 the title Russian Liberation Army (*Russkaia Osvoditelnaina Armiia* – ROA) was used to cover all the disparate Eastern volunteers. It was never really an army in any true sense, and was opposed by the non-Russians who had no desire to support Russian hegemony.

Vlasov, who was captured in 1942, hoped to raise a large national force to fight alongside the Wehrmacht against the Red Army. It was he who emerged as the ROA's leader. Vlasov inaugurated the Committee for the Liberation of the Peoples of Russia (*Komitat Osvozhniia Narodov Rosso* – KONR) in Prague on 14 November 1944. KONR dreamed of a Russian Army of twenty-five divisions encompassing the 650,000 Russian troops in German service, but only two were formed. Both the KONR and the SS coveted Pannwitz's Cossacks. However, the German Army would not hand over either the ROA or their Russian auxiliary battalions

Vlasov ended up with just two weak divisions, an air corps with no planes and the German Kalmyk Cavalry Corps. Only the 600th Panzergrenadier Division was brought up to strength, while the 605th Panzergrenadier Division ended up containing the remains of the hated Kaminski RONA brigade. Also, the Russian Defence Corps (*Russisches Schutzkorps Serbien* – RSS), which was incorporated into the German Army in 1942, was ordered to wear ROA arm shields three years later.

Ukraine hoped it would gain independence by helping Hitler's war machine, and about 180,000 Ukrainians served the Wehrmacht. In late 1942, some 70,000 Ukrainians were recruited into the German *Schuma* (Police), with 35,000 serving in seventy-one Schuma battalions, which included some Cossack forces, conducting anti-partisan duties. A year later, Ukraine supplied 30,000 men to form the 14th SS Grenadier Division.

The Ukrainian Liberation Army (*Ukrainske Vyzvolne Viysko* – UVV) was little more than a German propaganda tool, while two Ukrainian divisions numbering 40,000 men were designated the Ukrainian National Army (UNA) in 1945, but it was never effective. The Ukrainian Insurgent Army (*Ukrains'ka Povstans'ka Armiia* – UPA), created in 1944 and numbering perhaps 20,000–30,000 men, fought both the Red Army and the Wehrmacht.

Intelligence chief, Colonel Gehlen was well placed to appreciate the necessity of relying on foreign volunteers:

> As we could not replace all our losses rapidly and increasing demands were being made on our manpower, our commanders recruited Russians, Ukrainians and other nationalities, as auxiliaries for various types of duty: voluntarily they acted as drivers, ammunition carriers, cooks, interpreters and the like. [...] By mid-1943 there were about 320,000, of which a large number were actually fighting alongside our troops; the 18th Army alone had 47,000.[2]

In 1941 German-Soviet 'volunteers' basically fell into two categories – *Hiwis* or *Hilfswillige* (auxiliary volunteers) and *Osttruppen* (Eastern Troops) – who were integrated in formed units into the German forces for rear-area security. Major von Loringhoven recalled, 'In my battalion, several dozens of Russian prisoners worked as cooks or truck drivers. These *hiwis* were treated like German soldiers and received the same rations.'[3] The bulk of these 'volunteers' were Balts, Caucasians, Cossacks and Ukrainians.

Hitler also encouraged the nationalist feelings of the Soviet Asian population, because they were outside his sphere of planned occupation, and the Germans also raised *Ostlegionen* (Eastern Legions) which, along with supporting services, totalled at least 175,000 men. The Asians supplied auxiliary services such as the 20,000-strong Boller Brigade and 10,000-strong Construction Battalions.

Throughout the war, Hitler remained very reluctant to organise national armies from former Red Army personnel, even though the potential existed. Gehlen noted:

> As a result of the work of these various officers, of Vlasov's own work and of the initiative of our front-line commanders in the east, by early 1943 we had between 130,000 and 150,000 'eastern troops,' organised into 176 battalions and thirty-eight independent companies. At that time, as a result of a policy decision higher up, there was no amalgamation of these into larger formations.[4]

By 1943 the *Osttruppen* were 427,000 strong, the equivalent of thirty German divisions. Furthermore, the Luftwaffe may have recruited up to 300,000 Soviets. On the whole, Soviet volunteers wore German uniforms with varying national arm shields. In total, 650,000 former Soviet subjects served in Nazi uniform. The *Osttruppen*, however, were never really trusted. Hitler deliberately avoided unification and many were sent to Western Europe. This proved to be a blow to their morale, as they had volunteered to fight Stalin's Communism not the democracies of Britain and America.

In comparison to other Eastern Front allies, the Cossack, Russian and Ukrainian volunteers pale into insignificance. It is notable that, even excluding security forces, over 3 million Europeans and non-Europeans volunteered to serve Hitler. Overall, however, these foreign volunteers made little decisive contribution to the German war effort. In particular, the collapse of the Romanian, Italian and Hungarian armies north-west of Stalingrad spelt the beginning of the end for Germany on the Eastern Front. This, in turn, spelt the end of Cossack, Russian and Ukrainian aspirations to see an end to Soviet control.

Even the Italians on the Eastern Front had their own small Cossack force. Italy's contribution to Hitler's war against Russia, despite Mussolini's desire to share in the glory, was ill-fated and embarrassing. The 60,000-strong Italian Expeditionary Corps in Russia (*Corpo Spedizione Italiano in Russia* – CSIR) suffered from numerous inadequacies, particularly in leadership and equipment. By 1942, a second corps had been despatched, creating the 229,005-strong Italian 8th Army. The latter formed a voluntary Cossack squadron at Millerovo in September 1942, expanding it to battalion strength to become the *Gruppo Autonomo Cosacchi Savoia* (GACS). The Italian forces collapsed in December 1942 while defending the Don Front, north of Stalingrad, and were sent back to Italy. The GACS also withdrew into Italy and was eventually absorbed by the German Cossack units at Tolmezzo.

At the end of the Second World War, a heartrending scene took place in British-administered Austria when 50,000 Cossacks and their families were handed over to the Red Army. They had been serving the Waffen-SS in Yugoslavia and the Wehrmacht in Italy. Despite their pleas, they and their kin were sent back home to face the brutality of the Gulag or firing squad.

Cossacks were some of the most feared and respected of all Hitler's Soviet allies. When Barbarossa was launched, 100,000 Cossacks were serving the Red Army. Immortalised by the likes of Mikhail Sholokhov's *And Quiet Flows the Don* and Leo Tolstoy's *The Cossacks and the Raid*, the Cossacks have a long and proud martial tradition. They also have a long and chequered relationship with Moscow, which makes their prominent betrayal during the Second World War much easier to comprehend. Furthermore, the Cossacks had long memories. In particular, bitter memories of Soviet collectivisation and Stalin's Great Purge of the Red Army during the 1930s, in which the new-founded Cossack Corps was disbanded and their lands appropriated.

During the Russian Revolution and subsequent Civil War, the Don, Kuban and Terek Cossacks established their own anti-Bolshevik governments. The Ural and Orenburg Cossacks also turned against Moscow. A commander of the Transbaikal Cossacks even ruled eastern Siberia with Japanese assistance. This independence was short-lived, as by 1920 the pro-tsarist White forces had collapsed. The Cossacks were not officially forgiven for their adherence to the tsarist cause until the late 1930s when Cossack units began to appear in the Red Army, and they were subsequently to fall victim to Stalinist paranoia.

In 1935, Georgi Zhukov and his 4th Cavalry Division was transferred from the 3rd Cavalry Corps to the newly formed 6th Cossack Corps. The following year, the division was renamed the 4th Don Cossack Division and all its men adopted Cossack uniforms. Regularly involved in military manoeuvres, Zhukov recalled, 'It was invariably well prepared and always earned praise from the higher command'.[5]

Zhukov was appointed commander of the 3rd Cavalry Corps in 1937, but was then offered the 6th Cossack Corps. He accepted because it included his 4th Don Cossacks as well as the 6th Chongar Cossack Division, which Zhukov had fought alongside during the Civil War. Zhukov showered the corps in praise, 'In combat readiness the 6th Cossack Corps was better than any other unit'.[6] Within a year Zhukov, destined for greater things, was deputy commander of the Byelorussian Military District and in 1940 was appointed commander of the Kiev Special Military District. He does not recount the fate of the Cossack Corps, a victim of Stalin's Red Army Purge.

Just before the outbreak of the Second World War, Stalin's attention had been drawn to the Don Cossacks when they revolted north of Rostov at Shakhty, declaring an independent republic in early 1941. It was short-lived once Stalin's internal security force, the NKVD, arrived on the scene. After the initial German advance into the Soviet Union, about 70,000 Don Cossacks deserted the Red Army, probably spurred on by events at Shakhty and the Great Purge. This must have been particularly galling for Zhukov. In August 1941, a whole Soviet Cossack regiment under Major Kononow defected to become the Wehrmacht's 5th Don Cossack Regiment.

In September 1942, General Helmuth von Pannwitz, a German cavalry officer, began to explore the possibility of raising an independent Cossack division. Eventually he was to organise a Cossack Corps of 52,000 men, with a further 18,000 serving as militia under General Domanov. Appointed commander of Cossack units, Pannwitz resettled the Cossack families first in Poland at Mielau (Mlawa) and then to northern Italy at Tolmezzo, in Friuli.

By April 1943 Pannwitz had gathered von Jungschutz and Lehman regiments from Army Group South, and the Kononow and Wolff regiments from Army Group Centre. On being moved to Poland, they were formed into the 1st Cossack Division, consisting of two brigades. Pannwitz increased his men's morale and esteem by allowing them to wear their traditional clothing. In fact, Pannwitz was so popular that he was elected *Feldataman*, a post traditionally held by the tsar.

A year later, the division was disappointed to find that it was not to fight Stalin's Red Army, but Tito's partisans in Yugoslavia. The two brigades then formed the nucleus of the 1st and 2nd Cossack Divisions, which became the 14th Cossack Corps (it was re-designated the 15th SS Cossack Cavalry Corps at the end of 1944, although there was no actual physical reorganisation). There were already Russians serving the Germans in Yugoslavia. In Serbia in 1941, White Russian exiles raised the Russian Defence Corps (*Russisches Schutzkorps Serbien* – RSS) to help fight Tito's Communist partisans. By 1944, it numbered 11,197 strong, but was relegated to guard duties.

The Cossack Corps was to be the largest within the *Osttruppen* and continued to expand. An unnumbered brigade of Cossack infantry, made up of two regiments with a number of other units, were reorganised around the 5th Don Cossack Regiment to create (on paper) the 3rd Cossack Division. In 1945, the 630th Infantry Regiment (Cossack) that had been sent to defend the *Festung Europa*, or Atlantic Wall, was added to the 3rd Division.

Hitler's Cossack Cavalry Corps, however, was not destined for the huge battles of the Eastern Front. After being invaded by the Axis Powers, Yugoslavia was dismembered – the 55th Corps from the German 12th Army controlled Eastern Croatia and Serbia; while the Italian 2nd and 9th Armies occupied Western Yugoslavia. In July 1941, a revolt broke out in Montenegro, spreading to Slovenia, Bosnia and Serbia. The Germans launched a counter-attack, crushing the revolt by September. In mid-1942 they attacked Tito's headquarters but he escaped; his forces were again attacked in 1943. Then, in September 1943, the battered Italian Army declared an armistice and about half of Yugoslavia was liberated, this forced the Wehrmacht to implement Operation *Konstantin* (Constantine), the full occupation of the Balkans and Greece.

Hitler's 2nd Panzer Army, including the new 1st Cossack Division, faced the partisans. Kononow, who had been promoted to lieutenant colonel, was still serving with his 5th Don Cossack Cavalry Regiment. Upon arriving in Yugoslavia, the division went into action north-west of Belgrade and soon gained a reputation for brutality. Then, in November they were deployed north to Osijek, followed by Brod.

The Cossacks were involved in Operation *Treibjagd* (Driving Hunt) against the partisans and Operation *Kugelblitz* (Ball Lightning), launched in December 1943 against eastern Bosnia, western Serbia, Slovenia and the Adriatic Islands. The operation was designed to be a decisive stroke against the Communist partisans in the west and north-west. It lasted until February 1944 and drove the partisans back toward Bosnia, capturing Dalmatia and all the offshore Adriatic Islands except Vis. The new Cossack Corps was then redeployed to relieve the 11th SS Panzer Grenadier Division at Sisak in Croatia.

By 1944 the Germans were on the defensive and the corps was used to guard the Zagreb–Belgrade Railway, a vital link with Greece. The Germans did, however, launch one last offensive against Tito's forces – Operation *Herbstgewitter* (Autumn Storm), directed against Bosnia. Field Marshal Maximilian Freihrr von Weichs' Army Group F also conducted Operation *Maibaum* (May Pole) to cover Army Group E's withdrawal from Greece. The partisans did all they could to hamper the Germans' retreat, so that Soviet Marshal F.I. Tolbukhin's 3rd Ukrainian Front could cut them off as he advanced through Romania and Bulgaria.

With the fall of Belgrade in October, Pannwitz's Cossack Corps remained in Croatia to counter Soviet incursions. At last they found themselves fighting the Red Army. On 25 December 1944 the Cossacks successfully destroyed the Soviet 133rd Rifle Division's bridgehead on the River Drava. Many of those taken prisoner joined them. Also during 1944, Domanov's Cossack forces were withdrawn from the Eastern Front to Tolmezzo to fight Italian partisans. Another force of former Soviet POWs, the 162nd Turkoman Division, was also fighting on the front line in Italy with the Germans.

At the beginning of 1945, five divisions of Latvian, Estonian, Ukrainian and White Russians were established as Waffen-SS formations. The improvised Turkestan and Caucasus brigades had been absorbed into the SS and Heinrich Himmler had his eye on Pannwitz's three Cossack divisions. Although the corps was renamed in 1944, it remained unchanged and was not redeployed. The SS simply became responsible for resupplying the corps. This was a paper transformation and the Cossacks were never looked upon as full members of the Waffen-SS.

The Cossacks gained a bad reputation in Poland, as well as Yugoslavia and Italy. An unknown number of Cossacks (the majority of them were probably Ukrainians) took part in the brutal suppression of the Warsaw Uprising in 1944. Lieutenant General Reiner Stahel's German garrison included 900 renegade Ukrainians, Cossacks and Turkomen former POWs.

German reinforcements despatched to Warsaw included SS-Brigadeführer Bratislav Kaminski's RONA Brigade, part of the 29th Waffen-SS Grenadier Division – it numbered 1,585 Cossacks and Ukrainians. Kaminski, a Red Army deserter, governed Lokot Province in central Russia for the Germans from 1942–44, keeping it free from partisans. His brigade had contributed to the deaths of 7,000 partisans in 1944, during a series of brutal operations. In Poland, his unit was supported by SS-Oberführer Oskar Dirlewanger's anti-partisan brigade (36th SS Division), some 2,500 strong. It included two battalions of 865 released criminals and three battalions of former Soviet POWs.

After the war, German officers involved at Warsaw laid the blame firmly on Kaminski and Dirlewanger. At the time, Kaminski was court-martialled and executed for his actions by his commanding officer, while his men were transferred to the KONR and the 30th SS (*Russische Nr2*) Division. Other accounts state that the SS dressed Kaminski's death up as a Polish ambush, with his bullet-riddled car daubed in animal blood to conceal his fate from his unit's officers.

The problem of Soviet collaboration was so great that the Red Army carried out major repressive operations against its own civilian population during the war. Stalin swiftly purged those who had collaborated with the Nazis, as Alexandr Solzhenitsyn recalled:

Within the overall wave of those from formerly occupied areas, there followed, one after another, the quick and compact wave of the nationalities which had transgressed:

1   In 1943, the Kalmyks, Chechens, Ingush, and Balkars.
2   In 1944, the Crimean Tartars.

They would not have been pushed out into eternal exile so energetically and swiftly had it not been that regular army units and military trucks were assigned to help the Organs [NKVD]. The military units gallantly surrounded the auls, or settlements, and within twenty-four hours, with the speed of a parachute attack, those who had nested there for centuries past found themselves removed.[7]

The Muslim populations of the North Caucasus and Lower Volga area suffered for their collaboration with Hitler after being liberated by the Red Army. As early as the end of 1943, Stalin ordered the deportation of the Muslim nations, who were arbitrarily accused of 'collaboration with the occupying forces'. In November 1943, some 80,000 people, the entire Karachai population of Stavropol Krai, were forcibly deported to special settlements in Central Asia. In just four days at the end of December 1943, the Kalmyks were also herded into freight trains and moved to Siberia by the NKVD. By the end of the following year, the 5,000-strong German Kalmyk Cavalry Corps (mainly ex-Red Army soldiers) had withdrawn into Poland.

The same fate befell the Chechen, Ingush, Karabardin, Balkar and Crimean Tartars in 1944. The Tartars, in particular, represented the largest Muslim group in the European part of the Soviet Union and 35,000 of them served the Germans. After visiting the liberated Crimea, Alexander Werth noted, 'The 500,000 Crimea Tartars were, before long, to be deported *en masse* – women, children and all – to "the east" for having collaborated with the Germans.'[8] In total, about 1 million people were deported and over fifteen Red Army divisions were tied up during a crucial phase of the war, when they would have been better employed fighting the Germans rather than repressing largely defenceless civilians.

Even Russian exiles who were not Soviet citizens were not safe. 'At the end of 1944, when our army entered the Balkans,' says Solzhenitsyn, 'and especially in 1945, when it reached central Europe, a wave of Russian émigrés flowed through the channels of the Gulag.'[9]

By March 1945, the 1st Cossack Division was still defending the Drava against Soviet attacks while the 2nd was engaging partisans in the Papuk Mountains. The last major German operations conducted in Yugoslavia were *Waldrausch* (Forest Fever) and *Waldteufel* (Forest Devil), but with the approaching Red Army the struggle against Tito was nearly over. There then followed a mad scramble as the Cossack Cavalry Corps, Cossack militia, the KONR, the RSS and most of the UNA sought desperately to surrender to the Western Allies rather than the Red Army. Even so, under the February 1945 Yalta Agreement the Western Allies had promised to surrender all Soviet collaborators in their area of responsibility – there were to be only three exceptions.

The Germans surrendered in Italy on 29 April 1945, leaving Allied military officials to deal with the vast Cossack encampment at Tolmezzo. The 162nd

Turkoman Division surrendered near Padua and was repatriated by ship. Upon the approach of the British, Damanov and Krasnov retreated with their men to Lienz in Austria to surrender. They numbered approximately 24,000 Cossacks and 5,000 Caucasians. The Cossack Cavalry Corps also withdrew into Austria to Wolfsburg, 160km east of Lienz. The British duly handed both forces back to the Red Army in June. The first to be surrendered were Domanov, Krasnov and another White Cossack leader, Andrei Shukro. General Pannwitz nobly went with his men and was hanged on 16 January 1947, along with Domanov, Krasnov and Shukro.

Only the RSS, KONR Air Corps and UNA avoided repatriation. The Russians of the RSS were entirely White Russian émigrés (although technically Yugoslav citizens and therefore Tito's responsibility) and the 4,500 who laid down their arms in Austria were set free. General Maitsev's 8,000-strong KONR Air Corps would not give up until they were given a guarantee by the Americans, which was honoured (Maitsev himself was repatriated in 1946, as were 3,000 men from the 2nd KONR Division).

The UNA's 1st Division ended the war in Austria (the 2nd was not so fortunate and found itself in Czechoslovakia). They were able to argue that their former Polish status made them exempt, and 10,000 men escaped. A group of Ukrainian deserters from the 14th SS Division and comrades of the 1st Division, along with some UPA troops, also made it to the American Zone of Germany and safety, as late as 1946–47. However, the salvation of these men was nothing compared to the 2 million Russians who were handed over, both during and after the war.

The fate of the Cossacks and the other volunteer units must be kept in perspective in the light of the huge logistical problems facing the Western Allies at the end of the war. For example, Field Marshal Montgomery observed:

> In the area occupied by 21 Army Group [in north-western Europe] there were appalling civilian problems to be solved. Over one million civilian refugees had fled into the area before the advancing Russians. About one million German wounded were in hospital in the area, with no medical supplies. Over one and a half million unwounded German fighting men had surrendered to 21 Army Group on 5th May and were now prisoners of war, with all that that entailed. [10]

Concerning the problem of Soviet citizens, he went on to note:

> In addition to these prisoners, we had over one million Displaced Persons, nearly all from the east. Some 400,000 of these were Russians and we could

reasonably hope that Zhukov would take these off our hands. But the remaining 600,000 would probably remain with us for all time.[11]

Stalin was determined to punish all those who had betrayed the Soviet Union. Commenting on Vlasov, Stalin claimed he was 'at very least a large obstacle on the road to victory over the German fascists'. In fact, Vlasov was considered such a threat that the NKVD even recruited a major from a penal colony to infiltrate the Vlasov movement with a view to eventually assassinating him. However, in his memoirs Marshal Zhukov recalled the decision on Vlasov's fate, 'It was decided to capture him alive to make him pay in full for his treason'.

In January 1945, Vlasov's two KONR divisions had about 50,000 men under arms. At the end of the month, it was declared that they were the sole responsibility of the KONR and no longer formed part of the German Army, thereby leaving them to their fate. Presumably re-badging the Russian RSS security forces in Serbia signalled the same thing. The Waffen-SS had expected to be given control of Vlasov's divisions, but in the closing months of the war they had more pressing matters to worry about. Colonel Gehlen was dismissive of Vlasov's efforts:

> Born of opportunism and despair, the Vlasov army was doomed to failure from the start. On 10 February 1945 the first and only two Russian infantry divisions, numbers 600 and 605, were formally handed over to Lieutenant General Vlasov by General Köstring, who had succeeded Hellmich as General of the Volunteer units.[12]

Ironically, the 600th Division, numbering about 20,000 men with a few of Kaminski's tanks under Vlasov and General Bunichenko, ended up fighting the SS alongside the Czech insurgents in Prague in May 1945. Ultimately though, they found themselves disowned by both sides and then had to fight their way out of the city alongside the SS. General Zverev, commanding the 605th Division, was captured by the Soviets, although some of his men reached the Americans.

Upon surrendering to the Americans, the 600th Division was handed back to the Soviets on 13 May 1945. Reportedly, the Soviets hanged large numbers of them there and then. The Americans surrendered Vlasov and his staff two days later. Marshal Zhukov recalls:

> Vlasov was captured while riding in a car in the retreating column. Hidden under a heap of bundles and covered with a blanket, he pretended to be a sick soldier. But he was given away by his own bodyguards. Later Vlasov and his associates were tried by Military Tribunal and executed.[13]

Radio Moscow announced the execution of Vlasov, Bunichenko and ten others on 12 August 1946. Vlasov had paid in full for his treason.

The Dirlewanger Brigade was in Hungary by 1945. When the 8th Panzer Division, north of Budapest, failed to stop the Soviet advance the brigade fled. The survivors surrendered to the Red Army on 29 April 1945, and when the Soviets discovered their identity they massacred the lot. Dirlewanger died of unspecified causes while under arrest in June 1945.

The Red Army also found the Kalmyk Cavalry Corps, now part of the KONR, reorganising at Neuhammer. Those who were not shot or hanged were sent to join their compatriots in Siberia.

Stalin's vengeance on those who had betrayed the Soviet Union was predictable immediate death, or the slow death of the Gulag. Solzhenitsyn says:

All during 1945 and 1946 a big wave of genuine, at-long-last, enemies of the Soviet government flowed into the [Gulag] Archipelago. (These were the Vlasov men, the Krasnov Cossacks, and Muslims from the national units created under Hitler.) Some of them had acted out of conviction; others had been merely involuntary participants.

Along with them were seized *not less than one million fugitives from the Soviet government* – civilians of all ages and of both sexes who had been fortunate enough to find shelter on Allied territory, but who in 1946–1947 were perfidiously returned by the Allied authorities into Soviet hands.[14]

Stalin cared little about the fate of Pannwitz and Domanov's Cossacks or Vlasov, Kaminski and Dirlewanger's renegade Russians, or indeed the myriad of other units who had signed their own death warrants by serving the Wehrmacht and Waffen-SS. The Cossacks proved better than the Germans in their allotted anti-partisan role as their sturdy horses were ideal in the Balkan Mountains. When the Soviets and Bulgarians finally advanced into Yugoslavia, the Cossacks were used in a conventional role and were able to fight the Soviets with some distinction.

Hitler's most flamboyant Soviet volunteers were undoubtedly the Don, Kuban, Siberian and Terek Cossacks, of whom well over 80,000 served Nazi Germany. Driven by nationalism, monarchism and a desire to resist Stalin's Communist State, these men gained a tough reputation in Italy, Poland, the Soviet Union and Yugoslavia, but at the end of the war they and their families paid a terrible price for their collaboration. When the British Army surrendered them up it seemed a tragic end to such a colourful formation, but in the eyes of the Soviet Union they were traitors. While the Cossacks proved to be some of the most loyal and skilled of the foreign fighters, they also inflicted some of the most appalling atrocities of the Second World War. However, those who stayed loyal to the Russians were no better.

Overall, the 'Cossacks' most important contribution to Hitler's war effort was that they freed large numbers of the Wehrmacht from auxiliary and police duties, which helped lengthen the war. As a people, Zhukov bore the Cossacks no malice, recollecting in his memoirs, 'Though more than 30 years have passed … I still retain the warmest recollections of the command personnel, and men of the K. Ye. Voroshilov 4th Don Cossack Division.'[15] Stalin undoubtedly thought otherwise.

As a postscript to this sad tale, in 1996 the Russian Main Public Prosecutor reportedly rehabilitated Pannwitz. During his trial, he had been accused of shooting five Soviet partisans. The Public Prosecutor asserted that a Croatian court of justice had passed the death sentence and that there was no proof that Pannwitz or his troops had conducted war crimes against Soviet troops or civilians. No mention was made of the Yugoslavs, Italians or Poles who had died at the hands of Hitler's Cossacks.

SLAUGHTER ON THE EASTERN FRONT

Lieutenant General Eberhard Kinzel's suicide was understandable, as he had known from the very start that Hitler and his cronies simply could not win a war of attrition against a country the size of the Soviet Union. He had the misfortune of witnessing not only the beginning of the terrible slaughter on the Eastern Front but also its bloody climax on the streets of Berlin. He felt bad that Heinrici had abandoned Reymann's garrison to its miserable fate, but there was nothing they could do. Busse and Wenck were in an impossible position, yet Hitler in his final madness refused to believe their armies had given all they could.

Such were the pressures of war that Kinzel's marriage broke down and he abandoned his wife and two children. Choosing to die together, he first shot his girlfriend in the head and then pulled the trigger on himself. Theirs was one of thousands of such tragedies enacted across defeated Nazi Germany. General de Guingand felt responsible for Kinzel's death because he allowed him to keep his pistol. 'Without knowing it I no doubt helped him on his way,' recalled Guingand. 'He wore an eyeglass and was in every respect the typical Prussian General Staff officer. If he had lived he might have made a fortune in Hollywood.'[1]

In contrast Reinhard Gehlen, who was equally culpable, set about saving his neck. He copied all his secret Soviet intelligence files on the Red Army with the intention of selling his services to the Americans. This he did, and went on to become the head of West Germany's Intelligence Service.

General Erich Marcks, who had drafted the initial plans for Barbarossa, did not survive the war. Recovering from his injuries sustained on the Eastern Front, he got himself posted to France. Marcks was subsequently killed while serving as a corps commander in Normandy on 12 June 1944 – just six days after the D-Day landings and the opening of the Allies' long-awaited second front.

Ironically, this did not greatly help Stalin and the Red Army, which had torn the heart out of the Wehrmacht on the Eastern Front by August 1944.

Both Jodl and Keitel, two of the key architects of Operation Barbarossa, were hanged following the Nuremberg War Crimes Trials in 1946. General Halder, the only man who tried to put a stop to Hitler's military madness by speaking up, was retired and placed on the reserve list in the summer of 1942. Two years later, he was arrested following the 20 July 1944 assassination attempt on Hitler. Although not involved, Halder was implicated in earlier plots against the Führer and thrown into prison. At the end of the war he was handed over to the Americans and helped with the reconstruction of Germany.

Zeitzler, like Halder before him, never managed to get Hitler to moderate his strategic conduct of the war. Five times he tried to resign and each time Hitler refused, until Zeitzler claimed ill health in the summer of 1944. 'Hitler's distrust of him grew so great that he finally let him go,' said Guderian.[2] The Führer was so angry that he had Zeitzler thrown out of the army. Eventually captured by the British, he remained a POW until early 1947 and served as a witness during the Nuremberg Trials.

Zeitzler felt that Keitel had the 6th Army's blood on his hands. He and Jodl could have tried to sway Hitler's decision not to permit it to escape from Stalingrad, but they chose not to. After the war, Major von Loringhoven, who was miraculously ordered out of Stalingrad at the last minute and escaped the Führerbunker, was held as a prisoner with Zeitzler. They discussed the situation and Loringhoven recalled:

> At a meeting of a select few, including Keitel and Jodl, Zeitzler had pleaded eloquently for such an operation. Visibly impressed by his presentation, Hitler hesitated and asked Jodl and Keitel for their advice. In contrast to Jodl, who gave a vague response, Keitel argued unequivocally against a break-out from Stalingrad by 6th Army. [...] Given this endorsement of his own views, Hitler had refused to sanction Zeitzler's proposals.[3]

After the war, Timoshenko and Zhukov sought to exonerate themselves of any blame for failing to hold Barbarossa. Both claimed that they did not see the intelligence reports coming from diplomatic sources. 'Did the Defence Commissariat and the General Staff know anything about the reports Stalin was getting through these channels?' wrote Zhukov. 'Marshal Timoshenko assured me that he, at any rate, had known nothing about them. And I, too, declare as the then chief of staff, that I had no knowledge of them.'[4]

As these reports came through the Soviet Foreign Ministry this is quite conceivable, but it is hard to believe that Military Intelligence deliberately kept the

General Staff in the dark. Timoshenko and Zhukov must have been aware of the work being conducted by Golikov. In addition, the military district HQs kept them well informed of German border activity. Yet Zhukov insisted that the Soviet Union did not know about Operation Barbarossa – he went on record as saying claims that they had full knowledge was 'pure fiction'. However, this is at odds with Timoshenko and Zhukov's heroic efforts to get the Red Army into a battle-ready condition during early 1941.

Golikov, who had help persuade Stalin that invasion was not imminent, after fighting in defence of Moscow went on to command both the Bryansk and Voronezh Fronts during 1942 and 1943. Stalin's fall guy after Stalingrad and Kharkov, he was not given another combat command. Golikov complained personally to Stalin about his treatment at Stalingrad and Stalin almost dismissed Yeremenko for his conduct. It was only after Khrushchev intervened and explained that Golikov had lost his nerve that Stalin spared Yeremenko.

Golikov spent the rest of the war in Moscow, out of harm's way, where he was responsible for the repatriation of Soviet POWs – which usually meant a one-way ticket back to the Red Army or to the Gulag. He continued to serve with the military until his retirement in 1962. Likewise, Admiral Kuznetsov, who had said Hitler would not attack, remained commander-in-chief of Soviet naval forces until the end of the war.

Budenny, who had done great harm to the defence of the Soviet Union, survived the disasters of Uman and Kiev. Clearly another Stalin favourite, he went on to briefly command the Reserve Front and the North Caucasus Front. From the summer of 1943 he was packed off to do his ideal job as inspector of the cavalry. General Biriuzov, who had despaired at the Red Army gaining the wrong lessons from the Winter War, also survived the war only to be killed in a plane crash in 1964.

The hard men of Europe, who were deluded by Hitler that Barbarossa was a good idea and that victory was achievable, all paid the price. Italian partisans executed Mussolini just two days before Hitler took his own life. Antonescu was toppled in the summer of 1944 and was put on trial for war crimes two years later and executed.

Tragically, Jewish novelist and playwright Iosif Hechter, who chronicled the war from the Romanian perspective, was killed in a road accident on 29 May 1945.

Horthy, having swapped sides, was permitted to go into exile in Portugal where he wrote his memoirs.

Mannerheim was elected Finnish President in 1944, but resigned shortly after the end of the war. Due to ill health, he spent much of the rest of his life in hospital in Switzerland. Tiso was put on trial in Czechoslovakia as a Nazi collaborator and hanged in 1947.

Resistance to Hitler by King Boris III of Bulgaria had proved futile. Following a meeting with the Führer in the summer of 1943, he was allegedly poisoned for refusing to declare war on the Soviet Union and deport Bulgarian Jews.

Hitler was clearly seduced by how easily Europe had fallen to the Wehrmacht's triumphant blitzkrieg during 1939–41. The initial creation of the Soviet reserve front and reserve armies by Timoshenko and Zhukov gave warning of Stalin's enormous manpower reserves. Hitler chose to ignore this, and the massive strategic depth of the Soviet Union. The generation of further reserve fronts in 1942 and again in 1943 inevitably spelt defeat, first at Stalingrad and then Kursk. Ultimately, Hitler simply could not compete with Stalin's resources.

Barbarossa was to have been a quick and decisive campaign. After the intoxicating success of the summer of 1941, by the winter, Hitler's plans had become horribly unravelled. When he launched Barbarossa, his replacement army had about 450,000 men available, his fuel reserve had just three months' worth of petrol and one month of diesel. He gambled with the fate of his nation and lost.

By August 1941, although Hitler's losses were but a fraction of those endured by Stalin, they were still significant, totalling 440,000, of whom 94,000 were dead. Crucially by the end of the year only 217,000 replacements had been allotted and they still had to reach their designated units. Hitler would not hear of it when General Halder, chief of General Staff, recommended breaking up twelve existing infantry divisions to provide much-needed replacements for other battered units.

When the Battle of Kiev ended on 26 September 1941, the German official news service claimed the pocket had given up 665,000 Red Army prisoners, 884 tanks and 3,718 field guns and mortars. Staggeringly, five Soviet armies amounting to fifty divisions had been wiped off the Red Army's order of battle. Subsequently, the Soviets contested these figures, claiming they lost no more than 175,000 men. The general feeling is that Moscow was trying to play down the situation, rather than the Germans overinflating their victory. Despite the efforts of Khrushchev and Budenny, Stalin remained content to leave these vast forces to their fate. When he did relent, it was too late and thousands were killed trying to escape, including General Kirponos.

Stalin steadfastly refused to learn from this. Nonetheless, in some instances this produced dividends, such as in the case of the garrison of the Black Sea port of Odessa. Surrounded by the Romanian Army on 5 August 1941, General Petrov's Special Maritime Army held out until 16 October, inflicting 100,000 casualties on their attackers. During the two battles of Vyazma and Bryansk the Germans claimed to have captured 657,000 prisoners, 1,241 tanks and 5,396 pieces of artillery. This massive victory, coupled to the fact that the Soviets in many instances had shown little fighting spirit, convinced Hitler that his advance on Moscow would be swift.

To Halder's alarm, he found that their escalating casualty figure had risen to 686,000, of whom 145,000 had been killed and 29,000 were missing. From the remaining wounded, about two-thirds were expected to return to duty at some point. From 22 June to 26 November 1941 Hitler lost 187,000 men killed and missing on the Eastern Front. His wounded totalled 555,000, of whom only two-thirds might be expected to return to their units.

The official Soviet history, *The Great Patriotic War of the Soviet Union*, recorded German casualties sustained before Moscow during 16 November to 5 December 1941 as 155,000 (55,000 dead and over 100,000 wounded and frost-bitten). Equipment losses amounted to 777 panzers, 297 field guns and mortars and 1,500 aircraft. The Red Army's general winter offensive of 1942 routed fifty German divisions (i.e. they lost over half their manpower and equipment); by the Germans' own admission this totalled almost 400,000 men.

From 27 November 1941 to 31 March 1942 Germany's killed and missing amounted to 108,000 and 268,000 wounded, giving a total of 376,000. However, the weather also took its toll, with 228,000 frostbite cases and over 250,000 sick. This meant that 900,000 men were lost, of whom only half could be replaced. By the close of the winter fighting of 1941–42, Hitler's casualties had reached over 1.6 million, not including sick, and he simply did not have enough replacements.

By the end of September 1941, the Wehrmacht had accounted for over 2 million Soviet troops, 22,000 guns, 18,000 tanks and 14,000 aircraft. Between 22 June 1941 and 20 March 1942, the Red Army lost 3,461,000 captured alone. Hitler let 1,981,000 of these men die in captivity and another 1,308,000 died or disappeared in transit. By this stage total losses were in the region of 6 million; Stalin, however, had the ability to replace such appalling losses.

German estimates of Soviet manpower proved horribly wrong; they had assumed by December 1941 the Red Army would be able to muster 300 divisions, and Stalin managed twice that. This incredibly enabled him to shrug off the loss of 200 divisions and 4 million men by the end of 1941 – effectively the Red Army's entire peacetime strength. No other army has ever achieved such a feat and it is little short of a miracle.

By the end of 1941 the Soviet mobilisation system had provided 285 rifle divisions, eighty-eight cavalry divisions, twelve re-formed tank divisions, 174 rifle brigades and ninety-three tank brigades. This gave the Red Army the equivalent of 592 divisions. Stalin's manpower, despite all the terrible losses, had risen from 5,373,000 on 22 June to 8 million by December. These included ninety-seven divisions transferred from the Far East and twenty-five 'People's Militia' divisions raised from Muscovites and Leningraders. Also, by the end of the first six months of the war Soviet military academies had provided 192,000 new officers, easily making up for the detrimental effects of Stalin's purges and combat losses.

Colonel Gehlen estimated that Stalin had in the region of 17–19 million able-bodied men available to the Soviet armed forces. Taking into account Soviet losses since Barbarossa and as a result of the Winter War with Finland, he calculated the Soviet Union had suffered 7,530,000 casualties up to 1 May 1942. This left Stalin with at least 9.5 million men with which to wage the war. He had 7.8 million troops under arms, of whom 6 million were in the Red Army, 1.5 million in the air force and 300,000 in the navy. This meant that, on paper, Stalin could still call on 1.7–2 million men.

In his memoirs, General von Mellenthin lauded the Wehrmacht's accomplishments and recognised the lack of manpower was its undoing:

> The achievements of the German soldiers in Russia clearly prove that the Russians are not invincible. In the late autumn of 1941 the German Army was definitely in sight of victory in spite of vast spaces, the mud and slush of winter, and our deficient equipment and inferior numbers. Even in the critical years of 1944–45 our soldiers never had the feeling of being inferior to the Russians – but the weak German forces were like rocks in the ocean, surrounded by endless waves of men and tanks which surged around and finally submerged them.[5]

Nevertheless, it would be spurious to claim that Stalin's victory was based purely on superior numbers. The Red Army deserves more credit than that. Von Mellenthin goes on to claim:

> Experience gathered in the war shows that the Germans fought successful actions with a strength ratio of 1:5, as long as the formations involved were more or less intact and adequately equipped. Success was sometimes achieved with an even more unfavourable strength ratio, and it is unlikely that any other Western army could do better.[6]

Praise indeed. It was the Germans themselves who recognised that the Soviet victory was also in part due to the Red Army's ability to learn and adapt. General Kleist assessed:

> The men were first-rate *fighters* from the start, and we owed our success simply to superior training. They became first-rate *soldiers* with experience. They fought most toughly, had amazing endurance, and could carry on without

most of the things other armies regard as necessities. The Staff were quick to learn from their early defeats, and soon became highly efficient.[7]

Kleist also acknowledged the vast improvement in Soviet equipment:

> The Russians' weakest period had been in 1942. They had not been able to make up their 1941 losses, and throughout the year they were very short of artillery in particular. [...] But from 1943 on their equipment position became better and better.[8]

The Soviets' preference for standardisation of equipment also paid dividends. Captain von Senger, who after losing an arm on the Eastern Front served as adjutant to the Inspector of Panzer Forces, noted:

> Our panzer division in 1942 had twelve different types of armoured vehicle and twenty types of other vehicle. The Russian armoured corps then had mostly only one type of tank, the T-34, and one other vehicle, the Ford truck! [...]
>
> This simplicity of the Russian organisation had its drawbacks, but also its advantages, compared with the German – which suffered from having too many types of vehicle, of varying performance and design, thus complicating movement calculations as well as spare part supplies.[9]

Soviet troops also proved to be very fatalistic – if ordered to fight to the last, they often did – whereas German troops would disobey such orders when resistance became futile. This Soviet characteristic was observed very early in the war, but few appreciated its implications, as General Blumentritt observed:

> It was in this war, however, that we first learnt to realise what 'Russia' really means. The opening battle in June, 1941, revealed to us for the first time the new Soviet Army. Our casualties were up to fifty per cent. The OGPU [NKVD] and women's battalion defended the old citadel at Brest-Litovsk for a week, fighting to the last, in spite of bombardment with our heaviest guns and from the air. Our troops soon learnt to know what fighting the Russians meant. The Führer and most of our highest chiefs didn't know. That caused a lot of trouble.[10]

Some German generals felt that they should not have dallied on the flanks and mounted Operation Typhoon much sooner. Nonetheless, if Kirponos' armies had not been surrounded at Kiev, then Stavka would have had an extra

500,000 troops with which to threaten Army Group Centre's flank. Also, if the 4th Panzer Group had been released from Leningrad sooner, that would have eased the pressure there.

Not only did Hitler underestimate Stalin's manpower, he also grossly underestimated Soviet industrial capacity and resilience. Prior to Barbarossa commencing, General Thomas, OKW's armaments expert, wrongly assessed that Stalin would lose most of his military factories once the invasion had reached Moscow. This he believed would prevent Stalin from re-equipping the Soviet armed forces. Hitler and Thomas deliberately chose to ignore the possibility of these factories escaping before they were overrun by the Wehrmacht. Furthermore when they did escape Hitler's grasp and resumed work they easily outstripped German military production.

In these circumstances, Stalin could afford to trade bodies for military gain – Hitler could not. Operation Spark, conducted to break the blockade of Leningrad from mid-January 1943 till the end of the month, while a success, cost the Red Army a staggering 115,082 casualties, including 33,940 dead, captured or missing and 81,142 wounded from a force of 302,800. The Germans lost 12,000 killed.

Axis losses from 22 June 1941 to mid-November 1942 amounted to almost 2 million officers and men. To put this into perspective, during the First World War German casualties were just over 1.9 million. According to Zhukov, German losses in the Volga–Don–Stalingrad area, just from 19 November 1942 to 2 February 1943, amounted to thirty-two divisions destroyed, with another sixteen having lost 50–75 per cent of their effective strength. This totalled about 1.5 million men, 3,500 tanks and assault guns, 12,000 guns and 3,000 aircraft.

On the twenty-fifth anniversary of the Red Army on 23 February 1943, in his Order of the Day, Stalin proclaimed:

When Hitlerite Germany began the war against the USSR she enjoyed numerical superiority in troops already mobilised and ready for battle as compared with the Red Army. It was here that she had the advantage. In twenty months, however, the situation has changed in this sphere also. In the defensive and offensive battles, the Red Army, since the beginning of the war, has put out of action about 9,000,000 German-fascist officers and men, of which no less than 4,000,000 were killed on the battlefield.

The Romanian, Italian and Hungarian armies hurled by Hitler on to the Soviet–German front have been completely routed. In the last three months alone the Red Army has routed 112 enemy divisions, killing more than 700,000 men and taking over 300,000 prisoners.[11]

However accurate these figures were, they illustrated a trend that could not be ignored. Stalin recognised that Hitler did not have the resources to replace such manpower losses, and even if he did, Germany simply did not have the time to assemble or train them.

The Great Patriotic War of the Soviet Union records that in the period from November 1942 to March 1943 the Red Army destroyed over 100 enemy divisions, claiming that the German General Staff acknowledged losses of 1.2 million. The Soviets claim the Axis lost 1.7 million men, 3,500 tanks, 24,000 field guns and 4,300 aircraft during the winter campaign. The Battle of Kursk, which ran from 12 July to 23 August 1943, lasted fifty days and again according to Soviet sources cost the Germans thirty divisions, including seven panzer divisions. Zhukov recorded that German casualties amounted to 500,000 men, 1,500 tanks, 3,000 guns and more than 3,700 aircraft.

Across the Eastern Front, Hitler and his generals simply could not match the Red Army's swelling manpower in the face of continuing heavy losses. In the north, from mid-July to mid-October 1943, it expanded from 734,000 men (with 491,000 in reserve) to 893,000 (with 66,000 in reserve). By contrast, Army Group North had 601,000 troops in the field, down from 760,000. To make matters worse, the replacement and reinforcement requirements of Army Groups Centre and South were always considered a priority, meaning that it was regularly stripped of units.

The near total annihilation of Army Group Centre in June 1944, in the space of just under two weeks, cost Hitler 670,000 men – 300,000 dead, 250,000 wounded and about 120,000 captured. Only about 20,000 troops escaped. In addition, he lost 2,000 panzers and 57,000 other vehicles. Stalin's losses were 60,000 killed, 110,000 wounded and about 8,000 missing, 2,957 tanks, 2,447 artillery pieces and 822 aircraft.

Hitler's defence of East Prussia proved particularly dogged. Between 13–29 March 1945 the Red Army claimed to have killed 93,000 enemy troops and captured over 46,000. When Königsberg finally capitulated, the garrison lost 42,000 dead and 92,000 taken prisoner. The Soviets claimed to have destroyed twenty-five German divisions and routed another twelve. Hitler's last desperate counter-offensive in Hungary in March 1945 cost the German armed forces 40,000 troops, 500 tanks and 300 guns and mortars.

At the very end, fighting losses were simply colossal. In the battle from the Oder to Berlin alone, Zhukov and Konev lost around 100,000 men. The cost of overrunning the Nazi capital was simply enormous, the entire offensive cost the Red Army 81,116 killed; in addition, another 280,251 were wounded or sick. Included in that total are Polish forces which lost 2,825 killed or missing, and 6,067 wounded.

Initial Soviet estimates based on kill claims, placed German losses at 458,080 killed and 479,298 captured. The number of civilian casualties is unknown. Rampaging Soviet troops raped an estimated 100,000 women, and murdered innocent civilians along with Nazi Party officials. During the Berlin operation, the Germans destroyed over 800 Soviet tanks and self-propelled guns, most were lost on the very streets of Berlin itself.

The official Soviet history claims that during the Berlin operation the Red Army destroyed seventy infantry, twelve panzer and eleven motorised divisions, capturing 480,000 prisoners, 1,500 tanks and assault guns, 8,600 field guns and mortars and 4,500 aircraft. It puts the losses for the 1st and 2nd Byelorussian and 1st Ukrainian fronts between 16 April and 8 May 1945 at almost 300,000 killed and wounded, as well as 2,156 tanks and self-propelled guns, 1,220 field guns and mortars and 527 aircraft.

The conquest of Czechoslovakia during the final death throes of Hitler's Third Reich was intended to neutralise the 900,000 enemy troops there, equipped with 2,200 tanks, 10,000 field guns and mortars and about 1,000 aircraft. Soviet operations conducted on Czechoslovak territory from September 1944 to May 1945 cost the Red Army 140,000 dead. There was never any let-up in the bloodletting on the Eastern Front. From January to May 1945 the German Army lost over 1 million dead. The Red Army smashed ninety-eight divisions and overran another fifty-six. When Germany surrendered, another ninety-three divisions finally laid down their weapons.

The Red Army received no respite at the end of the Second World War. In early August 1945, Stalin drove the Japanese from the Mongolian border, Manchuria and Korea. In just twenty-three days, the Red Army destroyed the Japanese Kwantung Army at the cost of another 32,000 Soviet and 84,000 Japanese lives.

The scale of the losses on the Eastern Front are inconceivable, although total casualty estimates vary enormously. Published estimates of Soviet military war dead, including missing in action, POWs and Soviet partisan losses, range from 8.6 to 10.6 million. An additional 127,000 were killed during the Winter War with Finland. According to Soviet research, 13,684,692 Soviet civilians died during the war: of these, 7,420,000 were killed as a result of the fighting; 4,100,000 died under the Nazi occupation, and another 2,164,313 died after being deported (the Germans deported 5,269,513 Soviet civilians).

The Red Army's irrevocable losses amounted to 8,668,400 (this includes all services): these comprised 5,226,800 killed in action; 1,783,300 missing in action or died in captivity; 1,102,800 who died of their wounds and 555,5000 non-combat fatalities. Figures include navy losses of 154,771 and non-combat deaths include 157,000 sentenced to death by court martial. The Red Army's wounded totalled 14,685,593, including 2,576,000 permanently disabled. The Soviets also lost about 5 million captured, from whom 2,775,700 missing in action or POWs eventually returned to the ranks.

In total, 26.6 million Soviet soldiers and civilians died as a result of Barbarossa. Some 2.4 million people were officially considered missing in action and of the 9.5 million buried in mass graves, 6 million were unidentified. In comparison, German deaths amounted to 10,223,700 (German military dead have been estimated at about 5 million); France 328,671; Britain 462,762 and America 292,100. Soviet sources list the deaths of 474,967 of the 2,652,672 German POWs.

Equipment losses and, therefore, raw materials were equally massive. The Red Army lost 96,500 tanks and self-propelled guns and 218,000 field guns and mortars. The Soviets also lost over 106,400 aircraft including 88,300 combat types. On all fronts, Germany lost an estimated 116,875 aircraft, of which 70,000 were total losses and the remainder significantly damaged.

The Red Air Force claimed to have destroyed 55,000 German aircraft and dropped 30,450,00 bombs. Soviet air defence forces claimed another 7,000 aircraft, 40 per cent of which were brought down by anti-aircraft artillery fire. Soviet losses should be measured against a total of 3,125,000 combat sorties, of which only 168,000 were ground–attack sorties against enemy transportation. Other organisations flew an additional 3,852,000 sorties, including 350,000 flights by Soviet naval aviation and 109,000 flights in support of Soviet partisans.

The Soviet Navy lost 137 vessels, including about 100 submarines, while the Germans lost 840 vessels (the bulk of which were submarines). Soviet torpedo boats, submarines and naval aircraft claimed over 700 enemy vessels. Space does not permit the coverage of naval operations on the periphery of the Eastern Front, however, the Soviet Baltic fleet lost a battleship, fifteen destroyers, thirty-nine submarines, forty minesweepers, and many smaller ships. Hitler's forces lost 3 battleships, 3 cruisers, 19 destroyers, 48 submarines, 67 minesweepers, 129 smaller warships and landing craft, and 160 merchantmen; the Finns lost a monitor, 6 mine sweepers, 39 merchantmen and about a dozen smaller ships.

Hitler's Axis allies likewise paid a terrible price for the war in the east. Hungary suffered about 310,000 casualties, of whom 110,000 were fatalities and 200,000 were missing in action or captured. However, the Soviets claim to have taken 513,700 prisoners, of whom 54,700 died in captivity. Similarly, Romania lost about 100,000 killed and 200,000 captured. Slovak forces lost 7,000 troops on the Eastern Front, although another 30,000 men were also lost serving in the Hungarian Army. Significant casualties were then incurred fighting the Germans. The Finns, in their unequal struggle, lost 59,151.

Poland, caught in the middle, suffered its own agony, losing 239,800 soldiers and resistance fighters. During the 1939 invasion, killed and missing amounted to about 95,000 and 130,000 wounded, including 17,000–19,000 killed by the Soviets in the Katyn Massacre. Polish forces in exile lost 33,256 killed in action, 8,548 missing in action, 42,666 wounded and 29,385 interned. The Warsaw Uprising cost 16,000 Polish resistance fighters and 120,000 civilians.

Overall, civilian losses were 2.9 million in Poland and about 2.5 million in the Polish areas annexed by the Soviet Union. An official Polish report in the late 1940s assessed that 6,028,000 people died at the hands of the Nazis (including 123,178 military deaths, 2.8 million Poles and 3.2 million Jews), out of a population of 27 million ethnic Poles and Jews. About 108,000 Poles of German descent were also killed serving with the Wehrmacht on the Eastern Front. The Soviet occupation of eastern Poland from 1940–41 resulted in about 350,000 deaths (previously assessed as high as 1 million) and about 100,000 Poles were killed in 1943–44 during the massacres in Volhynia by the Ukrainian Insurgent Army.

In Moscow, the Red Army was feted for its achievements. Stalin held a reception for all his commanders on 24 May 1945. The following month, units of the Red Army triumphantly rolled through Moscow's Red Square, and this culminated in 200 captured Wehrmacht flags being symbolically placed at the foot of Lenin's mausoleum.

Despite his almost complete disregard for human life, Stalin ensured his people were rewarded for their sacrifice. To honour those who had fought on the Eastern Front the Soviet government awarded the 'Victory over Germany in the Great Patriotic War of 1941–45' medal to 13,660,000 Soviet soldiers. Seven million men received other decorations including the Orders of Lenin, the Red Banner and Red Star. Medals for valour and merit were granted to 7,580,000 servicemen. Those who fought behind enemy lines were also recognised. Over 127,000 partisans, from a force of 250,000 men at its peak, received the 'Partisan of the Great Patriotic War' medal. Over 184,000 were decorated with other awards.

After the devastation wrought by Operation Barbarossa, Stalin had every reason to be bitter. He saw no reason to seek reconciliation with the defeated Axis countries. His response to the pain and suffering his country had endured at the hands of Germany and her satellites was to draw an iron curtain across Eastern Europe and to impose a totalitarian political system that in many ways mirrored the Nazis. Hitler and Stalin's war also led to a new conflict, known as the Cold War. The Red Army, however, stood proud in the knowledge that it had turned utter disaster into a victory that changed the political shape of Europe and ensured the security of the Soviet Union.

Appendix I

Glossary of Key Military Operations 1941–45

(This does not include the numerous smaller operations conducted by the Germans against Soviet partisans.)

1941	
Barbarossa (Redbeard)	22 June 1941, Nazi invasion of the Soviet Union.
Lachsfang (Salmon Trap)	1 July–September 1941, combined German and Finnish operation to take the Murmansk Railway between Kandalaksha to the north and Belomorsk to the south.
Silberfuchs (Silver Fox)	1 July 1941, German offensive supported by the Finns to capture Kandalaksha on the White Sea to isolate Red Army forces in the Kola Peninsula.
South-Western Front operations toward Dubno	1–2 July 1941, Soviet counter-attack during Barbarossa.
Western Front operations toward Lepel	6–11 July 1941, Soviet counter-attack during Barbarossa.
South-Western Front operations toward Nogorod-Volynskii	10–14 July 1941, Soviet counter-attack during Barbarossa.
Leningrad Strategic Defensive Operation	10 July–30 September 1941, Red Army offensive in the Leningrad area designed to stop Army Group North.
Western Front counter-strokes along the Dnepr	13–17 July 1941, Soviet counter-attack during Barbarossa.
North-Western Front operations at Stolb'tsy	14–18 July 1941, Soviet counter-attack during Barbarossa.

South-Western Front's offensive around Korosten	5–8 August 1941, Soviet counter-attack during Barbarossa.
Western Front's Smolensk Offensive	11 August–9 September 1941, Soviet counter-attack during Barbarossa.
Staraia Russa Offensive	12–23 August 1941, Soviet offensive south of Leningrad.
Western Front's El'nia Offensive	30 August–8 September 1941, Soviet counter-attack during Barbarossa.
Bryansk Front's Roslavl-Novozybkov Offensive	30 August–12 September 1941, Soviet counter-attack during Barbarossa.
Georg	1 September 1941, operation launched by Army Group North to force Leningrad to surrender by starving the defenders.
Siniavino Offensive	10 September–28 October 1941, Soviet offensive south-east of Leningrad.
Taifun (Typhoon)	30 September–5 December 1941, culmination of Barbarossa German offensive against Moscow.
Trappenfang (Bustard Trap)	November 1941, German operation to secure the Kerch Peninsula at the eastern end of the Crimea.
Tikhvin Strategic Offensive	10 November–30 December 1941, Soviet offensive south-east of Leningrad.
Moscow Counter-Offensive	5 December 1941–7 May 1942, Red Army offensive to defeat the Germans before Moscow.
1942	
Bryansk Front's Orel-Bolkhov Offensive	7 January–18 February 1942, part of the Soviet winter offensive.
Bryansk Front's Kursk-Oboian Offensive	January–February 1942, part of the Soviet winter offensive.
Siniavino	7 January–late March 1942, unsuccessful Soviet offensive to liberate Leningrad.
Liuban Offensive	7 January–30 April 1942, Soviet offensive south of Leningrad which was designed to trap elements of Army Group North, but instead led to the encirclement of the Soviet 2nd Shock Army.
Rzhev–Vyazma Strategic Offensive	8 January–20 April 1942, Red Army offensive before Moscow.
Toropets-Kholm Offensive	9 January–6 February 1942, Red Army offensive south of Lake Ilmen, which helped create the Kholm and Demyansk pockets.
North-Western Front's Demyansk Offensive	6 March–9 April 1942, part of the Soviet winter offensive.

Kreml (Kremlin)	Early 1942, deception plan to divert attention from Operation *Blau* and to convince the Red Army that Hitler's summer offensive would be directed at Moscow.
Raubtier (Beast of Prey)	March 1942, offensive by the German 18th Army to counter the Red Army offensive north of Novgorod on the northern shore of Lake Ilmen.
Brückenschlag/Landbrücke (Bridge Blow or Land Bridge)	21 March–21 April 1942, Army Group North's operation to relieve the seven divisions of the German II Corps trapped in the Demyansk pocket. The pocket was sustained by the Luftwaffe until reached by ground forces, led Hitler to believe the 6th Army at Stalingrad could be maintained in such a way.
Eisstoss (Ice Pick)	March–April 1942, Luftwaffe offensive against the Soviet Baltic Fleet.
Mars I	Romanian reinforcements for the Axis Summer Offensive.
Mars II	Italian reinforcements for the Axis Summer Offensive.
Mars III	Hungarian reinforcements for the Axis Summer Offensive.
Trappenjagd (Bustard Hunt)	8–15 May 1942, German operation to eliminate the Red Army from the Kerch Peninsula in the Crimea prior to taking Sevastopol.
Orkan (Hurricane)	8 May–9 July 1942, designed to secure the Germans' right flank prior to their main Summer Offensive. Operation was conducted to drive the last of the Soviets from the Crimea and secure Sevastopol.
Fridericus I	17–29 May 1942, reduction of the Izyum Salient by Gruppe von Kleist prior to the launching of the German Summer Offensive.
Bolkhov Offensive	5–12 June 1942, small Soviet summer offensive.
Sturgeon	7 June–4 July 1942, German conquest of Sevastopol.
Wilhelm (William)	10–15 June 1942, German 6th Army offensive toward Volchansk, north-east of Kharkov. Preliminary operation in support of Operation *Blau*.

Fridericus II	22–26 June 1942, designed to clear the Red Army from the Kupyansk area and securing a bridgehead over the River Oskol.
Wirbelwind (Whirlwind)	June 1942, offensive planned by Army Group B to be conducted by the German 2nd Army and 4th Panzer Army in the Sukhinichi area. It was not conducted as *Blau* I overtook it.
Blau I (Blue 1, originally designated Siegfried)	28 June–7 July 1942, northern part of the German Summer Offensive, advancing east of Kursk and taking Voronezh. Designed to protect the left flank of the German 6th Army.
Blau II (Blue 2)	28 June–22 July 1942, 6th Army's drive on Stalingrad.
Blau III (Blue 3 – also known as *Clausewitz*, *Dampfhammer*/ Steam Hammer or *Maus*/ Mouse)	7–22 July 1942, attack between Izyum on the River Donets and Taganrog on the Sea of Azov. Designed to protect the right flank of the 6th Army.
Edelweiss	Part of *Blau* III intended to capture Baku and the Caspian oilfields, only reached the Caucasus Mountains.
Bryansk Front Counter-Offensive	June–July 1942, Soviet counter-offensive in response to Operation *Blau*.
Western Front Offensive	July–August 1942, Soviet offensive in response to Operation *Blau*.
Braunschweig (Brunswick)	July 1942, German Caucasus offensive.
Blucher	July 1942, crossing of the Straits of Kerch by the German 11th Army from the Crimea into the Kuban region. Designed to support the 17th Army's attempts to capture the Maikop oilfields and the port of Batumi on the Black Sea.
Seyditz	July 1942, German offensive near Belyy by the 9th Army as part of the effort to flatten out the front line west of Moscow.
Rösselsprung (Knight's Move)	1–10 July 1942, German air and naval offensive in support of Operation *Blau* against Allied convoys delivering supplies to the Soviet Union.
Nordpol (North Pole)	Plan for Army Group Centre to capitalise on the exhaustion of the Red Army's winter offensive at Moscow and to secure exposed German flanks. Was launched on 2 July as *Feuerzauber*, but was not followed up due to requirements of *Blau*.
Zhizdra Offensive	6–14 July 1942, small Soviet summer offensive.

Southern Front defensive battles in the Voroshilovgrad Operation	6–24 July 1942, Soviet operations in response to Operation *Blau*.
Fischreiher (Heron)	22 July–18 November 1942, extension of *Blau* II, pushing the 6th Army across the Don to Stalingrad on the Volga.
Nordlicht (Northern Light)	German plan to take Leningrad, but was shelved after the Soviet offensive on 19 August, south of Lake Ladoga. Efforts were diverted to thwarting this Soviet drive.
Moorbrand (Swamp Fire)	July/September 1942, operation conducted by Army Group North's 18th Army to stop Soviet relief attempts to Leningrad, particularly Operation Siniavino.
Klabautermann (Bogey Man)	July–November 1942, operations by German and Italian light naval forces against the Soviet Ladoga Naval Flotilla. Intended to cut the Soviet naval supply route across Lake Ladoga.
Siniavino Offensive	19 August–20 October 1942, Soviet offensive south-east of Leningrad designed to relieve the besieged city.
Wintermärchen (Winter Tales)	September 1942, offensive planned by Army Group A for the Italian 8th Army to launch against the Soviet bridgehead over the Don, but was never conducted.
Donnerschlag (Thunderclap)	December 1942, proposed break-out by the 6th Army and part of the 4th Panzer Army from Stalingrad to link up with Army Group Don. Hitler vetoed the plan.
Uranus	19–30 November 1942, Red Army offensive to isolate and surround the German forces attacking Stalingrad.
Mars, Rzhev-Sychevka Operation	25 November–20 December 1942, Red Army offensive to destroy the Germans in the Rzhev salient.
Great Saturn	December 1942, Red Army operation to trap the German 6th Army at Stalingrad.
Little Saturn	December 1942, Soviet destruction of the Italian 8th Army holding the south bank of the River Don.
Wintergewitter (Winter Storm or Winter Tempest)	12–23 December 1942, German attempt to relieve those forces trapped at Stalingrad.

1943	
Koltso (Ring)	9 January–2 February 1943, Soviet operation to wipe out the German 6th Army trapped in the Stalingrad pocket. The latter, cut in half, surrendered on 31 January and 2 February.
Siniavino Offensive (Operation Spark)	12–30 January 1943, successful Red Army offensive to break the blockade of Leningrad.
Gallop	29 January 1943, large-scale Soviet raid behind German lines toward Zaporozhe on the Dnepr following Stalingrad.
Star	1 February–26 March 1943, Red Army offensive to recapture Kharkov, Belgorod and Kursk.
Staraia Russa Offensive	4–19 February 1943, Soviet offensive south of Leningrad.
Demyansk Offensive (Operation Polar Star)	15–28 February 1943, Red Army offensive to destroy Army Group North and liberate the Leningrad region.
MGA-Siniavino Offensive	22 June–22 August 1943, Soviet offensive south-east of Leningrad.
Zitadelle (Citadel)	2–12 July 1943, German operation leading to the Battle of Kursk; was designed to wrest back the strategic initiative from the Red Army by pinching off the Soviets' bulge in the front line at Kursk.
Operation Kutuzov/Orel Strategic Counter-Offensive	12 July–18 August 1942, Red Army offensive to destroy the Germans' Orel bulge north of Kursk in the aftermath of the defeat of Operation *Zitadelle*.
Belgorod-Kharkov Strategic Offensive (Operation Polkovodets Rumyantsev)	3–23 August 1943, Red Army counter-offensive following Operation *Zitadelle* against the southern sector of the Kursk bulge.
Mirgorod Direction Offensive	3–23 August 1944, part of the above.
Smolensk Strategic Offensive	7 August–2 October 1943, Red Army offensive to clear the Germans from the Bryansk and Smolensk regions.
Lower Dnepr Offensive	24 August–23 December 1943, Red Army offensive designed to clear German forces from the eastern bank of the Dnepr.
Dnepr-Carpathian Strategic Offensive	24 December 1943–14 April 1944, a series of Red Army offensives to clear Ukraine and Moldova.
Zhitomir-Berdichev Offensive	24 December 1943–14 January 1944, Soviet attack west and south-west of Kiev.

1944	
Kirovograd Offensive	5–16 January 1944, Soviet liberation of Kirovograd.
Leningrad-Novgorod Strategic Offensive	14 January–1 March 1944, Soviet offensive which pushed Army Group North away from Leningrad.
Korsun–Shevchenkovsky Offensive	24 January–17 February 1944, Soviet attack south of the Korsun Salient.
Rovno-Lutsk Offensive	27 January 1944–11 February 1944, Soviet attacks toward Lvov and Ternopol.
Nikopol-Krivoi Rog Offensive	30 January–29 February 1944, Soviet attack toward these two cities.
Proskurov-Chernovtsy Offensive	4 March–17 April 1944, Soviet attack toward these two cities.
Uman-Botoshany Offensive	5 March–17 April 1944, Soviet attack toward these two cities.
Bereznegovatoye-Snigirevka Offensive	6–18 March 1944, Soviet attack toward Odessa and the Romanian border.
Margarethe I	9 March 1944, occupation of Hungary by the Germans to ensure their ally did not defect to the Soviet Union.
Margarethe II	German contingency plan to occupy Romania if it attempted to defect to the Soviet Union; the plan was pre-empted by the arrival of the Red Army, and Romania declared war on Germany on 25 August leading to the loss of Army Group North Ukraine.
Polesskoe Offensive	15 March–5 April 1944, Soviet attack toward Polesskoe.
Odessa Offensive	26 March–12 April 1944, Soviet attack to liberate Odessa.
Crimean Strategic Offensive	8 April–12 May 1944, series of Soviet offensives to liberate the Crimea.
Battle of Targul-Frumos	2–4 May 1944, unsuccessful Soviet attack on German forces north of Jassy.
Vyborg Offensive	10 June–15 July 1944, Soviet offensive to push the Germans and Finns away from Leningrad and the Karelian Isthmus.
Bagration Offensive	23 June–29 August 1944, Soviet operation launched by the Red Army to clear the Germans from Byelorussia and liberate Minsk.
Minsk Offensive	29 June–4 July 1944, part of Operation Bagration designed to liberate Minsk.

Lvov–Sandomierz Offensive	13–29 July 1944, Red Army offensive to drive the Germans from western Ukraine and eastern Poland.
Stanislav Offensive	13–27 July 1944, Red Army offensive forming part of the wider Lvov-Sandomierz operations.
Narva Offensive	24–30 July 1944, Red Army offensive to drive the Germans away from the city of Narva.
Lublin–Brest Offensive	28 July–2 August 1944, Red Army offensive in support of Bagration and Lvov–Sandomierz to drive the Germans from central eastern Poland.
Doppelkopf	16–27 August 1944, German counter-offensive in Lithuania.
Hubertus	German defensive plans for Moldavia and Bukovina, particularly between the Yablonitse Pass and Korneshti. Intended to stop the Red Army breaching the Carpathians and breaking into central Romania and wheeling north-west over the Alps into Hungary and Austria.
Jassey-Kishinev Strategic Offensive	20–29 August 1944, Red Army offensive into eastern Romania.
Skorpion	September 1944, German plan for former Soviet General Andrei Vlasov to assume command of all captured Soviets, in order to raise forces to fight the Red Army.
Belgrade Strategic Offensive	14–21 September 1944, Red Army offensive into Yugoslavia.
Debrecen Offensive	6–28 October 1944, Red Army offensive into Hungary.
Panzerfaust	16 October 1944, German seizure of Budapest's Burberg Castle and the arrest of Hungarian leader, Admiral Miklós Horthy.
Gumbinnen (Goldap) Operation	16–27 October 1944, Red Army's first attempt to penetrate the defences of East Prussia.
Eisenhammer (Iron Hammer)	November 1944, Luftwaffe offensive against Soviet munitions factories.
1945	
Konrad	1–20 January 1945, German attempts to relieve the Budapest garrison.
Vistula–Oder Offensive	12 January–2 February 1945, Red Army offensive that took it from the Vistula in Poland to the Oder, east of Berlin.

East Prussia Offensive	13 January–9 May 1945, Red Army's renewed effort to subdue East Prussia and capture Königsberg.
Hannibal	23 January–8 May 1945, German naval evacuation of East Prussia which moved over a million people to Germany and German-occupied Denmark.
Lower Silesian Offensive	8–24 February 1945, Red Army operation designed to clear Lower Silesia and take the provincial capital, Breslau.
Kosnitz-Köslin Offensive	10 February–6 March 1945, Red Army offensive.
Sonnenwende (Solstice)	15–18 February 1945, German counter-attack in Arnswalde and Stargard to keep open communications between Pomerania and East Prussia.
East Pomeranian Strategic Offensive	24 February–4 April 1945, Red Army offensive designed to clear German forces from East Pomerania and East Prussia.
Arnswalde-Kolberg Offensive	1–18 March 1945, Red Army offensive.
Gemese	1–12 March 1945, German counter-attacks in Silesia to retake Lauban and Striegau.
Frühlingserwachen (Spring Awakening)	6–15 March 1945, the Germans' last offensive of the war, designed to restore the front on the south-eastern approaches to Vienna.
Danzig Offensive	7–31 March 1945, Red Army offensive.
Braunsberg Offensive	13–29 March 1945 destruction of the German Heiligenbeil pocket prior to the assault on Königsberg.
Upper Silesian Offensive	15–31 March 1945, designed to clear German forces from Upper Silesia.
Altdam Offensive	18 March–4 April 1945, Red Army Offensive.
Vienna Offensive	2 April–13 April 1945, Red Army offensive to capture the Austrian capital.
Berlin Strategic Offensive	16 April–2 May 1945, the Red Army's final assault on Berlin.
Battle of the Seelow Heights	16–19 April 1945, Red Army offensive to penetrate Berlin's outer defences.
Battle of Berlin	19 April–2 May 1945, Red Army offensive to overcome Berlin.
Prague Strategic Offensive	5 May–11 May 1945, last major Soviet offensive of the war to capture Prague.

ESTIMATES OF HITLER'S PRINCIPAL EUROPEAN EASTERN FRONT ALLIES

Nationality	Number
Estonia	38,000
Finland	400,000
Hungary	200,000
Italy	229,000
Lithuania	13,000
Latvia	31,200
Romania	300,000
Slovakia	20,000
Spain	18,700
Total	1,249,900
(Includes regular and police units)	

Appendix 3

Estimates of Hitler's Principal Soviet Eastern Front Allies

Nationality	Numbers
Armenians, Georgians & other Caucasians	110,000
Committee for the Liberation of the Peoples of Russia (KONR)	50,000
Cossack Cavalry Corps & militia	80,000
Crimea Tartars	35,000
Kalmyk Cavalry Corps	5,000
Ostlegion	175,000
Osttruppen	427,000
Russian Defence Corps in Serbia (RSS)	11,200
Russian National Liberation Amy (RONA)	6,000
Turkomen	110,000
Ukrainian National Army (UNA)[*]	40,000
Ukrainian Insurgent Army (UPA)[**]	25,000
Total [***]	1,074,200

[*] The total number of Ukrainians serving the Germans is estimated to have been approximately 180,000 men.

[**] Fought both the Germans and Soviets at various times.

[***] Total is a very conservative figure as losses in Appendix 6 outstrip this number.

German Losses and Replacements, December 1941 – September 1942

Army Group	Losses	Replacements
North	375,800	272,800
Centre	765,000	481,400
South	547,300	415,100
Total	1,688,100	1,169,300

Appendix 5

Stalin's Reserve Armies, Spring 1942

Reserve Army	Location	Activated as	Commander
1st Reserve	Tula	64th Army	Vasili Chuikov
2nd reserve	Vologda	1st Guards Army	Kirill Moskalenk
3rd Reserve	Tambov	60th Army	Maxim Antonyuk
4th Reserve	Kalinin	38th Army	Nikandr Chibisov
5th Reserve	East of the Don	63rd Army	Vasili Kuznetsov
6th Reserve	East of the Don	6th Army	Fedor Kharitonov
7th Reserve	Stalingrad	62nd Army	Vladimir Kolpakchi
8th Reserve	Saratov	66th Army	Rodion Malinovsky
9th Reserve	Gorky	24th Army	Dmitri Kozlov
10th Reserve	Ivanovo	5th Shock Army	Markian Popov
3rd Tank Army	West of Tula	3rd Tank Army	Prokofi Romanenko
5th Tank Army	East of Orel	5th Tank Army	Aleksandr Lizukov

These forces equated to over 1 million men. In response to Hitler's summer 1942 offensive, the 5th Tank was moved south and three field armies were moved north up the Don. Then the 1st and 7th Reserve Armies were deployed to defend the Great Bend of the Don as the 64th and 62nd Armies respectively. To protect the Moscow–Stalingrad rail line, the 2nd Reserve was activated as the 1st Guards. To counter Paulus's thrust to northern Stalingrad, Stalin deployed the 9th Reserve as the 24th Army and the 8th Reserve as the 66th Army. Elements of the 1st Reserve, as well as the 21st, 38th, 51st and 57th Field Armies, were also involved in the defence of Stalingrad.

Axis Losses on the Eastern Front 1941–45

Nationality	Total Dead	Killed & Missing in Action	Captured	Died in Captivity
Germany	4,374,000	4,000,000	3,300,000	374,000
Hungary	300,000	1,00,000	500,000	200,000
Italy	82,000	32,000	70,000	50,000
Osttruppen[*]	215,000	215,000	1,000,000	unknown
Romania	281,000	81,000	500,000	200,000
Totals	5,178,000	4,428,000	5,450,000	824,000

★   Includes all Soviet nationalities.

APPENDIX 7

RED ARMY AND SOVIET ALLIED FORCES' LOSSES ON THE EASTERN FRONT 1941–45

Nationality	Total Dead	Killed & Missing in Action	Captured	Died in Captivity
Soviet Union	10,600,000	6,600,000	5,200,000	3,600,000
Bulgaria	10,000	10,000	unknown	unknown
Poland	24,000	24,000	unknown	unknown
Romania	17,000	17,000	80,000	unknown
Totals	10,651,000	6,651,000	5,280,000	3,600,000

APPENDIX 8

RED ARMY LOSSES BY OPERATION 1941–45[*]

Operation	Losses[**]
The Defence of Kiev, July–September 1941	700,564 casualties; 411 tanks, 28,419 artillery pieces and 343 aircraft.
Battle of Smolensk, July–September 1941	344,926 casualties; 1,348 tanks, 9,290 artillery pieces and 903 aircraft.
The Defence of Moscow, September–November 1941	658,279 casualties; 2,785 tanks, 3,832 artillery pieces and 293 aircraft.
Siege of Sevastopol, October 1941–July 1942	200,481 casualties; no data on equipment losses.
Rzhev–Vyazma Offensive, January–April 1942	776,889 casualties; 957 tanks, 7,296 artillery pieces and 550 aircraft.
Kharkov Offensive, May 1942	277,190 casualties; 652 tanks, 1,646 artillery pieces and n/a aircraft.
Battle of Stalingrad, July–November 1942	643,842 casualties; 1,426 tanks, 12,137 artillery pieces and 2,063 aircraft.
Stalingrad Offensive, November 1942–February 1943	485,777 casualties; 2,915 tanks, 3,591 artillery pieces and 706 aircraft.
Rzhev-Sychevka Offensive, November–December 1942	215,674 casualties; 1,655 tanks, n/a artillery pieces and n/a aircraft.
Kharkov-Belgorod Offensive, March–August 1943	255,566 casualties; 1,864 tanks, 423 artillery pieces and 153 aircraft.
Battle of Kursk, May–July 1943	177,847 casualties; 1,614 tanks, 3,929 artillery pieces and 459 aircraft.

Lower Dnepr Offensive, September–December 1943	754,392 casualties; 2,639 tanks, 3,125 artillery pieces and 430 aircraft.
Leningrad-Novgorod Offensive, January–April 1944	313,953 casualties; 462 tanks, 1,832 artillery pieces and 260 aircraft.
Crimean Offensive, April–May 1944	84,819 casualties; 171 tanks, 521 artillery pieces and 179 aircraft.
Byelorussian Offensive, June–August 1944	770,888 casualties; 2,957 tanks, 2,447 artillery pieces and 822 aircraft.
Baltic Offensive, September–November 1944	280,090 casualties; 522 tanks, 2,593 artillery pieces and 779 aircraft.
Budapest Offensive, October 1944–February 1945	320,082 casualties; 1,766 tanks, 4,127 artillery pieces and 293 aircraft.
Vistula–Oder Offensive, January–February 1945	194,191 casualties; 1,267 tanks, 374 artillery pieces and 343 aircraft.
East Prussian Offensive, January–April 1945	584,778 casualties; 3,525 tanks, 1,644 artillery pieces and 1,450 aircraft.
Vienna Offensive, March–April 1945	177,745 casualties; 603 tanks, 764 artillery pieces and 614 aircraft.
Berlin Offensive, April–May 1945	361,367 casualties; 1,997 tanks, 2,108 artillery pieces and 917 aircraft.
Prague Offensive, May 1945	52,498 casualties; 373 tanks, 1,006 artillery pieces and 80 aircraft.

* Courtesy Russell W. Schulke Jr, compiled from David Glantz's figures.

** Figures used in the text for both sides are predominantly taken from the official Soviet history.

NOTES

Chapter 1

1   Cited in Hugh Trevor-Roper (ed.), *Hitler's War Directives 1939–1945*, pp.93–94.
2   Nikita Khrushchev, *Khrushchev Remembers*, p.160.
3   Andre Stuchenko, 'In the Frunze Military Academy', cited in Seweryn Bialer (ed.), *Stalin and his Generals: Soviet Military Memoirs of World War II*, pp.81–82.
4   Alexandr Solzhenitsyn, *The Gulag Archipelago*, p.24.
5   *Ibid.*, p.99.
6   Biriuzov, 'In the 30th Red Banner Division', cited in Seweryn Bialer, op. cit., pp.84–85.
7   Solzhenitsyn, op. cit., p.448.
8   *Ibid.*, p.76.
9   Cited in Vadim Rogovin, *Stalin's Terror of 1937–1938*, p.202.
10 Biriuzov, *Stalin & His Generals*, p.137.
11 Zhukov, *Marshal of the Soviet Union G. Zhukov, Reminiscences and Reflections*, Volume 1, p.172.
12 *Ibid.*
13 Alexander Werth, *Russia at War*, p.51.

Chapter 2

1   Voroshilov, cited in Zhukov, *Reminiscences and Reflections*, Volume 1, p.177.
2   *Ibid.*, pp.177–78.
3   *Ibid.*, p.178.
4   Stalin, reported by *Novyi Mir*, Moscow.
5   Halifax & Craster, *Speeches on Foreign Policy*, p.340.
6   *Ibid.*, p.350.
7   Khrushchev, *Khrushchev Remembers*, p.154.
8   *Ibid.*
9   Halifax, op. cit., p.351.
10 Solzhenitsyn, op. cit., p.77.
11 Kuznetsov, cited in Eloise Engle and Lauri Paananen, *The Winter War: The Russo-Finnish Conflict, 1939–40*, p.146.

12 Khrushchev, op. cit., p.157.
13 Engle & Paananen, *The Winter War*, p.147, quoting N.N.Voronov, *Na Sluzhbe Voennoi* (Moscow, 1963), pp.157–58.
14 Biriuzov, *Stalin & His Generals*, p.137.
15 Voronov, *ibid.*, p.133.
16 Biriuzov, *ibid.*, p.137.

Chapter 3

1 Pontin, *Churchill*, pp.524–25, & Gilbert, *Churchill: A Life*, p.700.
2 Halifax, *Speeches on Foreign Policy*, p.291.
3 Cited in Hugh Trevor-Roper (ed.), *Hitler's War Directives 1939–1945*, p.86.
4 Field Marshal Erich von Manstein, *Lost Victories*, p.181.
5 Cited in Colonel Albert Seaton, *The German Army 1933–45*, p.163.
6 Hitler in Trevor-Roper, op. cit., pp.93–94.
7 General Heinz Guderian, *Panzer Leader*, p.214.
8 *Ibid.*
9 Seaton, op. cit., p.163.
10 Hitler in Trevor-Roper, op. cit., pp.96–97.
11 Manstein, op. cit., p.176.
12 *Ibid.*, p.177.
13 *Ibid.*, p.175.
14 Guderian, op. cit., p.142.
15 *Ibid.*, p.143.
16 Cited in Seaton, op. cit., p.168.
17 *Ibid.*, p.166.
18 Gehlen, *The Gehlen Memoirs*, p.50.
19 *Ibid.*, p.65.
20 Trevor-Roper, *Hitler's War Directives 1939–1945*, p.178.
21 Gehlen, p.65.
22 *Ibid.*, p.66.
23 Herling, *A World Apart*, p.176.
24 Loringhoven, *In the Bunker with Hitler*, p.29.

Chapter 4

1 Mihail Sebastian, *Journal 1935–44*, p.322.
2 Field Marshal Erich von Manstein, *Lost Victories*, p.206.
3 Sebastian, op. cit., p.350.
4 *Ibid.*, p.359.
5 *Ibid.*, p.364.
6 *Ibid.*, p.369.
7 Herling, op. cit., p.3.
8 Khrushchev, *Khrushchev Remembers*, p.194.
9 Stalin, cited in Montefiore, *Stalin: The Court of the Red Tsar*, p.298.
10 *Ibid.*
11 *Ibid.*, p.315.

12   Stalin, cited in Andrew & Mitrokhin, *The Mitrokhin Archive*, p.271.

13   Zhukov, *Reminiscences and Reflections*, Vol. 1, p.258.

14   Churchill, cited in Hough, *Winston and Clementine*, p.547.

15   Werth, op. cit., p.150.

16   Voronov, *Stalin and His Generals*, p.207.

17   Herling, op. cit., p.175.

18   Evseev, cited Merridale, *Ivan's War*, p.72.

Chapter 5

1   Jones, *Most Secret War*, p.205.

2   Cited in Cradock, *Know Your Enemy*, p.21.

3   *Ibid.*

4   Bialer, *Stalin & His Generals*, p.187.

5   *Ibid.*, p.188.

6   *Ibid.*, p.209.

7   *Ibid.*

8   Boldin cited in Werth, *Russia at War 1941–1945*, p.157.

9   Werth, *Ibid.*, p.143.

10   Bialer, *Stalin & His Generals*, p.208.

11   *Ibid.*, p.240.

Chapter 6

1   Khrushchev, *Khrushchev Remembers*, p.166.

2   Stalin, cited in Montefiore, *Stalin: The Court of the Red Tsar*, p.362.

3   Khrushchev, op. cit., pp.166–67.

4   Beria, cited in Knight, *Beria, Stalin's First Lieutenant*, p.108.

5   Timoshenko and Zhukov, cited in David Glantz, *Barbarossa Hitler's Invasion of Russia 1941*, p.242.

6   Mikoyan, cited in Merridale, *Ivan's War*, p.88.

7   Bialer, *Stalin & His Generals*, p.208.

8   Semenyak, BBC Interview cited in Laurence Rees, *World War Two Behind Closed Doors*, p.91.

9   Gilbert, op. cit., p.701.

10   *Ibid.*

11   Stewart, *His Finest Hours*, p.103.

12   Rees, op. cit., p.93.

13   Schroeder, *He was My Chief*, p.87.

14   *Ibid.*, p.89.

15   *Ibid.*, p.95.

16   Stalin, quoted in *Soviet Russia Today*, August 1941.

17   Herling, op. cit., p.175.

18   Jonathan Bastable, *Voices from Stalingrad*, p.16.

19   Stalin, *On the Great Patriotic War of the Soviet Union, Speeches, Orders of the Day, and Answers to Foreign Press Correspondents*, pp.7–8.

Chapter 7

1 Hitler in Trevor-Roper, op. cit., p.146.
2 Fedyuninsky, 'With Zhukov to Leningrad', cited in Bialer, op. cit., pp.430–31.
3 Georgi K. Zhukov, *Marshal Zhukov's Greatest Battles*, p.29.
4 Sebastian, *Journal 1935–1944*, p.369.
5 Manstein, op. cit., pp.206–07.
6 *Ibid.*, p.535.
7 *Ibid.*, p.214.
8 *Ibid.*, p.225.
9 *Ibid.*, p.228.

Chapter 8

1 Beloborodov, cited in Axell, *Russia's Heroes*, p.145.
2 Account given by General Blumentritt, von Kluge's chief of staff, to B.H. Liddell Hart, *The Other Side of the Hill*, p.285.
3 Zhukov, *Marshal Zhukov's Greatest Battles*, p.59.
4 Kerr, *The Russian Army*, p.26.
5 *Ibid.*
6 *Ibid.*
7 Vasily Grossman, *A Writer at War: with the Red Army 1941–1945*, p.56.
8 General Heinz Guderian, *Panzer Leader*, p.256.
9 Stalin, *On the Great Patriotic War of the Soviet Union*, p.11.
10 Stalin, speech 7 November 1941, *Ibid.*, pp.22–23.
11 Kerr, op. cit., p.9.
12 Guderian, op. cit., pp.254–55.
13 Henry, cited in Bastable, *Voices from Stalingrad*, p.20.
14 Edelman, cited in Andrew Nagorski, *The Greatest Battle: The Fight for Moscow 1941–42*, p.240.
15 Guderian, op. cit., p.248.
16 *Ibid.*
17 *Ibid.*, p.252.
18 Zhukov, op. cit., p.74.
19 Zhukov cited in Colonel Albert Seaton, *The Battle for Moscow*, p.188, from G.K. Zhukov, *Vospominaniya I Razmyshleniya* (London: 1969), pp.373–74.
20 Blumentritt, cited in Liddell Hart, op. cit., p.286.
21 *Ibid.*, p.287.
22 Anonymous, cited in Alan Clark, *Barbarossa The Russian–German Conflict – 1945*, p.173, quoting Colonel E. Leyderrey, *The German Defeat in the East* (Her Majesty's War Office 1952), p.47.
23 Zhukov, op. cit., p.83.
24 Grossman, op. cit., p.63.
25 Hofmann, 'The Battle for Moscow 1941', cited in H.A. Jacobsen & J. Rohwer (eds), *Decisive Battles of World War II*.
26 Zhukov, 'First Victory', cited in Bialer, op. cit., p.335.
27 Zhukov, op. cit., p.103.

28 Herling, op. cit., p.178.
29 Stalin, cited in Rodric Braithwaite, *Moscow 1941: A City and its People at War*, p.324, quoting G. Zhukov, *Vospominaniya I Razmyshleniya*, Vol. 2, (Moscow: 2002), pp.42–43.

Chapter 9

1 Ciano, cited in William L. Shirer, *The Rise and Fall of the Third Reich*, p.910, quoting Count Galeazzo Ciano, *The Ciano Diaries, 1939–1943*, (New York 1946), pp.442–43.
2 Loringhoven, *In the Bunker with Hitler*, p.109.
3 Shirer, op. cit., p.910.
4 *Ibid.*, p.915.
5 Hitler in Trevor-Roper, op. cit., p.178.
6 *Ibid.*, pp.178–79.
7 Khrushchev, op. cit., pp.186–87.
8 *Ibid.*, p.188.
9 Manstein, op. cit., p.240.
10 Merridale, op. cit., p.131.
11 Schroeder, op. cit., pp.111–12.
12 Zhukov, *Reminiscences and Reflections*, Vol. 2, p.78.
13 *Ibid.*, p.79.
14 Shirer, op. cit., p.909, quoting Paulus' testimony at Nuremberg, Hitler made this comment on 1 June 1942, almost a month before the German Summer Offensive started.
15 Kleist, cited in Bastable, op. cit., p.26.
16 Khrushchev, op. cit., p.193.
17 *Ibid.*
18 *Ibid.*
19 Golikov, cited in Craig, *Enemy at the Gates*, p.81.
20 Khrushchev, op. cit., p.193.
21 Simonov, cited in Beevor, *Stalingrad*, p.127.
22 Kerr, *The Russian Army*, p.111.
23 Chuikov, cited in Axell, *Russia's Heroes*, p.172.
24 Kerr, op. cit., p.112.
25 Khrushchev, op. cit., p.190.

Chapter 10

1 Shirer, op. cit., p.917.
2 Hitler in Trevor-Roper, op. cit., p.182.
3 Liddell Hart, op. cit., pp.308–99.
4 Shirer, op. cit., p.915.
5 *Ibid.*
6 Manstein, op. cit., 293.
7 Mellenthin, op. cit., p.199.
8 Zhukov, *Reminiscences and Reflections*, Vol. 2, p.111.

9   Mellenthin, op. cit., p.199.
10 Shirer, op. cit., p.919.
11 Bastable, op. cit., p.144.
12 Stalin, *On the Great Patriotic War of the Soviet Union*, p.48.
13 Gehlen, op. cit., p.70.
14 Anonymous, cited in Zhukov, op. cit., pp.124–25.
15 Bastable, op. cit., p.154.
16 Kerr, *The Secret of Stalingrad*, pp.212–13.
17 Anonymous, cited in Zhukov, op. cit., p.125.
18 Bastable, op. cit., p.172.
19 Zhukov, op. cit., p.122.
20 Bastable, op. cit., p.173.
21 *Ibid.*, p.158.
22 *Ibid.*, p.162.
23 Gehlen, op. cit., p.74.
24 Kerr, *The Secret of Stalingrad*, p.219.
25 Paulus to Hitler, cited in Heinrich Graf von Einsiedel, *The Onslaught: The German Drive to Stalingrad*, p.184.
26 Mellenthin, op. cit., p.226.

Chapter 11

1   Manstein, op. cit., p.350.
2   *Ibid.*, p.329.
3   Colonel Helmut Ritgen, *The 6th Panzer Division 1937–45*, p.28.
4   Shirer, op. cit., p.927.
5   Mellenthin, op. cit., p.233.
6   Ritgen, op. cit., p.33.
7   Bastable, op. cit., pp.202–03.
8   Kerr, *The Russian Army*, p.119.
9   Guderian, op. cit., p.275.
10 Shirer, op. cit., p.929.
11 Bastable, op. cit., p.225.
12 Mellenthin, op. cit., p.250.
13 Cited in Peter Abbott and Nigel Thomas, *Germany's Eastern Front Allies 1941–45*, p.4.
14 Loringhoven, *In the Bunker with Hitler*, p.36.
15 *Ibid.*, p.38.
16 Don HQ Daily Bulletin, cited in Bastable, op. cit., p.247.
17 *Ibid.*, p.248.
18 Stalin, op. cit., p.49.
19 Paulus, Bastable, p.28
20 Stalin, op. cit., p.50.
21 Sebastian, op. cit., p.542.
22 Walter Kerr, *The Secret of Stalingrad*, p.242.
23 Werth, op. cit., p.500.
24 Drebber, cited in Kerr, *The Russian Army*, p.126.

25 Zhukov, op. cit., pp.142–43.
26 Schroeder, op. cit., p.105.

Chapter 12

1   Manstein, op. cit., p.436.
2   Zhukov, op. cit., p.147.
3   Mellenthin, op. cit., p.253.
4   Guderian, op. cit., p.307.
5   Liddell Hart, op. cit., p.321.
6   Zhukov, op. cit., p.152.
7   *Ibid.*, p.176.
8   Gehlen, op. cit., p.82.
9   *Ibid.*, p.83.
10 *Ibid.*, pp.84–85.

Chapter 13

1   Zhukov, op. cit., Vol. 2, p.182.
2   Grossman, op. cit., p.238.
3   Zhukov, *Marshal Zhukov's Greatest Battles*, p.236–7.
4   Bergström, *Kursk – The Air Battle: July 1943*, p.109.
5   Ritgen, op. cit., p.35.
6   Mellenthin, op. cit., p.277.
7   Stalin, op. cit., p.64.
8   Shtemenko, 'Rituals of Victory,' cited in Bialer, op. cit., p.360.
9   Sajer, *The Forgotten Soldier*, pp.209 & 229.
10 *Ibid.*, p.228.
11 Shtemenko, in Bialer, op. cit., p.363.
12 Guderian, in Bergström, op. cit., p.121.
13 Gehlen, op. cit., p.86.
14 Zhukov, *Marshal Zhukov's Greatest Battles*, p.256.
15 Stalin, op. cit., p.78.

Chapter 14

1   Werth, *Russia at War*, p.751.
2   *Ibid.*, p.752.
3   *Ibid.*, p.753.
4   Shtemenko, *The Soviet General Staff at War 1942–1945*, p.317.
5   Belov, cited in Merridale, *Ivan's War*, p.238.
6   Army Group Centre, cited in Lieutenant General Gerd Niepold, *Battle for White Russia: The Destruction of Army Group Centre June 1944*, p.23.
7   Jordan, cited in Ian Baxter, *Operation Bagration: The Destruction of Army Group Centre June–July 1944*, p.4.
8   *Ibid.*

9 *Ibid.*

10 Busch, cited in Paul Carell, *Scorched Earth: The Russian–German War, 1943–1944*, p.581.

11 Basil Liddell Hart, *History of the Second World War*, p.580.

12 Sebastian, op. cit., p.601.

13 Drescher, cited in Paul Adair, *Hitler's Greatest Defeat*, p.153.

14 Guderian, op. cit., p.341.

Chapter 15

1 George Bruce, *The Warsaw Rising*, p.172.

2 Stalin, *Ibid.*, p.62.

3 Soviet government statement, *ibid.*, p.63.

4 Davies, op. cit., p.165.

5 Zhukov, op. cit., Vol. 2, p.301.

6 Bruce, op. cit., p.183

Chapter 16

1 Shirer, op. cit., p.850.

2 Cited in Alan Bullock, *Hitler: A Study in Tyranny*, p.649.

3 Sebastian, op. cit., p.527.

4 Bastable, op. cit., p.173.

5 German staff officer, *ibid.*, p.153.

6 German staff officer, *ibid.*, p.155.

7 Manstein, op. cit., p.535.

8 *Ibid.*

9 Sebastian, op. cit., p.589.

10 Loringhoven, op. cit., p.117.

11 Guderian, op. cit., p.367.

12 *Ibid.*

13 *Ibid.*, p.607.

14 *Ibid.*

15 *Ibid.*, p.608.

16 *Ibid.*, pp.609–10.

17 Loringhoven, op. cit., p.118.

18 Hindy, cited in Ungváry, *Battle for Budapest*, p.71.

Chapter 17

1 Guderian, op. cit., p.382.

2 *Ibid.*, pp.382–83.

3 Cited in G.M. Gilbert, *Nuremberg Diary*, p.157.

4 Schroeder, op. cit., p.174.

5 Guderian, op. cit., p.443.

6 Guderian's interrogation by the US 7th Army, cited in Chester Wilmot, *The Struggle for Europe*, p.622.

7 Cited in Shirer, op. cit., p.1108, from Boldt's own book *In the Shelter with Hitler*, published in London in 1948.
8 Guderian, op. cit., p.389.
9 Dittmar in Liddell Hart, op. cit., p.328.
10 Steiger cited in Will Fey, *Armor Battles of the Waffen-SS 1943–45*, pp.226–27.
11 *Ibid.*, p.230.
12 *Ibid.*
13 Pfeffer-Wildenbruch in Ungváry, op. cit., p.145.
14 Lehoczky, in Ungváry, op. cit., p.152.
15 Sulyánsky in Ungváry, op. cit., p.154.
16 Dietrich, cited in Charles Messenger, *Hitler's Gladiator: The Life and Times of Oberstgruppenführer and Panzergeneral-Oberst der Waffen-SS Sepp Dietrich*, pp.166–67.
17 *Ibid.*, p.170.

Chapter 18

1 Trevor-Roper, *Hitler's War Directives*, pp.290–91.
2 Sajer, *The Forgotten Soldier*, p.475.
3 Hax, cited in Georg Gunter, *Last Laurels: The German defence of Upper Silesia January–May 1945*, p.186.
4 Guderian, op. cit., p.418.
5 *Ibid.*
6 Gehlen, op. cit., p.122.
7 Lasch, cited in Denny, *The Fall of Hitler's Fortress City*, p.225.
8 *Ibid.*, p.227.
9 Gehlen, op. cit., p.17.
10 *Ibid.*, p.125.
11 Hitler in Trevor-Roper, op. cit., p.300.
12 Reymann, cited in Cornelius Ryan, *The Last Battle*, p.298.
13 Kinzel, *ibid.*, p.176.
14 Kempka, *I was Hitler's Chauffeur*, p.60.
15 Cited in Ryan, op. cit., p.287.
16 Weidling, cited in Zhukov, *Reminiscences and Reflections*, Vol. 2, p.365.
17 Popiel, cited in Ryan, op. cit., p.306,
18 *Ibid.*
19 Grossman, op. cit., p.334,
20 Reymann, cited in Ryan, op. cit., p.314,
21 *Ibid.*

Chapter 19

1 Schroeder, op. cit., p.176.
2 *Ibid.*, p.179.
3 Zhukov, 'On the Berlin Axis', cited in Bialer, op. cit., p.507 & Zhukov, *Greatest Battles*, p.286.
4 Zhukov, *Greatest Battles*, p.286.

5 Kempka, op. cit., p.58.

6 Lucas, *Hitler's Commanders*, p.199.

7 Reitlinger, *The SS Alibi of a Nation 1922–1945*, p.433, citing Steiner's interrogation in Georges Blond's *L'agonie de l'Allemagne*, Paris, 1952, p.287.

8 Ryan, op. cit., p.374.

9 Fest, *Inside Hitler's Bunker*, pp.67–68.

10 Ryan, op. cit., p.351.

11 Fest, op. cit., p.68.

12 Loringhoven, *In the Bunker with Hitler*, p.152.

13 Konev, 'Strike from the South', cited in Bialer, op. cit., p.528.

14 Grossman, op. cit., p.338.

15 Loringhoven, op. cit., p.167.

16 *Ibid.*, p.153.

17 Keitel, cited in Bullock, *Hitler: A Study in Tyranny*, p.790.

18 Loringhoven, op. cit., p.168.

19 German Radio, *ibid.*, p.168.

20 Propaganda Ministry, Trevor-Roper, *The Last Days of Hitler*, p.197.

21 Toland, *Adolf Hitler*, p.876.

22 Loringhoven, op. cit., p.168.

23 Ryan, op. cit., p.404.

24 Bialer, op. cit., p.532.

25 Ryan, op. cit., p.313.

26 Stalin, cited in Ryan, p.390, from Milovan Djilas, *Conversations with Stalin* (London 1962).

27 O'Donnell, *The Berlin Bunker*, p.145.

28 Hitler, in McKay, *The Lost World of Bletchley Park*, p.145.

29 Grossman, op. cit., p.338.

30 Montgomery, *The Memoirs of Field Marshal Montgomery*, p.335.

31 Warren, cited in Hamilton, *Monty: The Field Marshal 1944–1976*, p.501.

32 Thompson, *ibid.*, p.511.

33 Montgomery, *ibid.*, p.524.

34 de Guingand, *Operation Victory*, p.456.

35 Montgomery, *The Memoirs*, p.340.

36 Zhukov, *Greatest Battles*, p.290.

37 Lucas, *Last Days of the Reich*, p.245.

38 Stalin's Victory Address, 9 May 1945.

Chapter 20

1 Khrushchev, op. cit., p.182.

2 Gehlen, op. cit., p.96.

3 Loringhoven, op. cit., p.39.

4 Gehlen, op. cit., p.101.

5 Zhukov, *Reminiscences and Reflections*, Vol. 1, p.159.

6 *Ibid.*, p.172.

7 Solzhenitsyn, op. cit., p.84.

8 Werth, *Russia at War*, p.753.

9   Solzhenitsyn, op. cit., p.84.
10 Montgomery, *The Memoirs*, p.356.
11 *Ibid.*, pp.381–82.
12 Gehlen, op. cit., p.106.
13 Zhukov, *Reminiscences and Reflections*, Vol. 2, p.411.
14 Solzhenitsyn, op. cit., p.85.
15 Zhukov, *Reminiscences and Reflections*, Vol. 1, p.164.

Chapter 21

1   de Guingand, op. cit., p.461.
2   Guderian, op. cit., p.275.
3   Loringhoven, op. cit., pp.110–11.
4   Zhukov, *Reminiscences and Reflections*, Vol. 1, p.274.
5   Mellenthin, op. cit., p.365.
6   *Ibid.*, p.366.
7   Kleist, cited in Liddell Hart, *The Other Side of the Hill*, p.329.
8   Liddell Hart, paraphrasing General Kleist, *ibid.*, p.331.
9   von Senger, *ibid.*, pp.332–33.
10 Blumentritt, *ibid.*, p.338.
11 Stalin, *On the Great Patriotic War of the Soviet Union*, p.53.

BIBLIOGRAPHY

Memoirs & Reportage

Abdulin, Mansur, *Red Road from Stalingrad: Recollections of a Soviet Infantryman*, translated from Russian by Denis Fedosov and edited by Artem Drabkin (Barnsley: Pen & Sword, 2004).

Bessonov, Evgeni, *Tank Rider into the Reich with the Red Army*, translated from Russian by Bair Irincheev (London: Greenhill Books, 2003).

Bialer, Seweryn (ed.), *Stalin & His Generals: Soviet Military Memoirs of World War II* (London: Souvenir Press, 1970).

De Guingand, Major General Sir Francis, *Operation Victory* (London: Hodder and Stoughton, 1947).

Gehlen, General Reinhard, *The Gehlen Memoirs: The First Full Edition of the Memoirs of General Reinhard Gehlen 1942–1971*, translated from German by David Irving (London: Collins, 1972 [first published in a shorter edition in German, Mainz: V. Hase und Koehler Verlag, 1971]).

Gilbert, G.M., *Nuremberg Diary* (London: Eyre & Spotiswoode, 1948)

Grossman, Vasily, *A Writer at War: with the Red Army 1941–1945*, translated from Russian and edited by Anthony Beevor & Luba Vinogradova (London: Harvill Press, 2005).

Guderian, General Heinz, *Panzer Leader*, translated from German by Constantine Fitzgibbon (London: Michael Joseph, 1952/London: Futura 1982).

Halifax, Viscount & H.H.E. Craster (ed.), *Speeches on Foreign Policy* (London: Oxford University Press, 1940).

Herling, Gustav, *A World Apart*, translated from Polish by Joseph Marek (William Heinemann 1951/Oxford: Oxford University Press, 1987).

Kempka, Erich, *I was Hitler's Chauffeur: The Memoirs of Erich Kempka*, translated from German by Geoffrey Brooks (Barnsley: Frontline Books, 2012 [first published in German as *Ich Habe Adolf Hitler Verbrant*, Munich: Kyrburg, 1951]).

Kerr, Walter, *The Russian Army: Its Men, its Leaders and its Battles* (London: Victor Gollanz, 1944).

Khrushchev, Nikita, *Khrushchev Remembers* (London: Andre Deutsch Ltd, 1974).

Liddell Hart, B.H., *The Other Side of the Hill: Germany's Generals: Their Rise and Fall, with their own Account of Military Events, 1939–1945* (London: Cassel & Co., 1948, revised and enlarged edition 1951).

Loringhoven, Bernd Freytag von, with François d'Alançon, *In the Bunker with Hitler* (London: Weidenfeld & Nicolson, 2006 [first published in French as *Dans le Bunker de Hitler*, Paris: Editions Perrin, 2005]).

Manstein, Field Marshal Erich von, *Lost Victories*, translated from German and edited by Anthony G. Powell (Elstree: Greenhill Books/Lionel Leventhal, 1987 [first published in German as *Verlorene Siege*, Bonn: Athenaum-Verlag, 1955]).

Mellenthin, Major General F.W. von, *Panzer Battles*, translated from German by H. Betzler and edited by L.C.F. Turner (London: Cassell, 1955/London: Futura, 1984).

Montgomery, Field Marshal Bernard, *The Memoirs of Field-Marshal Montgomery* (London: Collins, 1958).

O'Donnell, James P., *The Berlin Bunker* (London: JM Debt & Sons, 1979).

Polyakov, A., *Westbound Tanks* (London: Hutchinson, 1943).

Ritgen, Colonel Helmut, *The 6th Panzer Division 1937–45* (Oxford: Osprey, 1982).

Sajer, Guy, *The Forgotten Soldier: War on the Russian Front, a True Story* (London: Weidenfeld & Nicolson, 1971/London: Cassell 1999 [first published in French as *Le Soldat Oublie*, Robert Laffont, 1977]).

Schroeder, Christa, *He was my Chief: The Memoirs of Adolf Hitler's Secretary*, translated from German by Geoffrey Brooks (Barnsley: Frontline Books, 2012 [first published in German as *Er war mein Chef: Aus dem Nachlass der Sekretärin von Adolf Hitler*, Munich: Langden Müller in der F.A. Herbig Verlagsbuchhandlung GmbH, 1985]).

Sebastian, Mihail (pen name of Iosif Hechter), *Journal 1935–44* (London: William Heinemann, 2001 [first published in Romanian in 1996 and French in 1998]).

Shtemenko, General S.M., *The Last Six Months: Russia's Final Battles with Hitler's Armies in World War II*, translated from Russian by Guy Daniels (London: William Kimber, 1978).

Shtemenko, General S.M., *The Soviet General Staff at War 1942–1945* (Moscow: Progress Press, 1970).

Stalin, Marshal J., *On the Great Patriotic War of the Soviet Union. Speeches, Orders of the Day, and Answers to Foreign Press Correspondents* (London: Hutchinson, 1943).

Stalin, Marshal J., *War Speeches, Orders of the Day, and Answers to Foreign Press Correspondents during the Great Patriotic War, July 3rd, 1941–June 22nd, 1945* (London: Hutchinson, 1946).

Trevor-Roper, H.R., *The Last Days of Hitler* (London: Macmillan & Co, 1947/London: Pan, 1965). (This is based on Trevor-Roper's official investigation into the fate of Hitler conducted in September 1945.)

Trevor-Roper, H.R. (intro), *Hitler's Table-Talk: Hitler's Conversations Recorded by Martin Bormann* (London: Weidenfeld & Nicolson, 1953/Oxford: Oxford University Press, 1988).

Trevor-Roper, H.R. (ed.), *Hitler's War Directives 1939–1945* (London: Sidgwick and Jackson, 1964/London: Pan, 1983 [first published in German as *Hitler's Weisungen für die Kriegführung 1939–45, Dokumente des Oberkommandos der Wehrmacht*, edited by Walter Hubatsch and published by Bernard und Graefe Verlag, Frankfurt on Main]).

Werth, Alexander, *The Year of Stalingrad* (London: Hamish Hamilton, 1946).

Werth, Alexander, *Russia at War 1941–1945* (London: Barrie & Rockliff, 1964).

Zhukov, Georgi, *Reminiscences and Reflections*, Volumes 1 & 2, translated from Russian by Vic Schneierson (Moscow: Progress Publishers, 1985 [first published in Russian in 1974]).

Zhukov, Georgi, *Marshal Zhukov's Greatest Battles*, translated from Russian by Theodore Shabad and edited by Harrison E. Salisbury (London: Macdonald, 1969 [first published in Russian in *Voyenno-Istoricheskii Zhurnal*, Moscow: Ministry of Defence, June 1965, August, September and October 1966 and August and September 1967; and in *Stalingradskaya Epopeya*, Moscow: Military Publishing House, 1968]).

Other Published Material

Abbot, Peter, & Eugune Pinak, *Ukrainian Armies 1914–55* (Oxford: Osprey, 2004).

Abbott, Peter, & Nigel Thomas, *Germany's Eastern Front Allies 1941–45* (London: Osprey, 1982).

Abbott, Peter, & Nigel Thomas, *Partisan Warfare 1941–45* (London: Osprey, 1983).

Adair, Paul, *Hitler's Greatest Defeat: The Collapse of Army Group Centre June 1944* (London: Arms and Armour, 1994/London: Rigel, 2004).

Ailsby, C., *SS Hell on the Eastern Front, The Waffen-SS War in Russia 1941–1945* (Staplehurst, 1998).

Ailsby, C., *Barbarossa: The German Invasion of Russia 1941* (Hoo: Grange Books, 2005).

Ailsby, C., *Images of Barbarossa* (London: Brassey's, 2002).

Allen, W.E.D., & Paul Muratoff, *The Russian Campaigns of 1944–45* (Harmondsworth: Penguin Books, 1946).

Andrew, Christopher, & Mitrokhin, *The Mitrokhin Archive* (London: Penguin, 1999).

Antill, Peter, *Berlin 1945: End of the Thousand Year Reich* (Oxford: Osprey, 2005/2006).

Applebaum, Anne, *Gulag: A History of the Soviet Camps* (London: Allen Lane, 2003).

Armstrong, Col. R., 'Spring Disaster: The Red Army's Kharkov Offensive', *Military Review* (May 1992).

Axell, Albert, *Russia's Heroes 1941–45* (London: Constable, 2001).

Barber, J., & A. Dzeniskevich (eds), *Life and Death in Besieged Leningrad, 1941–44* (London: Palgrave Macmillan, 2005).

Bastable, Jonathan, *Voices from Stalingrad: Nemesis on the Volga* (Newton Abbot: David and Charles, 2006).

Beevor, Anthony, *Stalingrad* (London: Viking, 1998).

Beevor, Anthony, *Berlin: The Downfall 1945* (London: Viking, 2002).

Bekker, Cajus, *The Luftwaffe War Diaries*, translated and edited by Frank Ziegler (London: Macdonald, 1967/London: Corgi Books, 1972 [originally published in German as *Angriffshöhe 4000*, Hamburg: Gerhard Stalling Verlag, 1964]).

Bellamy, Chris, *Absolute War: Soviet Russia in the Second World War* (London: Macmillan, 2007).

Bergström, C., *Kursk – The Air Battle: July 1943* (Hersham: Ian Allen, 2007).

Bergström, C., *Bagration to Berlin: The Final Air Battles in the East 1944–1945* (Hersham: Ian Allan, 2008).

Bishop, Chris, & Chris McNab (eds), *Campaigns of World War II Day by Day* (London: Amber Books, 2009).

Bonn, Keith E., *Slaughterhouse: The Handbook of the Eastern Front* (Bedford, USA: Aberjona Press, 2005).

Boyd, Alexander, *The Soviet Air Force Since 1918* (London: Macdonald and Jane's, 1977).

Braithewaite, Rodric, *Moscow 1941: A City and its People at War* (London: Profile Books, 2006).

Brendon, Piers, *The Dark Valley: A Panorama of the 1930s* (London: Jonathan Cape, 2000).

Brookes, Andrew, *Air War Over Russia* (Hersham: Ian Allan, 2003).

Bruce, George, *The Warsaw Rising* (London: Rupert Hart-Davis, 1972).

Bullock, Alan, *Hitler: A Study in Tyranny* (London: Odhams, 1952 [revised edition Pelican Books, 1962]).

Carell, P., *Scorched Earth: The Russian–German War, 1943–1944* (London: Corgi, 1971).

Carell, P., *Hitler Moves East, 1941–1943* (London: Ballatine Books, 1971).

Chaney Jr, Otto Preston, *Zhukov* (Newton Abbot: David and Charles, 1972).

Chant, Christopher, *The Encyclopaedia of Codenames of World War II* (London: Routledge & Kegan Paul, 1986).

Clark, Alan, *Barbarossa: The Russian–German Conflict 1941–1945* (London: Weidenfeld & Nicolson, 1995).

Clark, Lloyd, *Kursk: The Greatest Battle Eastern Front 1943* (London: Headline Review, 2011).

Collier, Richard, *The War that Stalin Won* (London: Hamish Hamilton, 1983).

Cornish, Nik, *Images of Kursk: History's Greatest Tank Battle, July 1943* (Staplehurst: Spellmount, 2002).

Cornish, Nik, *Armageddon Ost: The German Defeat on the Eastern Front 1944–5* (Hersham: Ian Allan, 2006).

Cradock, Percy, *Know Your Enemy: How the Joint Intelligence Committee Saw the World* (London: John Murray, 2002).

Craig, William, *Enemy at the Gates: The Battle for Stalingrad* (London: Hodder and Stoughton, 1973).

Davies, Norman, *Rising '44: The Battle for Warsaw* (London: Macmillan, 2003).

Davies, Norman, *Europe at War 1939–1945: No Simple Victory* (London: Macmillan, 2006).

Deichmann, General Paul, edited and with an introduction by Dr Alfred Price, *Spearhead for Blitzkrieg: Luftwaffe Operations in Support of the Army, 1939–1945* (London: Greenhill, 1996).

Denny, Isabel, *The Fall of Hitler's Fortress City: The Battle for Konigsberg, 1945* (St Paul: MBI Publishing, 2007/London: Greenhill Books, 2007).

Duffy, C., *Red Storm on the Reich: The Soviet March on Germany 1945* (New York: Da Capo Press, 1993).

Duffy, P., *Brothers in Arms* (London: Century, 2003).

Dunn, W., *Kursk: Hitler's Gamble, 1943* (Westport: Praeger, 1997).

Dunnigan, J., *The Russian Front: Germany's War in the East, 1941–45* (London: Arms and Armour Press, 1978).

Einsiedel, Heinrich Graf von (translated by Arnold J. Pomerans), *The Onslaught: The German Drive to Stalingrad* (London: Sidgwick& Jackson, 1984 [first published in German as *Der Überfall*, Hamburg, Hoffmann and Campe Verlag]).

Engle, Eloise, & Lauri Paananen, *The Winter War: The Russo-Finnish Conflict, 1939–40* (London: Military Book Society, 1973).

Erickson, John, *The Soviet High Command* (London: Macmillan, 1962).

Erickson, John, *The Road to Stalingrad: Stalin's War with Germany*, Volume 1 (London: Weidenfeld and Nicolson, 1975).

Erickson, John, *The Road to Berlin: Stalin's War with Germany*, Volume 2 (London: Weidenfeld and Nicolson, 1983).

Erickson, J., & D. Dilks, *Barbarossa, the Axis and the Allies* (Edinburgh: Edinburgh University Press, 1994).

Fest, Joachim, *Inside Hitler's Bunker: The Last Days of the Third Reich*, translated from German by Margot Bettauer Dembo (London: Macmillan, 2004/London: Pan, 2005 [originally published in German as *Der Untergang: Hitler und das Ende des Dritten Reiches*, Berlin: Alexander Fest Verlag, 2002]).

Fey, W., *Armor Battles of the Waffen-SS 1943–45* (Mechanicsburg, PA: Stackpole, 2003).

Forczyk, R., *Sevastopol 1942: Von Manstein's Triumph* (Oxford: Osprey, 2008).

Galitzky, K.N., *Fighting for East Prussia* (Moscow: Novosti Press, 1970).

Gilbert, Martin, *Churchill: A Life* (London: Pimlico, 2000).

Gladkov, Teodor Kirillovich, *Operation Bagration* (Moscow: Novosti Press, 1980).

Glantz, David M., *The Failures of Historiography: Forgotten Battles of the German–Soviet War (1941–1945)* (Fort Leavenworth, Kansas: Foreign Military Studies Office).

Glantz, David M., *Kharkov 1942: Anatomy of a Military Disaster Through Soviet Eyes* (Shepperton: Ian Allan, 1998).

Glantz, David M., 'The Red Army at War, 1941–1945: Sources and Interpretations', *The Journal of Military History* (July 1998).

Glantz, David M., *Barbarossa: Hitler's Invasion of Russia 1941* (Stroud: Tempus Publishing, 2001).

Glantz, David M., *The Siege of Leningrad 1941–1944: 900 Days of Terror* (London: Brown Partworks, 2001).

Glantz, D.M., & J.M. House, *When Titans Clashed: How the Red Army Stopped Hitler* (Kansas: 1995).

Glantz, D.M., & J.M. House, *The Battle of Kursk* (Lawrence: University Press of Kansas, 1999).

Glantz, D.M., & H.S. Orenstein, *The Battle for Kursk 1943: The Soviet General Staff Study* (London: Frank Cass, 1999).

Glantz, D.M., & H.S. Orenstein (trans. & ed.), *Belorussia 1944: The Soviet General Staff Study* (London: Frank Cass, 2001).

Granin, D.A., *Leningrad Under Siege* (Barnsley: Pen & Sword, 2007).

Groushko, M.A., *Cossack Warrior Riders of the Steppes* (London: Cassell, 1992).

Gunter, Georg, *Last Laurels The German Defence of Upper Silesia January–May 1945*, translated by C.F. Colton, additional material added to English edition by Duncan Rogers (Solihull: Helion, 2002 [originally published as *Letzter Lorbeer. Vorgeschichte und Geschichte de Kämpfe in Oberschlesien – von bis Mai 1945* by Oberschesischer Heimatverlag, Dülmen, Germany, 1974]).

Hamilton, Nigel, *Monty: The Field Marshal 1944–1976* (London: Hamish Hamilton, 1986).

Hastings, Max, *Armageddon: The Battle for Germany 1944–45* (London: Macmillan, 2004).

Hastings, Max, *All Hell Let Loose: The World at War 1939–1945* (London: Harper Press, 2011).

Haupt, Werner, *Army Group Centre: The Wehrmacht in Russia 1941–1945* (Atglen, PA: Schiffer Military History, 1997 [originally published in German as *Heeresgruppe Mitte*, Friedberg: Podzun-Pallas Verlag]).

Haupt, Werner, *Army Group North: The Wehrmacht in Russia 1941–1945* (Atglen, PA: Schiffer Military History, 1997 [originally published in German as *Heeresgruppe Nord*, Friedberg: Podzun-Pallas Verlag]).

Healy, Mark, *Kursk 1943: Tide Turns in the East* (Oxford: Osprey, 1993).

Hoeffding, O., *Soviet Interdiction Operations, 1941–1945* (Santa Monica: USAF Project Rand, November 1970).

Hough, Richard, *Winston & Clementine: The Triumphs & Tragedies of the Churchills* (London: Bantam Press, 1990).

Humble, Richard, *Hitler's Generals* (London: Arthur Barker, 1973).

Infield, Glenn B., *The Poltava Affair: The Secret World War II Operation that Foreshadowed the Cold War* (London: Robert Hale, 1974).

Irving, David, *The Rise and Fall of the Luftwaffe: The Life of Luftwaffe Marshal Erhard Milch* (London: Weidenfeld and Nicolson, 1973).

Jacobsen, H.A., & J. Rohwer (eds), *Decisive Battles of World War II* (New York: Putnam Pub Group, 1965).

Jones, Michael, *Leningrad State of Siege* (London: John Murray, 2008).

Jones, R.V., *Most Secret War: British Scientific Intelligence 1939–1945* (London: Hamish Hamilton, 1978).

Jukes, Geoffrey, *The Defence of Moscow* (London: Macdonald, 1970).

Jukes, Geoffrey, *The Eastern Front 1941–1945* (Oxford: Osprey, 2002).

Jurado, Carlos Caballero, *Foreign Volunteers of the Wehrmacht 1941–45* (London: Osprey, 1983).

Keagan, John, *Barbarossa: Invasion of Russia 1941* (London: Macdonald, 1971).

Kerr, Walter, *The Secret of Stalingrad* (New York: Doubleday, 1978/London: Macdonald and Jane's, 1979).

Kershaw, Robert, *War Without Garlands: Operation Barbarossa 1941–1942* (Hersham: Ian Allan, 2000).

Kirchubel, Robert, *Operation Barbarossa 1941 (3) Army Group Center* (Oxford/New York: Osprey, 2007).

Knight, Amy, *Beria, Stalin's First Lieutenant* (Princeton: Princeton University Press, 1993).

Kurowski, Franz, *Deadlock before Moscow Army Group Center 1942/1943* (West Chester, PA, USA: Schiffer Military History, 1992 (originally published in German as *Die Heeresgruppe Mitte 1942/43*, Freidberg: Podzum-Pallas Verlag]).

Liddell Hart, B.H., *History of the Second World War* (London: Cassell & Company, 1970).

Lubbeck, W., & D.B. Hurt, *At Leningrad's Gates: The Story of a Soldier with Army Group North* (Barnsley: Pen & Sword, 2006).

Lucas, James, *War on the Eastern Front 1941–1945: The German Soldier in Russia* (London: Jane's Publishing, 1979).

Lucas James, *Hitler's Commanders: German Bravery in the Field, 1939–1945* (London: Cassell, 2000).

Lucas, James, *Hitler's Enforcers: Leaders of the German War Machine 1933–1945* (London: Arms & Armour Press, 1996/ London: Brockhampton Press, 1999).

Lucas, James, *Last Days of the Reich: The Collapse of Nazi Germany, May 1945* (London: Arms & Armour, 1986/London: Cassell, 2000).

Mackintosh, Malcolm, *Juggernaught: A History of the Soviet Armed Forces* (London: Secker & Warburg, 1967).

Mathews, R., *Hitler: Military Commander* (London: Arcturus, 2003).

McKay, Sinclair, *The Lost World of Bletchley Park* (London: Aurum Press Ltd, 2013).

Merridale, Catherine, *Ivan's War: The Red Army 1939–1945* (London: Faber & Faber, 2005).

Messenger, Charles, *Hitler's Gladiator: The Life and Times of Oberstgruppenführer and Panzergeneral-Oberst der Waffen-SS Sepp Dietrich* (London: Brassey's Defence Publishers, 1988).

Messenger, Charles, *The Art of Blitzkrieg* (Shepperton: Ian Allan, 1976 [second edition, 1991]).

Minasyan, M.M. (ed.), *Great Patriotic War of the Soviet Union 1941–45*, translated from Russian by David Skvirsky and Vic Schneierson (Moscow: Progress Publishers, 1974).

Mitcham Jr, Samuel W., *Hitler's Field Marshals and their Battles* (London: William Heinemann, 1988).

Montefiore, Simon Sebag, *Stalin: The Court of the Red Tsar* (London: Weidenfeld & Nicolson, 2003/Phoenix, 2004).

Nagorski, Andrew, *The Greatest Battle: The Fight for Moscow 1941–42* (London: Aurum Press, 2007).

Newton, S.H., *Kursk, the German View* (West View Press, 2003).

Niepold, Lieutenant General Gerd, *Battle for White Russia: The Destruction of Army Group Centre, June 1944* (London: Brassey's, 1987).

Nipe, G., *Last Victory in Russia: The SS-Panzerkorps and Manstein's Kharkov Counter-offensive – February–March 1943*, (Atglen, PA: Schiffer, 2000).

Nipe, G., *Platz der Leibstandarte: A Photo Study of the SS Panzergrenadier Division 'Liebstandarte SS Adolf Hitler' and the Battle for Kharkov January–March 1943* (Canada: Presidio Press, 2002).

O'Balance, Edgar, *The Red Army* (London: Faber & Faber, 1964).

Overy, Richard, *Russia's War* (London: Allen Lane, 1998).

Overy, Richard, *The Dictators: Hitler's Germany, Stalin's Russia* (London: Allen Lane, 2004).

Overy, Richard, & A. Wheatcroft, *The Road to War* (London: BBC Books, 1989).

Pervov, A.G., 'Improvements in Command and Control of the Red Army Air Forces during the Pre-War and Great Patriotic War Years', *Voyenno-Istoricheskii Zhurnal* online, Vol. 2006, No. 1.

Pontin, Clive, *Churchill* (London: Sinclair-Stevenson, 1994).

Popov, I., *The Great Patriotic War of the Soviet People 1941–1945* (Stanford Overseas Studies, Fall 2007).

Quarrie, Bruce, *Hitler's Samurai: The Waffen-SS in Action* (London: Patrick Stephens, 1985).

Quarrie, Bruce, *Hitler's Teutonic Knights: SS Panzers in Action* (London: Patrick Stephens, 1986).

Quarrie, Bruce, *Weapons of the Waffen-SS: From Small Arms to Tanks* (London: Patrick Stephens, 1988).

Rayfield, Donald, *Stalin and his Hangmen: An Authoritative Portrait of a Tyrant and Those Who Served Him* (London: Viking, 2004).

Read, A., & D. Fisher, *The Fall of Berlin* (London: Norton, 1993).

Rees, Laurence, *World War Two Behind Closed Doors: Stalin, the Nazis and the West* (London: BBC Books, 2008).

Reinhardt, Klaus, *Moscow, the Turning Point? The Failure of Hitler's Strategy in the Winter of 1941–42* (Oxford: Berg, 1992).

Reitlinger, Gerald, *The SS Alibi of a Nation 1922–1945* (London: William Heinemann, 1956/London: Arms and Armour Press, 1981).

Restayn, Jean, *The Battle of Kharkov: Winter 1942–1943* (Canada: Fedorowicz, 2000).

Riasanovsky, Nicholas V., *A History of Russia* (New York: Oxford University Press, 1993).

Ripley, Tim, *Steel Storm: Waffen-SS Panzer Battles on the Eastern Front 1943–1945* (Stroud: Sutton Publishing, 2000).

Roberts, Geoffrey, *Stalin's General: The Life of Georgy Zhukov* (London: Icon, 2013).

Rogers, Duncan, & Sarah Williams (ed.), *On the Bloody Road to Berlin: Front-Line Accounts from North-West Europe and the Eastern Front 1944–45* (Solihull: Helion, 2005).

Rogovin, Vadim Zakharovich, *Stalin's Terror 1937–1938: Political Genocide in the USSR* (Oak Park, MI: Mehring Books, 2009).

Ruffner, Kevin Conley, *Luftwaffe Field Divisions 1941–45* (Oxford: Osprey, 1990).

Ryan, Cornelius, *The Last Battle* (London: Collins, 1966).

Salisbury, Harrison E., *The 900 Days: The Siege of Leningrad* (London: Secker & Warburg, 1969).

Scurr, J., *Germany's Spanish Volunteers 1941–45: The Blue Division in Russia* (London: Osprey, 1980).

Seaton, Albert, *The Battle for Moscow* (New York: Stein & Day, 1971).

Seaton, Albert, *Stalin as Warlord* (London: BT Batsford, 1976).

Seaton, Albert, *The Fall of Fortress Europe 1943–1945* (London: BT Batsford, 1981).

Seaton, Albert, *The German Army 1933–45* (London: Weidenfeld & Nicolson, 1982).

Service, Robert, *Stalin: A Biography* (London: Macmillan, 2004).

Shirer, William L., *The Rise and Fall of the Third Reich* (London: Secker & Warburg, 1960).

Slepyan, Kenneth, *Stalin's Guerrillas: Soviet Partisans in World War II* (Kansas: University Press of Kansas, 2006).

Solzhenitsyn, Alexandr, *The Gulag Archipelago 1918–1956* (London: Collins/Harvill Press and Fontana, 1974 [translated from Russian by Thomas P. Whitney]).

Stewart, Graham, *His Finest Hours: The War Speeches of Winston Churchill* (London: Quercus, 2007).

Sweeting, C.G., *Blood and Iron: The German Conquest of Sevastopol* (Potomac, 2005).

Taylor, Brian, *Barbarossa to Berlin: A Chronology of the Campaigns on the Eastern Front 1941 to 1945*, Volume 2, 'The Defeat of Germany 19 November 1942 to 15 May 1945' (Staplehurst: Spellmount, 2004).

Toland, John, *Adolf Hitler* (New York: Doubleday 1976/Ware: Wordsworth, 1997).

Tolstoy, N., *Victims of Yalta* (London: Corgi, 1979).

Tucker-Jones, Anthony, *Stalin's Revenge: Operation Bagration & the Annihilation of Army Group Centre* (Barnsley: Pen & Sword Books, 2009).

Ungváry, K., *Battle for Budapest: 100 Days in World War II*, translated from German by Ladislaus Löb (London: IB Tauris & Co., 2003 [first published in Hungarian as *Budapest Ostroma*, Budapest: Corvina, 1998 and in German as *Die Schlacht um Budapest 1944/45*, Munich: FA Herbig Verlagsbuchhandlung GmbH, 1999]).

Voyetekhov, Boris, *The Last Days of Sevastopol*, translated from Russian by Ralph Parker & V.M. Genne (London: Cassell, 1943).

Williamson, G., *German Military Police Units 1939–45* (Oxford: Osprey, 1989).

Williamson, G., *The SS: Hitler's Instrument of Terror* (London: Sidgwick & Jackson, 1994).

Willmott, H.P., *June 1944* (Poole: Blandford Press, 1984).

Wilmot, Chester, *The Struggle for Europe* (London: Collins, 1952).

Winchester, C., *Ostfront: Hitler's War on Russia 1941–45* (Oxford: Osprey, 1998).

Wood, A., *Stalin and Stalinism* (London: Routledge, 1990).

Zaloga, Steven, *Bagration 1944: The Destruction of Army Group Centre* (Oxford: Osprey, 1996).

Ziemke, Earl Frederick, *The Battle for Berlin: End of the Third Reich* (New York: Ballatine, 1968).

Documentary Films & Interviews

Adamovich, Alexandr, & Sergei Gusev (writer/director), *The Battle of Kursk – Parts 1 & 2* (Discovery Civilisation in Association with Russian Television and Radio, 2003/2012).

Barrett, Matthew (executive producer), *WWII in Colour: Hitler Strikes East* (Nugus Martin Productions/IMG Entertainment, 2009).

Barrett, Matthew, *WWII in Colour: The Soviet Steamroller* (Nugus Martin Productions/IMG Entertainment, 2009).

Barrett, Matthew, *WWII in Colour: Victory in Europe* (Nugus Martin Productions/IMG Entertainment, 2009).

Donskaya, Tatiana, & Alexander Lyutenkov (writer/director), *The Stalingrad Apocalypse: No Win Situation* (Discovery Civilisation in Association with Russian Television and Radio, 2003/2012).

Drozdova, Marina & Sasha Kiselev (writer/director), *The Elbe Day* (Discovery Civilisation in Association with Russian Television and Radio, 2005/2012).

Elsmore, Philip (narrator), *Battles: The Eastern Front – 1944–1945, The Campaign in the East* (Boulevard Entertainment, 2006).

Zainetdinov, Ruslan, & Denis Skvortsov (writer/director), *The Brest Fortress* (Discovery Civilisation in Association with Russian Television and Radio, 2007/2012).

Zanin, Yuri, & Irina Malyarov (writer/director), *Leningrad – The Secrets of the Blockaded City* (Discovery Civilisation in Association with Russian Television and Radio, 2004/2012).

Zanin, Yuri, & Irina Malyarov (writer/director), *Prague '45: The Last Battle with the Third Reich* (Discovery Civilisation in Association with Russian Television and Radio, 2004/2012).

ACKNOWLEDGEMENTS

My thanks to Chrissy McMorris managing editor at The History Press and commissioning editors Tim Newark and Michael Leventhal for making this book possible. Likewise my copy-editor Andrew Latimer was a highly professional and patient pair of hands throughout the process of putting it together. The fine plate section and cover photos were made possible by the generosity of Scott Pick in making his photographic collection available. Lastly I would like to thank my good friend and artist Saul Cumiskey who provided the initial designs for the maps. He admirably tackled the complexity of it all with a great degree of welcome clarity.

INDEX

By the same author ...

ANTHONY TUCKER-JONES

KURSK 1943

HITLER'S BITTER HARVEST

978 0 7509 8448 5

The History Press

The destination for history
www.thehistorypress.co.uk